Wildflowers of Alberta

A Guide to Common Wildflowers and Other Herbaceous Plants

Wildflowers
of ALBERTA

*A Guide to
Common
Wildflowers
and Other
Herbaceous
Plants*

Kathleen 🖉
Wilkinson

Illustrations by Joan Williams
Keys by Linda Kershaw

THE UNIVERSITY OF ALBERTA PRESS   LONE PINE PUBLISHING

Published by
   The University of Alberta Press
   141 Athabasca Hall
   Edmonton, Alberta T6G 2E8
and
   Lone Pine Publishing
   206, 10426-81 Avenue
   Edmonton, Alberta T6E 1X5

Printed in Canada   5   4   3   2   1

Canadian Cataloguing in Publication Data

Wilkinson, Kathleen, 1950-
   Wildflowers of Alberta

   Includes bibliographical references and index.
   ISBN 0-88864-298-9

   1. Wild flowers—Alberta. 2. Wild flowers—Alberta—Identification. I.
Title.

QK203.A4W543 1999   582.13'097123   C97-910328-2

Printed and bound by Kromar Printing Ltd., Winnipeg, Manitoba.
Colour separations and filmwork by Elite Lithographers, Edmonton, Alberta.

The University of Alberta Press acknowledges the support received for its program from the Canada
Council for the Arts. The Press also gratefully acknowledges the financial support of the Government
of Canada through the Book Publishing Industry Development Program for its publishing activities.

THE CANADA COUNCIL | LE CONSEIL DES ARTS
FOR THE ARTS | DU CANADA
SINCE 1957 | DEPUIS 1957

Contents

This book is dedicated to my father, Al Mattick,
for his constant support and encouragement.

Acknowledgements

I would like to express my sincere appreciation to the many people who have contributed to making this book a reality:

Joan Williams for her drawings (and patience!); all the photographers who supplied slides; Julie Hrapko, Dr Jim Pojar and Dr David Murray for technical review of the manuscript; Donna Cherniawsky for clarification on the genus *Petasites* and revisions to the composite family key; Ian Macdonald for reference material and helpful discussion; Derek Johnson for reviewing the keys; Dr C.C. Chinnappa for taxonomic clarification and access to the University of Calgary herbarium to examine plant specimens; Beryl Hallworth for supplying valuable reference material; the University of Alberta Press, particularly Glenn Rollans, Director, for taking on the project; Leslie Vermeer for editing the manuscript; Bruce Timothy Keith for doing the design and layout; and the Sport, Recreation, Parks and Wildlife Foundation for its financial support of this project. Thank you also to my husband, Ken, and son, Brian, for patiently (most of the time!) accompanying me on botanizing expeditions.

Introduction

The purpose of this book is to introduce the interested observer to the wealth of plant life in Alberta, in a colourful, up-to-date, easy-to-use, handy-sized format. Nearly 1600 species of plants are currently known to occur in Alberta, but it was not feasible to include them all in this book. The species represented within include the most common native herbaceous species (although a few introduced and weedy species have been included, as well as some dwarf shrubs) and the most interesting from a medicinal, technological or ethnobotanical perspective. (Shrubs more than 30 cm in height and trees have been described by the author in *A Habitat Field Guide to Trees and Shrubs of Alberta* [Edmonton: Lone Pine Publishing, 1990]).

A total of 246 species in 66 families are described and illustrated in detail, with more than 450 colour photographs and, in several cases, with line drawings to highlight specific features. Numerous other species are also mentioned in less detail.

To enhance the book's value to the non-botanist, technical terms have been avoided when possible. Where it has been necessary to use botanical terminology, brief definitions are given in the text, and the illustrated glossary offers more detailed explanations.

This book has been written primarily for beginning to intermediate naturalists and presents basic information for most of the major plant families. For information on such technically difficult groups as grasses, sedges, mosses, lichens and liverworts, check the Selected References, pp 341-42.

Readers familiar with *Flora of Alberta* (Moss 1983) will notice several new species that have been discovered since *Flora* was published. In most cases, these new species are rare in the province, and the information regarding their distribution has been taken from *Plant Species of Special Concern*, November 1996 edition.

All plants (and animals) are identified scientifically by a universally accepted Latin name composed of two parts. For example, the scientific name of three-flowered avens is *Geum triflorum*. The first part, *Geum*, indicates the group or genus (pl. genera), in this case the avens, of related plants to which this particular species belongs. The second part, *triflorum*, is the species or specific name and tells us that we are dealing with three-flowered avens. Scientific names usually describe some aspect of the plant and often have interesting origins. *Geum* is said to be derived from the Greek *geyo* (to stimulate), because the shredded roots of a Mediterranean *Geum* species were used as a stimulant, while *triflorum*, Latin for "three-flowered," refers to the plant's flower arrangement.

In theory, each species has one scientific name used in all the countries of the world. Unfortunately, taxonomists occasionally disagree; also, as knowledge accumulates, revisions are made to scientific nomenclature. The scientific names used in this book are those of *The Vascular Plants of British Columbia*, as this flora lists the most recent names and taxonomy for our western Canadian plants. These names have often been derived from Kartesz (1994) and from material presented in *The Flora of North America* (1993-1997), but not always, as the taxonomy and nomenclature presented in these standard references are not always considered applicable to our western species. For those more familiar with the nomenclature in *Flora of Alberta* (a technical text used by professional botanists, written by E.H. Moss in 1959 and revised by J.G. Packer in 1983), a list of the old names and their more update-to-date equivalents is provided on page 329.

In addition to scientific names, common or popular names are listed for each species in the book. The most common ones used in the province (usually those listed in *Alberta Plants and Fungi—Master Species List and Species Group Checklists,* published by Alberta Environmental Protection, 1993) appear in boldface type; other, less familiar names are also included. The plants are listed by families (groups of related genera) in Englerian order. In this system, named after German taxonomist Heinrich Engler, families are organized from what was considered in Engler's time to be most primitive to most advanced. Within each family, the genera and species are arranged in alphabetical order of their scientific names. In general, species that are closely related (and thus usually similar in appearance) are listed together, a feature which may help in identification.

The habitat and range, flowers, fruit, leaves and growth habit are described for each species. Features most helpful in identification have been highlighted in the text. But everyone, at one time or another, experiences the joy of identifying a plant only to discover that it cannot possibly occur where it was found. No matter how much it looks like a picture of bog laurel, if you found it growing on a sand dune in southern Alberta, it's not bog laurel. Most plants are found in specific habitats, although some may occur over a wide range of climatic, soil and moisture conditions.

Various concepts have been used to describe plant and animal habitats. This book divides Alberta into four major habitat types or natural regions, based on climate and vegetation characteristics (see map on page XII). These regions are prairie, aspen parkland, boreal forest and Rocky Mountains. The Rocky Mountains have been subdivided (in order of increasing elevation) into montane, subalpine and alpine zones. The climatic conditions and characteristic plants of each region are described on pp XIII to XVIII. Vegetation descriptions refer to natural landscapes in the areas and not to habitats altered significantly by human activities.

The natural regions where each plant occurs are listed at the top of the species account. Although a specific plant may be shown as occurring on the prairie, it may occur there only in riverine shrub or tree communities. The natural region designations are therefore meant to show where the plant may be found on a gross scale, and should be supplemented by more specific information provided in the habitat description.

Blooming periods listed in the species descriptions indicate when plants of that species have been observed in flower in Alberta (based on personal experience and herbarium specimen data) and do not refer to the length of flowering time.

Having identified a plant, it's interesting to learn something about it, something that gives it character and sets it apart from other plants. How did it get its name? Is it edible? Does it have medicinal properties? Where is it found throughout the world? Such questions are answered below each plant description. Most of the information in this section is derived from other published works, and readers who would like to pursue these aspects further should see the Selected References on pp 341–42.

ᪧ ᪧ ᪧ

A word of caution: **Do not eat any part** of a wild plant unless you are positive that you have identified it correctly as an edible species. Plants may contain potent chemicals, and what is safe for one person to eat or use may be unsafe or even fatal for another. Sample a very small amount at first and allow at least 24 hours to see if any adverse reaction occurs.

Do not attempt to treat yourself for any medical condition using wild plants. The medicinal uses, particularly those by native peoples, have not been verified and are included here for historic interest only.

Although many attractive and unusual flowers and plants are noted in this book, please **do not pick them**. Indiscriminate picking has decimated the populations of many of our lovely wildflowers in easily accessible locations. Likewise, do not attempt to transplant species: they frequently have particular habitat requirements, such as dependent relationships with site-specific fungi, that cannot be met in your garden. Please take only photographs, so that others can enjoy our plants for years to come. If you are interested in growing native wildflowers in your garden, there are several reputable suppliers. The Alberta Native Plant Council produces an annual list of native plant material suppliers for a nominal cost.

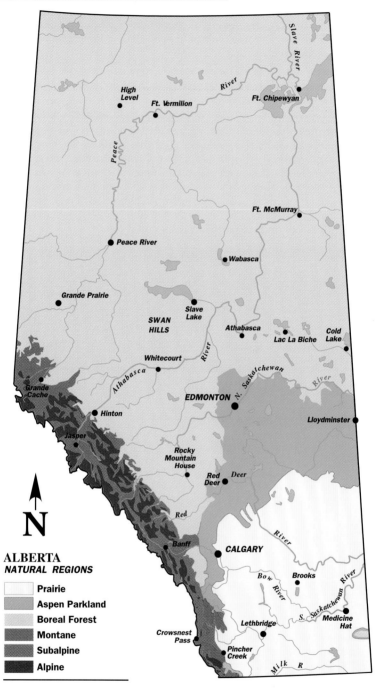

Source: *Modified from Natural Regions and Sub-regions of Alberta. Alberta Parks Services, Alberta Environmental Protection, 1994.*

PRAIRIE

The prairie, dominated by grasses, occupies most of the southern quarter of Alberta and is characterized by low annual rainfall, high winds and a frost-free period ranging from approximately 115 days in the warm, dry southeast to 90 days in the cooler, wetter, northern and western portions.

The southeastern section of the prairie is the driest, hottest and has the least snow accumulation. Warm winter chinooks are frequent and are a major factor in inhibiting tree growth except in areas of higher moisture, such as north-facing coulee slopes, and along streams and rivers. The landscape is flat to rolling, covered primarily by blue grama grass, spear grasses and wheat grasses, with splashes of colour provided by yellow composites, pink cushion cactus and old man's whiskers, wild blue flax and slender blue beard-tongue. Look for such drought-tolerant shrubs as sagebrush, rabbit-brush and greasewood here. In shaded ravines are shrubs that require more moisture, such as buckbrush, wolf-willow, saskatoon, hawthorn and choke cherry.

To the west, lower summer temperatures, deeper snow cover and more precipitation result in more luxuriant growth. Blue grama grass, cactus and sagebrush gradually disappear, replaced by lupines, sticky geranium, northern bedstraw and Canada goldenrod. On the western edge of the grassland, fescues and oat grasses become dominant, and more trees and shrubs, such as poplar, choke cherry, currants and gooseberries, appear. The gradual presence of aspen poplar groves signifies the beginning of the aspen parkland region.

ASPEN PARKLAND

To the north and west of the prairie lies a region of intermingled grassland and aspen groves known as the aspen parkland. This region receives more precipitation (particularly during the summer months) and has lower winter temperatures, fewer chinooks and longer snow cover than the adjacent prairie. The aspen parkland is transitional between prairie and boreal forest to the north and between prairie and the Rocky Mountains to the west.

The region features groves of aspen, with occasional balsam poplar, white spruce and paper birch. Shrubs, including saskatoon, buckbrush, roses, wolf-willow, choke cherry and beaked hazelnut, are common, while wild sarsaparilla, asters, goldenrods, wild vetch, Solomon's-seal, peavine, violets, fairybells, tall mertensia and cow parsnip are frequent in the herbaceous understory.

BOREAL FOREST

The boreal forest is the largest natural region in Alberta, covering most of the northern half of the province and extending southward in a wedge between the Rocky Mountains in the west and aspen parkland to the east. The boreal forest is also the largest natural region in Canada, stretching in a wide band across the country from Newfoundland to British Columbia. Winters are cold and long, due to the influence of arctic air masses, and summers range from warm in the south to cool in more northerly areas. Most of the annual precipitation falls as rain in the summer, allowing trees to flourish. White spruce, aspen poplar and balsam fir are present throughout upland areas while black spruce, swamp or bog birch, tamarack and balsam poplar are characteristic of more poorly drained sites. Lodgepole pine is common in the southwest, where the boreal forest is transitional to the montane natural region. In dry, sandy areas in central and northeastern sections, look for jack pine, bearberry, blueberry and lichen communities. In wet, cold muskegs, black spruce and *Sphagnum* moss are abundant, with scattered tamarack, dwarf birch, Labrador tea, marsh cinquefoil, buckbean, bog rosemary and bog cranberry.

THE ROCKY MOUNTAINS

THE MONTANE ZONE occupies a small area of the province along lower elevation river valleys in the mountains and in patches in the western foothills. It is drier and warmer than either the subalpine or alpine zones, due to the strong influence of Pacific air masses.

Montane forests tend to be open, especially in the southern part of this zone, with trees interspersed with grassy areas. Douglas-fir and limber pine are characteristic southwestern montane species, but they are usually less abundant than lodgepole pine, white spruce and aspen poplar. Shrubs such as junipers, Canada buffaloberry and shrubby cinquefoil may be locally common, with willows in moist locations along creeks and rivers.

Reed grasses, hairy wild rye, hedysarum, showy aster, milk-vetch and veiny meadow rue occur in the shade of trees, while rough fescue, spear grasses, oat grasses, northern bedstraw, fleabanes, sages, three-flowered avens and cinquefoils are common in grassy patches. Low-lying areas are dominated by sedges and willows.

The foothills, although primarily montane, are transitional between prairie, aspen parkland, boreal forest and the Rocky Mountains, and may have plants characteristic of all four natural regions.

THE SUBALPINE ZONE: As elevation increases, the climate becomes cooler and wetter, with increased snowfall. These conditions suit the growth of dense forests of white and Engelmann spruce and subalpine fir, although after fires these species are temporarily replaced by stands of lodgepole pine. Lodgepole pine seedlings, unlike spruce and fir, are not shade tolerant; thus, spruce and fir will eventually dominate the forest once again. In the deep shade of the trees, shrub growth is sparse and consists of such species as false azalea, Labrador tea and occasional bracted honeysuckle, rock willow, bristly black currant and Canada

buffaloberry. Feather-mosses, on the other hand, thrive in these moist, shady conditions and form a thick, soft carpet punctuated by grouseberry, arnica, bronzebells, bunchberry, wintergreens and twinflower.

At higher elevations, Engelmann spruce replaces white spruce, and subalpine fir becomes more frequent. In the upper regions of the subalpine zone, stronger winds and intense sun increase moisture stress, and the tree cover thins out. High altitude trees, such as white-bark pine and subalpine larch, may appear in small numbers. As the subalpine zone merges with the alpine, tree growth is reduced to scattered islands of stunted, bushy, wind-flagged Engelmann spruce and subalpine fir called *krüppelholz*.

THE ALPINE ZONE lies above treeline (the limit of contiguous tree cover), where tree growth is limited to occasional *krüppelholz* islands. Alpine soils are frequently low in nutrients. Winters are cold and summers are cool; even during July and August the temperature may dip below zero. Although these conditions inhibit the growth of trees and tall shrubs, many herbaceous species and dwarf shrubs have adapted to survive and even flourish here.

Wide species diversity is possible over short distances in response to differences in levels of snow accumulation, snow melt patterns, wind exposure, drainage and soil development. Where snow accumulation is great and snow does not melt until late in the season, sedges predominate, often forming a dense, hummocky turf. Where snow accumulation is somewhat less, moist meadows support a wide array of colourful flowers including heathers, valerian, paintbrushes, louseworts, buttercups, veronica, groundsels and gentians. Better drained, exposed areas are dominated by carpets of white mountain avens.

At higher elevations, where high-intensity solar radiation, strong winds and the low moisture-holding capacity of the soils produce drought conditions during the short growing season, plant cover is limited to species that take shelter in crevices or have compact, cushion growth forms, such as whitlow-grasses, saxifrages, moss campion and mountain chickweed. At the highest elevations, only hardy lichens can exist, forming isolated patches of colour as they cling tenaciously to boulders and rubble.

How To Use This Guide For Field Identification

1. If you know your specimen belongs to one of the major families described in this book, turn to the keys for the major families (pp 293–328). Work through the keys to determine the correct genus and species. Note that keys to genera and species are provided for only the fifteen largest families in the book; not all species found in Alberta are mentioned in the keys and the book.

2. If you don't know which family your specimen belongs to, compare the live specimen with the photographs and drawings in this book. Species that look similar tend to be closely related and will usually be found together in this book. It may also be helpful to look at the species index by flower colour (pp 343–49).

3. Once you think you've found a visual match, read the text description, paying particular attention to the size, flower, fruit, leaf details, habitat and range. If you are unsure of a term, check the glossary (pp 331–40). Helpful identifying features are highlighted in the text.

4. To find out about a plant whose common or scientific name you know, check the species index (pp 351–63).

5. If this book has piqued your curiosity and you would like further information, consult the selected references (pp 341–42).

stiff club-moss
Lycopodium annotinum L.
BOREAL FOREST, MONTANE, SUBALPINE

HABITAT AND RANGE: Moist to dry woods, thickets, open mountain slopes, bogs. Widespread in Alberta.

REPRODUCTIVE STRUCTURES: The bright-yellow spores are borne in kidney-shaped spore cases (*sporangia*) which occur in the axils of specialized leaves called *sporophylls*. The sporophylls and their sporangia are arranged in club-like, **stalkless, solitary spikes** called *strobili* (singular *strobilus*).

LEAVES: Numerous, small (3 to 10 mm long), **spreading to sometimes overlapping, stiff, backward-bent**, evergreen, linear to lance-shaped, with tiny, 1-nerved spines at the tip.

stiff club-moss   (BA)

GROWTH HABIT: Low, evergreen, moss-like herb that trails on the ground with long, **prostrate stems**. Erect branches simple or forked, up to 25 cm tall.

The genus name arises from the Greek *lycos* (wolf) and *pous* (foot), because of the appearance of the branching shoot-tips of several of the species. *Annotinum* means "1 year old." ✍ Small amounts of a related species, mountain club-moss (*L. selago*), were chewed by certain native peoples of the western United States for their narcotic effect; this species contains high concentrations of **toxic alkaloids**. ✍ The Blackfoot are said to have dusted club-moss spores on wounds and also inhaled them to stop nosebleeds. ✍ Club-moss spores have also been used to make theatrical explosives and to prevent pills from sticking to one another in closed containers.

The plant has gained popularity recently for use in Christmas decorations. ✍ Another related species, ground-cedar (*L. complanatum*), is also common in the province. Its cones are borne on long stalks, and it has flattened, somewhat cedar-like leaves in 4 rows. ✍ There are over 200 species of *Lycopodium* in the world, mostly in tropical and subtropical regions. Of these, 8 occur in Alberta.

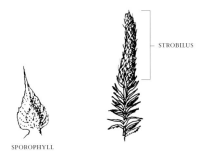

STROBILUS

SPOROPHYLL

reproductive structures of stiff club-moss

ground-cedar   (BA)

prairie selaginella, evergreen spikemoss, dwarf club-moss
Selaginella densa Rydb.

PRAIRIE, ASPEN PARKLAND, BOREAL FOREST, MONTANE, SUBALPINE, ALPINE

prairie selaginella (CWA)

HABITAT AND RANGE: Dry grassland, exposed hillsides, stony places; to above treeline in the mountains. Predominantly in the southern half of the province.

REPRODUCTIVE STRUCTURES: Spore cases (*sporangia*) are organized into sharply **4-sided, elongate, terminal, erect "cones"** (*strobili*), 1 to 3 cm long. There are 2 kinds of spores (large *megaspores* and small *microspores*) in the same "cone," but in separate sporangia.

LEAVES: Stiff, **densely crowded and overlapping in spirals, with long, white bristles on leaf tips and often tiny hairs on the margins. Noticeably 1-nerved on back.** Pale gray-green to bright green, sometimes yellowing with age, 2 to 3 mm long.

GROWTH HABIT: Small (main stems up to 12 cm long), low-growing, **densely tufted, moss-like evergreen perennial** that appears in drier habitats than mosses. Has creeping, branched stems and forms dense mats.

The genus name *Selaginella* is the diminutive of *selago*, an ancient name of some species of club-moss (*Lycopodium*), which it resembles. *Densa* likely refers to the crowded leaf arrangement. ✐ The Alberta Blackfoot used a mixture containing prairie selaginella foliage to induce labour or expel the afterbirth. ✐ The plant may be helpful in controlling erosion but has no forage value. It tends to increase at the expense of more desirable range species and is often used as an indicator of overgrazing and/or drought conditions. ✐ There are 500 species of *Selaginella* in the world, most commonly in warm, moist regions; 3 other species occur in Alberta. Rock little club-moss (*S. rupestris*) is uncommon and Wallace's little club-moss (*S. wallacei*) is rare in the province. The former occurs primarily in the extreme northeast, while the latter grows only in the extreme southwest, in Waterton Lakes National Park. These 3 species are difficult to differentiate at a glance, and the ranges of the latter 2 may be wider than is currently indicated. ✐ Spiny-edged little club-moss or mountain-moss (*S. selaginoides*) is more widespread and may be distinguished from prairie selaginella by the lack of bristles at the end of its leaves.

common horsetail, field horsetail

Equisetum arvense L.

PRAIRIE, ASPEN PARKLAND, BOREAL FOREST, MONTANE, SUBALPINE, ALPINE

HABITAT AND RANGE: Moist woods, creeks, swamps, fens, river banks, along rail lines. Tolerant of poor soil. Widespread throughout Alberta and Canada.

REPRODUCTIVE STRUCTURES: **Terminal rounded cones** (*strobili*) up to 3 cm long, bearing numerous, tiny green spores.

LEAVES: Small, **fused into a sheath with only the 8 to 12 brown-to-black tips free**. The leaves usually lack chlorophyll; however, the green branches and stems are photosynthetic.

GROWTH HABIT: 2 kinds of stems arise from creeping, branched, black rootstocks. **Fertile stems erect, unbranched, thick, white or brownish**, 10 to 30 cm tall, appearing in spring. **Sterile stems** 10 to 50 cm tall, much-branched (in whorls), **green, slender, with 10 to 12 ridges**, appearing later in the season.

fertile stems of common horsetail (CWE)

The genus name is from the Latin *equus* (horse) and *seta* (bristle), because of the resemblance of the branching stem of some species to a horse's tail. *Arvense* means "field." ✍ Horsetails are regularly eaten by black bears and voles but are toxic to horses if consumed in large quantities as hay. ✍ The rough surface of the stem is due to crystals of silica which help to strengthen the plant. The abrasive stems were used like sandpaper for arrowheads and carved items, and early European settlers used bundles of horsetail stems to polish metal and floors. Some B.C. tribes used horsetail stems in basketwork, while the Alberta Blackfoot crushed the stems to make a light pink dye.

sterile stem of common horsetail (CWE)

common scouring rush (BA)

The succulent fertile shoots were eaten fresh or boiled by coastal tribes after the tough, outer fibres were discarded. Some native American peoples boiled the stems and used the resulting mixture as a shampoo to deter fleas, lice and mites. The heads of the reproductive shoots have been eaten to cure diarrhea. ◢ There are 20 species of horsetails in the world, 9 of which occur in Alberta. Common horsetail is similar to meadow horsetail (*E. pratense*); however, the latter has stem sheaths with teeth that have a broad, whitish margin, branch sheaths with 4 teeth and the lowest internode of each branch is usually as long as or shorter than the corresponding stem sheath. In contrast, common horsetail has brown teeth lacking white margins on the stem sheath, 3-toothed branch sheaths and lowest internodes generally much longer than the corresponding stem sheaths. Another widespread species, common scouring rush (*E. hyemale*), has sheaths that become grayish, with 2 black bands at the base and tip, and teeth that break off.

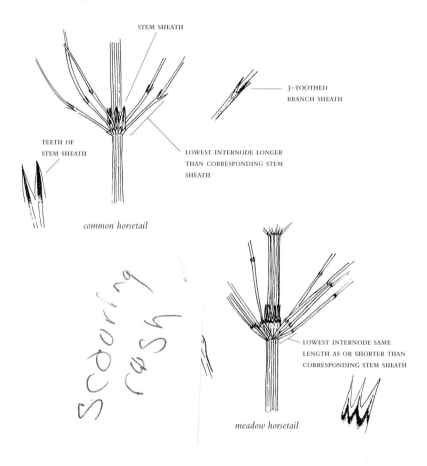

STEM SHEATH

3-TOOTHED
BRANCH SHEATH

TEETH OF
STEM SHEATH

LOWEST INTERNODE LONGER
THAN CORRESPONDING STEM
SHEATH

common horsetail

LOWEST INTERNODE SAME
LENGTH AS OR SHORTER THAN
CORRESPONDING STEM SHEATH

meadow horsetail

fragile bladder fern
Cystopteris fragilis (L.) Bernh.
PRAIRIE, ASPEN PARKLAND, BOREAL FOREST, MONTANE, SUBALPINE, ALPINE

HABITAT AND RANGE: Moist to dry rocky ledges, talus slopes, cliffs, crevices, woods. Widespread in Alberta.

REPRODUCTIVE STRUCTURES: *Sporangia* are grouped in small, rounded clusters called *sori*. The **sori are partially covered with a membraneous hood called an *indusium*.**

LEAVES: Blades lance-shaped in outline, tapered at both ends, 10 to 25 cm long, **at least twice as long as wide**, bi to tripinnate, smooth or with inconspicuous glands. **Basal pinnae about equal size.** Stipes narrow, pale yellow or tan, scaly at base, **shorter than the blades.**

fragile bladder fern   (JH)

GROWTH HABIT: Tufted perennial from thick, unbranched rhizome. Stipes up to 30 cm tall.

*C*ystopteris is from the Greek *kystis* (bladder) and *pteris* (fern), referring to the membraneous indusium covering the sori, while *fragilis* (brittle) describes the stipes. ✐ Some native peoples applied fragile bladder fern to wounds and made the plant into tea to relieve upset stomachs. ✐ There are about 10 species of *Cystopteris* in the world, widely distributed. The other Alberta species, the provincially rare mountain bladder fern (*C. montana*) of northern Alberta, has a leaf blade nearly or fully as wide as long and basal pinnae unequal in size.

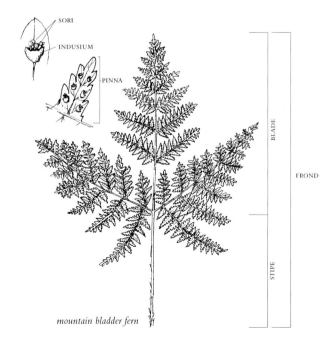

mountain bladder fern

oak fern
Gymnocarpium dryopteris (L.) Newn.
BOREAL FOREST, MONTANE, SUBALPINE

oak fern (DJ)

HABITAT AND RANGE: Moist forests, thickets, stream banks, rocky slopes. Mainly in the northern half of the province but also in the Rocky Mountains of southwestern Alberta and the Cypress Hills.

REPRODUCTIVE STRUCTURES: *Sori* small, rounded, with **no membraneous covering**.

LEAVES: Fronds usually solitary. Blades **broadly triangular** in outline, 5 to 25 cm broad and 5 to 18 cm long (usually wider than long), with **3 stalked, mostly bipinnate** divisions. Blades hairless, smooth to slightly glandular along the central stalk. **Lowest pair of pinnae large and asymmetrical**. Stipe narrow, shiny, pale yellow, equal to or longer than the blade, lacking glands.

GROWTH HABIT: Yellow-green perennial from **slender, blackish, branched, scaly rhizome**. Stipes to 50 cm tall. May form a dense carpet in suitable locations.

The name *Gymnocarpium* is from the Greek *gymnos* (naked) and *karpos* (fruit) because the sori lack indusia. *Dryopteris* is from the Greek *drys* (tree, especially an oak) and *pteris* (fern), although the plant actually does not grow on or near oaks. This species is sometimes included in the genus *Dryopteris*, where it is known as *Dryopteris disjuncta*. ✎ The Cree used crushed oak ferns as a mosquito repellent and to soothe mosquito bites. ✎ There are 3 species of *Gymnocarpium* widespread in the northern hemisphere. The only other Alberta species, northern oak fern (*G. jessoense*), has a finer blade that is glandular on both sides, and the 2 lower divisions are about half as long as the terminal one. The stipe is glandular and not shiny. Northern oak fern occurs on limestone and shale ledges and on rocky slopes; it is extremely rare in Alberta, known only from the extreme northeast of the province.

common cattail
Typha latifolia L.
<small>PRAIRIE, ASPEN PARKLAND, BOREAL FOREST, MONTANE</small>

HABITAT AND RANGE: Shallow, standing or slow-moving water in marshes, or at lake, stream or river edges. Widespread in Alberta.

FLOWERS: Very small, unisexual, with no petals or sepals. **Female (*pistillate*) flowers in a dense, sausage-shaped spike** to 15 cm long and 3 cm in diameter. **Male (*staminate*) flowers occur above the female on the same stalk**, in a much narrower cluster, to about 10 cm long. Male flowers blow away after the pollen is shed, leaving a bare upper stalk. July.

FRUIT: Tiny (1 mm long) achenes on narrow stalks. The achenes and their thin, long stalks make up the "fluff" which falls from the plant in the fall.

LEAVES: Alternate, basal, grayish green, sword-like. Long (25 to 50 cm), flat, **8 to 20 mm broad**, erect, spongy, parallel-veined, sheathing at base.

GROWTH HABIT: Erect perennial herb with pithy stem, 1 to 2 m tall from coarse, white, creeping rhizome.

common cattail   (BA)

The genus name is from *Typhe*, the ancient Greek name for the plant. *Latifolia* means "broad-leaved." ✿ The stems and leaves have been used for packing material, mats and chair seats, while the leaves have been fashioned into hats, bags and capes. The fluffy seed heads may be used as a soft absorbent in infants' diapers, to stuff mattresses and pillows and to start fires. The Blackfoot used the down from cattail heads as a dressing for burns. The American Sioux treated smallpox pustules with cattail down and coyote fat. ✿ The mature flower heads can be soaked in kerosene to make torches. The rhizomes, young leaf blades and young flower spikes were eaten by many native tribes. The young shoots are quite delicious when boiled with butter. The young rootstocks can be peeled and eaten raw or boiled, and the flowers can be boiled and eaten like corn on the cob. The pollen makes an excellent flour (when mixed with wheat flour) and can be baked into bread or made into pancakes. Cattails should not be eaten from areas where there is any danger of contamination from fertilizers, other chemicals or sewage. ✿ Cattails provide important cover and food for birds, waterfowl, ducks, geese, muskrats and moose. ✿ There are 9 or 10 species of *Typha* in the world, mainly in temperate and tropical areas. Only 2 species are found in Alberta. Lesser cattail (*T. angustifolia*) has the female and male flowers slightly separate; in common cattail they are continuous. Lesser cattail also usually has narrower (3 to 10 mm) leaves. It is rare in Alberta, known from only a single location in northwestern Alberta.

seaside arrow-grass, salt-grass, goose-tongue
Triglochin maritimum L.
<small>PRAIRIE, ASPEN PARKLAND, BOREAL FOREST, MONTANE</small>

seaside arrow-grass (LK)

HABITAT AND RANGE: Saline marshes, fens, wet meadows, mud flats, moist gravelly areas. Widespread throughout Alberta.

FLOWERS: **Narrow, terminal, long (to more than 15 cm), dense cluster of small greenish flowers, each consisting of 6 deciduous, petal-like segments.** Flower stalks extend along stem in ridges. Stamens 6. May to August.

FRUIT: **Usually 6-parted,** round to cylindrical, 4 to 6 mm long, composed of 3 to 6 follicles which separate at maturity and fall from the stem. Elongate seeds, 1 per follicle.

LEAVES: **All basal, grass-like, linear, erect, slightly fleshy,** sheathing at the base, up to 50 cm long and 1.5 to 4.0 mm broad.

GROWTH HABIT: Erect perennial with a leafless stem, 10 to 100 cm tall or more, from a stout, woody rhizome covered with persistent leaf-bases. The **leaf stalks and flower stems are whitish (sometimes mottled with purple)** and fleshy near the ground.

The scientific name is from the Greek *treis* (three) and *glochis* (point), as the fruit of some species is 3-pointed. *Maritimum* means "of the sea" and refers to the plant's wetland habitat. ✍ The mature leaves and flower stalks are **poisonous** (they can produce hydrocyanic acid) and have caused livestock poisoning. ✍ The whitish leaf bases were eaten by several coastal B.C. tribes, and the seeds of some species have been dried and eaten. Eating the seeds and leaf bases is not recommended, however, due to the **potential for poisoning**. ✍ There are 12 species of *Triglochin*, widely distributed throughout the world. The other Alberta species, slender arrow-grass (*T. palustris*), is similar but has tapering, 3-compartmented, round to cylindrical fruits and is generally a smaller, less robust plant.

(a)   *(b)*

fruits of (a) seaside arrow-grass, (b) slender arrow-grass

arum-leaved arrowhead, wapato
Sagittaria cuneata Sheldon
PRAIRIE, ASPEN PARKLAND, BOREAL FOREST, MONTANE

HABITAT AND RANGE: Shallow ponds, lakeshores, semi-open marshes, ditches, creeks, slow moving water. Widespread in Alberta.

FLOWERS: **Lower flower heads female, upper male. Male flowers showy, white, with petals in 3s** and numerous stamens. Petals broadly oval, to about 1 cm long. **Female flowers develop first and occur in ball-like clusters** on shorter stalks than the male flowers. Sepals green, to 8 mm long. June to August.

FRUIT: Flattened achenes up to 2.5 mm long, each with distinct erect, tiny (0.2 to 0.4 mm long) beak, in a dense, round head to 1 cm long, which is first green then black.

LEAVES: All basal. **Emergent leaves arrow-shaped**, up to 12 cm long

arum-leaved arrowhead   (JH)

and 6 cm wide, with long leaf stalks. Basal lobes usually much shorter than upper. Floating leaves linear to oval or heart-shaped. Submersed leaves simple, tapered at both ends, and much narrower than emergent leaves. Veins of lower leaves often have noticeable cross-walls.

GROWTH HABIT: Perennial, 20 to 50 cm tall, with slender rhizomes and small tubers up to 5 cm in diameter. Plants have **milky juice** and usually lack stem leaves.

Wapato (or wapatoo) is named after an island in the Columbia River in the United States, where the plant is common. The genus name *Sagittaria* is from the Latin *sagitta* (arrow); the common name "arrowhead" refers to the arrow-shaped leaves. The specific name *cuneata* means "wedge-shaped," referring to the starchy tubers at the ends of the rootstocks. ✐ Wapato was an important trade item for North American natives. Using their toes, native women rooted out the tubers, which rose to the surface where they could be collected. The large, starchy tubers were boiled

arum-leaved arrowhead (leaves only)   (CWE)

and roasted. Wapato is cultivated in the Orient alongside rice patties; the tubers are eaten sliced like water chestnuts. They are also eaten by ducks, geese and musk-rats. ✍ There are 20 species of *Sagittaria*, mainly of temperate and tropical regions; 2 occur in Alberta. Broad-leaved arrowhead (*S. latifolia*) is larger and taller than arum-leaved arrowhead, has achenes with larger beaks (0.5 to 1.5 mm) extending at right angles to the body, rather than erect, and has mature male and female flower stalks of equal length. Broad-leaved arrowhead is rare in the province and has been iden-tified only from a few locations in north-central Alberta.

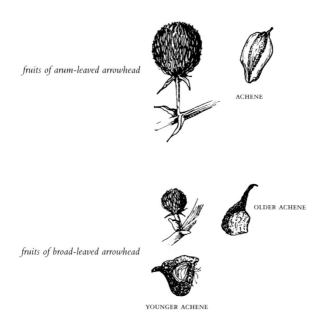

fruits of arum-leaved arrowhead

ACHENE

OLDER ACHENE

fruits of broad-leaved arrowhead

YOUNGER ACHENE

common great bulrush, softstem bulrush, tule
Scirpus validus Vahl
PRAIRIE, ASPEN PARKLAND, BOREAL FOREST

HABITAT AND RANGE: Marshes, muddy banks, pond, river and lake margins. Salt-tolerant. Widespread in Alberta.

FLOWERS: Spikelets in often **drooping clusters** of 1 or more at the ends of stalks that are up to 6 cm long. Each spikelet to 1 cm long, **with shiny, reddish-brown scales to 3.5 mm long, each with a prominent midvein that often ends in a short spine. Scale margins entire to fringed with hairs.** Sepals and petals reduced to 6 reddish bristles. Stem extends beyond flower cluster as an **erect involucral bract for up to 10 cm.** June to August.

FRUIT: Gray-brown achenes to about 2 mm long, with barbed bristles arising from the base. Each achene broadly oval with a short beak at tip, tapered to a narrow base.

LEAVES: Short-bladed or bladeless, green to brownish sheaths at base of plant.

GROWTH HABIT: Stout, rhizomatous perennial to 3 m tall, with **soft, easily crushed, thick, round stems that are broadest at base.**

common great bulrush (JH)

*S*cirpus is from the classical Latin name of the plant. *Validus* means "strong." ✍ The roots are edible and can be pounded into flour. Some native tribes crushed and boiled them to make a syrup. Young shoots may be eaten raw or boiled, and the seeds ground into a meal. The Blackfoot dug and ate tubers from related prairie bulrush (*S. maritimus* var. *paludosus*; *S. paludosus* in Moss 1983). ✍ There are about 175 species of *Scirpus* in the world, widely distributed; 14 species occur in Alberta, of which 5 are rare. Great or hardstem bulrush (*S. acutus*) is similar to common great bulrush and often grows in the same locations; however, as the name suggests, hardstem bulrush has a stem not easily compressed between the fingers. In addition, the inflorescence is usually erect, as opposed to drooping, and the scales are pale with reddish brown stripes and torn-looking. Prairie or alkali bulrush has distinctly 3-angled, pale-green stems that have leaves along the lower portion and large spikelets (1 to 2.5 cm) with lens-shaped achenes surrounded at base by notched scales. It is often seen growing on saline or alkaline mudflats.

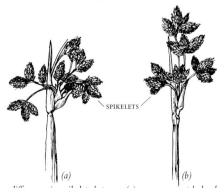
SPIKELETS
(a) *(b)*
differences in spikelets between (a) common great bulrush and (b) great bulrush

water arum, wild calla, water calla

Calla palustris L.

Aspen Parkland, Boreal Forest

water arum (in flower)   (CWa)

HABITAT AND RANGE: Shallow water of wet bogs, sloughs and ditches; primarily in boreal forests in the northern half of the province.

FLOWERS: Tiny, yellowish, in a **dense cylindrical spike (*spadix*) up to 2.5 cm long**, surrounded by a large, showy, **white, oval bract (*spathe*)** up to 4 cm long, with a long, pointed tip. The spathe rots away as the fruit develops. No petals or sepals. Stamens 6. June to July.

FRUIT: **Berry-like, red, in dense heads** 1.5 to 5 cm long. Few seeds.

LEAVES: All basal. Shiny green, broad, parallel-veined, up to 10 cm long, **heart-shaped or rounded at the base. Long-stalked, with leaf stalks twice as long as the blades.**

GROWTH HABIT: Perennial herb up to 20 cm tall from a long, thick rootstock.

The genus name *Calla* is from the Greek *kallos* (beautiful); the species name *palustris* means "of the marsh." This plant is related to the calla lilies sold in florist shops and to the skunk cabbage seen in B.C. coastal forests. ✐ The fruit was eaten dried and boiled by certain tribes of the northern United States; however, water arum **can cause rashes** if touched and **produces burning and edema** if swallowed. It contains needle-like crystals of calcium oxalate which can become embedded in mucus membranes. ✐ Only this species of *Calla* is found in Alberta and Canada, ranging from Alaska and the Yukon east to Prince Edward Island and south to Florida. It also occurs in Eurasia.

water arum (in fruit)   (BA)

wire rush, Baltic rush

Juncus balticus Willd.

<small>Prairie, Aspen Parkland, Boreal Forest, Montane, Subalpine</small>

wire rush (LA)

HABITAT AND RANGE: Wet saline and sandy shores, meadows, marshes, and bogs. Widespread in moist sites.

FLOWERS: Brownish inflorescence, 2 to 4 cm long, **appearing on the side of the stem**. Each flower consists of 3 scale-like sepals and 3 petals that are similar in appearance, 4 to 5 mm long, dark brown, pale or greenish. Stamens 6, enclosed by sepals and petals. June to August.

FRUIT: 3-valved, reddish brown, **oval capsule, to 3 mm long, with pointed tip. Capsule enclosed by sepals and petals**, contains many seeds, each about 0.5 mm long.

LEAVES: Light to dark-green, **bladeless leaves with brown, shiny, sheathing bases**. Basal sheaths bladeless or with very short blade (less than 1 cm long).

GROWTH HABIT: Slender perennial, variable in appearance, up to 60 cm tall from creeping, thick rootstock. Stems round to slightly flattened, up to 5 mm thick at base. Often found in large colonies.

The name wire rush is likely derived from the stiff, wiry growth form. *Juncus* originates from the Latin or Greek name for rush, and *balticus* likely means "of the Baltic." ✒ The Blackfoot made a brown dye from the stems of this plant. ✒ There are over 200 species world-wide, in wet places; 22 species are found in Alberta, of which 8 are provincially rare. ✒ Toad rush *(J. bufonius)*, another widespread species, is a very small (5 to 30 cm tall), much-branched annual.

toad rush

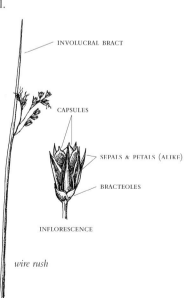

INVOLUCRAL BRACT

CAPSULES

SEPALS & PETALS (ALIKE)

BRACTEOLES

INFLORESCENCE

wire rush

This widely distributed family is particularly abundant in warm temperate and tropical regions and includes many beautiful ornamentals such as tulips, lilies and hyacinths, as well as the familiar vegetables onions, garlic and asparagus. Most lilies are perennial herbs growing from bulbs, fleshy roots or rhizomes. The flower parts are usually in 3s, and the 3 sepals and 3 petals are often alike and petal-like in appearance. There are usually 6 stamens. The leaves are usually parallel-veined and basal, alternate or whorled. Fruits are papery capsules with many seeds or fleshy, few-seeded berries. *(See key for this family beginning page 293.)*

nodding onion
Allium cernuum Roth
ASPEN PARKLAND, MONTANE, SUBALPINE, ALPINE

HABITAT AND RANGE: Dry, rocky slopes, open woods and thickets from the Peace River country south to the United States border.

FLOWERS: 8 to 12 or more, **in loose, nodding clusters** at the end of the stem. Flowers composed of **6 pinkish to white, petal-like segments, each about 6 mm long**. Stamens 6. May to August.

FRUIT: Dry, 3-lobed capsule, 3 to 4 mm long with dull black, flattened seeds, each up to 3 mm long.

LEAVES: Numerous, long, narrow, **circular in cross-section**, bright green, smooth, 2 to 4 mm wide. **Strongly scented.**

GROWTH HABIT: Erect perennial, 10 to 50 cm tall, from a slender pinkish bulb that sometimes is covered with a parallel-veined membrane. **Flower stalk nods when the flowers are present but becomes erect before the seeds mature.**

nodding onion (DJ)

*A*llium is the Latin name for garlic, from the Celtic *all* (hot or burning), because it irritates the eyes. The species name *cernuum* refers to the crook in the flower stem. ✍ Nodding onion gives off an onion odour when crushed and is one of the better-tasting wild onions. Both leaves and bulb may be eaten but **do not confuse this plant with the highly poisonous death camas** (described on pp 32-33), which has no onion odour and has flowers in racemes, not umbels (see illustrated glossary page 331). ✍ The bulbs were dug before flowering by several native tribes, and were eaten raw, cooked or added to soups and stews; however, eating too much of any of the wild onions, especially prairie onion, can cause an **upset stomach**. The crushed bulbs were also used to relieve insect stings. Bears, ground squirrels and marmots also find them a tasty addition to their diets. ✍ There are 500 species of *Allium* in the world, all of them in the northern hemisphere; 4 occur in Alberta. Prairie onion (*A. textile*) has an upright, rather than nodding, stalked, usually white flower; while wild chives (*A. schoenoprasum* L. var. *sibiricum*) has a more compact, pink or purple flower and hollow leaves (at least near the base). Geyer's onion (*A. geyeri*) usually has pink flowers, leaves that are not hollow and a fibrous, net-like bulb-coat. This species is rare, found only in the extreme southwest of the province.

prairie onion (DJ)

wild chives (CWE)

15

mariposa lily, three-spot tulip, pointed mariposa
Calochortus apiculatus Baker
Montane, Subalpine

mariposa lily (CWe)

HABITAT AND RANGE: Open coniferous woods, dry, sandy or gravelly slopes, moist fescue grassland in the montane zone. Restricted to the southwestern corner of the province.

FLOWERS: 1 to 5 flowers per plant. Petals **3, spreading, yellowish white, up to 3 cm long, fringed at the margin**. Each petal **hairy on the inner surface** with a **purplish gland at the base**. The 3 sepals, which appear between the petals, are greenish white, narrow, prominently veined and about 2.5 cm long. Stamens 6, large, white. Stigma 3-lobed. June to July.

FRUIT: **3-ridged, nodding capsule** with many yellowish seeds.

LEAVES: **Single basal leaf** flat, up to 30 cm long, 5 to 15 mm broad, tapering at both ends. Blue-green, prominently veined. Bracts lance-shaped, 1 to 5 cm long.

GROWTH HABIT: Erect, single-leaved perennial, up to 30 cm tall from a scaly bulb.

*M*ariposa means "butterfly" in Spanish and the markings on certain mariposa petals are like the markings on a butterfly's wings. The purple glands at the base of each petal give the flower the name three-spot tulip. *Calochortus* is from the Greek *kallos* (beautiful) and *chortos* (grass); *apiculatus* refers to the slender-tipped anthers. ✍ The bulbs and flower buds were eaten raw, roasted or boiled by some British Columbian native tribes. The dried bulbs could be stored for long periods or pounded into a flour. The Blackfoot treated them as a famine food. ✍ There are 60 species of *Calochortus*, all in North and Central America. Only this species occurs in Alberta. The closely related sego lily (*C. nuttallii*), the state flower of Utah, is said to have saved many Mormon settlers from famine in the mid 1800s, when crops were destroyed by insects.

blue camas, common camas, wild hyacinth, sweet camas

Camassia quamash (Pursh) Greene

MONTANE, SUBALPINE

HABITAT AND RANGE: Wet meadows and streambanks in the southwestern corner of the province.

FLOWERS: Numerous, in a loose terminal cluster. Petals and sepals **in 3s**, similar in appearance, **dark-blue or purplish**, narrow, tapered at both ends, up to 4 cm long. Stamens 6, with long filaments and yellow anthers. May to June.

FRUIT: 3-angled oval capsule up to 18 mm long, with shiny black seeds.

LEAVES: Leaves basal, narrow, 5 to 25 mm broad and up to 40 cm long.

GROWTH HABIT: Smooth, showy perennial up to 60 cm tall from a white bulb with brown scales. Often occurs in **large colonies**.

blue camas   (CWA)

Camas is from *chamas*, a Nootka or Chinook word meaning "sweet," because of the sweet-tasting bulbs. *Quamash* is a native name for the plant. ✦ The bulbs were a major source of food and a valued trade item for many tribes, including Alberta's Blood and Blackfoot. Many battles were fought over the right to collect bulbs in specific locations. In some cases, collecting the bulbs was a festive occasion, with dances honouring the camas. The bulbs were often baked in pits and relished for their high sugar content. The Flathead of Montana boiled the bulbs to produce a type of coffee. ✦ Victoria, B.C. was once called *Camosun* or "place for gathering camas." ✦ **Take care** not to confuse this bulb with the **poisonous death camas,** which has cream-coloured flowers (see pp 32-33). When the flowers are missing, death camas and blue camas are hard to distinguish because the leaves and bulbs of both species are similar in appearance. ✦ There are 5 species of *Camassia*, all found in North America. Only this species grows in Alberta.

corn lily, queen's cup, bluebead lily, one-flowered clintonia

Clintonia uniflora (Schult.) Kunth

MONTANE, SUBALPINE, ALPINE

corn lily   (JH)

HABITAT AND RANGE: Moist, shaded coniferous forests; often on cold, acidic soils. Mainly in the southwestern part of the province.

FLOWERS: A single flower per plant (occasionally 2). **White, 2 cm long, composed of 6 petal-like segments**, each 7 to 9-nerved and rounded at the tip. Stamens 6 with long (4 to 5 mm), yellow anthers; filaments hairy at base. June to July.

FRUIT: Attractive, **dark-blue**, many-seeded berry, 6 to 10 mm long on a **long stalk**.

LEAVES: 2 to 5, **basal**, oblong, 7 to 25 cm long. Shiny above, softly hairy beneath, rounded or abruptly sharp-pointed at tip.

GROWTH HABIT: Perennial, up to 15 cm tall from slender rhizome. Often forms dense colonies.

The common name bluebead lily comes from the dark-blue, bead-like fruit. This plant is named after DeWitt Clinton, an American naturalist and former governor of New York state. *Uniflora* refers to the single flower. ✒ The berries are not palatable but were used by the Lillooet people as an eye medicine and by the Lower Thompson as a blue dye. ✒ There are 6 species of *Clintonia* in the world, 4 in North America and 2 in Asia. Only this species occurs in Alberta.

corn lily   (BA)

fairybells, rough-fruited fairybells

Disporum trachycarpum (S. Wats.) B. & H.

ASPEN PARKLAND, BOREAL FOREST, MONTANE, SUBALPINE

HABITAT AND RANGE: Shaded, moist poplar woods, stream banks, thickets, moist riverine prairie. Widespread and common in Alberta.

FLOWERS: **Paired and drooping,** tubular, on stout stalks at tips of branches. Petal-like segments 6, **greenish white to cream-coloured,** pointed, curved, oblong, narrowed at base, 12 to 20 mm long. Stamens 6. May to June.

FRUIT: **Orange or bright scarlet-red, 3-compartmented berry** with a **bumpy surface,** 6 to 10 mm in diameter. Few seeds.

rough-fruited fairybells   (CWE)

LEAVES: Alternate, wavy-margined, **broadly oval, with prominent parallel veins.** Abruptly narrowed at base and often clasping the stem. Pale green, **smooth above,** with spreading hairs along the margins and hairy beneath when young; up to 12 cm long and 5 cm wide.

GROWTH HABIT: Branched perennial reaching 60 cm tall from prominent rhizome. **Stem fuzzy-hairy,** scaly below.

The genus name comes from the Greek *dis* (double) and *spora* (seeds), meaning 2 seeds (some species have 2 seeds per fruit compartment). The species name *trachycarpum* means "rough-fruited." ✿ The berries are edible but rather tasteless, and were eaten by the Blood and Blackfoot of Alberta and the Shuswap of B.C. They are enjoyed by many rodents and birds. ✿ There are 15 species of *Disporum* in the world, chiefly in Asia; 2 occur in Alberta. Oregon fairybells (*D. hookeri*), restricted to the extreme southwest of Alberta, has leaves that are hairy above and an ovate, rather than rounded, fruit that lacks the bumpy surface of fairybells. ✿ Fairybells is similar to 2 other members of the lily family. It can be distinguished from clasping-leaved twisted-stalk (*Streptopus amplexifolius*), described on page 27, because, as the name suggests, the latter bears its flowers and fruits on a twisted stalk. The flowers of twisted-stalk arise from the leaf-axils, while the flowers of fairybells appear at the ends of the branches. Fairybells can be distinguished from false Solomon's-seal (*Smilacina racemosa* var. *amplexicaulis*) because Solomon's-seal has flowers in a raceme and is generally unbranched.

rough-fruited fairybells   (JH)

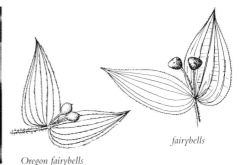

Oregon fairybells

fairybells

glacier lily, yellow avalanche lily, dogtooth violet

Erythronium grandiflorum Pursh

MONTANE, SUBALPINE, ALPINE

glacier lily (BA)

HABITAT AND RANGE: Open woods, dry slopes, moist meadows and stream banks from montane to alpine elevations in the foothills and Rocky Mountains. Often observed growing **near melting snow banks**.

FLOWERS: **Nodding**, composed of similar, **bright-yellow** (sometimes pale or whitish) petals and sepals; each 2 to 5 cm long, 4 to 8 mm wide, tapered to the tip, **reflexed**. Stamens 6, with anthers that are reddish when immature but turn yellow to whitish with age. May to June.

FRUIT: Papery, **3-angled, oblong capsule**, 3 to 6 cm long, with many seeds.

LEAVES: **Usually 2, attached near base of stem**. Broadly oblong, 10 to 20 cm long, gently tapered to base, with pointed, closed, reddish tip. Parallel-veined, somewhat fleshy.

GROWTH HABIT: Smooth, herbaceous perennial, 10 to 40 cm tall from an elongated, bulb-like corm. Often grows in clumps.

*E*rythronium is from the Greek *erythros* (red), referring to the red or pink flowers of some species. *Grandiflorum* means "large-flowered." ✐ The corms are edible raw or cooked but are hard to dig out. The Blackfoot occasionally ate them, and they were dried by some American tribes as a winter food. They are a favoured food for bears. The leaves can be eaten raw or boiled. Neither corms nor leaves are recommended as food, however, as both **may cause vomiting** if eaten in quantity, and the corms of related species have caused poultry poisoning. ✐ The Blackfoot used the corms to treat boils. Pounded roots were applied as dressings for skin sores. The Blood used the leaves and flowers to produce a dye. ✐ There are 12 or 13 species of *Erythronium*, all but 1 in North America. Only this species occurs in Alberta.

fruit of glacier lily.

glacier lily (CWE)

yellowbell, yellow fritillary, yellow snowdrop
Fritillaria pudica (Pursh) Spreng.
PRAIRIE, MONTANE

HABITAT AND RANGE: Open mixedwoods, stream banks, dry coulee areas, dry coniferous forest. Occurs in the southwestern corner of the province.

FLOWERS: Usually 1 or 2 nodding flowers per stalk. Petals and sepals oblong to lance-shaped, **rounded at tips, bright yellow, fading to orange or purple**; to about 35 mm long and 10 mm wide. Glands at bases of sepals and petals. April to May.

FRUIT: Capsule erect on stem, **green and white striped when young, 3-compartmented, cylindrical** (sometimes triangular-shaped), up to 30 mm long, with many brownish seeds, each about 4 mm long.

LEAVES: 2 to 7 **blue-green, strap-shaped, nearly opposite, blunt-tipped leaves,** 3 to 16 cm long and up to 12 mm wide.

GROWTH HABIT: Erect, sweet-scented perennial up to 35 cm tall, from small, scaly bulb.

yellowbell (CWA)

Fritillaria is from the Latin *fritillus* (a dice-box), perhaps referring to the shape of the seed-capsule. *Pudica* means "bashful," in reference to the nodding habit. ✐ The bulbs, which were dug before the plants flowered, were eaten raw or cooked by native peoples and early European explorers. The green seed pods are also edible raw or cooked. ✐ The starchy roots and bulbs also provide food for bears, pocket gophers and ground squirrels. ✐ There are 50 species of *Fritillaria*, all in the northern hemisphere. Only this species is found in Alberta.

yellowbell (CWE)

western wood lily, wild tiger lily, chalice-cup lily

Lilium philadelphicum L. var. *andinum* (Nutt.) Ker.

PRAIRIE, ASPEN PARKLAND, BOREAL FOREST, MONTANE, SUBALPINE

western wood lily   (LF)

HABITAT AND RANGE: Moist meadows, dense to open woods and edges of aspen groves. Widespread except for the southeast and extreme north of the province.

FLOWERS: 1 to 5 flowers per plant. **3 bright-orange or orange-red petals and 3 similar sepals**, 2.5 to 7 cm long, **becoming yellowish, and black or purple-dotted at the bases.** Stamens 6; **anthers dark purple.** June to August.

FRUIT: Elongated, egg-shaped capsule, 2 to 4 cm long, with many flattened seeds.

LEAVES: Numerous, linear to narrowly lance-shaped, smooth, 3 to 10 cm long. Alternate on the stem except for the upper leaves, which are **in whorls**.

GROWTH HABIT: Erect, smooth, leafy perennial, 30 to 60 cm tall from a white, thick-scaled bulb.

L ilium is the Latin name for the plant. The species name originates from the fact that Linnaeus received his specimens of the plant from a student in Philadelphia; *andinum* means "pertaining to the Andes." ✿ Western wood lily, the floral emblem of Saskatchewan, is becoming increasingly rare because of overpicking. Picking removes leaves which then cannot make food for the bulb, and therefore the plant dies. The plants do not survive well if transplanted. ✿ The bulbs were eaten by some natives and early settlers as a substitute for potatoes, but they were considered rather bitter. The Blackfoot treated spider bites with a wet dressing of the crushed flowers. ✿ There are 75 species of *Lilium*, in north temperate zones, but only this species occurs in Alberta.

wild lily-of-the-valley, two-leaved Solomon's-seal

Maianthemum canadense Desf. var. *interius* Fern.

PRAIRIE, ASPEN PARKLAND, BOREAL FOREST, MONTANE

HABITAT AND RANGE: Moist to dry woods, riverine prairie, calcareous fens. Widespread except in the dry grasslands.

FLOWERS: Small, white, 4 to 6 mm wide, in short, terminal raceme. **4 petal-like segments**, each 2 mm long. Stamens 4. Faintly aromatic. May to July.

FRUIT: **Clusters of shiny, greenish (turning red with age), speckled, round berries, 3 to 6 mm wide**. Seeds 1 to 2.

LEAVES: Alternate. **1 to 3 (usually 2) stalkless or short-stalked stem leaves, plus 1 long-stalked basal leaf.** Leaf blades 2 to 8 cm long, usually **slightly hairy**, parallel-veined, oval, heart-shaped at base.

wild lily-of-the-valley   (CWA)

GROWTH HABIT: Low (to 20 cm tall), erect perennial from a creeping rhizome.

Maianthemum is from the Greek *maios* (May) and *anthemom* (flower), describing the time of flowering. *Canadense* refers to the plant's range from Labrador to B.C. and south, while *interius* means "in the inner part, on the inside." ✦ The berries of a related species, false lily-of-the-valley (*M. dilatatum*), were eaten by coastal peoples of British Columbia; however, the berries of this species are said to be **poisonous**. ✦ There are 3 species of *Maianthemum*, in northern temperate zones of the world. Only this species occurs in Alberta. ✦ Wild lily-of-the-valley may be confused with three-leaved Solomon's-seal (see page 25); however, the latter has long-stalked flowers in less dense clusters; flowers with 6 petal-like segments, each about 3 mm long; and broadly lance-shaped leaves.

wild lily-of-the-valley

three-leaved Solomon's-seal

Lily Family (Liliaceae)

star-flowered Solomon's-seal, wild spikenard
Smilacina stellata (L.) Desf.
PRAIRIE, ASPEN PARKLAND, BOREAL FOREST, MONTANE, SUBALPINE, ALPINE

star-flowered Solomon's-seal   (CWE)

HABITAT AND RANGE: Moist woods, river and stream banks, thickets, meadows, sandy areas, slopes. Very common.

FLOWERS: Few to several, **star-shaped**, in loose, short-stalked cluster up to 5 cm long, **often on zig-zag stem**. Petal-like segments 6, small (up to 6 mm long), white, narrowly oblong. Stamens 6, white with yellow tips. May to July.

FRUIT: Cluster of shiny **green berries with maroon stripes**, turning darker with age. Each berry 3-compartmented, up to 8 mm long.

LEAVES: Numerous, alternate, light-bluish green, often with whitish bloom. Broadly lance-shaped or oblong, gradually tapering to pointed tip, 2.5 to 12 cm long and 1 to 5 cm wide. Smooth (hairy beneath), stalkless, somewhat clasping. **Prominently parallel veined**, sometimes folded at the midrib.

GROWTH HABIT: Erect, leafy perennial, 15 to 70 cm tall, with creeping rhizomes. Stem sometimes reddish at base.

A theory of origin of the common name is from the plant's alleged use in sealing wounds. Another suggestion is that a cross-section of the root of a related Solomon's-seal resembles the six-pointed, star-shaped seal of King Solomon. The genus name is derived from *Smilax*, an ancient Greek name applied to another genus. *Stellata*

star-flowered Solomon's-seal (fruit)   (BA)

24

means "star-like" and refers to the shape of the tiny white flowers. ✔ The Thompson and Shuswap used the plants as a scent. The Blackfoot are said to have used the powdered roots of false Solomon's-seal (*S. racemosa* var. *amplexicaulis*) as a wound dressing. False Solomon's-seal berries are said to be edible, laxative and not very palatable; the Blood, however, used them to induce abortion and relieve swellings. ✔ There are 20 species of *Smilacina*, mainly in Asia; 3 occur in Alberta. False Solomon's-seal has wider leaves and its flowers grow in a branched cluster (*panicle*) rather than attached to the stem by short stalks (*raceme*). Three-leaved Solomon's-seal (*S. trifolia*) usually has flowers on longer stalks and only 3 broadly lance-shaped leaves; it is generally shorter than the other 2 species.

false Solomon's-seal (CWE)

three-leaved Solomon's-seal (BA)

bronzebells, mountain-bells

Stenanthium occidentale A. Gray

MONTANE, SUBALPINE, ALPINE

bronzebells (CWE)

HABITAT AND RANGE: Moist woods, stream banks, cliffs, meadows and slopes in the Rocky Mountains.

FLOWERS: **In loose, drooping terminal clusters of 3 to 10 or more. Flowers greenish or reddish, 8 to 15 mm long, bell-shaped.** Petals and sepals alike, narrowly lance-shaped with tips turned back. Withering-persistent, sweet-scented. Stamens 6. 1 or 2 lance-shaped bracts below the inflorescence and below each flower. June to July.

FRUIT: Capsule 15 to 20 mm long, lance-shaped, membraneous, greenish; 3-beaked, with long, persistent style. Seeds light brown, about 3 mm long.

LEAVES: **Few, mainly basal. Narrow, pale green, lighter underneath, reddish at base, tapered at both ends**; somewhat resembling grass leaves. Prominently parallel-veined, especially underneath, 15 to 30 cm long, usually 3 to 30 mm broad.

GROWTH HABIT: Erect, slender-stemmed perennial up to 50 cm tall from an elongated bulb.

The genus name is from the Greek *steno* (narrow) and *anthos* (flower). The species name *occidentale* means "western." ✱ The Thompson people of British Columbia believed this plant to be **poisonous**. ✱ There are 5 species of *Stenanthium*, all in North America. Only this species occurs in Alberta.

clasping-leaved twisted-stalk
Streptopus amplexifolius (L.) DC.
BOREAL FOREST, MONTANE, SUBALPINE

HABITAT AND RANGE: Moist, mossy, coniferous woods, stream banks and thickets. In the Rocky Mountains, Cypress Hills and boreal forest.

FLOWERS: **In leaf axils, solitary or occasionally in pairs, on twisted stalks. Sepals and petals narrowly oblong, joined to form pale-yellow or greenish, bell-shaped flowers that are reflexed at tips,** 8 to 12 mm long. Stamens 6, unequal. June to July.

FRUIT: **Green (maturing to orange or red), smooth, 3-compartmented berry on stalk with 1 twist.** Berries up to 1.5 cm long, 8 mm across. Seeds 3 to 15, straw-coloured, prominently grooved, about 3 mm long.

LEAVES: Alternate, stalkless. **Broadly oval, pointed at the tip, clasping at base, parallel-veined.** Entire or with minute teeth on the margins. Bright green above, **with a whitish bloom beneath.** Can grow to 12 cm long, 6 cm wide.

GROWTH HABIT: Usually branched, spreading perennial, 30 to 100 cm tall from thick rhizome. **Stems thick, often zig-zagged,** sometimes hairy (but not at stem joints), occasionally with reddish spots.

clasping-leaved twisted-stalk   (CWE)

S*treptopus* is from the Greek *streptos* (twisted) and *pous* (foot), referring to the twisted flower stalks. *Amplexifolius* means "clasping leaf," from the Latin *amplexor* (to surround). ✐ There are 7 species of *Streptopus* in the world, in temperate North America and Eurasia; 3 occur in Alberta. The other Alberta species, rose mandarin (*S. roseus*) and small twisted-stalk (*S. streptopoides*), are much shorter (less than 30 cm tall), have hairy stem joints and are rare in Alberta, known only from the Smoky-Athabasca River area. Although both have reddish flowers, rose mandarin frequently has segmented hairs along the leaf margins, with petals and sepals 6 to 10 mm long, while small twisted-stalk has nearly transparent teeth, with petals and sepals about 2.5 to 4.5 mm long.

clasping-leaved twisted-stalk   (CWE)   *rose mandarin*   (DJ)

sticky false asphodel
Tofieldia glutinosa (Michx.) Pers.

<small>Aspen Parkland, Boreal Forest, Montane, Subalpine, Alpine</small>

sticky false asphodel   (CWa)

HABITAT AND RANGE: Wet areas, calcareous bogs, meadows, stream banks, lake shores. Common in the Rocky Mountains and boreal forest.

FLOWERS: **In 3s in a short, dense, terminal cluster** that is 1 to 7 cm long and 1 to 2 cm thick. Sepals and petals alike, oblong, white to greenish, 3 to 6 mm long. Stamens 6, anthers dark. June to August.

FRUIT: Plump, membraneous, reddish or yellowish capsule, 4 to 8 mm long, with numerous **tailed seeds**.

LEAVES: **Basal, linear to lance-shaped, grass-like**, 5 to 20 cm long, 3 to 8 mm broad. May have 2 or 3 short, sheathing stem leaves.

GROWTH HABIT: Erect, slender, tufted perennial up to 50 cm high from a short rootstock. **Stem with sticky glands under the inflorescence.** Dark, fibrous remains of old leaves at base of plant.

This plant resembles the European asphodel, hence the common name. *Tofieldia* honours the British 18th-century botanist Thomas Tofield, and *glutinosa* refers to the sticky stem below the flower. ✍ There are 15 species of *Tofieldia* in the world, in the north temperate zone and in the Andes of South America; of these, 2 occur in Alberta. Dwarf false or bog asphodel (*T. pusilla*) is found from the montane to alpine tundra. It is shorter (5 to 20 cm tall), and has a smooth stem and seeds without tails; its flowers occur singly rather than in 3s.

green false hellebore, Indian hellebore

Veratrum viride Ait. ssp. *eschscholtzii* (A. Gray) Löve & Löve
(*Veratrum eschscholtzii* (R. & S.) A. Gray in Moss 1983)

BOREAL FOREST, MONTANE, SUBALPINE, ALPINE

HABITAT AND RANGE: Moist forest, thickets,
swamps, avalanche chutes, open slopes,
wet meadows of the Rocky Mountains
and boreal forest.

FLOWERS: **In long (3 to 7 cm), open, drooping
clusters. Petal-like segments 6, greenish,
white-hairy on margins and fuzzy-hairy
beneath,** up to 10 mm long. Stamens 6, yellow-
tipped. Flowers have slight odour. Late June to
September.

FRUIT: 3-compartmented, beaked, oval, smooth
capsule, 2 to 3 cm long. Seeds numerous, 8 to 10
mm long.

LEAVES: **Large (to more than 30 cm in
length)**, dull green, with long, closed sheaths at
base. **Each leaf broadly elliptic** with pointed
tip, **prominently parallel-veined**, smooth above,
ciliate on veins and soft, white-hairy beneath.
Leaves reduced upward.

GROWTH HABIT: **Tall (to 2 m), stout, often
fuzzy-hairy perennial with many leaves.**
Smooth below to rather woolly-hairy above
(including the flowers).

false hellebore (DJ)

The genus name is from the Latin name
for hellebore, derived from *vere* (true)
and *atrum* (black), because of the black roots
of true hellebore. *Viride* means "green," while
eschscholtzii honours Dr. Eschscholtz, a Russian doctor and naturalist of the 19th
century. ✐ Green false hellebore contains **toxic alkaloids**, particularly in the young
shoots and roots, and can cause symptoms similar to heart attack. People have died
from eating it, and it was used by Alberta Blackfoot to commit suicide. The plant,
which is most dangerous early in the growing season, has also caused accidental
poisonings of cattle and sheep. ✐ Green false hellebore was used externally as an
anaesthetic and blistering agent by some B.C. native peoples, and the rootstock was
dried and powdered by Montana natives and sniffed as a decongestant. The Blackfoot
took it to relieve headaches. Early American settlers boiled the roots and combed
the resulting liquid through their hair to kill lice. False hellebore was also used medicinally in the U.S. as a heart depressant and spinal paralyzant. ✐ The Lillooet are said
to have used the stem fibres to weave bags and pouches. ✐ There are about 12 species of *Veratrum* in the western hemisphere; only this species occurs in Alberta.

bear grass, Indian basket grass

Xerophyllum tenax (Pursh) Nutt.

MONTANE, SUBALPINE, ALPINE

bear grass (CWA)

HABITAT AND RANGE: Dry forest, open woods, meadows, roadsides and clearings. Restricted to the extreme southwestern corner of Alberta.

FLOWERS: Numerous, **in dense terminal clusters, blooming from the lowest end of the cluster first**. Petal-like segments 6, creamy-white, lance-shaped, spreading, each about 6-10 mm long. Yellow stigma and **long-protruding stamens**. Fragrant. Late May to August.

FRUIT: 3-compartmented, oval, dry capsule, up to 7 mm long. 2 to 5 seeds per compartment.

LEAVES: **Narrow (to 4 mm broad), basal leaves in large clumps, each leaf up to 60 cm long. Rough-hairy on margins, deeply grooved,** thickened. Green above with white rib underneath. **Stem leaves reduced, linear with flared, white-margined, purple-mottled base.**

GROWTH HABIT: **Tall, grass-like, densely tufted, robust, evergreen perennial with thick, hollow stem**; up to 1.5 m tall. Often occurs in colonies.

The genus name is from the Greek *xeros* (dry) and *phyllon* (leaf), in reference to the tough leaves. *Tenax* also refers to the tough or "tenacious" leaves. ✍ Northwestern U.S. tribes dried and bleached the leaves to weave hats and baskets. The Blackfoot used a potion of the boiled roots as a hair tonic and to ease sprains. The chewed roots have been made into a poultice for wounds. ✍ Bears are said to like the soft new leaves in spring. ✍ There are 2 species of *Xerophyllum* in the world, the other occurring in eastern North America.

bear grass (CWE)

soapweed, yucca, soaproot, Spanish bayonet, beargrass
Yucca glauca Nutt.
PRAIRIE

HABITAT AND RANGE: Dry, exposed slopes on well-drained, often sandy or gravelly soils. Known in Alberta from only 2 localities in the Milk River region.

FLOWERS: 25 to 30, showy, **bell-shaped, in large, drooping, terminal clusters. Sepals and petals alike, cream-coloured or greenish white, leathery, up to 5 cm long.** Stamens 6. Flowers are almost closed during bright, sunny days and open at night. June to July.

FRUIT: Oblong, cream-coloured, 3-ribbed, woody capsule, 5 to 7 cm long, with layers of numerous black seeds. Each seed thin, flat, 10 to 12 mm long, with tiny net veins.

LEAVES: Numerous, spreading, simple, alternate, **evergreen, persistent. Stiff, narrow basal leaves up to 60 cm long, with sharp, hard tips. Margins whitish, inrolled, with a few shredding, stiff fibres.** Older leaves drooping.

GROWTH HABIT: Coarse, erect or prostrate perennial, up to 1 m tall from a woody rootstock. Plants occur singly or in clumps.

soapweed (CWA)

The name soapweed stems from the fact that the plants contain *saponin*, and the leaves and roots can produce a soap-like lather when rubbed in water. *Yucca* is supposedly derived from the Caribbean name for cassava, a different species, while *glauca* means "glaucous" (covered with a whitish or bluish, waxy bloom, like a prune). *◢* The Blackfoot pounded and mixed the roots with water to make a soap or shampoo (believed effective against dandruff and skin irritation). The roots were also used medicinally to treat sprains, cuts and saddle sores. *◢* Unripe fruit was baked or dried by some North American natives. Although some parts of the plant are edible, eating it is not recommended because the plant acts as a **laxative.** The leaves contain salicyclic acid (the active ingredient in many pain relievers), and the roots contain saponin. *◢* Yucca leaves have fibres that can be used, after soaking, to make rope. *◢* The plant provides shade and nest sites for small mammals, birds and reptiles.

◢ Soapweed, which is rare in both Alberta and Canada, can be fertilized only by a particular moth that feeds on it. *◢* There are 30 species of *Yucca* in dry, often desert areas. Only this species is found in our province.

soapweed (CWE)

white camas, mountain death camas, smooth camas

Zigadenus elegans Pursh

PRAIRIE, ASPEN PARKLAND, BOREAL FOREST, MONTANE, SUBALPINE, ALPINE

white camas (JH)

HABITAT AND RANGE: Moist grassland, grassy slopes, open woods. Widespread in the southern half of Alberta.

FLOWERS: Many, lily-shaped, in an open cluster; foul-smelling and withering-persistent. **Sepals and petals alike, greenish white with heart-shaped, yellow-green nectaries near the base**, spreading, narrowly oblong, **8 to 11 mm long. Sepals and petals attached to the middle of the ovary.** Stamens 6, prominent, white. June to August.

FRUIT: Dry, 3-lobed capsule, 1.5 to 2 cm long, with many small, angled, straw-coloured seeds, each 5 to 6 mm long.

LEAVES: **Several basal, pale-green, grass-like, with prominent midveins.** Few small stem leaves, 10 to 25 cm long, narrow, V-shaped, alternate.

GROWTH HABIT: Slender, erect perennial 30 to 60 cm tall. **Has an onion-like bulb with no onion smell.**

The genus name *Zigadenus* is derived from the Greek *zygos* (yoke) and *aden* (gland), which describes a 2-lobed nectary near the base of each petal and sepal. *Elegans* means "elegant" and refers to the attractive petals. The derivation of the term camas is explained on page 17. ✒ All parts of this plant contain **toxic alkaloids**, especially the bulb, and eating it has caused many fatalities, particularly in sheep. ✒ The Blackfoot

white camas

death camas

treated sprains, bruises and rheumatism with a wet dressing of related death camas bulbs (*Z. venenosus* var. *gramineus*). The Okanagan peoples used mashed death camas bulbs as an arrow-poison. ✿ There are 15 species of *Zigadenus* in the world, mainly in North America and Asia; 2 occur in Alberta. Death camas has cream-coloured to yellowish flowers that are shorter (less than 7 mm long), in a tight cluster. The sepals and petals have broadly oval to circular nectaries that are attached below the ovary. Death camas is a less robust, narrower-leaved, **more poisonous** plant than white camas.

death camas (CWA)

blue-eyed grass, common blue-eyed grass

Sisyrinchium montanum Greene

PRAIRIE, ASPEN PARKLAND, BOREAL FOREST, MONTANE, SUBALPINE

blue-eyed grass   (LF)

HABITAT AND RANGE: Moist grassland and woods, river and stream banks, ditches, edges of sloughs. Common.

FLOWERS: 1 to 5 flowers per stem, on stalks usually 19 to 30 mm long. Each flower consists of **6 violet or pale-purple, notched and/or awned, petal-like segments surrounding a bright-yellow centre.** Stamens 3. **Flowers arise from a pair of erect, greenish bracts of unequal length, both inflated at base.** Blooms in June and July but each flower lasts only a day.

FRUIT: **Round, greenish to brown, 3-compartmented capsule**; up to 6 mm long with many small, black seeds.

LEAVES: Narrow, mainly basal, long, **grass-like, 1 to 4 mm wide, with transparent margins at the base.**

GROWTH HABIT: Erect, slender, tufted perennial, 6 to 40 cm tall. **Stems flattened, slightly winged.** Plants often found with remains of old, dried-up leaves at base. Frequently forms large colonies.

The common name is derived from the fact that the plant looks like a grass with a blue flower. *Sisyrinchium* means "swine snout," from the Greek name for a plant whose roots were relished by pigs, while *montanum* means "of the mountains." ✿ There are 50 to 60 species of *Sisyrinchium* in North and South America and the West Indies; 2 species occur in Alberta. Rare pale or northern blue-eyed grass (*S. septentrionale*) is a species of southern Alberta and may be distinguished by its narrower leaves, paler, often white flowers and shorter flower stalks (14 to 18 mm).

northern blue-eyed grass   (JH)

Orchid Family (Orchidaceae)

This primitive but very large (20,000 to 35,000 species) family of perennials has the most representatives in the warm, humid tropics; however, 26 species occur in Alberta. Except for the lady's-slippers and the calypso orchid, most of our species do not have the spectacular flowers we associate with cultivated specimens. Each flower has 3 often petal-like sepals (sometimes 1 is modified) and 3 petals: 2 alike and 1 modified to form a lip or spur. Many orchids have distinctive features to enhance pollination by insects, and a lack of specialized pollinators may account for the rarity of some species (including our mountain lady's-slipper).

The leaves are simple, sheathing and entire, or sometimes reduced to scales. The fruit is a 3-valved, papery capsule with many seeds, a necessary characteristic of primitive plants as the tiny seeds lack stored food. Each orchid seed therefore depends on the presence of a specific fungus growing within its tissues for germination and subsequent development, as the fungus transfers nutrients from the soil into the developing seedling. The roots also have fungal growths, which facilitate absorption of water and minerals from the soil. The reason that many orchid transplants are unsuccessful is that these specific fungi are lacking in the soil to which the plant is transplanted. Better to enjoy our orchids in their natural habitat!

Besides supplying us with many strikingly beautiful and unusual flowers, this family provides us with the widely used flavouring vanilla. *(See key for this family beginning page 295.)*

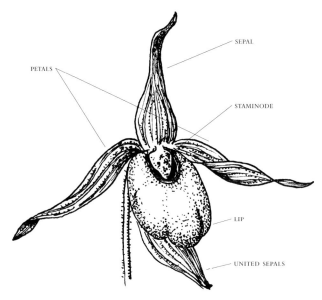

pale coralroot, northern coralroot

Corallorhiza trifida Châtelain

ASPEN PARKLAND, BOREAL FOREST, MONTANE, SUBALPINE, ALPINE

pale coralroot   (CWE)

HABITAT AND RANGE: Moist woods, bogs. Widespread in wooded areas throughout Alberta.

FLOWERS: 3 to 15, up to 10 mm long, spread out on thick stalks in a cluster at the end of the stem. Lateral petals and sepals similar, 4 to 6 mm long, **yellow or greenish yellow** to nearly white, 1-nerved. **Lip 3-lobed near base, often with pale-red dots.** Lip shorter (3.5 to 4.5 mm long) than the lateral petals. June to August.

FRUIT: Reflexed, oval capsule up to 1 cm long.

LEAVES: Reduced to **sheathing scales** at base.

GROWTH HABIT: Erect, **pale-yellow to greenish yellow** perennial, up to 25 cm tall from extensive **coral-like rhizomes.** All coral-roots are saprophytic, meaning they absorb nutrients from decaying organic matter.

*C*orallorhiza is from the Greek *korallion* (coral) and *rhiza* (root). *Trifida* refers to the 3-lobed lip. ✍ The orchid family is one of the largest plant families in the world, with over 400 genera and more than 20,000 species, mostly in tropical regions. ✍ There are 15 species of *Corallorhiza*, 3 of which occur in Alberta. Spotted coralroot (*C. maculata*) has a longer (5 to 9 mm), white, usually purple-spotted lip and a larger, reddish or purplish stem. Striped coralroot (*C. striata*) has a purple to reddish, striped flower. Both spotted and striped coralroot are taller and have larger flowers than pale coralroot.

spotted coralroot   (CWA)

striped coralroot   (SR)

striped coralroot   (CWA)

yellow lady's-slipper, yellow moccasin flower

Cypripedium calceolus L.
<small>ASPEN PARKLAND, BOREAL FOREST, MONTANE</small>

HABITAT AND RANGE: Bogs, damp woods, streambanks. Primarily a species of central Alberta.

FLOWERS: Usually 1 (sometimes 2), with a leaf-like bract below. **Sepals and lateral petals similar, greenish yellow to brownish, wavy-margined and twisted**, 3 to 6 cm long. **Lower sepals fused together. Lip pouch-shaped, bright yellow, often purple-dotted around the puckered opening**, 2 to 4 cm long. Scented. A white-lipped form of this plant is rare in the province. May to July.

FRUIT: Dry, prominently veined, green (becoming brown) capsule, 2 to 3 cm long, with short, white hairs. Contains many seeds.

LEAVES: Alternate, 2 to 4 per stem. Broadly elliptic, slightly clasping, 5 to 15 cm long and up to 6 cm broad. Finely hairy and often glandular; prominently veined.

GROWTH HABIT: Showy, sparsely hairy, often glandular perennial, 15 to 40 cm tall from a thick rhizome. Solitary or occurring in clumps.

yellow lady's-slipper   (CWE)

*C*ypris was another name for Venus, and *pedilon* (foot) refers to the flower lip shape. *Calceolus* means "a small shoe." ✿ Yellow lady's-slipper was used by some North American natives as a sedative and nerve medicine, and was listed in the U.S. Pharmacopoeia as an antispasmodic and nerve tonic until 1916. The leaf and stem

stemless lady's-slipper   (CWA)

hairs **can cause rashes** in some people. ✐ Picking has caused a large decline in numbers of lady's-slippers throughout Canada. ✐ There are 25 species of *Cypripedium* in the world, native to temperate North America and Eurasia; 4 occur in Alberta. Stemless lady's-slipper (*C. acaule*), a provincially rare species found occasionally in extreme northeastern Alberta, has a pink-lipped flower and a leafless stem. Another species rare in the province is mountain lady's-slipper (*C. montanum*), which is similar to yellow lady's-slipper but has a white lip and usually 2 or more flowers per plant. Sparrow's-egg lady's-slipper (*C. passerinum*) has a whitish or pink lip and shorter (to 1.5 cm), more rounded, green sepals and petals. It is more widely distributed and more common than the preceding 2 species.

mountain lady's-slipper   (CWE)

sparrow's-egg lady's-slipper   (CWE)

western rattlesnake plantain, rattlesnake plantain

Goodyera oblongifolia Raf.

BOREAL FOREST, MONTANE, SUBALPINE

HABITAT AND RANGE: Shaded dry or moist coniferous woods. Mainly in montane to subalpine habitats in the Rocky Mountains.

FLOWERS: **Small (sepals and petals 6 to 8 mm long), white or greenish, in dense, twisted or 1-sided, spike-like clusters,** 5 to 10 cm long. Flowers 2-lipped: upper lip minutely 2-lobed, lower lip blunt with incurved margins and pinkish guidelines. Blooms at bottom of cluster first. July to September

FRUIT: Dry, sparsely hairy, ribbed capsule, 1 cm long with many pale-brown, narrow seeds, each about 1 mm long.

LEAVES: Alternate. Stem leaves scale-like, greenish beige, short-hairy. Basal leaves lance-shaped, dark green above, **often with white, mottled midvein and whitish lateral veins**. Smooth, paler beneath, **3 to 7 cm long** including abruptly narrowed, winged leaf stalk.

GROWTH HABIT: Single-stemmed, stiff-hairy perennial, up to 40 cm tall from short rhizome. Often grows in small clumps.

rattlesnake plantain (CWₐ)

The name rattlesnake comes from the mottled white markings on the leaves, which reminded early European settlers of the markings on a rattlesnake. Plantain comes from the Latin *planta* (foot), because of the broad, flat, foot-like leaves. As with true plantains, the leaves of this plant grow close to the ground. The genus name commemorates the 17th-century English botanist John Goodyer, while *oblongifolia* refers to the oblong leaves. ✐ The United States Mohegan tribe used the mashed leaves to prevent thrush in infants. Some North American peoples chewed the root and applied it to bites from rattlesnakes and other poisonous reptiles. ✐ There are 25 species of *Goodyera*, widely distributed in the world; 2 are native to Alberta. Lesser or northern rattlesnake plantain (*G. repens*) has a shorter inflorescence (3 to 6 cm), shorter leaves (1 to 3 cm), which are less marked with white, and a more pouch-like lip. It is much more widespread in Alberta than western rattlesnake plantain.

northern twayblade

Listera borealis Morong.

ASPEN PARKLAND, BOREAL FOREST, MONTANE, SUBALPINE

northern twayblade   (CWE)

HABITAT AND RANGE: Moist coniferous woods, banks, lakeshores; often found on cold, acidic soil in the Rocky Mountains, Cypress Hills, aspen parkland and boreal forest.

FLOWERS: 3 to 15 flowers in terminal, open, bracted cluster. Petals and sepals somewhat similar, greenish brown, 1-nerved, curved backwards. Petals narrower and shorter than sepals. **Lip slightly hairy, oblong, cleft into 2 rounded lobes; broadest at base, 7 to 12 mm long.** Sepals 4 to 6 mm long. June to August.

FRUIT: Small, greenish capsule, about 5 mm long, with many seeds.

LEAVES: **2 paired or slightly separate leaves near the middle of the stem. Blade lance-shaped to oval, rounded at the tip, 2 to 5 cm long.** A few bladeless sheaths enclose the base.

GROWTH HABIT: Delicate plant, 7 to 25 cm tall. Stem slightly 4-sided, smooth below leaves and sparsely glandular-hairy above.

Twayblade refers to the 2 blades of the stem leaves. The genus name commemorates Dr. Martin Lister, an English naturalist of the 1600s, and *borealis* indicates the plant's boreal or northern range. ✍ There are 20 species of *Listera* in the world, in cool temperate to subarctic regions of the northern hemisphere; 4 of these occur in Alberta. Western twayblade (*L. caurina*) and broad-lipped twayblade (*L. convallarioides*), both mainly found in the extreme southwest, are rare in Alberta. Western twayblade has a smaller (5 mm versus 8 to 10 mm), less notched lip than broad-lipped twayblade. Heart-leaved twayblade (*L. cordata*) has a more deeply divided lip than the other species, with heart-shaped to broadly triangular leaves. Northern twayblade is the largest of the 4 and can be distinguished from the others by its broad, plate-like lip with 2 ear-like lobes at the base.

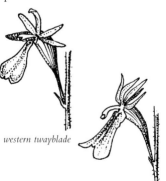

LIP TOOTHED NEAR BASE

northern twayblade

western twayblade

broad-lipped twayblade

heart-leaved twayblade

tall white bog orchid, fragrant white orchid

Platanthera dilatata Lindl. ex Beck
(*Habenaria dilatata* (Pursh) Hook. in Moss 1983)
BOREAL FOREST, MONTANE, SUBALPINE

HABITAT AND RANGE: Wet ground, open or shaded woods, bogs, fens. Banks, sedge meadows, pond edges. Mainly in the Rocky Mountains, Cypress Hills and north of the North Saskatchewan River.

FLOWERS: **White to greenish, sweet-scented, in long (up to 30 cm) spike-like cluster.** Petals hooded. **Lip diamond-shaped or oblong, drooping, spurred, dilated at base**, 5 to 8 mm long. Sepals 3-nerved. Upper sepal oval and hooded, lower sepals spreading and twisted. June to September.

FRUIT: Dry, greenish to brown, prominently veined capsule, up to 12 mm long, with masses of tiny, light-brown seeds.

LEAVES: Short at base, longest at middle of plant, shorter at top. Lower leaves oblong to lance-shaped, usually 4 to 15 cm long, somewhat fleshy. Prominently parallel-veined.

GROWTH HABIT: Smooth perennial up to 1 m tall, with hollow, leafy stems.

tall white bog orchid   (CWE)

*P*latanthera means "broad anther," from the Greek *platy* (broad) and *anthera* (anther). *Dilatata* means "dilated" or "expanded," perhaps in reference to the expanded lip margin. ✐ The Shuswap of British Columbia used tall white bog orchid as a poison for coyotes and grizzlies. ✐ 5 species of *Platanthera* are native to Alberta. Northern green bog orchid (*P. hyperborea*; *Habenaria hyperborea* in Moss 1983) has green flowers and shorter (2 to 10 cm) leaves. Blunt-leaved bog orchid (*P. obtusata*; *Habenaria obtusata* in Moss 1983) has no stem leaves and only a single (sometimes 2) long (4 to 12 cm), rounded oval to lance-shaped leaf at the base, with greenish white flowers. Round-

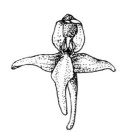

tall white bog orchid

northern green bog orchid

bracted bog orchid

leaved bog orchid (*P. orbiculata*; *Habenaria orbiculata* in Moss 1983) has 2 nearly round leaves that lie close to the ground and no stem leaves. Slender bog orchid (*P. stricta*; *Habenaria saccata* in Moss 1983) has a long (usually more than 10 cm), narrow inflorescence of many green flowers with a short, often purplish lip. It is rare, found only in the extreme southwest of the province. Another orchid with a similar narrow inflorescence that is found in the extreme southwest (and also farther north) is Alaska bog orchid (*Piperia unalascensis*; *Habenaria unalascensis* in Moss 1983). It has 1-nerved sepals and no stem leaves, in contrast to slender bog orchid, which has leaves along the stem and 3-nerved sepals. ✍ Bracted bog orchid (*Coeloglossum viride* ssp. *bracteatum*; *Habenaria viridis* var. *bracteata* in Moss 1983) was, until recently, included in the same genus as tall white bog orchid. It differs from the latter by having a greenish flower with a 2 to 3-toothed lip, long bracts below each flower and broader, more oval-shaped leaves.

tall white bog orchid   (CWᴀ)   *Alaska bog orchid*   (CWᴀ)   *bracted bog orchid*   (CWᴇ)

hooded ladies'-tresses

Spiranthes romanzoffiana Cham.

ASPEN PARKLAND, BOREAL FOREST, MONTANE, SUBALPINE

HABITAT AND RANGE: Moist woods, stream banks, bogs, wet meadows. Widespread in Alberta.

FLOWERS: In **spirally twisted, dense spike**. Each flower is greenish, white or cream-coloured, 6 to 10 mm long, attached directly to the stem. **Upper sepal and lateral petals form an arched hood.** Lip to 12 mm long, bent downward. **Lower sepals sticky-hairy, often with reflexed tips.** Bracts 7 to 20 mm long, whitish or greenish. **Flowers vanilla-scented.** June to August.

FRUIT: Small capsule, to about 7 mm long, with many tiny, shiny brown seeds.

LEAVES: Several, near the base of the stem. Narrowly lance-shaped to oblong, blunt-tipped, 5 to 25 cm long. Reduced upward to sheaths.

GROWTH HABIT: Robust, smooth perennial, 10 to 60 cm tall, with enlarged, fleshy roots.

hooded ladies'-tresses (CWₐ)

The original meaning of tresses was "braid," and the flower spikes grow in a braid-like pattern, hence the common name. The genus name is from the Greek *speira* (coil) and *anthos* (flower), referring to the spiral inflorescence. The species name honours Russian Count Romanzoff, an early patron of science. ✐ There are between 100 and 200 species of *Spiranthes*, depending on the taxonomic authority, mostly in temperate areas of the Old and New World; 2 are native to Alberta. Northern slender ladies'-tresses (*S. lacera*) differs from hooded ladies'-tresses in having flowers in a single spiral in loose clusters, rather than 2 to 3 spirals in tight clusters, and oval to oblong, rather than lance-shaped, leaves. It is rare in Alberta.

hemp, marijuana
Cannabis sativa L.

marijuana   (BA)

HABITAT AND RANGE: Waste ground. Introduced in Alberta.

FLOWERS: **Male and female flowers inconspicuous, on separate plants.** Male flowers in clusters in upper leaf axils. Female flowers stalkless, in clusters on short, leafy branches from upper leaf axils. Sepals 5, distinct, glandular-hairy. Stamens 5.

FRUIT: Achene 3 to 5 mm long, enclosed by a pale, veiny membrane.

LEAVES: Simple, alternate above, **palmately compound below**, composed of **5 to 9 narrow, toothed leaflets, 5 to 20 cm long**. Leaflets tapered at both ends, **glandular, with tiny white spines**.

GROWTH HABIT: Erect, perennial herb, 1 to 4 m tall, although heights of 9 m have been recorded elsewhere for fibre hemp.

Cannabis is the Latin and Greek name for the plant, and *sativa* means "cultivated." *Cannabis sativa* var. *sativa* is low in tetrahydracannabinol (THC) and is used to make hemp, while *Cannabis sativa* var. *indica*, higher in THC, is the narcotic plant used to make marijuana. Fibre hemp research plots have been grown in Alberta since 1995. Hemp can be used to make rope, textiles, paper products and construction materials, and the seed produces oils for industrial and edible uses. ☙ Marijuana has **hallucinogenic properties** and contains toxic alkaloids in the plant resin. It was once listed in the U.S. Pharmacopoeia as a sedative, analgesic and narcotic; it was also used as an antispasmodic by the British and East Indians. The plant is bitter tasting and therefore not readily eaten by livestock; however, poisoning of horses has been reported. ☙ This species, introduced from Asia, is the only *Cannabis* grown in Alberta and Canada.

common nettle, stinging nettle

Urtica dioica L. ssp. *gracilis* (Ait.) Selander

PRAIRIE, ASPEN PARKLAND, BOREAL FOREST, MONTANE, SUBALPINE

HABITAT AND RANGE: Moist mountain forests, thickets, moist meadows, disturbed ground. Widespread in Alberta and Canada from sea level to subalpine elevations.

FLOWERS: **Green, inconspicuous, small, in drooping clusters from the leaf axils.** There are 4 sepals and no petals. **Both male and female flowers are usually found on the same plant.** June to July.

FRUIT: Small, flat, lens-shaped achene, 10 to 15 mm long.

LEAVES: **Opposite, simple, toothed, wrinkled.** Narrowly lance-shaped to nearly oval, up to 15 cm long. Shiny above, tapered to the tip and covered with stinging hairs. Leaf stalk to half as long as the blade. Stipules present.

common nettle (CWE)

GROWTH HABIT: Rhizomatous, erect, square-stemmed perennial, from 60 cm to more than 2 m tall.

The genus name is from *uro* (to burn), because of the stinging hairs. The species name is derived from the Greek *di* (two) and *oikos* (dwelling), as the male and female flowers sometimes occur on separate plants. *Gracilis* means "graceful," perhaps referring to the narrow, drooping leaves. ✒ The Sioux prepared a diuretic from a mixture containing the root, and the Okanagan made poison arrows by boiling them in water with nettle roots. The bristly hairs on the stems and leaves contain an oil high in formic acid. The oil is released on contact and causes a burning sensation. The term *urtication* refers to the rubbing of the arms and legs with nettles, practised by native North Americans and Europeans to soothe arthritis, rheumatism and similar complaints. ✒ The stems can be dried in the sun and were an important source of fibre for coastal tribes in B.C., who used them to make snares, fishing lines and nets, and for early European settlers, who wove them into nets, paper and cloth. The fibres have also been used in tattooing. ✒ The Alaska Tlingit made a red dye by boiling nettles with urine. ✒ Surprisingly, common nettle leaves and stems are tasty and lose their stinging properties when boiled; they are high in Vitamins A and C, protein and certain minerals. The young shoots have been boiled and eaten by B.C. native peoples. Nettle tea contains iron and Vitamin C and has been drunk to treat sore throats, asthma and gout. It must not be brewed too long and must be taken in **moderation** as too much causes a burning sensation. Nettles have also been brewed into beer or wine. ✒ The presence of nettles usually indicates fertile soil. ✒ There are 25 to 30 species of *Urtica*, widely distributed throughout the world. The only other Alberta *Urtica*, annual small or dog nettle (*U. urens*), was introduced to the province and is much smaller (20 to 40 cm in height) than stinging nettle.

pale comandra, bastard toadflax

Comandra umbellata (L.) Nutt.

PRAIRIE, ASPEN PARKLAND, BOREAL FOREST, MONTANE, SUBALPINE

pale comandra   (LF)

HABITAT AND RANGE: Dry slopes, open grassland and open pine woods. Often on well-drained, gravelly or sandy soils. Widespread in both Alberta and Canada.

FLOWERS: In small terminal clusters, composed of **5 whitish green, cream-coloured or pinkish sepals**; each 3 to 5 mm long. No petals. Stamens 5, with **cobwebby bases**. May to June.

FRUIT: Round, hard, **olive-green to reddish (becoming bluish with age)**, dry, berry-like, 4 to 8 mm long. Seeds light brown, smooth, 5 to 7 mm long.

LEAVES: Numerous, alternate, simple. **Pale gray-green, often with a white bloom**, slightly fleshy, broadest in the middle and tapering to both ends, up to 40 mm long. Stalkless or nearly so.

GROWTH HABIT: Erect, leafy, branched perennial up to 40 cm tall from a thick, white, underground rootstock. Parasitic on the roots of other plants. Spreads to form colonies.

The common name bastard toadflax is puzzling, as the plant is not the least bit similar to toadflax (see page 215). The name *Comandra* originates from the Greek *kome* (hair) and *andros* (man), referring to the hairy bases of the stamens. *Umbellata* relates to the shape of the clusters of flowers, although they are not technically umbels. ✐ Some native tribes ate the berries of pale comandra, and native children sucked nectar from the flowers. ✐ There are 2 or 3 (depending on whose taxonomy you follow) species of *Comandra* in the world. Northern comandra (*Geocaulon lividum*), which is included by some botanists within this genus, is similar in appearance. It flowers in 3s, however, usually in the upper leaf axils, and bright-red fruit, rather than the purplish or brownish mature fruit of pale comandra. Northern comandra usually occurs in moister habitats.

northern comandra   (EJ)

Buckwheat family members are often weedy annuals or perennials, frequently with inconspicuous flowers. The flowers, which are usually small and numerous in dense clusters, are often greenish white or pinkish. Petals are lacking. There are 3 to 6 petal-like segments and 4 to 9 stamens. Fruits are 3-angled or flattened achenes, with a single seed. The leaves are chiefly alternate but are sometimes opposite or whorled, and typically have sheathing stipules at the base called *ocreae* (singular, *ocrea*). Another characteristic feature of the buckwheats is that the stems often have swollen nodes. While few members of this family are economically important, buckwheat and rhubarb are notable exceptions. *(See key for this family beginning page 297.)*

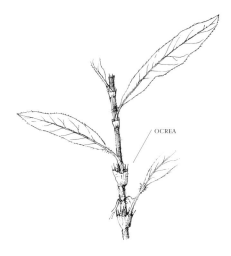

OCREA

yellow umbrella–plant, sulphur plant, yellow buckwheat

Eriogonum flavum Nutt.

yellow umbrella-plant   (CWA)

HABITAT AND RANGE: Dry, often sandy or rocky outcrops to alpine elevations, eroded slopes, badlands and exposed ridges. Very common in Alberta south of the Red Deer River.

FLOWERS: Usually in **umbrella-shaped clusters** (compound umbels), with **large, leafy bracts at base**. Flowers small, numerous, **fuzzy-hairy, pale yellow or rose-tinged**. Stamens 9, protruding. June to August.

FRUIT: Hairy 3-angled achenes, 3 to 5 mm long.

LEAVES: Basal, stalked, thick, 3 to 5 cm long. **Dark green above but appearing white or felty on the underside due to the dense hairs.** Narrowly oblong, broadly lance-shaped or spoon-shaped, with a **prominent yellow midvein. Leaf-stalks reddish.**

GROWTH HABIT: **Fuzzy-hairy**, tufted perennial, 10 to 30 cm tall from stout, woody base. Occasionally forms thick mats.

The common name refers to the umbrella-like appearance of the flower. The genus name comes from the Greek *erion* (wool) and *gony* (knee or joint). *Flavum* means "yellow." ✐ The umbrella–plants have an unpleasant smell but their nectar is relished by bees and produces a strongly flavoured, buckwheat-like honey. ✐ The Hopi used an infusion of umbrella-plants to stop bleeding after childbirth. According to the Blackfoot, eating too much of the root would cause the nose to bleed. ✐ There are 150 species of *Eriogonum* in the world, all but 1 native to North America; 5 occur in Alberta. Provincially rare silver-plant (*E. ovalifolium*) has a simple, rather than compound, umbel of white flowers; it appears gray-coloured due to the dense, whitish hairs. Sulphur buckwheat or subalpine umbrella-plant (*E. umbellatum*) has a large, compound umbel and smooth, pale-yellow or greenish white flowers. Both occur in the southern Rocky Mountains.

silver-plant   (CB)

sulphur buckwheat   (IM)

mountain sorrel, alpine sorrel

Oxyria digyna (L.) Hill

SUBALPINE, ALPINE

HABITAT AND RANGE: Moist, rocky alpine and subalpine slopes and meadows; often along streams and on gravelly soil.

FLOWERS: Small, green or red, in dense clusters. No petals. Sepals 4, inner erect, 4 to 6 mm long, outer bent backward. Stamens 6. June to July.

FRUIT: **Red, papery sepals surround lens-shaped, broad-winged achene**, 4 to 6 mm broad.

LEAVES: Simple; mainly basal, on long stalks. **Often reddish-tinged, kidney or heart-shaped, smooth with wavy margin**, to 5 cm across. **Stipules form loose sheaths.**

mountain sorrel (CWA)

GROWTH HABIT: Low-growing (5 to 30 cm), erect, usually branched perennial from thick, fleshy root. Often grows in clumps.

Sorrel comes from the Old High German *sur* (sour), due to the acid flavour of the leaves. The generic name is from *oxys* (sour), also because of the tart taste. *Digyna* refers to the 2 partitions of the fruit. ✿ The leaves are tasty raw and were useful in preventing scurvy, being high in Vitamins A and C. They add a tangy taste and crisp texture to salads, and chewing them is said to alleviate thirst. The leaves **should not be eaten in large quantities**, however, because they contain salts of oxalic acids which can damage the kidneys. ✿ Mountain sorrel was prized as a vegetable by the Inuit and eaten fresh or preserved in seal oil. Many North American peoples fermented the leaves with those of other species to make a sauerkraut-type mixture. ✿ Sorrel is also eaten by caribou, muskoxen, geese, hares and lemmings. ✿ This is the only species in this genus. It is found in arctic and alpine regions of Eurasia and North America.

mountain sorrel (IM)

water smartweed
Polygonum amphibium L.
PRAIRIE, ASPEN PARKLAND, BOREAL FOREST, MONTANE, SUBALPINE

water smartweed   (BA)

HABITAT AND RANGE: Shallow water of ponds, marshes, ditches and shores throughout the province.

FLOWERS: In a dense, **oblong, terminal cluster, up to 1.5 cm wide and 1 to 3.5 cm long**, on a thick, usually smooth stalk. **Petal-like oblong segments red to pink**, 4 to 5 mm long. Stamens 8, protruding. July to August.

FRUIT: Brown to black, shiny, lens-shaped achenes, 2.5 to 3 mm long.

LEAVES: Numerous, alternate. Plants growing on land have lance-shaped leaves with short stalks. Floating plants have waxy, broader, long-stalked leaves. Leaf blades narrowly oblong to lance-shaped, up to 15 cm long, rounded or pointed at the tip, with a prominent midvein. **Leaves have sheaths at their bases called *ocreae* (singular *ocrea*), which are hairy and often bristly at the tip.**

GROWTH HABIT: Aquatic or terrestrial, smooth to slightly hairy perennial with trailing, rooting stems. Flowering branches up to 80 cm long. **Often forms attractive green and red or pink mats on lakes.**

The name smartweed is from the ancient *arsmart* because of the irritating effect on human "arses" when used as a poultice or to treat piles. *Polygonum* originates from the Greek *poly* (many) and *gonu* (knee), because of the swollen nodes of some species. *Amphibium* refers to the plant's aquatic habitat. ✍ Water smartweed has been used medicinally to treat piles and skin diseases. The tuberous roots of many *Polygonum* species were eaten roasted or boiled by both the Inuit and other aboriginal peoples. The Blackfoot added the roots of related western bistort (*P. bistortoides*)

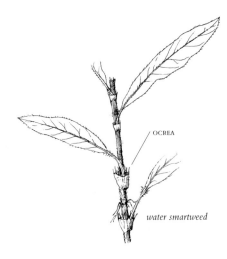

OCREA

water smartweed

to soups and stews. ❧ Water smartweed achenes are an important food source for waterfowl and gamebirds. ❧ There are 150 species of *Polygonum* in the world, widespread but mainly in temperate regions. Approximately 18 species occur in Alberta. Alpine bistort (*P. viviparum*) is a terrestrial perennial that usually has pinkish purple, bulb-like projections below white or pink sterile flowers; it is primarily found in the mountains. The flower "bulbs" can produce a new plant while still attached to the parent plant. Wild buckwheat (*P. convolvulus*) is a common annual weed with trailing branches and arrowhead-shaped leaves.

alpine bistort   (JH)

wild buckwheat   (BA)

narrow-leaved dock, willow dock

Rumex salicifolius Weinm.
(*Rumex triangulivalvis* (Dans.) Rech. f. in Moss 1983)
PRAIRIE, BOREAL FOREST, MONTANE

narrow-leaved dock   (BA)

HABITAT AND RANGE: Moist ground, depressions, gravel flats, coniferous woods, stream banks, pond edges, disturbed areas. Widespread in Alberta.

FLOWERS: **Inconspicuous, greenish brown to pinkish,** lacking petals. Flowers have inner and outer rings, each of 3 segments. Inner 3 segments form valves. Stamens 6.

FRUIT: Achene 3-angled, smooth, 2 mm long. **Valves 3 to 6 mm long, triangle-shaped, with grain-like thickenings.**

LEAVES: Numerous, alternate, entire. Pale green, often with whitish bloom. **Narrowly lance-shaped and tapered at both ends,** usually folded, 5 to 15 cm long. Lower leaves with short stalks, upper without.

GROWTH HABIT: Erect, often branched, 1 to many-stemmed perennial, 30 to 60 cm tall.

*R*umex is from the Latin name and *salicifolius* means "leaves like willow" (*Salix* species). ✐ The young leaves, which have an astringent, lemony flavour, can be cooked and eaten and are high in Vitamins C and A, potassium and iron. They are also high in tannic and oxalic acids and **should be eaten in moderation.** Oxalic acids have caused livestock poisoning. ✐ The seeds were eaten by the Inuit. The Blackfoot boiled the plant and used the liquid to reduce swelling. The roots are rich in tannins and have also been used for tanning deerskins by some tribes. A mixture of the root boiled in water was used as a toothpaste and to treat syphilis and leprosy. ✐ The leaves of related sheep sorrel (*R. acetosella*) were chewed as a snack by the Thompson of B.C. Related

western dock (BA)

western dock (*R. occidentalis*), also known as Indian rhubarb, was used by coastal tribes as a vegetable and also as a medicinal poultice. The Blackfoot crushed the green leaves of curled dock (*R. crispus*) to make a poultice for boils. Curled dock seeds have been used as a substitute for, or in mixtures with, tobacco. ✐ In the Middle Ages, docks were used for poultices and relief of burns. ✐ There are 125 species of *Rumex* in the world, widely distributed; 15 occur in Alberta. Wild begonia (*R. venosus*), an attractive species often seen along roadsides and on sandy dunes in the dry southeastern prairie, has large (1 to 3 cm across), rosy-pink valves. Western dock, a much less attractive but more widespread species, has long, tapered, rhubarb-like leaves and small (5 to 8 mm long), reddish, net-veined valves that lack grain-like thickenings.

wild begonia (CWA)

winter-fat, winter sage, white sage
Eurotia lanata (Pursh) Moq.
<small>PRAIRIE</small>

winter-fat   (CW<small>A</small>)

HABITAT AND RANGE: Dry, often sandy, saline or alkaline soil in prairie badlands, grasslands and the foothills.

FLOWERS: Small, in **yellow-orange or green ball-like clusters from the leaf axils. Male and female flowers separate on the stem, female below male.** Stamens 4. Late June to August.

FRUIT: Thin-walled, slightly inflated, hairy, enclosed by 2 bracts. Each fruit contains a single seed, 2 to 3 mm long.

LEAVES: Alternate, entire, occurring singly and in whorls. **Gray-green, densely hairy, with simple and star-shaped hairs. Linear to narrowly lance-shaped**, rounded at the tip, 2 to 3 mm wide, with **margins curled under**. Upper leaves up to 5 cm long, short-stalked; basal to 12 cm long. Midvein prominent.

GROWTH HABIT: Leafy perennial, **woody and shreddy at base**, up to 45 cm tall from a tap root. Pale gray, **soft white-woolly throughout**, with hairs often turning reddish with age. Occurs in clumps.

This plant's high protein and mineral content makes it excellent winter forage for livestock; hence the common name winter-fat. *Eurotia* is from the Greek *euros* (mold), in reference to the soft-hairy, mold-like covering; *lanata* means "hairy." ✐ The Blackfoot soaked the leaves in warm water to make a shampoo and also brewed them into a tea. Some American tribes treated fevers with a potion from the leaves. ✐ Winter-fat is drought-tolerant and helps to control erosion; it is frequently used for reclamation. ✐ There are 3 species of *Eurotia* in the world; the others are Eurasian. Winter-fat is similar to some sages in appearance (particularly sagebrush); however, winter-fat leaves are turned under at the margins and densely hairy underneath, and the plant lacks the characteristic sage aroma.

winter fat

sagebrush

samphire, glasswort, saltwort

Salicornia europaea L. ssp. *rubra* (A. Nels.) Breit.

PRAIRIE, ASPEN PARKLAND, BOREAL FOREST

HABITAT AND RANGE: Beaches, saline mud flats, saline marshes, edges of alkaline lakes and ponds. Of scattered occurrence across Alberta.

FLOWERS: Tiny and inconspicuous. Flower cluster 1 to 5 cm long, with **flowers in groups of 3, sunken into the stem. Central flower of each cluster protrudes above the others.** June to September.

FRUIT: Sparsely hairy, enclosed in spongy calyx. Seed about 1 mm long.

LEAVES: Tiny, **scale-like, broadly triangular-shaped**.

GROWTH HABIT: **Succulent, branched annual** up to 25 cm tall, with a **distinctly segmented appearance.** Joints 1 to 2 mm long and wide. **Red-coloured at maturity.**

samphire   (JH)

The name glasswort describes the plant's historic use for the manufacture of glass and soap products (*wort* is an early English word meaning "plant"). *Salicornia* is said to be from the Latin *sal* (salt), due to its salty habitat, and *cornu* (horn), because of its branched, horn-like appearance. *Europaea* means "of Europe," while *rubra* means "red." ✐ The succulent stem tips can be eaten raw, and the plant has been used as a pickle or relish. Certain North American peoples ground the seeds of members of this genus into flour. ✐ Ducks and geese eat the stems and seeds. ✐ There are about 12 species of *Salicornia*, primarily of coastal salt marshes or saline and alkaline lakes. In Alberta, only this species occurs.

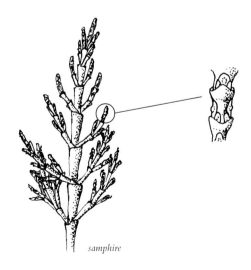

samphire

western spring beauty
Claytonia lanceolata Pursh
MONTANE, SUBALPINE, ALPINE

western spring beauty   (CWE)

HABITAT AND RANGE: Edges of moist woods and stream banks from foothills to alpine meadows (**often in snow bank areas**); usually on rich soil. Occurs in the Rocky Mountains and Cypress Hills.

FLOWERS: 1 to 20 in loose, terminal, often 1-sided, short-stalked clusters. **Flower-stalks erect when flowering, drooping in bud and fruit.** Petals 5, 5 to 12 mm long, **pinkish with long, darker lines or nearly white**, notched at the tip and joined at the base. Sepals 2, oval, cup-shaped. Stamens 5, with pink anthers, attached to the bases of the petals. May to August.

FRUIT: 3-valved, papery capsule with 3 to 6 black, shiny seeds.

LEAVES: **2 nearly opposite leaves per stem, linear to lance-shaped**, bright green, parallel-veined, succulent, up to 15 mm wide. Sometimes also with 1 or 2 basal leaves that have their leaf stalks underground.

GROWTH HABIT: Short (5 to 20 cm), often reddish or purplish-stemmed, perennial herb from round, thick corm. Variable in size, with alpine plants usually smaller than those from lower elevations. Sometimes grows in large clumps.

Despite the common name, this species doesn't usually flower here until July at high elevations. The genus name honours John Clayton, a 17th-century botanist who collected plants in the United States, while the species name refers to the lance-shaped leaves. ✿ The edible corms, sometimes called Indian potatoes, can be eaten raw or boiled. The Blackfoot dug them in the spring and ate them fresh or roasted as an important source of carbohydrates. The green leaves are also edible, and both leaves and roots were prized by the Inuit. ✿ The corms are eaten by grizzly bears and rodents, and the flowers and leaves are enjoyed by mountain sheep, deer, elk and moose. This plant has nectar sacs at the base of the petals, which attract insects such as bees. ✿ There are 10 species of *Claytonia* in North America, mostly in arctic-alpine regions. There are 2 species in Alberta. Alpine spring beauty (*C. megarhiza*), found on scree slopes and in rock crevices at high elevations, has many basal leaves that are spoon-shaped (broadest at the tip) and a large, fleshy root.

alpine spring beauty

mouse-ear chickweed, field mouse-ear chickweed
Cerastium arvense L.
PRAIRIE, ASPEN PARKLAND, BOREAL FOREST, MONTANE, SUBALPINE, ALPINE

HABITAT AND RANGE: Dry grassland, rocky and disturbed ground, slopes. Often occurs on gravelly or calcareous soil. Widespread in southern Alberta, of scattered occurrence in the north.

FLOWERS: Few to many per plant, in loose clusters on thin stalks that are 1 to 3 cm long. Petals 5, white, 10 to 15 mm long, **with a notched tip. Green lines on the petals** serve as nectar guides for insects. **Sepals 5, glandular,** ⅓ as long as petals. Stamens 10. May to July.

FRUIT: Curved, cylindrical capsule, up to 12 mm long, with many golden to reddish brown seeds.

mouse-ear chickweed   (CWA)

LEAVES: **Numerous, in pairs, extending halfway up the stem. Narrowly linear to lance-shaped,** usually hairy, **1-nerved,** sometimes with tiny glands. Slightly grayish in colour, 1 to 4 cm long. **Lower leaves usually have tufts of small leaves in the axils.**

GROWTH HABIT: Slender, densely hairy to smooth, often glandular, **tufted perennial,** 10 to 30 cm tall on trailing stems. Can form large colonies.

The upper part of the leaf resembles a mouse's ear, hence the common name. The scientific name originates from the Greek *keras* (horn), referring to the shape of the seed capsule. *Arvense* means "field." ✄ There are 100 species of *Cerastium* in the world, mostly in north temperate Eurasia, with 3 native and 1 introduced species in Alberta. Alpine chickweed (*C. beeringianum*) is similar to mouse-ear chickweed but has broader leaves and frequently a more spreading form; it is restricted to high alpine habitats.

alpine chickweed   (LA)

alpine chickweed   (LK)

long-leaved chickweed, long–leaved stitchwort, starwort

Stellaria longifolia Muhl.

PRAIRIE, ASPEN PARKLAND, BOREAL FOREST, MONTANE

long-leaved chickweed   (BA)

HABITAT AND RANGE: Moist, shady grassland, stream banks, meadows. Widespread in the province except in the southeastern prairie.

FLOWERS: Usually many flowers on **wide-spreading flower stalks**. Petals 5, white, notched, up to 6 mm long. Sepals 3-nerved, with whitish edges, each about 3 mm long. Stamens 10. May to August.

FRUIT: Capsule yellowish green, about 4 mm long, with round, reddish brown, bumpy seeds about 1 mm long.

LEAVES: Opposite, spreading to ascending, non-stalked. **Narrow (to about 2.5 mm wide), linear to lance-shaped, tapered at both ends, up to 5 cm long.** Smaller leaves in axils.

GROWTH HABIT: Branched, delicate, spreading perennial, 10 to 50 cm tall. Stems 4-angled. Forms mats.

*S*tellaria is from the Latin *stella* (star), because of the star-shaped flower. The name chickweed relates to the fact that chickens (and other birds) enjoy the plant's leaves and capsules. *Longifolia* means "long-leaved." ✐ There are about 100 species of *Stellaria* in the world, mainly in the north temperate zone; 10 occur in Alberta. The closely related common chickweed (*S. media*), an annual with round, stalked basal leaves, is a common weed; the young leaves and shoots are edible and are popular in Europe, where the plant originates. Young spring plants are preferable and can be cooked as a potherb. The leaves can also be made into a tea. Long-stalked chick-weed (*S. longipes*), a variable species, usually has a purplish black capsule and shorter (1 to 3 cm) leaves that are broadest at the base.

common chickweed   (LK)

yellow pond-lily, yellow water-lily, cow-lily

Nuphar variegatum Engelm. ex Durand

ASPEN PARKLAND, BOREAL FOREST

HABITAT AND RANGE: Sheltered bays, ponds, lakes, slow-moving streams. From the Red Deer River north to the Northwest Territories.

FLOWERS: **Solitary on long stalk.** Petals numerous, small. **Sepals 6, showy, greenish yellow on the outside, often red-tinged on the inside, up to 3.5 cm long.** Stamens numerous, yellow, surrounding a **large pistil**. June to July.

FRUIT: Hard capsule, 3 to 5 cm long with many seeds. Seeds brownish, 5 mm long.

LEAVES: **Floating,** simple, 7 to 15 cm long. **Waxy on the surface; round and broadly oval to heart-shaped at base.** Leaf stalks long and flat-tened.

yellow pond-lily (CWA)

GROWTH HABIT: **Aquatic** perennial with thick rootstock and cord-like stems.

Nuphar is from the Persian *nenuphar* or the Arabic *naufar*, referring to a water lily. The species name *variegatum*, meaning "with patches of different colours," describes the sepals. Seeds of related northwestern species were ground into flour by native peoples, and the rootstocks were boiled, baked, peeled and eaten raw, or ground into flour for bread and porridge. ✿ The rootstocks were used medicinally by some Montana tribes to treat venereal disease, to make poultices and to treat bruises and cuts on horses. ✿ The leaves provide shade and cover for fish, the seeds are eaten by ducks and beavers, and muskrat eat both leaves and stems. ✿ There are 15 species of *Nuphar* in the world's north temperate zones. Only this species occurs in Alberta.

yellow pond-lily (CWA)

Buttercup Family (Ranunculaceae)

Plants in this large family are mainly herbs, with some climbing vines and shrubs; they often contain poisonous alkaloids. The leaves are simple or compound, mostly alternate and deeply divided. Although many of the flowers are showy, petals are sometimes lacking; the 3 to 15 sepals are sometimes petal-like. Stamens are numerous, and the fruits are follicles, achenes or berries. Anemones, delphiniums, columbines and clematis are a few well-known garden buttercup family members. *(See key for this family beginning page 298.)*

monkshood

Aconitum delphinifolium DC.

MONTANE, SUBALPINE, ALPINE

HABITAT AND RANGE: Moist mixed and coniferous woods and meadows in the mountains; to alpine elevations. Restricted in Alberta to the northern Rockies.

FLOWERS: Numerous, irregular, **showy, dark-blue to purple flowers in short, terminal clusters. Sepals 5, petal-like, blue; lower drooping, upper forming a hood.** Upper 2 petals concealed by hood, lower 3 petals small or absent. Stamens numerous. June to August.

FRUIT: Pod-like follicle, smooth or sparsely hairy fruit that opens along 1 side. Up to 1 cm long including beak at tip.

LEAVES: Alternate, simple, **deeply palmately lobed. Lower leaves long-stalked.**

GROWTH HABIT: Finely hairy to smooth perennial herb, up to 70 cm tall from short tuber. Stem reddish at base.

monkshood   (LA)

Monkshood describes the shape of the upper sepal. *Aconitum* is from the ancient Greek name. The Greek *acon* means "dart," as the plant has been used to make poison for tipping arrows. *Delphinifolium* means "with leaves like delphinium." ⌀ The entire plant is **poisonous**, especially the leaves, seeds and tubers, which contain alkaloids that cause paralysis, decrease blood pressure and body temperature, and **can prove fatal** within hours. Fortunately, it is not very palatable and is therefore normally avoided. Monkshood was once included in the U.S. Pharmacopoeia because of its uses as an irritant and anaesthetic; however, its toxicity outweighed its therapeutic effects. ⌀ There are 50 to 100 species of *Aconitum* in the north temperate zones of North America, Europe and Asia. Only this species is found in Alberta.

red or white baneberry

Actaea rubra Ait. (Willd.)

ASPEN PARKLAND, BOREAL FOREST, MONTANE, SUBALPINE

baneberry   (CWE)

HABITAT AND RANGE: Moist, shady woods and thickets; often found along streams and in ravines. Widespread in the province except in the dry southeast.

FLOWERS: In dense, **cone-shaped, terminal or axillary clusters** on stalks up to 3 cm long. Petals 4 to 10, linear, white, deciduous. Sepals 3 to 5, white (sometimes reddish-tinged at tip), petal-like, 4 mm long. Stamens numerous, pale yellow. May to June.

FRUIT: Large cluster of many-seeded, **shiny red or white berries** (greenish when immature or sometimes on drying), 0.5 to 1 cm long. Seeds reddish brown, tightly packed, to about 3 mm long.

LEAVES: Large compound leaves with **leaflets usually in 3s**. Each leaflet somewhat oval-shaped, lobed and sharply toothed on the margins, hairy along the veins underneath, up to 40 mm long. Lower leaves and leaflets on wide-spreading stalks.

GROWTH HABIT: Tall, often branching, thick-stemmed, leafy, herbaceous perennial, 20 to 75 cm tall.

*B*ana was the Anglo-Saxon word for "murderer" or "destroyer" and the name baneberry was likely applied to this plant because of the poisonous berries. *Actaea* comes from the Greek *aktaia* for the elder tree, as the leaves are similar in shape to elder leaves, while *rubra* is from the Latin "red," referring to the berry colour. ✐ The berries, leaves and roots are all **poisonous** in sufficient amounts, **causing severe gastroenteritis** and **paralyzing the respiratory system**. ✐ The Blackfoot boiled the roots and drank the resulting liquid to treat coughs and colds. Baneberry was used in many sacred ceremonies by the Cheyenne, and nursing mothers drank a tea made from the boiled roots to increase milk production. The Thompson drank a potion of the roots as a cure for syphilis and rheumatism, but too strong a dosage was said to kill. ✐ There are 6 species of *Actaea*, all in the north temperate zone, but only this species occurs in Alberta.

baneberry (red fruits)   (BA)

baneberry (white fruits)   (JH)

Canada anemone
Anemone canadensis L.
PRAIRIE, ASPEN PARKLAND, BOREAL FOREST

HABITAT AND RANGE: Moist grassland, edges of aspen poplar groves, riverine thickets, sandy shores. Found throughout Alberta.

FLOWERS: No petals. **5 white, petal-like sepals 1 to 2 cm long, rounded at the tip and with soft hairs underneath.** Stamens numerous, conspicuous, yellow. Several flowering stems may branch upward from a distant whorl of leaf-like bracts. June to July.

FRUIT: **Tightly packed, beaked achenes with short styles, in a green, round head** up to 1 cm long.

Canada anemone (CWE)

LEAVES: Toothed and deeply divided into 3 to 5 lobes, on long leaf stalks. Light green, 4 to 7 cm wide, with fine hairs above and below. Prominently veined. **Involucral leaves attached directly to the stem in a whorl.** Basal leaves several, incised.

GROWTH HABIT: Hairy-stemmed perennial, 20 to 70 cm tall from a bulbous taproot. Often grows in dense patches.

The origin of the genus name is uncertain but is believed to originate from the Greek word *anemos* (wind), perhaps because the wind disperses the long-plumed fruits of some anemones. *Canadensis* is Latin for "of Canada." ✿ Anemones are alleged to have arisen from the tears shed by Venus over the slain god Adonis. In the Near East, anemones were a symbol of illness, and in some cultures, a symbol of sorrow and pain. ✿ The whole plant is **poisonous**, causing **skin irritation** and, if ingested, **inflammation and ulceration**, followed by **severe gastroenteritis**. Some species of anemone contain the substance *anemonin*, said to be a potent antiseptic, and the pounded, boiled roots of some anemones have been used to treat wounds. ✿ There are approximately 100 species of *Anemone* in the world, mostly in the northern hemisphere; 10 of these are found in Alberta, and 3 are described in detail in this book. Canada anemone is sometimes confused with wild white geranium (see photo page 126); however, wild white geranium has sepals and petals, while Canada anemone has only sepals. Small wood anemone (*A. parviflora*) has small (1 to 3 cm broad), 3-parted, dark-green, wedge-shaped leaves on long stalks from the base of the plant; a white (frequently tinged with blue or pink) flower; and a head of densely hairy achenes. It is found primarily in the mountains, up to alpine elevations.

ACHENE

small wood anemone (BA)   *fruits of Canada anemone*

cut-leaved anemone, wind-flower
Anemone multifida Poir.

PRAIRIE, ASPEN PARKLAND, BOREAL FOREST, MONTANE, SUBALPINE, ALPINE

HABITAT AND RANGE: Grassland and open woods, south-facing slopes; from moist fescue prairie to alpine meadows. Widespread in Alberta.

FLOWERS: **1 to 4 hairy flowering stalks from whorl of leaf-like bracts.** No petals. **Sepals 5 to 8, broadly oval, petal-like, varying in colour from white or yellow to red or blue, 12 to 20 mm across.** June to July.

FRUIT: **Achenes in a rounded head, about 1 cm wide, which forms a large, cottony mass later in the season.**

LEAVES: **Palmate, with deeply incised, silky-hairy leaflets,** each up to 4 cm long. **Upper bract-like leaves attached directly to the stem, basal with long stalks.**

GROWTH HABIT: Softly hairy perennial, 15 to 50 cm tall from a thick rootstock.

Wind-flower refers to the method of travel of the fluffy achenes, while the species name *multifida*, meaning "many-cleft," refers to the deeply divided leaves. The origin of *Anemone* is explained on page 65. ✿ Long-fruited anemone (*A. cylindrica*) occurs in many of the same habitats as wind-flower but has longer (2 to 4 cm), denser, cylindrical clusters of achenes. It has 5-parted, more wedge-shaped leaves with wider segments and greenish or cream-coloured flowers.

cut-leaved anemone   (LA)

long-fruited anemone   (DJ)

cut-leaved anemone   (CWE)

prairie crocus, pasque flower, prairie anemone

Anemone patens L. ssp. *multifida* (Pritzel) Hult.
(*Anemone patens* in Moss 1983)
PRAIRIE, ASPEN PARKLAND, MONTANE, SUBALPINE

HABITAT AND RANGE: Dry grassland, open woods, south-facing slopes. Prefers well-drained soil. Widespread throughout Alberta.

FLOWERS: Petal-like sepals 5 to 7, **delicate pale-lavender to whitish, 2 to 4 cm long**. Styles long, soft, greenish. Stamens numerous, yellow. Late April to early June.

FRUIT: Cluster of club-shaped achenes, 3 to 4 mm long, attached to **feathery styles, 2 to 4 cm long**.

LEAVES: Basal leaves much-divided, long-stalked, covered with long, white hairs. **Whorl of numerous, shorter, narrow, hairy leaves below the flower. Leaves develop after the flower.**

prairie crocus   (BA)

GROWTH HABIT: Soft-hairy perennial up to 40 cm tall from a thick, woody tap root. Stems 1 to several, elongating after flowering. May form large colonies.

Prairie crocus is the floral emblem of Manitoba and the state flower of South Dakota. The common name pasque flower alludes to the fact that the flower is in bloom at Easter time in much of its range (*Pasque* is an old French word for this religious festival). The origin of the genus name is discussed on page 65. The species name *patens* means "spreading" or "outspread," perhaps in reference to the sepals in bloom. *Multifida*, meaning "many-cleft," describes the deeply divided leaves. ✿ The Thompson people of B.C. held crocus flowers to the nose to stop nosebleeds, and several tribes applied the crushed leaves to wounds and burns as a counter-irritant. The U.S. Pharmacopoeia listed prairie crocus as a diuretic and expectorant until 1905. A drug derived from the chopped whole plant can induce vomiting and act as

western chaliceflower   (CWE)

western chaliceflower   (CWA)

a depressant to the nervous system and heart. Many anemones contain a substance called *protoanemonin*, an irritating oil that produces **rashes**. ✿ Related western chaliceflower (*A. occidentalis*) has long-hairy stems and finely dissected, hairy leaves. The petals are white, up to 2 cm long and very hairy underneath. The hairy growth habit helps to keep the plant warm in its cold subalpine to alpine meadow habitat. Its comical shaggy head of plumed achenes gives it another common name: towheaded babies.

fruit of prairie crocus

blue columbine

Aquilegia brevistyla Hook.

<small>ASPEN PARKLAND, MONTANE, BOREAL FOREST</small>

HABITAT AND RANGE: Deciduous, coniferous and mixed woods; meadows, thickets and riverine prairie. Widespread in the province from the Bow River north.

FLOWERS: Usually several-flowered. Each flower attractive, nodding or ascending, with **yellowish or white petals and 5 purplish, reflexed sepals**. Nectar-producing **spur (nectary) purplish, hooked, 5 to 8 mm long**. Involucral bracts 3 to 5, up to 3 cm long. Stamens numerous. May to July.

FRUIT: Group of 5 hairy, beaked pods, 2 to 3 cm long, that open along 1 side, called *follicles*.

LEAVES: Leaflets blue-green, in 3s, with scalloped tips. Basal leaves long-stalked. Stem leaves few.

GROWTH HABIT: Perennial with slender, slightly purplish, somewhat glandular-hairy stems, up to 80 cm tall from branching rootstocks.

blue columbine (JH)

The name columbine comes from *columba* (dove), because the 5 petals were thought to appear like a group of doves. The genus name may be from the Latin *aquila* (eagle), because of the long, claw-like spur on the flower, which supposedly resembles an eagle's talons. Another possible origin is that *Aquilegia* is taken from *agua* (water) and *legere* (to collect), as little drops of nectar collect at the ends of the spurs. *Brevistyla* refers to the short style. ✐ The roots of blue columbine were occasionally boiled and eaten by early American settlers during famines, and closely related species have been used as a shampoo and an aphrodisiac. ✐ Bumblebees and butterflies enjoy the sweet nectar of blue columbine. ✐ There are 70 species of *Aquilegia*, mainly in the northern hemisphere. Of these, 4 are found in Alberta. The only other blue-flowered columbine in the province is the rare, shorter (usually less than 20 cm tall) Jones' columbine (*A. jonesii*), found in alpine screes of the Waterton area. Yellow columbine (*A. flavescens*) has yellow, usually nodding flowers and is primarily a species of the mountains. Sitka columbine (*A. formosa*) usually has reddish sepals and yellow petals; it tends to be found at lower elevations than yellow columbine, and only in the northern Rockies (it is rare in Alberta). Yellow and Sitka columbine can interbreed where their ranges overlap.

yellow columbine (CWA)

Sitka columbine (DJ)

marsh-marigold
Caltha palustris L.
ASPEN PARKLAND, BOREAL FOREST

HABITAT AND RANGE: Marshes, wet meadows and woods, bogs. Often in shallow water of slow-moving streams and ditches. Widespread in the northern half of Alberta.

FLOWERS: Many-flowered with flowers 1.5 to 4 cm wide. **Sepals bright yellow, 5 to 9, showy, up to 2 cm long. No petals.** Stamens numerous, with long, yellow anthers. April to June.

FRUIT: Leathery, veiny, 6 to 12-compartmented, curved, pod-like, up to 15 mm long, with short beaks at the tip. Many-seeded.

LEAVES: Mostly basal. **Basal leaves long-stalked, dark green, thick, more than 6 cm across.** Stem

marsh-marigold   (CWA)

leaves stalkless or nearly so. **Blades round to kidney or heart-shaped**, with toothed, scalloped or entire margins.

GROWTH HABIT: Branched, perennial herb up to 60 cm tall with stout, hollow stems.

The name marigold comes from "Mary's gold," a reference to a yellow flower esteemed by the Virgin Mary. This plant is not a true marigold: true marigolds belong to the aster (composite) family. *Caltha* is from the Greek *kalathos* (goblet), a name used by the Greeks for some unknown wetland plant. *Palustris* is Latin for "of marshes or wet places." ✒ Some interesting common names for this (and closely related species *C. leptosepala*) include gools, horse blob and water goggles. ✒ The leaves were cooked and eaten by some North American natives and early settlers, and the leaves and roots are still eaten by some northern tribes. They are said to be bitter, however, and **possibly toxic**. The plants contain glucosides (supposedly lost in cooking) which have killed cattle, but the plant is distasteful to livestock due to its acrid juice. All parts of the mature plant are **poisonous** if ingested, and the sap can be **irritating** to the skin. The buds have been pickled as a substitute for capers.

✒ There are 20 species of *Caltha* in the world, mainly in wet habitats of the northern hemisphere; 2 other species occur in Alberta. Floating marsh-marigold (*C. natans*) has a similar range but has smaller white or pink sepals. Mountain marsh-marigold (*C. leptosepala*) is found only in the mountains and has white or bluish sepals and 1 or no stem leaves.

mountain marsh-marigold   (JH)

purple clematis, blue clematis, purple Virgin's-bower

Clematis occidentalis (Hornem.) DC. ssp. *grosseserrata* (Rydb.) Taylor & MacBryde
(*Clematis occidentalis* (Hornem.) DC. var. *grosseserrata* (Rydb.) Pringle in Moss 1983)
PRAIRIE, ASPEN PARKLAND, BOREAL FOREST, MONTANE

purple clematis (CWE)

HABITAT AND RANGE: Shaded, moist riverine woods, open dry woods, thickets. Common in the western and central parts of the province.

FLOWERS: Solitary, usually long-stalked. Petals lacking. Sepals 4 to 5, petal-like, **pale purple with dark-purple veins, slightly hairy**, up to 6 cm long. Stamens numerous, pale whitish green, hairy. May to June.

FRUIT: Thin, greenish, hairy achenes, in a thick head, with **long (4 cm or more), feathery styles.**

LEAVES: **Compound, in 3s on long stalks.** Leaflets dull above, glossy underneath, **wrinkly; margins wavy**, occasionally toothed. Heart-shaped at base, up to 9 cm long. Stipules small, pointed.

GROWTH HABIT: **Climbing,** slightly hairy, reddish-stemmed vine that attaches to other plants with **narrow tendrils**.

*C*lematis is from the Greek *klema* (a vine branch or tendril) and alludes to the climbing habit. *Occidentalis,* meaning "of the western hemisphere," is from the Latin *occidere* (to set, in reference to the sun). *Grosseserrata* means "large-toothed," referring to the leaf margins. ✐ The Blackfoot called this plant *sto-o-kat-sis* (ghost's lariat), because it entangled them when they walked through it. The whole plant is **toxic** if swallowed, and the sap is a **skin irritant**. ✐ The Blackfeet of the United States are said to have used an infusion of the white inner bark of related western clematis (*C. ligusticifolia*) to treat fever and to have chewed the leaves to treat colds and sore throats. The bark of western clematis was woven into bags, mats and capes by interior British Columbia tribes, and the Flathead of Montana and the Okanagan of British Columbia rubbed the leaves into a lather to produce a soap and shampoo. ✐ There are 200 species of *Clematis,* mainly of the temperate northern hemisphere; 2 other species occur in Alberta. The native western clematis has white flowers and 5 to 7 leaflets, while the naturalized yellow clematis (*C. tangutica*) has yellow flowers and 5 leaflets.

western clematis (CWE)

yellow clematis (BA)

low larkspur
Delphinium bicolor Nutt.
PRAIRIE, MONTANE, SUBALPINE

HABITAT AND RANGE: Poplar thickets, open woods, moist grassland and slopes; occurs on well-drained to moist, heavy soil. From the North Saskatchewan River south to the Montana border.

FLOWERS: 1 to 15 irregular flowers per plant in long, lax spike. Petals 4, in pairs. **Upper pair plus upper sepal light purple, forming a spur. Lower petals shallowly 2-lobed, large and dark blue-purple. Calyx 15 to 25 mm long, composed of 5 sepals, lower dark blue-purple.** May to June.

FRUIT: Clustered, pod-like follicles, each curved, usually about 15 to 20 mm long, with the remains of the style at the tip. Pale green to brown, hairy or smooth, with numerous dark-brown seeds, 2 to 2.5 mm long.

LEAVES: Few stem leaves, more basal leaves. **Leaflets deeply dissected,** softly hairy, lighter underneath, up to 20 mm long.

GROWTH HABIT: Short-hairy to nearly smooth, sometimes glandular, few-flowered perennial, **15 to 70 cm tall,** with thick, slightly fleshy roots.

low larkspur (BA)

*D*elphinium is derived from the Greek *delphin* (dolphin), as the plant's nectaries are said to resemble old pictures of dolphins, while *bicolor* means "two-coloured," in reference to the different colours of the sepals and petals. The common name larkspur originated from the resemblance of the spur on the flower to the spur on the foot of a lark. ✐ The leaves and seeds contain toxic alkaloids which have caused cattle losses. Sheep are less affected and are occasionally used to rid pastures of this plant. In humans, the plant **may cause rashes**. ✐ The Blackfoot dyed porcupine quills with a dye made from the flowers. Some American tribes applied crushed larkspur to their hair to repel lice. ✐ There are 200 species of *Delphinium*, widely distributed throughout the world; 2 other species occur in Alberta. Tall larkspur (*D. glaucum*), common in northern and western Alberta, is taller (1 to 2 m in height), with many flowers. Nuttall's larkspur (*D. nuttallianum*), restricted to southwestern Alberta, has petals more deeply notched than those of low larkspur and a calyx 15 to 25 mm long.

Nuttall's larkspur (CB)

tall larkspur (JH)

seaside buttercup, creeping buttercup, seaside crowfoot

Ranunculus cymbalaria Pursh

PRAIRIE, ASPEN PARKLAND, BOREAL FOREST, MONTANE

seaside buttercup   (BA)

HABITAT AND RANGE: Silty mud flats, shallow water, stream banks; lake, pond and river edges; moist meadows. Often found in saline conditions. Widespread in Alberta.

FLOWERS: **Petals 5, yellow to whitish, oval, 3 to 8 mm long, with nectary at base. Sepals 5, pale green with red-purple tinge**, shorter than petals. Stamens numerous, yellow. June to August.

FRUIT: Bright green, round to cylindrical group of achenes. Each **achene wrinkled, somewhat wedge-shaped, about 2 mm long, with curved tip**.

LEAVES: Mostly **basal**, smooth or hairy, thick, shiny, **oval to heart or kidney-shaped, with scalloped, occasionally reddish edges**. Blade 10 to 35 mm long, leaf stalk to 4 cm long or more.

GROWTH HABIT: Perennial, usually with several stems, up to 20 cm tall with fibrous roots and runners (*stolons*). Can form dense mats.

The name buttercup is likely derived from the bright-yellow flowers of several of the *Ranunculus* species. In some species the leaves are deeply incised and slightly resemble a bird's foot, hence the name "crowfoot." ✿ The genus name is from the Greek *rana* (frog), in reference to the wetland habitat. *Cymbalaria* means "pertaining to cymbals," perhaps because of the leaf shape. ✿ Buttercups contain alkaloids and some species are poisonous to cattle. Although the plants are relatively unpalatable and therefore usually avoided, some animals develop a taste for them. Hay containing buttercups is supposedly safe if the plant has dried and cured. ✿ Some species of buttercup were rubbed on arrows to poison them by the Thompson people of British Columbia. ✿ There are about 300 species of buttercup in the world, mainly in the northern hemisphere temperate and arctic regions; 26 are found in Alberta, mostly in moist habitats. 3 aquatic species occurring in Alberta are large-leaved water crowfoot (*R. aquatilis*), white water crowfoot (*R. circinatus*) and yellow water crowfoot (*R. gmelinii*). The first 2 species both have white flowers; however, the former has 15 to 25 beakless or minutely beaked achenes, while the latter has 30 to 80 achenes with beaks 0.3 to 0.5 mm long. They have recently been described as a single species (*R. aquatilis* var. *diffusus*) in *The Flora of North America*. Yellow water crowfoot has yellow flowers and palmately lobed or dissected leaves.

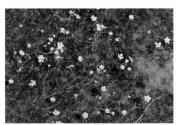

large-leaved water crowfoot   (EJ)

white water crowfoot   (CWA)

mountain buttercup, alpine buttercup, snowpatch buttercup
Ranunculus eschscholtzii Schlecht.
ALPINE, SUBALPINE

HABITAT AND RANGE: Moist meadows, subalpine forests and rocky slopes in the Rocky Mountains. Often occurring in areas of **snow drift accumulation and late snowmelt**.

FLOWERS: 1 to 4 per plant. Petals 5, yellow, **5 to 18 mm long**. Sepals 5, smooth or slightly hairy, **usually purplish-tinged**. Numerous stamens. July to August.

FRUIT: A round to cylindrical cluster of achenes. Each achene smooth or hairy with a thin, slender, straight to slightly curved beak.

LEAVES: Mainly basal, shallowly to **deeply lobed, round to kidney-shaped**. Blades 1 to 3 cm long.

mountain buttercup (CWE)

GROWTH HABIT: Smooth perennial (sometimes hairy in the inflorescence), 5 to 20 cm tall from large rootstock. Flowering stems usually without leaves, although the bracts are leaf-like. Often grows in large colonies.

The origin of the genus name *Ranunculus* is explained on page 72. *Eschscholtzii* honours J.F. Eschscholtz, a Russian doctor and naturalist of the 19th century. ✍ Certain buttercups contain oils that irritate the skin and have been used to cause blistering. The Montagnais of Nova Scotia and Newfoundland reportedly crushed the leaves and inhaled the vapours of buttercups to cure headaches. Some North American tribes pulverized buttercup roots, soaked them and used the pulp to treat wounds. ✍ Macoun's buttercup (*R. macounii*), a common and widespread species, is taller (30 to 70 cm), is usually quite hairy and has compound leaves with 3 leaflets, each leaflet further divided into lobes.

Macoun's buttercup

veiny meadow rue

Thalictrum venulosum Trel.

PRAIRIE, ASPEN PARKLAND, BOREAL FOREST, MONTANE, SUBALPINE

veiny meadow rue (BA)

HABITAT AND RANGE: Open aspen, coniferous and mixed woods, meadows, floodplains, thickets, moist or riverine prairie. Widespread in Alberta.

FLOWERS: Numerous, **small male and female flowers, usually on separate plants**. Male flowers consist of tiny (4 to 8 mm long) drooping, **yellowish, purplish or reddish stamens**, with anthers more than 1 mm long and filaments 3 to 5 mm long. Female flowers are composed of **green to purplish pistils**, about 6 mm long including style. No petals. Sepals 4 or 5, greenish white, deciduous, prominently veined, rounded at tips, about 4 to 5 mm long. **Flower stalks of different lengths.** May to July.

FRUIT: Broad-ribbed achenes, 3 to 5 mm long, ascending or erect, plump-looking, **in a tight, star-shaped cluster**. Achenes with persistent style (1 to 2.5 mm long), often with fine glandular hairs.

LEAVES: Alternate, compound basal and stem leaves, with **leaflets in 3s**. Each leaflet blue-green, paler below, smooth, **round to wedge-shaped at the base, with deep scallops at the tip. Leaflets usually broader than long**, 1 to 2.5 cm in length, **prominently veined**. Leaf stalks sheath the stem at the bases.

GROWTH HABIT: Erect perennial 20 to 100 cm tall.

The common name rue may refer to the plant's bitter taste. The genus name is derived from the Greek *thallo* (to grow green), referring to the bright-green early shoots. *Venulosum* describes the prominent veins on the underside of the leaf.

veiny meadow rue (male flowers) (CWE)

There are 100 or more species of *Thalictrum* in the world, mostly in north temperate woods and mountains; 4 are found in Alberta. Western meadow rue (*T. occidentale*) is similar to veiny meadow rue but has wide-spreading, rather than ascending, flower stalks; its flower stalks are all roughly the same length, and the filaments are 5 to 10 mm long, as opposed to 3 to 5 mm long. The veins of veiny meadow rue are also generally much more pronounced than in western meadow rue. The Montana Flathead chewed the seeds of western meadow rue and applied them as a perfume. The Blackfoot also kept seeds and foliage for their aroma, which likely repelled insects as well. Related species have been used as a stimulant to prepare horses for long journeys. ✎ Tall or purple meadow rue (*T. dasycarpum*) is usually more robust and frequently taller (to 1 m or more in height) than veiny meadow rue. Its 3–lobed leaflets are longer than they are broad and are hairy below, and the achenes are also usually hairy. The slender flat-fruited or few-flowered meadow rue (*T. sparsiflorum*) has flowers with both male and female parts, strongly flattened achenes and anthers less than 1 mm long.

veiny meadow rue (female flowers)   (LK)

globeflower

Trollius laxus Salisb.
(*Trollius albiflorus* (A. Gray) Rydb. in Moss 1983)
SUBALPINE, ALPINE

globeflower (JH)

HABITAT AND RANGE: Moist subalpine to alpine stream banks, coniferous woods and meadows of the Rocky Mountains.

FLOWERS: Large and attractive, up to 4 cm across. Petals 5 to 8, inconspicuous. **Sepals 5 to 10, pale creamy-white (sometimes bluish or pinkish on the outside), broad, rounded, 10 to 20 mm long,** surrounding a central core of numerous, dark-yellow stamens. June to August.

FRUIT: **Round cluster of greenish to purplish beaked follicles** that open along 1 side, 8 to 10 mm long. Follicles contain numerous shiny, round, tan seeds up to 2 mm long.

LEAVES: **Shiny, bright green (lighter underneath), 5 to 7-parted.** Lobed and often toothed at the tip, prominently veined, 4 to 8 cm long. Basal leaves long-stalked with broad, membraneous stipules. Stem leaves few (2 to 4), short-stalked. Upper leaves stalkless.

GROWTH HABIT: Hollow-stemmed, smooth, erect, herbaceous perennial, 10 to 40 cm tall from thick rootstock and fibrous roots. Many fibrous leaf sheaths at base of plant.

The sepals curve inward in inclement weather, making the flower appear round: hence the name "globeflower." *Trollius* is from the German *Trollblume* (globeflower) or after the Swedish *Troll* (a malignant supernatural being), because the plant contains **poisonous substances**. *Laxus* means "loose or with parts distinct or apart from one another," perhaps describing the rather open growth habit.
◢ There are 12 species of *Trollius* in northern temperate areas. Only this species occurs in Alberta.

arctic poppy, alpine poppy

Papaver radicatum Rottb. ssp. *kluanensis* (D. Löve) D.F. Murray
(*Papaver kluanensis* D. Löve in Moss 1983)
ALPINE

HABITAT AND RANGE: Alpine shale slopes, rocky ledges, scree. Occurs in the Rockies from the Smoky River south to the Bow River.

FLOWERS: 2.5 to 3 cm broad on a **stalk covered with whitish to light-brown, spreading hairs. Petals 4 or 5, 1 to 2.5 cm long, thin, bright yellow, becoming pale green or brick-red** (plants formerly called *P. freedmanium*) with age. Flower bud covered with dark-brown hairs, solitary on long stalk, nodding in bud but straightening out later so the flower petals can face the sun. Pistil with several united stigmas that form a star shape. Stamens about 25, the same length as the pistil. Sepals 2, deciduous. July to August.

arctic poppy   (JH)

FRUIT: **Papery, oval capsule 1 to 2 cm long, covered with long, brown bristles.** Capsule opens by small pores to release many pale-brown, curved seeds, up to 1.5 mm long.

LEAVES: Numerous, basal, finely dissected, up to 7 cm long including stalk. Blade and stalk covered with **long hairs**.

GROWTH HABIT: Tufted, long-hairy perennial to 10 cm tall with milky juice and no stem leaves.

*P*apaver is the Latin name for the plant, perhaps from the Greek *papa* (pap), referring to the milky juice, or the Sumerian *pa pa*, the noise supposedly made when chewing poppy seeds. *Radicatum* is derived from the Latin *radix* (root) and may refer to the plant's perennial rootstocks, from which grow tufted plants. *Kluanensis* means "of Kluane." Arctic poppy is the more common of our 2 native poppies (Freedman's poppy, *P. freedmanianum* in Moss 1983, is now considered a synonym of arctic poppy). Dwarf or alpine poppy (*P. pygmaeum*) has leaves that are sparsely hairy above and nearly smooth below, has smaller petals (less than 1 cm long) and occurs in Alberta only in Waterton Lakes National Park. Both arctic and dwarf poppy are rare in Alberta. ✿ Substances **toxic to humans** are present in both the foliage and seed pods of poppies. ✿ There are about 50 *Papaver* species in the world, mainly in temperate and subtropical Eurasia and Africa. Both the orange to red-flowered Iceland poppy (*P. nudicaule*), 20 to 30 cm tall, and the white to purple-flowered opium poppy (*P. somniferum*), 30 to 100 cm tall, are occasionally seen in Alberta as garden escapes.

Iceland poppy   (DJ)

golden corydalis, yellow corydalis

Corydalis aurea Willd.

<small>ASPEN PARKLAND, BOREAL FOREST, MONTANE, SUBALPINE</small>

golden corydalis (JH)

HABITAT AND RANGE: Open woods, roadsides, shores, banks, disturbed ground; often on gravelly soils. Widespread in Alberta except on the prairie.

FLOWERS: In bracted clusters. **Irregularly shaped (somewhat like a pea family flower), yellow,** 10 to 18 mm long. Petals 4, **outer pair slightly inflated and keeled at the tip.** 1 of the outer pair of petals with a spur 4 mm long. Sepals 2, small, yellowish white. Stamens 6. May to July.

FRUIT: Narrow, 2-valved, somewhat wrinkled, drooping or spreading capsule, 15 to 25 mm long with many shiny, black seeds, 2 to 3 mm long.

LEAVES: Alternate. Light blue-green, 7 to 10 cm long, twice or more **pinnately dissected**.

GROWTH HABIT: Erect or spreading, branched, leafy biennial or annual, 10 to 50 cm tall.

The name *Corydalis* is from the ancient Greek name of the crested lark (*korydallis*). It was thought that the upper petal appeared crested or that the spur of the petal resembles the spur of the lark. *Aurea* means "golden," in reference to the petal colour. ✿ Some *Corydalis* species are called fume-root because of the nitrous odour of the roots. Certain native peoples steamed the roots of this species and inhaled the smoke to clear congestion. ✿ There are approximately 100 species of *Corydalis* in the world, mostly in the northern hemisphere; 2 of these occur in Alberta. Pink corydalis (*C. sempervirens*) is taller and more erect, has pinkish flowers that are tinged with yellow and bears ascending, rather than spreading or drooping, capsules. It is said to be slightly poisonous to sheep and is suspected of having caused livestock losses.

pink corydalis (BA)

bee plant, spider-flower, pink cleome, stinking clover, Rocky Mountain bee plant, clammyweed

Cleome serrulata Pursh

PRAIRIE, ASPEN PARKLAND

HABITAT AND RANGE: Common in the southern half of the province in disturbed areas (**especially on rodent mounds**) and along roadsides. Often occurs on sandy soils.

FLOWERS: **Mass of pinkish or purplish to white flowers in rounded terminal cluster.** Petals 4, each 8 to 12 mm long. **Stamens 6, pinkish or white, protruding.** Sepals 4. Flower clusters elongate in fruit. June to September.

FRUIT: Oblong, 2-valved capsule, 2.5 to 5 cm long with projection at tip. Capsule droops on curved stalk. Seeds gray-black, 3 to 4 mm long, with a wrinkled surface.

LEAVES: Compound, **of 3 lance-shaped to oval, dark-green, smooth, mostly entire leaflets, 2 to 7 cm long**. Lower leaves long-stalked, upper stalkless or nearly so.

GROWTH HABIT: Somewhat shrubby, malodorous, smooth to sparsely hairy, freely branched annual with pale-green stems. Up to 80 cm tall from a tap root. Often found in large clumps.

bee plant   (CWA)

The plant is attractive to bees because it produces large amounts of nectar, hence the common name. The origin of the genus name is obscure but may be from the Greek *kleos* (glory). *Serrulata* refers to the occasionally finely toothed leaves. ✒ Bee plant was an important food plant for many western North American natives. The young, tender shoots and leaves were cooked as a potherb (the water was changed several times to decrease the unpleasant odour). The boiled plant left a residue which was occasionally used as a food but was more often used as a paint or dye (frequently for pottery). The seeds could be ground into gruel or flour. Alberta Blackfoot made a tea to reduce fever from the plant. ✒ There are approximately 100 species of *Cleome* in the world, mainly in the tropics. Only this species occurs in Alberta.

Mustard Family (Brassicaceae or Cruciferae)

Many food plants, such as broccoli, cabbage, cauliflower, canola, the familiar condiments mustard and horse radish, and numerous troublesome weeds, including stinkweed, shepherd's-purse, flixweed, pepper grass and hoary cress, number among the 2500 or more members of the mustards. They are mostly herbs with watery, often pungent juice and often have forked or star-shaped hairs. The leaves are simple and alternate, and the flowers have 4 petals in a Maltese-cross shape, hence the former family name, Cruciferae, from the Latin *crux, crucis* (cross). There are 2 short stamens and 4 longer ones, and 4 sepals. Fruits are generally pod-like with 2 chambers and may be short and more or less round (*silicles*), as in sand bladderpod, or elongated and narrow (*siliques*), as in reflexed rock cress. *(See key for this family beginning page 300.)*

SILICLE

reflexed rock cress

Arabis holboellii Hornem.

PRAIRIE, ASPEN PARKLAND, BOREAL FOREST, MONTANE, SUBALPINE

HABITAT AND RANGE: Widespread in the prairies, especially on gravelly slopes, and in dry to moist open woods. Occurs throughout Alberta.

FLOWERS: **On spreading or reflexed stalks**, in a terminal cluster. **Petals 4, pink to white**, 5 to 10 mm long. Sepals 2 to 4 mm long, with whitish margins.

FRUIT: **Long (up to 7 cm), straight to curved, pod-like fruits** called *siliques*, **on spreading to reflexed stalks**. Seeds slightly winged, flattened, 1 to 1.5 mm long.

LEAVES: Entire to distantly toothed. Basal leaves hairy, short-stalked, **in a rosette. Stem leaves numerous, clasping** (particularly the upper), 1 to 4 cm long.

GROWTH HABIT: Biennial or perennial herb, 10 to 70 cm tall; **often with short, stiff, spreading hairs that sometimes occur in star-like clusters**. Some plants appear grayish due to their abundant whitish hairs.

reflexed rock cress (LF)

The name rock cress describes the habitat of many *Arabis* species. *Arabis* is said to be derived from Arabia, where many rock cresses are found, while *holboellii* commemorates Danish botanist-naturalist Carl Peter Holbøell (1795-1856). ✍ All rock cresses are edible, but smooth species are preferred to hairy. They have a sharp tang, somewhat similar to radishes. ✍ There are 100 species of *Arabis* in the world, from desert to alpine habitats in the northern hemisphere; 9 of these occur in Alberta. A species mainly of sandy areas in the boreal forest and northern mountains, lyre-leaved rock cress (*A. lyrata* ssp. *kamchatica*) may be distinguished from reflexed rock cress by its erect or spreading-ascending, shorter siliques (1.5 to 4 cm) and its more incised or lobed leaves. Lyall's rock cress (*A. lyallii*) is a much smaller (5 to 25 cm) purple to deep pink-flowered species of dry alpine habitats. ✍ Although there are 32 genera and approximately 98 species of the mustard family in Alberta, only a few species are mentioned in this book. Most of our native mustards are not particularly attractive plants and/or are weedy.

lyre-leaved rock cress (LK)

Lyall's rock cress (LA)

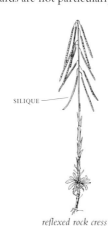

SILIQUE

reflexed rock cress

golden whitlow-grass

Draba aurea Vahl in Horn.

<small>BOREAL FOREST, SUBALPINE, ALPINE</small>

golden whitlow-grass   (BA)

HABITAT AND RANGE: Rocky slopes, open woods, clearings, ridges, alpine meadows. Throughout the Rocky Mountains and also in the western boreal forest.

FLOWERS: In short to long clusters on stalks 3 to 20 mm long. Lowest flowers may have bracts below. **Petals 4, pale to bright yellow, 4 to 6 mm long.** Sepals 2 to 3.5 mm long. Stamens 6. June to August.

FRUIT: Softly hairy to smooth, **often twisted pods** called *silicles*. **Silicles narrowly to broadly lance-shaped, 7 to 20 mm long and 2 to 4 mm broad, with persistent style 0.3 to 1.5 mm long.** Numerous shiny, tan seeds, about 1 mm long.

LEAVES: Numerous, densely hairy, entire to distantly toothed. Basal leaves stalked, in a rosette, lance-shaped, 1 to 5 cm long. Stem leaves few to many, essentially stalkless, sometimes clasping, oval to broadly lance-shaped.

GROWTH HABIT: Short-lived, 1 to several-stemmed perennial, 10 to 50 cm tall from an erect or curved base. **Hairy with a mixture of simple, forked and star-shaped hairs.**

*D*raba is derived from *drabe* (acrid), in reference to the sap of some members of the mustard family. *Aurea* means "golden," describing the petal colour. *Draba* species were used to treat "whitlows" (inflammation of the finger tips or toe nails), hence the name "whitlow-grass" (in ancient times the term grass was used interchangeably with plant). ⚘ Most of our *Draba* species are tufted subalpine to alpine plants, whose low height and hairiness enable them to survive these cold, often dry environments. They are difficult to tell apart and usually leaf hair characteristics and style length must be examined under a microscope to differentiate species. ⚘ There are about 300 species of *Draba*, mainly of temperate to arctic North America and Eurasia; 24 species are found in Alberta, chiefly in the mountains. Annual whitlowgrass (*D. nemorosa*) or woods draba is a small (up to 35 cm), yellow-flowered annual, occurring on moist to dry open ground throughout the province. ⚘ The Blackfoot used a mixture containing the root of related Yellowstone draba (*D. incerta*) to stop nosebleeds and induce abortions.

SILICLE

Yellowstone draba

annual whitlow-grass   (CWA)

prairie rocket
Erysimum asperum (Nutt.) DC.
PRAIRIE, ASPEN PARKLAND

HABITAT AND RANGE: Dry, sandy grasslands, primarily in the southern quarter of Alberta.

FLOWERS: In terminal, rounded cluster. **Petals bright yellow to orangish**, pleasant-scented, 15 to 25 mm long. Flower stalks **thick, ascending or widespreading**. May to August.

FRUIT: **Long (usually 5 to 10 cm), narrow (up to 2 mm), 4-angled pod** called a *silique*. Erect or spreading silique contains numerous tan seeds, wingless or wing-margined, each less than 1 mm long.

LEAVES: Simple, **thick, stiff, gray-green**. Basal leaves numerous, in rosette, entire to wavy-toothed, to 8 cm or longer. Stem leaves alternate, narrowly lance-shaped to linear, entire to slightly toothed.

GROWTH HABIT: Erect, robust perennial, simple or branched from the base, up to 45 cm tall. The **grayish appearance of the plant is due to the thick, white, mainly 2-forked hairs**.

prairie rocket (JH)

The genus name is from *erysio* (to draw), as in to draw out pain, because the acrid juices of *Erysimum* species were used in poultices. *Asperum* means "rough," likely in reference to the stiff hairs. ✿ There are 80 species of *Erysimum* in the north temperate zone, mainly Eurasian; 3 other species occur in Alberta. Wormseed mustard (*E. cheiranthoides*) has much shorter petals (2 to 5 mm long) and shorter fruits (1 to 3 cm long). Historically, the seeds of this species were crushed and given to children to drink to kill worms. Small-flowered rocket (*E. inconspicuum*) is similar to wormseed mustard but has longer petals (6 to 12 mm). Alpine wallflower or purple alpine rocket (*E. pallasii*) has pinkish purple, sweet-scented flowers in the centre of a rosette of leaves and is found only in dry alpine habitats.

alpine wallflower (RF)

83

sand bladderpod
Lesquerella arenosa (Richards.) Rydb.

PRAIRIE, ASPEN PARKLAND, MONTANE

sand bladderpod   (DJ)

HABITAT AND RANGE: Dry, often sandy or gravelly, exposed grassland, eroded slopes, disturbed areas. Common in the southern half of Alberta.

FLOWERS: Many flowers per plant, in loose, open clusters. **Petals 4, bright yellow**, sometimes pinkish or purple-tinged, with dark-yellow veins, up to 10 mm long. Sepals 4, yellowish green, about 6 mm long. May to June.

FRUIT: **Round**, gray-green, hairy, **bladder-shaped** *silicle*, 3 to 6 mm long, usually **drooping on a curved stalk. Style persistent**, 2.5 to 4 mm long. Seeds slightly flattened, about 1 mm long.

LEAVES: Mainly in a **basal rosette**. Basal leaves linear to spoon-shaped, gradually tapered to base, grayish, hairy with star-shaped hairs, entire or distantly toothed, up to 8 cm long. Stem leaves oval to broadly lance-shaped.

GROWTH HABIT: Tufted, short (5 to 25 cm), spreading, grayish annual or perennial. Usually with **several stems from a tap root**.

Bladderpod undoubtedly refers to the round, bladder-like fruit. The genus name commemorates Leo Lesquereux, a 19th-century American botanist, and *arenosa* means "of sand or sandy places." ✿ There are 50 species of *Lesquerella* in the world, all in the western hemisphere; 3 occur in Alberta. Spatulate bladderpod (*L. alpina*) has an S-shaped stalk attached to at least some of the fruits. Northern bladderpod (*L. arctica*) has fruit stalks that are erect and straight or only slightly curved.

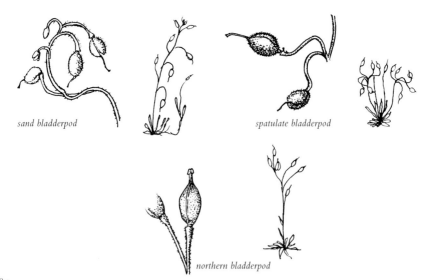

sand bladderpod

spatulate bladderpod

northern bladderpod

silver rock cress, alpine smelowskia, fernleaf candytuft
Smelowskia calycina (Stephan.) C.A. Mey. var. *americana* (Rydb.) Drury & Rollins
SUBALPINE, ALPINE

HABITAT AND RANGE: Rocky ledges and crevices, alpine scree, ridges; in the Rocky Mountains.

FLOWERS: In terminal clusters on ascending-to-erect, short stalks. Cluster elongates as fruit develops. **Petals whitish, sometimes tinged with pink or purple, spoon-shaped, 4 to 8 mm long.** Sepals 2 to 3 mm long, soon deciduous. Stamens 6. May to August.

FRUIT: Narrow, dark, hairy pods called *siliques*, **5 to 12 mm long, tapered at both ends, with persistent style 0.3 to 1 mm long.** Seeds 6 to 10, tan, about 3 mm long.

LEAVES: Variable, from oval to divided into many segments. **Bluish green to grayish with fine, branched hairs.** Basal leaves 1 to 10 cm long including slender stalks. **Stalks equalling or longer than blades, fringed with long, stiff hairs near the base.** Stem leaves similar but smaller, finely dissected and short-stalked or stalkless.

silver rock cress   (CWA)

GROWTH HABIT: Usually mat-forming perennial, **covered with old leaves at the base.** Stems several, 5 to 20 cm tall, with long, soft, and shorter, branched, hairs that give the plant a felt-like appearance.

The genus name commemorates Russian botanist Timotheus Smelowsky (1770-1815). *Calycina* means "belonging to the calyx" or "with a well-developed calyx." This plant is sometimes called fernleaf candytuft in the United States because the leaves are fern-like in appearance. ✱ Silver rock cress is often affected by a rust fungus that produces numerous brown pustules on the leaves and stems, and causes the flowers to abort. ✱ There are 4 or 5 species of *Smelowskia*, occurring in western North America and Asia. Only this species is native to Alberta.

pitcher-plant

Sarracenia purpurea L.

BOREAL FOREST

pitcher-plant (BA)

HABITAT AND RANGE: Sedge fens in northeastern quarter of Alberta.

FLOWERS: Solitary on leafless stalk, nodding, 5 to 7 cm wide. **Petals 5, curved, dark reddish purple.** Style enlarged above, with tiny stigmas at angles. Stamens numerous. Sepals 5, spreading. June to July.

FRUIT: Granular capsule, 2 to 3 cm broad, with numerous, pale-brown, bumpy seeds, up to 1.5 mm long.

LEAVES: **Several, basal, modified to form "pitchers."** Each leaf 10 to 20 cm long, bluish green, **blotched with red or purple, prominently veined. Blade forms hood at the top.** Insects fall into the pitcher and are frequently drowned in a pool of water at the base. Downward pointing bristles inside prevent any survivors from crawling out.

GROWTH HABIT: Stemless, robust, carnivorous perennial, 20 to 45 cm tall.

Sarracenia honours Michael Sarrasin, an early French botanist and physician. *Purpurea* means purple, likely in reference to the petals. Devil's-boot, dumb-watches (because the surface of the stigma looks like the face of a watch) and frog-bonnet are additional common names applied to this plant. *◢* Pitcher-plant is the floral emblem of Newfoundland, where it is known as Indian-cup, Indian-jug or Indian-pipe. *◢* This plant was once regarded as a smallpox cure by tribes in the Great Lakes region of Canada and the United States. An infusion of the roots was thought to offer immunity, shorten the term of the disease, cure it and prevent formation of deep "pits" in convalescence. *◢* There are 8 species of *Sarracenia* in the world, primarily in eastern North America. Only this species grows in Alberta, and it is considered rare here.

pitcher-plant (JH)

round-leaved sundew
Drosera rotundifolia L.
BOREAL FOREST

HABITAT AND RANGE: Mossy bogs, swamps, moist pine woods. Restricted to the northeastern part of the province.

FLOWERS: Open only in bright sunshine. Petals 4 to 8, small, inconspicuous, white to pinkish in a 1-sided cluster. Sepals 4 or 5, up to 5 mm long. July to August.

FRUIT: Brown to black capsule, 1 to 3 mm long, with many seeds.

LEAVES: In a basal rosette. Reddish green, **spoon-shaped, usually broader than long**, up to 3.5 cm long. Along the margins of the leaves are hairs with large, **reddish, sticky, short glands**. The colour attracts small insects that are trapped when the leaves curl inwards. The plant then secretes juices to digest the victim.

round-leaved sundew (CWE)

GROWTH HABIT: Carnivorous, herbaceous perennial up to 25 cm tall.

The name sundew likely originates from the plant's habit of opening the flowers only in sunlight and the shiny, dew-like sticky droplets on the leaf-margins. *Drosera* is from the Greek *droseros,* meaning "dew," and *rotundifolia* means "round-leaved." The plant is carnivorous to supplement the minerals, chiefly nitrogen and phosphorus, that are scarce in its nutrient-poor habitat. Most carnivorous plants of Alberta live in swamps, bogs and fens. ✎ There are 90 species of *Drosera* in the world, mainly in Australia and South Africa, but only 3 in Alberta. Both oblong-leaved sundew (*D. anglica*) and slender-leaved sundew (*D. linearis*) have leaves that are longer than broad and are provincially rare, found in northern and central Alberta.

slender-leaved sundew (CWE)

lance-leaved stonecrop, common stonecrop, sedum

Sedum lanceolatum Torr.

Prairie, Aspen Parkland, Montane, Subalpine, Alpine

lance-leaved stonecrop   (CWe)

HABITAT AND RANGE: Dry, rocky, open, shrubby slopes, meadows, dry grassland. Often in rock crevices or on gravelly soil. Chiefly found in the mountains, although of scattered occurrence elsewhere.

FLOWERS: Numerous, **star-shaped in dense, flat-topped to rounded cluster**, about 2.5 cm across. **Petals 4 or 5, bright yellow**, lance-shaped, 5 to 7 mm long. Stamens 8 to 10, yellow. Sepals 4 to 5, green, widely lance-shaped, joined at base, 4 mm long. June to August.

FRUIT: Green, 5-compartmented, erect, beaked pod that opens along 1 side to release tiny brown seeds, each about 1 mm long.

LEAVES: **Numerous, fleshy, overlapping**. Alternate on stem and basal. **Pale green to reddish, linear to lance-shaped**, up to about 1 cm long.

GROWTH HABIT: **Fleshy perennial with reddish stem**, up to 15 cm tall, surrounded by dense clump of basal leaves.

The name stonecrop refers to the plant's stony habitat. *Sedum* is from the Latin *sedere* (to sit) and alludes to the way the plant attaches to gravel. *Lanceolatum* is derived from the lance-shaped leaves. ✔ The succulent stems and leaves enable the plant to resist drought. ✔ Stonecrop can be eaten when young (but not in quantity) to combat hunger and thirst. The young leaves and shoots of many species have been used in salads or cooked as potherbs. Some stonecrops are still cultivated for food use in Holland. This plant is also eaten by pikas and rodents. ✔ There are 400 to 500 species of *Sedum*, mainly in the north temperate zone; 4 species occur in Alberta. Spreading stonecrop (*S. divergens*), rare in the province, has mostly opposite, oval to round leaves; narrow-petalled stonecrop (*S. stenopetalum*) has flattened, brownish leaves and spreading, rather than erect, fruits. Rose-root (*S. integrifolium*; *Tolmachevia integrifolia* in Moss 1983) has purple to reddish flowers and is found on subalpine to alpine rock faces.

rose-root   (CWe)

This widespread family of perennial herbs provides us with many ornamentals such as saxifrages, coral-bells and astilbe. The leaves are simple (sometimes lobed), usually alternate or often all basal. There are 4 or 5 separate or partly united sepals, and also 4 or 5 (sometimes none) petals. There may be twice as many stamens as petals, or there may be the same number of stamens as petals (in which case the stamens are positioned alternately with the petals). Fruits are mainly capsules. *(See key for this family beginning page 302.)*

green saxifrage, northern water-carpet, golden-saxifrage, northern golden-saxifrage

Chrysosplenium tetrandrum (Lund) Fries

BOREAL FOREST, MONTANE, SUBALPINE, ALPINE

green saxifrage   (CWA)

HABITAT AND RANGE: Rock crevices, wet banks, along streams, shady sites, seepage areas in the Rocky Mountains and boreal forest.

FLOWERS: Inconspicuous, 2 to 3 mm broad. Petals lacking. **Calyx 4-lobed, each lobe about 1 mm long, erect, greenish (often with purple spots)**, attached to the lower half of the ovary. Stamens 4 (sometimes 3). June.

FRUIT: **2-lobed, flattened, saucer-shaped capsule**, about 4 mm long. Seeds plump, sometimes ridged, glossy reddish brown, 0.5 to 1 mm long. The seeds are dispersed when water droplets hit the cups of the capsules.

LEAVES: Alternate, mainly basal, on slender stalks up to 3 cm long. **Blades oval to kidney-shaped, with 3 to 7 broad scallops,** yellow-ish green, smooth to sparsely hairy. Stem leaves 1 to 4, lobed, smooth.

GROWTH HABIT: Stoloniferous perennial with weakly erect stems, up to 20 cm tall.

*C*hrysosplenium originates from the Greek *chrysos* (gold) and *splen* (spleen), refer-ring to some supposed medicinal qualities of the plant. *Tetrandrum* applies to the flower parts in 4s. The common name water-carpet describes the mat-like form the plant assumes in wet habitats. ✍ There are 40 or more species of *Chrysosplenium*, chiefly in moist habitats of temperate to arctic North America, South America and Eurasia; 2 occur in Alberta. The other Alberta species, golden saxifrage (*C. iowense*), has yellow, spreading, green sepals.

Richardson's alumroot

Heuchera richardsonii R. Br.

PRAIRIE, ASPEN PARKLAND, BOREAL FOREST, MONTANE

HABITAT AND RANGE: Open sandy or gravelly grassland, rocky slopes, stream banks, crevices, moist prairie and aspen parkland. Common in the southern half of Alberta; occasional in the boreal forest.

FLOWERS: Numerous, on a leafless stem. Petals 5, inconspicuous, spoon-shaped, **purplish or pinkish**, glandular-hairy. **Petals the same length (5 to 10 mm) as or slightly longer than the 5 greenish, glandular-hairy sepals.** Stamens 5, often exserted. June to July.

FRUIT: Capsule brown, 2-beaked, 1 cm long, containing flat, dark-brown, oval seeds less than 1 mm long. Seed surface covered with **glandular spines**.

LEAVES: All basal, **round to heart-shaped**, 2.5 to 6 cm across, on long stalks. Somewhat **leathery, lobed and coarsely toothed**. Smooth or slightly hairy above, short stiff-hairy beneath. Stipules present.

GROWTH HABIT: Erect perennial herb, 30 to 40 cm tall from thick, scaly rootstock. **Stiff-hairy with tiny glands near the top.**

Richardson's alumroot (JH)

The common name refers to the alum-like, astringent quality of the rhizome. The genus name honours Dr. Johann von Heucher, a professor of medicine at the University of Wittenberg, while *richardsonii* refers to an early explorer, John Richardson. ✍ Some B.C. tribes used the roots of a related species, sticky alumroot (*H. cylindrica*), as a medicinal tea to treat "aching bones," tuberculosis, cuts and sores. The Alberta Blackfoot and Montana Flathead used a tea made from the roots to cure cramps and diarrhea. Early European settlers used alumroot to treat wounds, sores, ulcers and cancer, and the plant was also used to soothe saddle sores on horses. ✍ There are 35 species of *Heuchera* in the world, all in North America. Of the 4 that occur in Alberta, this is the only species with pinkish flowers. Sticky alumroot also has a large calyx (6 to 10 mm) but has a yellowish flower and petals that are absent or much shorter than the sepals. It occurs on rocky slopes and ledges in the mountains. Alpine alumroot (*H. glabra*) has a calyx 2 to 3.5 mm long and stamens strongly protruding from the white flower; it occurs rarely in the northern Rockies. Small-leaved alumroot (*H. parvifolia*), found in southern Alberta, also has a short calyx (2 to 3 mm long), but the stamens do not protrude from the white or yellowish flower.

sticky alumroot (JP)

bishop's-cap, mitrewort

Mitella nuda L.

ASPEN PARKLAND, BOREAL FOREST, MONTANE, SUBALPINE

bishop's-cap   (CWE)

HABITAT AND RANGE: Moist to dry forests, bogs, thickets, stream banks. Common and widespread in Alberta, except on the prairies.

FLOWERS: Several, tiny, in occasionally branched, loose, open cluster, 2 to 10 cm long. Petals greenish yellow, **deeply incised, antenna-like**. Calyx with **5 sepals, white to greenish, spreading, saucer-shaped**, each about 1.5 mm long. Stamens 10.

FRUIT: Capsule greenish, 2-valved, with few black, tiny, shiny seeds, each about 1 mm long.

LEAVES: Simple, basal, on long, hairy leaf stalks. Blades 1 to 3 cm long, heart to kidney-shaped, with **short lobes and rounded teeth. Upper and lower surfaces have stiff, short, bristly hairs**.

GROWTH HABIT: Erect, finely glandular-hairy perennial, with underground and above-ground prostrate stems, up to 20 cm tall. Usually with no stem leaves, although sometimes with 1 stalkless leaf near the base.

The common and genus names are derived from the Greek *mitra* (a cap), referring to the shape of the unopened seed capsule. The capsule slightly resembles a mitre, a tall, pointed, 2-peaked hat worn by bishops. *Nuda* means "naked." ✿ There are 12 species of *Mitella*, chiefly in western North America, Japan and northeastern Asia. Of the 4 found in Alberta, bishop's-cap is the only species with 10 stamens. Another common *Mitella* species in Alberta, five-stamened mitrewort (*M. pentandra*), has only 5 stamens, each opposite the green petals. It is primarily located in the Rocky Mountains. When the flowers are missing, it can be very difficult to distinguish between five-stamened mitrewort and sugarscoop (*Tiarella unifoliata*); however, sugarscoop usually has a more deeply lobed leaf, somewhat similar to that of a maple.

flower of five-stamened mitrewort

bishop's-cap   (EJ)

spotted saxifrage, common saxifrage, prickly saxifrage

Saxifraga bronchialis L. ssp. *austromontana* (Wieg.) Piper

MONTANE, SUBALPINE, ALPINE

HABITAT AND RANGE: Rocky crevices and rock faces, scree, open slopes; from the foothills to alpine elevations in the mountains.

FLOWERS: In open clusters at the top of the plant. **Petals 5, white (usually with red or yellow spots near the tip)**, oval, narrowed at base, 4 to 6 mm long. Stamens 10, white, tapered. Sepals 5, green to reddish, spreading, rounded at tip, 1 to 3 mm long. June to August.

FRUIT: **Small capsule, 4 to 5 mm long, with 2 divergent beaks.** Seeds dark brown, less than 1 mm long.

LEAVES: **Mainly basal, crowded,** 7 to 15 mm long. Bright green, **stiff, lance-shaped, roughened with tiny, sharp teeth on margins, sharp-pointed and spiny at tip.** Scattered, small, scale-like leaves on stem.

GROWTH HABIT: **Tufted, creeping** perennial herb, 5 to 15 cm tall. Leafy at base. Stems reddish, glandular-hairy (especially above) or smooth. **Often forms mats on rocks.**

spotted saxifrage (JH)

*S*axifraga is from the Latin *saxum* (rock) and *frangere* (to break). Saxifrages frequently grow on rocks and are thought capable of breaking rocks into soil. *Bronchialis* is derived from *bronchus* (division or branch) and refers to the branching, mat-like growth, while *austromontana* is from *australis* (southern) and *montana* (mountains). ✐ Saxifrages are frequently eaten by pikas. Several are grown in rock and alpine gardens. ✐ There are about 300 species of *Saxifraga* in the world, mainly in temperate and arctic regions; 16 species are found in Alberta, primarily in the mountains. Yellow mountain saxifrage (*S. aizoides*) has a yellow flower and a stem with entire (not toothed) spine-tipped leaves, 4 to 8 mm long; it occurs along alpine streams, on rocky slopes and on moist sand or gravel to above treeline. Three-toothed saxifrage (*S. tricuspidata*) lacks stem leaves, has stiff, wedge-shaped basal leaves with 3 spiny-tipped teeth and purple or orange-spotted white flowers.

yellow mountain saxifrage (CWₐ)

three-toothed saxifrage (CWₐ)

purple saxifrage
Saxifraga oppositifolia L.
<small>ALPINE</small>

purple saxifrage   (OP)

HABITAT AND RANGE: In the Rocky Mountains on **rocky talus slopes, ledges, alpine boulder fields.**

FLOWERS: Each solitary on short stem. **Petals 5, purple (sometimes pinkish or whitish), 5 to 8 mm long.** Sepals 5, oblong to broadly lance-shaped, joined at base, hairy on margins, 2 to 3 mm long. May to July, immediately after winter snow has melted or receded.

FRUIT: Small beaked capsule, 6 to 8 mm long. Seeds light brown, slightly veiny, 0.5 mm long.

LEAVES: **Opposite, stalkless; appearing whorled**, as opposed to most saxifrages, which have alternate or basal leaves. **Each leaf broadly wedge-shaped, bluish green, fleshy, bristly-hairy on margins, overlapping, 2 to 5 mm long.**

GROWTH HABIT: Leafy perennial herb **in dense cushions**; up to 10 cm tall. Stem occasionally hairy, often purplish.

The origin of the genus name is explained on page 93. The plant's opposite leaves are responsible for its species name (*folia* means "leaves"). The cushion-like, compact habit of purple saxifrage allows it to retain heat and withstand the drying winds and low temperatures of its high mountain habitats. ⚹ This plant is sometimes confused with moss campion (*Silene acaulis*). Both have a purplish flower and similar cushion form. Moss campion, however, has narrowly lance-shaped leaves, as opposed to purple saxifrage's overlapping leaves that come off the stem in 4s. ⚹ Red-stemmed or Lyall's saxifrage (*S. lyallii*) often has a noticeably dark-red or purplish stem, fan or wedge-shaped, stalked basal leaves and tiny (2 to 4 mm), white flowers (often marked with greenish yellow). It is frequently found growing in a bed of moist mosses at the edges of streams in subalpine to alpine locations.

moss campion   (LA)

Lyall's saxifrage   (LA)

laceflower, false mitrewort, foam flower

Tiarella trifoliata L.

<small>BOREAL FOREST, MONTANE, SUBALPINE</small>

HABITAT AND RANGE: Moist coniferous woods, stream banks, trailsides in the boreal forest.

FLOWERS: Often **in groups of 3 in long, open, glandular cluster. Petals 5, white or pinkish, narrowly awl-shaped, much longer than the sepals.** Sepals 5, white or pinkish, 1 to 2 mm long, glandular-dotted on back. Stamens 10, **protruding, with long, white, purplish-tipped filaments.** June to July.

FRUIT: Membraneous, crown-shaped capsule, about 7 mm long, that splits into 2 unequal parts, each containing few, nearly black, shiny seeds.

LEAVES: 2 to 4, compound, **usually with 3 leaflets. Middle leaflet usually 3-lobed and toothed.** Blades hairy with numerous, short, stiff hairs or smooth. Scalloped to toothed on the margins, teeth spiny. Long-stalked.

GROWTH HABIT: Graceful, attractive perennial, 20 to 40 cm tall from a scaly rootstock. Smooth or hairy below and glandular-hairy above. Often grows in clumps.

laceflower (JP)

M itrewort alludes to the shape of the un-opened capsules (referring to a bishop's cap or mitre). Foam flower describes the flower's appearance, like flecks of white foam on the shady forest floor. *Tiarella* is Latin, diminutive of the Greek *tiara* (an ancient Persian turban-like headdress), again describing the fruit appearance. *Trifoliata* refers to the compound leaf with 3 leaflets.

✍ There are 6 species of *Tiarella* in the world, mostly in North America; 2 occur in Alberta. Sugarscoop (*T. unifoliata*), with simple, shallowly to deeply 3 to 5-lobed leaves (somewhat like a maple leaf), grows primarily in the moist woods of the Rocky Mountains.

laceflower

sugarscoop

sugarscoop (JH)

northern grass-of-Parnassus, grass-of-Parnassus

Parnassia palustris L.

BOREAL FOREST, MONTANE, SUBALPINE

northern grass-of-Parnassus   (CWE)

HABITAT AND RANGE: Wet woodlands, pond edges, stream banks, bogs, ditches, river flats. Common, except on the prairies.

FLOWERS: **Solitary**, showy. **Petals 5, white to cream-coloured with 5 to 9 yellow or green lines, oval, 8 to 15 mm long,** longer than sepals. Sepals 5, up to 1 cm long, united at base. Stamens 5, with large anthers; alternate with petals. **5 sterile stamens (*staminodia*) with sticky tips** to attract pollinating insects. July to August.

FRUIT: Oval capsule, about 1 cm long, usually with 4 compartments. Seeds numerous, reddish brown, winged, patterned with net veins, about 1 mm long.

LEAVES: Entire. Basal leaves broadly oval, **truncate to heart-shaped at base,** tapered to rounded at tip, up to 3 cm long, attached to long stalks. **Stem leaf lacks stalk, usually clasping, up to 3 cm long.**

GROWTH HABIT: Smooth, several-stemmed perennial herb, **7 to 35 cm tall, with small leaf at or below middle.**

The origin of the common name is somewhat obscure, but historically the terms "grass" and "plant" were interchangeable. The genus name is from Mount Parnassus in Greece, the favourite retreat of the god Apollo. *Palustris* means "of wetlands." ✐ There are 15 species of *Parnassia* in temperate and arctic North America and Eurasia; 4 occur in Alberta, this species being the most common and widespread. Fringed grass-of-Parnassus (*P. fimbriata*) has petals with fringed-hairy margins; provincially rare small-flowered grass-of-Parnassus (*P. parviflora*) has leaves narrowed to the base, as opposed to heart-shaped or truncate; and small or Kotzebue's grass-of-Parnassus (*P. kotzebuei)* is much smaller (usually 10 cm tall or less), with 3-veined petals.

fringed grass-of-Parnassus   (CWE)

The rose family, composed of often-thorny herbs, shrubs and trees, includes many valuable fruits (apples, plums, cherries, pears, strawberries and raspberries) and ornamentals (roses, mountain ash, hawthorns, cinquefoils and spiraeas). The leaves are alternate, simple or compound, usually with stipules. Petals usually number 5, arising from a cup or saucer-like structure (*hypanthium*) at the top of the stem. Sepals also occur in 5s, often with alternate bractlets; there are numerous stamens. The crushed leaves of most members of the family produce an odour like bitter almonds. *(See key for this family beginning page 303.)*

agrimony

Agrimonia striata Michx.

agrimony (EJ)

HABITAT AND RANGE: Moist aspen woods, thickets. Also in drier habitats and sandy or rocky soil. Occurs in east-central Alberta and the Cypress Hills.

FLOWERS: Small in **dense, long (5 to 20 cm), narrow, bracted cluster** at top of stem. **Petals 5, bright yellow, 3 mm long.** Calyx 5-lobed. Sepals spread at flowering time, then curve inward. Stamens numerous. Stigmas large, 2-lobed.

FRUIT: Dry **achenes with hooks** that can adhere to clothing and fur.

LEAVES: **Compoundly pinnate with 5 to 9 major leaflets.** Upper leaflet up to 6 cm long, plus several smaller ones. Leaflets lance-shaped, large-toothed and pointed at the tip. Dark green, hairy; with **tiny, stalkless glands beneath** and prominent veins. Large (up to 2 cm long), usually toothed stipules.

GROWTH HABIT: Erect, brownish-hairy perennial, up to 1.2 m tall from stout rootstock.

The derivation of *Agrimonia* may be from *argemon* (white spot on the eye), which the plant supposedly cured, or the Hebrew *argaman* (red-purple). *Striata* means striped. Other common names for the plant include harvest-lice, snakeweed and sweethearts. ⌀ Agrimony has been used to treat diabetes, bladder problems, fever, jaundice and tapeworm. A related species that grows in England was combined with a mixture of "pounded frogs and human blood" as a remedy for internal bleeding. ⌀ Handling this plant can cause **rashes** and **skin irritation.** ⌀ There are 20 species of *Agrimonia*, mainly in the north temperate zone. Only this species occurs in Alberta.

chamaerhodos

Chamaerhodos erecta (L.) Bunge ssp. *nuttallii* (Pickering) Hult.

PRAIRIE, ASPEN PARKLAND, MONTANE

HABITAT AND RANGE: Dry slopes and grasslands, **often on sandy or gravelly soil**. Common in the southern half of the province.

FLOWERS: **Numerous, white to purple-tinged, in branched, bracted, flat-topped clusters.** Petals usually 5, deciduous, longer than sepals. Calyx 4 to 5 mm long, composed of lance-shaped sepals with shiny hairs. Stamens 5, opposite the petals. June to July.

FRUIT: Brownish or greenish, grainy, pear-shaped achenes, 1.5 to 2.5 mm long.

LEAVES: Forms **circular, leafy basal rosette in first year**, with more erect leaves, 1 to 3 cm long, in second year. **Basal leaves stalked, deeply dissected, glandular, long-hairy.** Stem leaves smaller, uppermost reduced to stalkless, dissected bracts. Remains of old leaves visible at base of plant.

chamaerhodos (TC)

GROWTH HABIT: Biennial, 10 to 30 cm tall, from woody tap root. Basal rosette forms in first year, followed by flowering shoot in second year. Glandular, hairy (particularly at top of plant) stem may be branched above or from the base. Sometimes stem and leaf tips are reddish or purplish-tinged.

*C*hamaerhodos is from the Greek *chamai* (on the ground) and *rhodon* (rose). *Erecta* likely refers to the erect stem. ✍ The basal rosettes create interesting tiny, circular tufts on often otherwise bare, sandy soil. ✍ There are 5 species of *Chamaerhodos* in the world. The other 4 are found in Siberia.

yellow mountain avens, yellow dryad, Drummond's dryad,
Drummond's mountain avens
Dryas drummondii Richards.

MONTANE, SUBALPINE

HABITAT AND RANGE: Gravelly stream and river banks, slopes and roadsides in the foothills and mountains.

FLOWERS: Usually **solitary, nodding**, often glandular-hairy. Petals 8 to 10, whitish to bright yellow, bell or cup-shaped, 8 to 12 mm long. Sepals 8 to 10, dark green, covered with **black, glandular hairs**. Stamens numerous. June to August.

FRUIT: Achenes about 5 mm long, with **long, shiny plumes that twist into a spiral in wet weather**.

LEAVES: Alternate, **leathery, wrinkly, dark green above, whitish-hairy beneath**. Oblong, rounded at the tip, **wedge-shaped at the base**, 1.5 to 3 cm long. **Margins scalloped** and **slightly rolled under**.

yellow mountain avens   (JH)

GROWTH HABIT: Hairy-stemmed dwarf shrub up to 30 cm tall. **Frequently spreads to form large mats.**

*D*ryas was the wood-nymph of Greek mythology; *drummondii* honours a Scottish naturalist who accompanied Franklin on an expedition in search of the Northwest Passage. ✿ There are 6 species of *Dryas* in Eurasia and North America, mainly in arctic or alpine habitats; 3 are found in Alberta. White mountain avens (*D. octopetala*) and northern or entire-leaved white mountain avens (*D. integrifolia*) both have showy, large (up to 1 cm across), white flowers and leaves that are squared-off to heart-shaped at the base. The latter usually has entire, as opposed to uniformly scalloped, leaf margins and lacks the wrinkly upper leaf surface seen in white mountain avens. Northern white mountain avens, the floral emblem of the Northwest Territories, may occur in the montane to alpine zone. White mountain avens occupies exposed alpine habitats and can hybridize with northern white mountain avens where both grow together.

yellow mountain avens in fruit

white mountain avens   (CWE)

wild strawberry

Fragaria virginiana Duchesne ssp. *glauca* (S. Wats.) Staudt.
PRAIRIE, ASPEN PARKLAND, BOREAL FOREST, MONTANE, SUBALPINE, ALPINE

HABITAT AND RANGE: Shaded to open gravelly soils and thickets from prairie to alpine habitats. Common and widespread in Alberta and Canada.

FLOWERS: **On leafless stem that is usually shorter than the leaves.** Petals 5, white, 5 to 10 mm long. Sepals 5, silky-hairy. Stamens numerous, yellow. May to June.

FRUIT: Fleshy "berry," 10 to 15 mm in diameter, **covered with sunken, seed-like achenes.**

LEAVES: Compound, with **3 leaflets** up to 3.5 cm long on short stalks or stalkless. Rounded to broadly oval,

wild strawberry (CWA)

toothed (**with terminal tooth usually shorter than lateral ones**), often with reddish marks at tip. Blue-green, **smooth above**, usually hairy below, often with a whitish bloom.

GROWTH HABIT: Low, tufted, creeping perennial up to 15 cm tall. Stems hairy with appressed to spreading hairs. **New plants can establish from reddish runners.**

Strawberry is said to be derived from the Anglo-Saxon name *streowberie* because the runners are strewn across the ground. *Fragaria* means "fragrance." *Virginiana* means "of Virginia," and *glauca* is from the Greek *glaukos*, alluding to the bloom on the leaves. ✿ Strawberry plants are rich in iron, potassium, calcium, sodium and Vitamin C. The fruit is delicious, with a more pronounced flavour than that of domestic strawberries, and the stems and leaf stalks are also edible in an emergency. The leaves have been dried and used in teas, but wilted leaves should be avoided as they **can be toxic.** The leaves have also been used to treat eczema and other skin diseases. The roots and leaves have been used as a diarrhea remedy, and extract of wild strawberry is still sold in drugstores for this purpose. ✿ The Blackfoot called the Hand Hills *Oht-tchis-tchis* or "Strawberry Hills." ✿ There are approximately 30 species of *Fragaria*, primarily in temperate regions of Eurasia and North America; 2 species occur in Alberta. Woodland strawberry (*F. vesca*) differs from wild strawberry by having spreading teeth on the leaf margins, the terminal tooth longer than the lateral ones, and a hairy upper leaf surface. The flowering stem of woodland strawberry at maturity is usually longer than the leaves, and the fruits are usually more oval in shape.

wild strawberry (BA)

wild strawberry

woodland strawberry

yellow avens

Geum aleppicum Jacq.

ASPEN PARKLAND, BOREAL FOREST, MONTANE

yellow avens   (CWA)

HABITAT AND RANGE: Moist woods, river and stream banks, thickets, meadows. Widespread in Alberta.

FLOWERS: Several in open clusters. Petals 5, **bright yellow**, up to 2.5 cm across. **Petals and sepals about the same length.** Sepals often reflexed, abruptly tapered to tip, 5 to 8 mm long. Stamens numerous. June to July.

FRUIT: Head of reddish brown, flattened achenes, 3 to 4 mm long, with long, white hairs. The **persistent, hooked styles give a burr-like appearance** and can attach to clothing and animal fur for seed dispersal.

LEAVES: **Compound, doubly toothed; terminal leaflet deeply 3-lobed and wedge-shaped at base.** Several, stalked basal leaves to 15 cm long, with 5 to 9 main segments and **many interspersed smaller ones.** Numerous stem leaves, lower ones with large leafy stipules.

GROWTH HABIT: Erect, hairy perennial up to 1 m tall from fibrous roots.

*G*eum is either from the Greek *geyo* (to stimulate), as shredded roots of a Mediterranean species were used for this purpose, or from the Latin name for the species. *Aleppicum* means "of Aleppo" (Syria). ⌀ The Inuit have eaten the roots of related species raw. ⌀ There are 50 species of *Geum*, mainly of north temperate and arctic regions; 4 occur in Alberta. Large-leaved avens (*G. macrophyllum*) differs from yellow avens in that the terminal leaf segment is rounded and much larger than the lateral leaf segments, and the style is glandular-hairy. Purple avens (*G. rivale*), a species of marshes and wet meadows, has purple flowers. Three-flowered avens or old man's whiskers (*G. triflorum*), which has distinctive flowers and leaves, is described and illustrated on page 103.

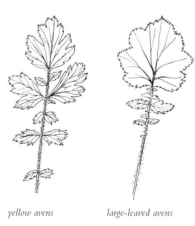

yellow avens   *large-leaved avens*

purple avens   (JH)

three-flowered avens, old man's whiskers, prairie smoke

Geum triflorum Pursh

HABITAT AND RANGE: Dry grassland, open woods, coulees. Common.

FLOWERS: 1 to 5 (most often 3), attractive, **usually nodding. Sepals pale rose in colour, cup-shaped, 5-lobed, containing 5 inconspicuous, pinkish or yellowish petals.** Stamens numerous. Mid-May to July.

FRUIT: Achenes with **feathery styles up to 4 cm long,** grouped into a head.

LEAVES: Alternate, compound, mostly basal. Soft, usually long-hairy, dark green, crowded, wedge-shaped, narrowly toothed, 15 to 20 cm long. 1 or 2 small, opposite, deeply divided stem leaves. Leaves die off during the summer.

GROWTH HABIT: Low-growing (20 to 40 cm tall), **softly hairy,** often reddish-stemmed perennial, from thick, scaly, black rootstocks. Often forms large colonies.

three-flowered avens   (LF)

The persistent styles on the fruit give the plant the name old man's whiskers, while prairie smoke describes either the plumed fruits or the appearance of the dusky, pinkish flowers. *Triflorum* refers to the 3 flowers, and the derivation of *Geum* is described on page 102. ✐ Certain British Columbia natives boiled the roots for tea and as a medicine for colds, flu and fever. The Blackfoot made an eyewash from the roots and used the crushed ripe seeds as a perfume.

three-flowered avens   (CWE)

partridgefoot, meadow spiraea, creeping spiraea

Luetkea pectinata (Pursh) Kuntze

SUBALPINE, ALPINE

partridgefoot   (JH)

HABITAT AND RANGE: Moist meadows, scree slopes at treeline; in the Rockies north of the North Saskatchewan River. **Often occurs where snow melts late in the season**, mainly on acid soil.

FLOWERS: In short, crowded cluster on leafy shoot. **Petals 5, white to cream-coloured, spoon-shaped to broadly oval, 3 to 3.5 mm long.** Sepals 5, triangular, white-hairy, lobes 2 mm long. Stamens 20, conspicuous. June to August.

FRUIT: Hard, **beaked, sparsely hairy, shiny fruit** that opens along 1 side to release smooth, tan seeds, each about 3 mm long.

LEAVES: Numerous, smooth, mainly basal, divided into narrow segments. Leaf stalks slightly wing-margined, 5 to 10 mm long. Stem leaves alternate. **Old leaves wither and persist for years.**

GROWTH HABIT: Somewhat **woody, tufted, ever-green** plant up to 15 cm tall. Trailing branches may form large mats more than 1 m across.

The genus name honours Count F.P. Luetke (1797-1882), a Russian sea captain and arctic explorer who circumnavigated the earth in the early 1800s. *Pectinata* means "with narrow divisions, comb-like," referring to the leaves. The finely divided leaves resemble the track of a partridge, hence the name partridgefoot. ✍ Partridgefoot looks similar to chamaerhodos (see page 99); however, chamaerhodos is a plant of the prairie, aspen parkland, montane foothills and mountain valley grasslands; partridgefoot is restricted to moist, shady habitats at high elevations in the northern Rocky Mountains. ✍ This is the only species of *Luetkea* in the world, found in North America in Alaska and northern Canada, in the mountains of British Columbia and Alberta and into the northwestern United States.

silverweed, silvery cinquefoil
Potentilla anserina L.
<small>Prairie, Aspen Parkland, Boreal Forest, Montane</small>

HABITAT AND RANGE: Moist meadows, ditches, mudflats, stream and river banks, lakeshores, slough margins. Tolerates salinity and alkalinity. Widespread.

FLOWERS: **Solitary on leafless stem.** Petals in 5s, bright yellow, rounded, 5 to 10 mm long. Sepals appearing between petals, pale green, hairy, 5 mm long. Stamens bright yellow, numerous. May to September.

FRUIT: Grooved or wrinkled achenes in a head-like cluster. A single seed per achene.

LEAVES: **Basal compound pinnate, up to 25 cm long, with 7 to 25 leaflets per leaf.** Each leaflet up to 3.5 cm long, **silky-hairy, dark green or sometimes silvery above, lighter on the underside. Margins deeply toothed.**

silverweed   (JH)

GROWTH HABIT: Low (up to 20 cm tall), **tufted to prostrate** perennial, from thick rootstock. **Reddish runners** (*stolons*) up to 60 cm long. May form extensive colonies.

The name silverweed comes from the silvery-gray leaf underside. Cinquefoil refers to the 5-parted leaves of many of the species. *Potentilla* is from the Latin *potens* (powerful), alluding to the supposed medical properties of this genus, and *anserina* means "of geese," either because the soft hairs resemble goose down or because the plant is eaten by geese (the plant is often found in habitats frequented by waterfowl). ✐ The roots may be eaten raw or cooked and were eaten by many North American natives, including the Alberta Blackfoot. The roots can also be used to produce a reddish dye. The Blackfoot used the runners as ties for leggings and blankets. Silverweed leaves have been steeped in boiling water to cure diarrhea. ✐ There are 200 species of *Potentilla* in the northern hemisphere, chiefly in the temperate zone; 30 species are found in Alberta. Early cinquefoil (*P. concinna*) is a short (usually less than 10 cm), spreading perennial with 5 to 9 wedge-shaped, pinnate to digitate leaflets per leaf and 2 to 5 yellow flowers, each 10 to 15 mm across, per plant. It is one of our early spring bloomers on dry, sandy prairie.

early cinquefoil   (CWE)

graceful cinquefoil

Potentilla gracilis Dougl. ex Hook.

PRAIRIE, ASPEN PARKLAND, BOREAL FOREST, MONTANE, SUBALPINE

graceful cinquefoil (DJ)

HABITAT AND RANGE: Grassland, thickets, slopes, open woods, meadows, disturbed sites in all habitats except alpine. Widespread.

FLOWERS: Several per plant. Petals 5, bright yellow, broad, notched, to more than 10 mm long. Sepals lance-shaped, smooth to hairy. Stamens 20. June to July.

FRUIT: Numerous achenes in a head. Each achene 1 to 2 mm long, smooth, shiny pale green to brownish.

LEAVES: Compound with 5 to 9 glandular leaflets, **shiny dark green above, much lighter and sparsely to densely hairy below**. Leaflets wedge-shaped at base to broadly lance-shaped, with margins toothed to deeply dissected. **Basal leaves long-stalked and palmate (spread like fingers from a central point).** Usually 1 or 2 stem leaves. Leaves variable in width, hairiness and margin characteristics, depending on variety.

GROWTH HABIT: Tufted perennial with **conspicuous brownish scales at base**. Several-stemmed, short-lived, reaching 70 cm tall from tap root.

The origin of cinquefoil and the derivation of the genus name are explained on page 105. *Gracilis* means "graceful," perhaps because of the attractive green leaves. ✿ 4 varieties of graceful cinquefoil are recognized in Alberta, differentiated chiefly on leaf characteristics. Variety *rigida* (Nutt.) S. Wats. has green, sparsely hairy leaves. Variety *pulcherrima* (Lehm.) Fern. has broader leaflets that are thickly white-hairy and have scalloped teeth on the margins. Variety *flabelliformis* (Lehm.) Nutt. has finely divided leaflets (at least ⅔ of the way to the midrib). Variety *gracilis* has narrowly to broadly lance-shaped leaflets with thick, tangled white hairs beneath and triangular teeth on the margins. ✿ White cinquefoil (*P. arguta*) has white to cream-coloured flowers and 7 to 11 pinnate leaflets on a long-stalked leaf. It is a glandular-hairy, robust plant, easily confused with sticky cinquefoil (*P. glandulosa*), which also often has cream-coloured flowers; however, sticky cinquefoil is a less robust plant with open, rather than contracted, flower clusters. ✿ Marsh cinquefoil (*P. palustris*) is easily distinguished from our many other cinquefoils by its dark-reddish purple flowers and wet, marshy habitat.

white cinquefoil (CWA)

marsh cinquefoil (JH)

sibbaldia
Sibbaldia procumbens L.
SUBALPINE, ALPINE

HABITAT AND RANGE: Open, dry to moist slopes, meadows, ridges; at high elevations in the Rocky Mountains. **Often in gravelly or rocky areas and/or where snow stays till late in the season.**

FLOWERS: Few. Petals 5, pale yellow, oval to spoon-shaped, up to 4 mm long. **Petals alternate with, and are half as long as, sepals.** Sepals 5, with alternating bracts. Stamens 5. June to early August.

FRUIT: Plump, brownish, pear-shaped to oval, shiny, smooth or lightly patterned achenes, about 1.5 mm long.

LEAVES: Each with 3 leaflets on long, slender stalks. **Leaflets widest at the tip and tapered to the base, 3 to 5-toothed at the tips**, 1 to 3 cm long. Sparsely hairy above and below, **often purplish beneath**.

sibbaldia (CWA)

GROWTH HABIT: **Tiny (usually less than 10 cm tall), densely tufted perennial** from short, creeping, woody rootstocks. **Leaf stalks and leaves often tinged reddish purple.** Often forms thick carpets in alpine meadows.

*S*ibbaldia is named after Sir Robert Sibbald (1641-1722), a professor of medicine in Edinburgh. *Procumbens* means "prone or flat on the ground," relating to the growth habit. ✿ There are 6 or 7 species of *Sibbaldia* in the world, from arctic to mountain habitats. The other species are all found in Asia. ✿ Sibbaldia may be confused with some high elevation mountain cinquefoils; however, sibbaldia generally has 5 stamens, shorter petals (less than 5 mm long) and leaflets prominently 3-toothed at the tip (but not on the sides). Cinquefoils usually have more than 10 stamens, petals longer than 5 mm and leaves toothed on tip and sides.

snow cinquefoil (JH)

A very large family of herbs or woody plants (about 14,000 species worldwide and the third in size after orchids and composites), the peas, or legumes, have been an important food source for people for thousands of years. Peas, beans and lentils are becoming increasingly popular in North America today as we strive for healthier nutrition, with more emphasis on vegetables and less reliance on meats for protein. Members of the pea family provide us with useful dyes and oils, and some, such as the familiar sweet pea and lupines, are attractive additions to the garden. Legumes are frequently used in reclamation, as the roots of many species have bacteria-containing nodules capable of producing nitrogen compounds from atmospheric nitrogen (a process called *nitrogen fixation*).

Pea flowers are typically composed of 5 petals arranged as standard, wings and keel. The keel usually encloses the pistil and normally 9 united and 1 separate stamen. The 5-lobed calyx is cup-shaped to tubular, and the fruit is usually a dehiscent pod called a *legume*. Leaves are alternate, usually pinnately or occasionally palmately compound, typically with stipules. *(See key for this family beginning page 305.)*

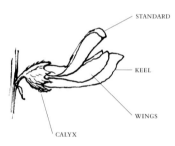

ascending purple milk-vetch, standing milk-vetch

Astragalus adsurgens Pallas ssp. *robustior* (Hook.) Welsh
(*Astragalus striatus* Nutt. in Moss 1983)

<small>PRAIRIE, ASPEN PARKLAND, BOREAL FOREST, MONTANE, SUBALPINE</small>

HABITAT AND RANGE: Grassland, rocky foothills, moist meadows. Widespread in Alberta

FLOWERS: Dense, round clusters, 4 to 5 cm long. Flowers **white or pale reddish to purplish, 14 to 18 mm in length.** Standard (see page 108 for pea family flower part definitions) has dark lines; keel is dark-tinged. Calyx 5 to 9 mm long, covered with white or black hairs. June to August.

FRUIT: Pod erect, membraneous, hairy, up to 15 mm long, with a **deep, indented groove on 1 side**. Seeds brown to black, kidney-shaped, 1 to 2 mm long.

ascending purple milk-vetch   (CWA)

LEAVES: Pinnately compound, gray-green, hairy. Leaves 4 to 12 cm long with clear, membraneous stipules. Leaflets 9 to 25, oblong, 1 to 2.5 cm long. Leaflets shortest near the tip of the leaf.

GROWTH HABIT: Tufted, **gray-green**, erect or spreading perennial, up to 40 cm tall. Stems leafy, branched. Many **hairs attached to the leaf or stem by the middle of the hair** as opposed to the end (best seen under a microscope or strong hand lens).

The Greek word *astragalus* means "ankle bone" and may refer to the pod shape of some species. Another theory of origin states that *Astragalus* comes from the Greek *astron* (star) and *gala* (milk), because when livestock grazed plants of this genus, their milk production was said to increase. *Adsurgens* means "rising up," in reference to the often ascending growth habit; *robustior* likely means "robust." ✍ The long roots of some milk-vetch species were eaten by some North American natives. ✍ Loose-flowered milk-vetch (*A. tenellus*) is found in similar habitats but has much shorter, yellowish flowers (7 to 9 mm) and narrower, more closely spaced leaflets. Ground-plum or buffalo bean (*A. crassicarpus*) is a prostrate, spreading plant with 17 to 25 narrowly oblong leaflets and yellowish white flowers with a purple-tinged keel.

loose-flowered milk-vetch   (CWA)

ground-plum (CWE)

The young pods, distinctively round and fleshy, were eaten raw or boiled by Alberta Blackfoot. ✍ Milk-vetches can be confused with locoweeds because their leaves and flowers are similar; however, the flowers of locoweeds are usually on leafless stalks and always have a pointed projection at the tip of the keel.

ground-plum (CWE)

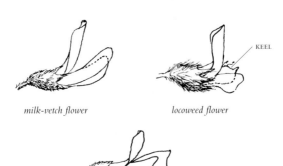

milk-vetch flower

locoweed flower

hedysarum flower

purple milk-vetch, field milk-vetch
Astragalus agrestis Dougl. ex D. Don
(*Astragalus dasyglottis* Fisch. ex DC. in Moss 1983)
PRAIRIE, ASPEN PARKLAND, BOREAL FOREST, MONTANE, SUBALPINE

HABITAT AND RANGE: Grassland, roadsides; often on sandy or gravelly soil. From prairie to alpine elevations.

FLOWERS: In dense, rounded clusters **from the leaf axils.** Petals purplish blue (occasionally white or pinkish), 17 to 20 mm long, **enclosed by a black-hairy (sometimes whitish) calyx,** up to 10 mm long. May to August.

FRUIT: Densely hairy, oval pods, up to 1 cm long.

LEAVES: 4 to 10 cm long, composed of **15 to 21 narrow, linear to elliptic leaflets,** from less than 5 mm to 2 cm long. Leaflets often notched at end, with long, whitish hairs. Stipules pale, up to 7 mm long.

GROWTH HABIT: Low, ascending or decumbent, often many-stemmed herb, with **long, white, appressed hairs**; 5 to 30 cm (usually les than 15 cm) tall, from long rootstocks.

purple milk-vetch (JH)

The derivation of *Astragalus* is explained on page 109. *Agrestis* is Latin for "pertaining to fields or cultivated land." ✿ The Cree and Stoney tribes ate the roots of related Indian milk-vetch (*A. aboriginum*). ✿ There are over 2000 species of *Astragalus*, many of which tend to concentrate selenium and can therefore cause livestock poisoning. 25 species of *Astragalus* may be found in Alberta; 3 of these are known high selenium concentrators: narrow-leaved milk-vetch (*A. pectinatus*), timber milk-vetch (*A. miser*) and two-grooved milk-vetch (*A. bisulcatus*). Narrow-leaved milk-vetch has 9 to 17 narrow, linear leaflets, 20 to 60 mm long; yellowish white flowers,

narrow-leaved milk-vetch (DJ)

about 2 cm long; and a reflexed, oblong pod, 8 to 15 mm long. It is common in the southeastern quarter of the province. Timber milk-vetch, mainly a mountain species in Alberta, has 9 to 21 shorter (5 to 30 mm) linear to lance-shaped leaflets; yellowish white to purple flowers, 6 to 14 mm long in open clusters; and a drooping pod, 2 to 2.5 cm long. Two-grooved milk-vetch has 11 to 27 lance-shaped to oblong leaflets; a dense cluster of (usually) purple to pale-purple or white flowers 11 to 15 mm long; and a drooping, 2-grooved pod, 15 to 22 mm long.

timber milk-vetch

two-grooved milk-vetch (LA)

wild licorice

Glycyrrhiza lepidota (Nutt.) Pursh

<small>PRAIRIE, ASPEN PARKLAND</small>

HABITAT AND RANGE: Moist grassland, river banks, slough margins, roadsides, disturbed areas. Often on sandy soil.

FLOWERS: **Yellowish white**, up to 15 mm long in an erect, dense cluster. **Upward-pointing standard encloses wings and keel** (see page 108 for an illustration of a typical pea family flower). Bottom flowers open first. Calyx tubular, about 7 mm long with narrow, long-tapered lobes. Stamens 10. June to July.

FRUIT: Conspicuous, **densely clustered**, oblong, flattened, **reddish brown, burr-like pods, 1 to 2 cm long, covered with hooked barbs** that aid seed dispersal. Pods contain 3 to 5 pea-like seeds, each about 3 mm long. The pods often persist over winter.

wild licorice   (CWA)

LEAVES: Alternate, **pinnately compound, with 11 to 19 sharp-pointed, lance-shaped to oval leaflets**. Leaflets dark green, **glandular-dotted underneath**, 2.5 to 4 cm long, longest near the base of the leaf. **When the leaf is broken, it has a lemony smell that helps to distinguish wild licorice from hedysarum** (see pp 114-15), which has similar leaves. Stipules 2 per leaf, narrowly pointed.

GROWTH HABIT: Robust, erect, reddish-stemmed, slightly hairy and frequently glandular perennial herb, 30 to 100 cm tall from a thick rootstock. Can form large colonies.

The rootstock has a slight licorice flavour, hence the common name. The genus name, meaning "sweet root," comes from the Greek *glykrrhiza: glykys* (sweet) and *rhiza* (root). *Lepidota* means "with small, scurfy scales" and refers to the small dots on the leaf surfaces. ✿ The roots (said to taste like sweet potato) were eaten raw or roasted by several North American peoples. The roots were also boiled into a tea drunk as a tonic by the Blackfoot and early European settlers. The Blackfoot also steeped the leaves in water and used the resulting liquid to treat earache. They applied the chewed leaves to wounds as a poultice. Wild licorice has been used as a cough remedy and expectorant, but is said to aggravate high blood pressure. ✿ The plant used for making commercial licorice is cultivated in southern Europe and does not grow wild in North America. A related licorice plant that grows in Europe is currently being investigated as a source of natural sweeteners. ✿ There are 12 species of *Glycyrrhiza*, widely distributed throughout the world. Only this species occurs in North America.

wild licorice   (CWA)

alpine hedysarum, sweet-broom, alpine sweet-vetch

Hedysarum alpinum L. ssp. *americanum* (Michx.) Fedtsch.

PRAIRIE, ASPEN PARKLAND, BOREAL FOREST, MONTANE, SUBALPINE, ALPINE

alpine hedysarum (JH)

HABITAT AND RANGE: Riverine prairie, moist, shaded to open woods, roadsides, foothill and mountain slopes to alpine elevations. Widespread.

FLOWERS: In long (up to 15 cm), usually drooping cluster that is interrupted near the base. Flowers **reddish pink to purplish** (more intensely coloured at higher elevations), sometimes cream-coloured with patches of darker colours. **Keel squared at the tip**, to about 17 mm long. Calyx 4 mm long, green with pink tinge, white-hairy, cup-shaped, **lobes unequal in length**. June to August.

FRUIT: Each composed of 2 to 5 **narrowly wing-margined, circular compartments, called** *loments*, per pod. Each loment smooth or some-times hairy, veined, up to 5 mm long and **3 to 5 mm wide**. Terminal loment with a pointed tip. Seeds dark, kidney-shaped, up to 3 mm long.

LEAVES: Alternate, pinnately compound leaves, 12 cm long; composed of 11 to 21 dark-green, nearly opposite, oval leaflets, each up to 35 mm long. **Prominently veined**, smooth, slightly hairy below, minutely glandular-dotted above. Stipules brownish, deciduous.

GROWTH HABIT: Leafy, erect, few-branched perennial up to 80 cm tall from woody tap root. May form large colonies where conditions are favourable.

northern hedysarum (LA)

sulphur hedysarum   (CWe)

The genus name is from the Greek *hedys* (sweet) and *aroma* (smell). *Alpinum* means "of the alpine," but this plant is also found at lower elevations. *Americanum* means "of America." ❧ Hedysarum roots are a favoured food for grizzlies (also for pikas and voles), and the plants are sometimes known as bear-root. Alpine hedysarum roots were collected by northern aboriginals and eaten raw, boiled or roasted, but related northern hedysarum roots are **extremely poisonous**. ❧ There are 100 species of *Hedysarum*, mainly in northern temperate zones, mostly Eurasian. There are 3 in Alberta. Sulphur or yellow hedysarum (*H. sulphurescens*) has yellow flowers, as opposed to pinkish. Northern hedysarum (*H. boreale*) has loments without winged margins, purplish flowers, often in 1-sided clusters, and narrowly tapered calyx lobes, nearly equal in length.

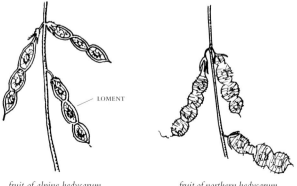

LOMENT

fruit of alpine hedysarum   *fruit of northern hedysarum*

cream-coloured vetchling, peavine
Lathyrus ochroleucus Hook.
PRAIRIE, ASPEN PARKLAND, BOREAL FOREST, MONTANE, SUBALPINE

cream-coloured vetchling (CWE)

HABITAT AND RANGE: Moist shaded woods, semi-open riverine prairie, thicket edges. Common in Alberta and across the prairie provinces.

FLOWERS: **Pale yellow, pea-like**, to about 20 mm long, in loose clusters of 5 to 10 from leaf axils. **Sepals united, pale green, up to 8 mm long, with lobes of different lengths.** Stamens 10. May to July.

FRUIT: Flattened, smooth, narrow pod up to 6 cm long. Seeds grayish brown, round, 3 to 4 mm long.

LEAVES: **Alternate, compound, with 6 to 10 leaflets per leaf. Leaflets often with whitish bloom**, oval with pointed tip, smooth, thick, 3 to 6 cm long. **Tendrils usually branched at the end of the leaf. Stipules large, up to ⅔ as long as leaflets, pointed.** Larger stipules toothed.

GROWTH HABIT: **Twining** perennial up to 1 m long, with **coiled tendrils** at the ends of the leaves and slightly angled stems.

*L*athyrus is from the ancient Greek name for this or some other member of the pea family. *Ochroleucus* means "yellowish white," alluding to the flower colour. ✍ This plant is palatable, although the seeds of several *Lathyrus* species have caused **poisoning** in livestock (particularly horses) and people. ✍ There are 150 species of *Lathyrus*, mainly in north temperate zones. Only 2 species occur in Alberta. Wild or purple peavine (*L. venosus*) has purple flowers, leaflets that are hairy beneath and smaller stipules that are less than ½ as long as the leaflets. ✍ The peavines may be distinguished from the vetches (*Vicia* species) by their larger leaves and stipules and by having a style hairy along the side rather than just at the tip, as in vetches.

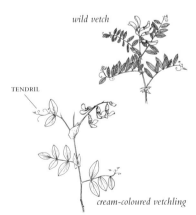

wild vetch

TENDRIL

cream-coloured vetchling

purple peavine (CWE)

silky perennial lupine, perennial lupine, silky lupine
Lupinus sericeus Pursh
PRAIRIE, MONTANE, SUBALPINE

HABITAT AND RANGE: Dry, often sandy or gravelly grassland, open woods, roadsides. Mainly in the southwestern corner of the province.

FLOWERS: Showy, in dense, long, terminal clusters. Each flower 9 to 12 mm in length, purple, tinged with blue (occasionally white or yellowish). **Standard reflexed, hairy on back. Keel strongly truncate, pointed at tip.** June to September.

FRUIT: **Clusters of pale-green (drying to brown), broad, softly furry, thick-walled pods, 2 to 3.5 cm long with a persistent style.** Each pod contains 4 to 6 lens-shaped, tan seeds, each seed about 6 mm long.

LEAVES: **Palmately compound**, alternate on stem, **long-stalked**. Leaflets 6 to 10, individual lobes narrow, 3 to 6 cm long. **Thickly silvery-hairy above and below.**

GROWTH HABIT: Leafy, erect, tufted perennial with stout stems, up to 80 cm tall. **Silky-hairy**, with reddish or silvery hairs appearing to be of 2 different lengths. Often grows in dense groups.

*L*upinus is derived from *lupus* (wolf), perhaps because lupines were believed to rob the soil of nutrients. *Sericeus* is from the Latin *sericus* (silk), referring to the soft, silky hairs that cover the plant. ✐ Lupine is actually a nitrogen fixer and adds this element to the soil. Both silky lupine and closely related silvery perennial lupine (*L. argenteus*)

silky perennial lupine   (CWa)

silky perennial lupine   (IM)

contain toxic alkaloids, particularly in the pods and seeds, and are **poisonous** to livestock, especially sheep. The rhizomes of some lupine species were eaten roasted by some coastal British Columbia tribes, including the Haida and Bella Coola. Too much, however, caused a drunken-like state. ✍ There are 100 species of *Lupinus* in the world, chiefly in North America; 8 of these species occur in Alberta. Alpine lupine (*L. lepidus*) has a standard that is smooth on the back and strongly curved backward, is usually less than 30 cm tall and is mainly found in the extreme southwest of the province. Annual lupine (*L. pusillus*) is a low-growing (5 to 25 cm tall) annual, with stems curved at the base and 2 light-brown, wrinkled seeds per pod. It is found on sandy soils and dunes in the southern quarter of the province. Silvery perennial lupine has a similar distribution to silky lupine, but is smooth to sparsely hairy, rather than densely hairy, on the back of the standard, and its leaves are sparsely hairy to smooth above.

alpine lupine   (DJ)

annual lupine   (CWE)

yellow sweet–clover
Melilotus officinalis (L.) Lam.
PRAIRIE, ASPEN PARKLAND, BOREAL FOREST, MONTANE, SUBALPINE

HABITAT AND RANGE: Roadsides, embankments, pastures, disturbed sites; often on gravelly soil. Introduced but common in the province.

FLOWERS: **In long, narrow, tapered clusters**, 3 to 12 cm long, at the top of the plant and from the leaf axils. Each flower **yellow**, 4 to 6 mm long, with standard, wings and keel typical of the pea family. **Standard and wings about the same length; wings attached to keel.** Stamens 10, in 2 sets of unequal length. Calyx white-hairy, 5-lobed, lobes of different lengths. May to September.

FRUIT: **Very wrinkled, oval, yellowish brown pod**, about 3 mm long excluding persistent style. Seeds round, dark, about 2 mm long.

LEAVES: Smooth to sparsely hairy **leaflets in 3s, to about 3 cm long, slightly toothed**. Stipules narrow, pointed, partially attached to the leaf stalk.

GROWTH HABIT: **Sweet-smelling annual or biennial**, 0.5 to 2.5 m tall, with smooth, leafy, branched stems from the tap root.

yellow sweet-clover (BA)

*M*elilotus is from the Greek *meli* (honey) and *lotos* (the name for some clover-like plant). *Officinalis* means "yellow," describing the flower colour. ❧ Sweet-clovers produce nectar that is an important source of food for honeybees. They are also nitrogen fixers and are often grown to add nitrogen to the soil. ❧ The sweet smell of sweet-clover comes from *coumarin*, a substance that can break down into compounds that prevent blood from clotting. Feeding hay containing spoiled sweet-clover can cause hemmorhaging in livestock. Research on this problem, however, led to the development of an anticlotting agent, *dicoumarin*, and the rat poison *warfarin*. ❧ There are 20 species of *Melilotus* in the world, native to Eurasia and Africa. There are 2 species in Alberta, both introduced. *M. officinalis* is native to the Mediterranean area and was introduced to North America as a forage crop. White sweet-clover (*M. alba*) has white flowers, a standard longer than the wings and a net-veined, but not wrinkly, seed pod. Alfalfa (*Medicago sativa*), another introduced member of the same family, grows in similar habitats and may be difficult to distinguish from sweet-clover when the flowers (dark purple to whitish) and coiled fruits are missing. In general, however, alfalfa has a leafier, shorter, less leggy appearance, and its leaves are usually toothed only near the tips, narrower and more wedge-shaped.

white sweet-clover (BA)

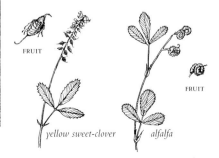
FRUIT

FRUIT

yellow sweet-clover   *alfalfa*

early yellow locoweed, silky locoweed
Oxytropis sericea Nutt. var. *spicata* (Hook.) Barneby
<small>PRAIRIE, ASPEN PARKLAND, MONTANE, SUBALPINE, ALPINE</small>

early yellow locoweed   (JH)

HABITAT AND RANGE: Prairie grass-land, dry hillsides, roadsides. Often on sandy soil. Common in the southern half of the province and also found in the Peace River country.

FLOWERS: 6 to 27, **pale yellow, pea-like, in dense terminal cluster on hairy, leafless stem**. Corolla usually 18 to 22 mm long, with noticeably flared wings, and **keel 10 to 20 mm long, with pointed appendage at tip**, a feature which distinguishes locoweeds from related milk-vetches (*Astragalus* spp.). Calyx lobed, with **black and lighter hairs**. May to June.

FRUIT: Oblong, short-hairy, **leathery**, beaked pods up to 2.5 cm long, with white and black hairs. Seeds kidney-shaped, greenish brown, up to 2 mm long.

LEAVES: **All basal**, 4 to 30 cm long, with **7 to 17 opposite, oblong, sharp-pointed leaflets**. Leaflets softly gray-green with white hairs, lance-shaped to oblong, keeled, tapered at both ends, 1 to 3 cm long.

GROWTH HABIT: Low-growing, silvery-hairy, tufted perennial with hairy, prominent stipules. Flower stalks 7 to 50 cm tall from a stout, brown, tufted rootstock.

This plant is poisonous to cattle, horses and sheep because of alkaloids that can cause blind staggers, giving affected animals the appearance of being *loco* (Spanish for "mad, foolish"). Large quantities of the plant must be eaten over long periods of time to produce this effect, however. *Oxytropis* is from the Greek *oxys* (sharp, bitter) and *tropis* (keel), in reference to the sharp-pointed tip on the keel. *Sericea* (silky) likely describes the soft hairs, and *spicata* (with spikes) refers to the inflorescence. ✍ The Blackfoot chewed the leaves to alleviate sore throats; however, this is not recommended due to the plant's **high alkaloid content**. The Okanagan used the flowers as bedding and flooring in their sweathouses. ✍ There are about 300 species of *Oxytropis* in the world, chiefly in western North America and Siberia; 9 species are found in Alberta. Late yellow locoweed (*O. monticola*) is similar in appearance but flowers later in the season and has smaller flowers (keels 11 to 15 mm versus 15 to 20 mm), more leaflets (17 to 33) and a papery pod. Another common species, showy locoweed (*O. splendens*), is recognized by its silky-hairy, grayish green leaves in whorls and its bluish to reddish flowers.

showy locoweed   (SR)

white prairie-clover
Petalostemon candidum (Willd.) Michx.
PRAIRIE, ASPEN PARKLAND

HABITAT AND RANGE: Sandy, dry or eroded slopes in badlands and grasslands; often on gravelly soil. Occurs in the southern third of the province.

FLOWERS: Terminal and on leafy branches. **Thick, short heads (up to 5 cm long) composed of tiny, white flowers, each 4 to 6 mm long.** Stamens 5, yellow, united. Calyx tubular, **10-ribbed, with hairy tips.** Blooms from bottom of flower cluster first. June to August.

FRUIT. Short (3 to 4 mm long) pod, enclosed by persistent calyx and containing 1 or 2 wrinkled, green-brown seeds.

LEAVES: Pinnately compound. **5 to 9 linear to oblong, blunt-tipped (often notched) leaflets, each 5 to 15 mm long.** Gray-green, **glandular-dotted beneath**.

GROWTH HABIT: Prostrate to erect, smooth, leafy, often many-stemmed perennial, 25 to 40 cm tall from very thick root. Branches reddish at base.

*P*etalostemon is from the Greek *petalon* (petal) and *stemon* (stamen), referring to the union of petals and stamens or to the presence of petal-like stamens. *Candidum* is from the Latin "to shine" and is a term often applied to white-flowered plants. ✒ This plant lacks the usual pea-type flower. The standard is typical but the other 4 petals are alike. ✒ Bruised leaves of prairie-clovers were steeped in water and applied to wounds by the Blackfoot. The leaves were also used to make tea and potions to prevent disease. ✒ There are 36 species of *Petalostemon* in North America, 2 of these occurring in Alberta. Purple prairie-clover (*P. purpureum*) has deep-pink to purple flowers and 3 to 5 narrower leaflets per leaf. Both purple and white prairie-clover occupy similar ranges and habitats in the southern half of Alberta. Purple prairie-clover can cause bloat in livestock if too much is eaten, but the plant is palatable and nutritious before it becomes woody with age.

white prairie-clover (LF)

purple prairie-clover (LF)

Indian breadroot

Psoralea esculenta Pursh

Indian breadroot (CWE)

HABITAT AND RANGE: Dry grassland, foothills, slopes; often on sandy soils. Scattered throughout the southern half of the province.

FLOWERS: Numerous, **light bluish purple,** up to about 1.5 cm long, in dense clusters, 2 to 10 cm long. **Wings scythe-shaped;** curved keel slightly shorter than the standard. Calyx 5 mm long, excluding 5 long-hairy, unequal lobes. Stamens 9 or 10. June to July.

FRUIT: Papery, oval, short, thick pod. Body about 8 mm long, half as long the slender beak. Seed dull brown, flattened, bean-like, 5 mm wide.

LEAVES: Alternate, **blue-green, palmately compound with 3 to 5 oblong to broadly lance-shaped leaflets,** each 2 to 6 cm long. **Leaflets mainly smooth above, hairy beneath,** not glandular-dotted, on hairy leaf stalks.

GROWTH HABIT: Short-stemmed, white-hairy perennial, 10 to 30 cm tall from an **enlarged tuberous root.**

Psoralea is from the Greek *psora* (itch or mange), referring to the rough, scabby glands of some species. *Esculenta* means "edible." ⌀ Indian breadroot was a well-known food to the Plains peoples and early European settlers. The roots and tubers were eaten raw, cooked in different ways, or sun-dried and stored. Alberta Blackfoot and Cree ate the roots roasted or dried them for winter use. They also ground them into meal to mix with soup. Some tribes made a pudding with breadroot flour and buffalo-berries, and teething children were sometimes given the root to chew on. ⌀ There are more than 100 species of *Psoralea*, mainly in warm, dry regions. Indian breadroot has longer flowers (up to 15 mm long, as opposed to 1 cm or less) than the other 2 Alberta species. Provincially rare silverleaf psoralea (*P. argophylla*) has darker-blue flowers and extremely hairy, usually silvery leaves. Scurf pea or lance-leaved psoralea (*P. lanceolata*) has narrower, very glandular-dotted leaves and is found on sandy soil or dunes.

scurf pea

silverleaf psoralea (LA)

golden bean, buffalo bean
Thermopsis rhombifolia Nutt. ex Richards.
PRAIRIE, ASPEN PARKLAND, MONTANE

HABITAT AND RANGE: Grassy hillsides, roadsides, ditches; often in exposed places or on sandy or unstable soils. Very common in southern Alberta.

FLOWERS: Several per plant in short, crowded clusters. Typical pea or legume shape flower, with **bright-yellow petals,** up to 2 cm long. The standard is about 1 cm long, with small black lines in the centre. Keel encloses 10 long stamens. Sepals 5. May to June.

FRUIT: **Flat, pale green to gray-brown curved pod, 4 to 8 cm with long style. Pod has pale hairs on the margins** and is somewhat constricted between seeds. Seeds in 1 row in the pod, kidney-shaped, dark brown to greenish, 3 to 4 mm long.

LEAVES: Alternate, compound leaves and clasping, opposite, stalkless, leaf-like stipules. Leaflets in 3s, **bluish green with a bloom,** silky-hairy to smooth, thick, to 4 cm long.

GROWTH HABIT: Smooth to hairy perennial, 15 to 40 cm tall. Stems simple, mostly unbranched. Can form large clumps from creeping rootstocks.

The genus name is from the Greek *thermos* (lupine) and *opsis* (resemblance), because the flowers are similar in shape to those of lupines. *Rhombifolia* means "with rhombic (diamond-shaped) leaves." ✐ The Blackfoot gave this plant the name buffalo bean because the buffalo bulls headed for

golden bean (BA)

their summer grazing grounds when it bloomed. The name buffalo bean is usually applied to another member of the pea family (*Astragalus crassicarpus*). ✐ Golden bean contains **poisonous alkaloids**, and children have become very ill from eating the seeds. It is suspected of causing livestock deaths, and grazing this plant in small amounts can cause a taint in the milk of dairy cows. ✐ There are only 8 species of *Thermopsis* in the world, chiefly in the United States and Asia. Only this species occurs in Alberta.

golden bean

white clover, Dutch clover, creeping Dutch clover

Trifolium repens L.

<small>PRAIRIE, ASPEN PARKLAND, MONTANE, SUBALPINE</small>

white clover (LA)

HABITAT AND RANGE: Introduced. Common in Alberta in lawns, pastures, roadsides.

FLOWERS: Typical pea family flowers **clustered on short, slender stalks in round heads, 1.5 to 2 cm broad. Individual flowers 5 to 9 mm long, white, often tinged with pink. Corolla turns brown and droops with age, but persists.** Calyx pale at base, with 5 greenish, long, narrow lobes. Stamens 10, in 2 groups. June to October.

FRUIT: 2 to 5-seeded pods, about 5 mm long with squarish, yellow seeds.

LEAVES: Alternate, long-stalked, **composed of 3 leaflets, 1 to 2.5 cm long**, with broad, sometimes indented tops and wedge-shaped to rounded bases. Margins finely toothed. Leaf stalks about the same length to much longer than leaflets. Stipules 3 to 10 mm long, united most of their length, upper part long-tapering, pointed.

GROWTH HABIT: Smooth to sparsely hairy perennial, **frequently with creeping, often rooting stems, 10 to 60 cm tall.**

The name clover may originate from *clava* (club), the triple-headed weapon carried by Hercules. *Trifolium* is from the Latin *tres* (three) and *folium* (leaf), describing the 3-parted leaves. *Repens* means "creeping." ✿ White clover originated in Eurasia and was introduced to North America for hay, pasture and soil improvement. ✿ Clover flowers can be brewed into a tea that has been prescribed to treat coughs or gas and to soothe bad nerves. The Alberta Blackfoot applied crushed leaves to wounds to stop bleeding. The young leaves and flowers can be eaten raw (in small quantities as they are **hard to digest**) and the rootstocks cooked, although they are said to be tough. The dried flowers and seeds of red and white clover were used to make bread during famines in Ireland. The blossoms have been used to flavour cheese and tobacco. The plant provides excellent clover honey. ✿ There are about 300 species of *Trifolium*, mostly of north temperate zones, particularly in western North America; 4, all introduced, are found in Alberta. Red clover (*T. pratense*) has dark-pink, larger (12 to 20 mm long) flowers, in essentially stalkless clusters. Alsike clover (*T. hybridum*) is a hybrid between red and white clover, with pinkish white, stalked flower heads and longer (2 to 4 cm) leaves. Yellow or hop clover (*T. aureum*) is an annual with yellow flowers.

red clover (BA)

wild vetch, American vetch
Vicia americana Muhl. ex Willd.
<small>PRAIRIE, ASPEN PARKLAND, BOREAL FOREST, MONTANE</small>

HABITAT AND RANGE: Shady riverine prairie, open woods, thickets, meadows; frequently on gravelly soil. Widespread throughout Alberta.

FLOWERS: **2 to 9 typical pea family flowers per cluster,** from leaf axils. Each 15 to 25 mm long, bluish purple to whitish, with a **dark purple-tinged keel that is much shorter than the attached wings.** Calyx of 5 red-tinged sepals, up to 5 mm long. Stamens 10. June to July.

FRUIT: Smooth, flat pod 2 to 4 cm long, tapered at both ends, with round brown or black seeds.

LEAVES: Alternate, pinnate, with **6 to 14 narrow to oval leaflets,** each up

wild vetch (CWE)

to 35 mm long. Each leaflet gray-green, lighter underneath, strongly veined, smooth to hairy, entire to sharply toothed at the tip. **Toothed stipules attached at the middle, pointed at the tip. Forked tendrils at the end of the leaf.**

GROWTH HABIT: Smooth, **twining** perennial herb, 30 to 80 cm long.

*V*icia is from the Latin *vincio* (to bind together), referring to the binding tendrils. *Vicia* was translated to Old North French *veche* and later became the English term *vetch*. *Americana* means "of America." ✍ Vetches can enrich the soil by building up nitrates, and they provide good forage for livestock, although some sources suggest that the seeds are poisonous. ✍ There are 200 species of *Vicia* in the world, widely distributed. The only other species found in Alberta, introduced tufted or bird vetch (*V. cracca*), has a 1-sided, many-flowered (15 or more) inflorescence and numerous (10 to 20 or more), generally narrower leaflets. It is a weedy plant and is often found along roadsides and on disturbed ground. ✍ Wild vetch differs from the vetchlings (*Lathyrus* species) because the vetches are hairy only at the tip of the rounded style, rather than along 1 side of the flattened style. Leaf and stipule differences between the species are illustrated on page 116.

tufted vetch (JH)

sticky purple geranium

Geranium viscosissimum Fisch. & Mey

PRAIRIE, ASPEN PARKLAND, MONTANE, SUBALPINE

HABITAT AND RANGE: Moist grassland, open woods, thickets. Occurs in the southwest part of the province and the Cypress Hills.

FLOWERS: Several, very showy, **on sticky-glandular stalks. Petals 5, rose-purple, deep pink or rarely white, with darker veins, 14 to 20 mm long**, hairy at the bases. Sepals 5, red-green, abruptly tapered, very long-hairy, **with bristly tips and sticky glands**. Stamens 10. Stigma dark purple. May to August.

FRUIT: Long-beaked (10 to 14 mm), **oblong, glandular-hairy capsule** that splits into 5 segments to release black, oblong, net-veined seeds, each 4 to 5 mm long.

sticky purple geranium   (CWE)

LEAVES: Opposite, mainly basal, dark green to gray-green. **Densely hairy above, underside of leaves hairy on veins only.** Long-stalked, often glandular, 5 to 12 cm wide. Sharply incised into 5 to 7 lobes.

GROWTH HABIT: Erect, smooth or sparsely hairy, slightly branched perennial herb, 20 to 90 cm tall from a woody rootstock. **Stems, inflorescence and lower leaf stalks usually glandular-hairy**.

Geranium is from the Greek *geranos* (crane), as the fruit of some members of this genus resemble a crane's bill. The species name refers to the sticky glands. ❧ There are approximately 200 species of *Geranium* in the world, mainly in temperate zones; 5 of these are found in Alberta. Bicknell's geranium (*G. bicknellii*) and wild white geranium (*G. richardsonii*) are quite common. Bicknell's geranium has small (5 to 7 mm long) pinkish purple petals that are longer than the sepals. Wild white geranium has large (10 to 18 mm long), usually pink or purple-veined white petals and smooth to hairy, non-sticky leaves.

wild white geranium   (CWE)

sticky purple geranium   (LF)

wild blue flax

Linum perenne L. ssp. *lewisii* (Pursh) Hult.
(*Linum lewisii* Pursh in Moss 1983)
PRAIRIE, ASPEN PARKLAND, BOREAL FOREST,
MONTANE, SUBALPINE, ALPINE

HABITAT AND RANGE: Dry, often sandy, exposed hillsides, grasslands, roadsides, gravelly river flats and open woods. Widespread.

FLOWERS: Several, terminal or scattered on upper branches. **Flower stalk often droops at the tip. Petals 5, pale purplish blue with darker guidelines, yellowish at base,** wedge-shaped, 10 to 20 mm long; deciduous early. Sepals 5, often whitish on the margins, 4 to 7 mm long. Stamens 5, united at the base. May to August.

wild blue flax (CWE)

FRUIT: Shiny, brown, many-compartmented capsule, 3 to 5 mm in diameter, with 8 to 10 shiny, dark-brown to black seeds.

LEAVES: Alternate, simple, stalkless, 1-nerved. Numerous, gray-green, **linear to lance-shaped,** up to 25 mm long.

GROWTH HABIT: Several-stemmed, delicate, smooth perennial, 20 to 70 cm tall from a woody rootstock and tap root.

*L*inum is from the Greek *linon* (thread), likely because flax is used to make thread. *Perenne* means "perennial," and *lewisii* honours Capt. Meriwether Lewis, who explored North America with Clark in the early 1800s. ✍ Flax has been cultivated for various uses, notably oil and linen, since ancient times. ✍ This species was used by some North American natives to treat boils, and an eye poultice was made from the fresh, crushed leaves. The British Columbia Thompson used wild blue flax as a shampoo. ✍ There are 100 species of *Linum* in temperate zones of the world; 3 of these occur in Alberta. Yellow flax (*L. rigidum)* has yellow flowers, is shorter and has glandular sepals. Common flax (*L. usitatissimum*) is an introduced annual with broader leaves and erect flower stalks. Both wild blue and yellow flax are suspected of causing livestock poisoning.

yellow flax (LF)

Seneca snakeroot

Polygala senega L.

PRAIRIE, ASPEN PARKLAND

Seneca snakeroot (BA)

HABITAT AND RANGE: Open woods and prairies, clearings in aspen poplar stands; usually on moist soil. Of scattered occurrence in Alberta from the Bow River north to the Peace River country.

FLOWERS: Numerous in dense, usually **tapered cluster**, up to 6 cm long. Petals 3, broad, **greenish white to white, sometimes pinkish**. Sepals 5; 2 inner sepals larger, often petal-like. Stamens 8, united below. June to July.

FRUIT: Broad, 2-seeded capsule. Seed hairy with whitish, 2-lobed appendage.

LEAVES: Numerous, simple, alternate. Lance-shaped to oval, 10 to 30 cm long. Lower leaves smaller, often scale-like. Margins entire, roughened or slightly toothed.

GROWTH HABIT: Several-stemmed perennial, 10 to 50 cm tall from a woody base.

The common name originates from the use of the plant to treat snakebite. *Polygala* is from the Greek *polys* (much) and *gala* (milk), as these plants were thought to enhance milk secretion; *senega* means "of the Seneca Indians." ✇ Seneca snakeroot was well known in the United States, where it was touted as a cure for pleurisy, pneumonia and gout, and as an expectorant for asthmatics and bronchitis sufferers. The Blackfoot used the root in a mixture to treat respiratory diseases. ✇ There are approximately 500 species of *Polygala* in the world; 2 species occur in Alberta. Rare fringed milkwort (*P. paucifolia*) differs from Seneca snakeroot in having 1 to 4 purplish flowers.

fringed milkwort (DJ)

crowberry, curlewberry

Empetrum nigrum L. ssp. *hermaphroditicum* (Lange) Böcher

ASPEN PARKLAND, BOREAL FOREST, MONTANE, SUBALPINE

HABITAT AND RANGE: Acidic rocks, muskegs, calcareous fens, moist woods and coniferous forest in the mountains and the northern half of Alberta.

FLOWERS: Perfect (having both stamens and pistils) or unisexual; crowded in the leaf axils. Petals 3, inconspicuous, sometimes lacking, purplish or reddish, 3 mm long, surrounded by 3 chaffy bracts similar to but smaller than sepals. Stamens 3. May to June.

FRUIT: Solitary or in groups of 2 to 5. **Shiny, black or purplish, acidic, berry-like**, with 6 to 9 compartments, each containing a seed. The fruit is juicy, but the seeds are hard and large.

LEAVES: Alternate or in whorls, spreading or reflexed. Smooth, **evergreen, shiny, glandular-hairy**.

crowberry (BA)

Linear-oblong, narrow, **4 to 8 mm long with deeply grooved white midvein beneath**. Margins turned under. Blades jointed with the leaf stalks.

GROWTH HABIT: Evergreen **dwarf shrub with trailing branches** up to 40 cm long. Branches slender, glandular-hairy to nearly smooth. Forms mats over mosses.

The common name refers to the black, crow-like colour of the berries, or possibly to the fact that crows eat it. *Empetrum* is from the Greek *en* (upon) and *petros* (rock), referring to the plant's habitat. *Nigrum* is Latin for "black," and *hermaphroditicum* is from "hermaphrodite," because the flower may be of either sex. ✐ British Columbia natives ate the berries fresh and dried (the flavour is said to be improved by freezing), while the Inuit ate the berries and brewed the twigs into a tea. Crowberry has been made into wine in Scandinavia. The berries are said to make excellent pies and jellies. ✐ There are 2 species of *Empetrum* in the world: this species in North America and Eurasia, the other in South America.

western jewelweed, common touch-me-not

Impatiens noli-tangere L.

ASPEN PARKLAND, BOREAL FOREST

western jewelweed (LA)

HABITAT AND RANGE: Scattered through the northern half of the province in moist woods and thickets, and along shady river and stream banks and lake margins.

FLOWERS: Mostly in 2s from upper leaf axils. **Pale yellowish, sparsely flecked with red or purple**, or unspotted, about 2.5 cm long. Perianth of 6 segments. Large spurred sac and 2 smaller segments are considered sepals. 3-lobed or notched parts are petals. **Sac-like sepal dilated, about 20 mm long, gradually narrowed into a down-curved spur, 6 to 10 mm long.** Stamens 5, more or less united around the stigma. July to August.

FRUIT: Pod-like, narrow capsule, up to about 2.5 cm long, that explodes open along 5 valves to eject numerous dark-brown seeds, each about 3 mm long.

LEAVES: Alternate, simple. **Blades thin**, somewhat egg-shaped, 3 to 12 cm long, on stalks 2 to 4 cm long. **Margins with large, rounded, spiny-tipped teeth.**

GROWTH HABIT: Annual, 50 to 150 cm tall, with succulent, leafy, often branched stems and watery juice.

The genus and species name refer to the explosive release of the seeds when the capsule is touched. *Impatiens* is Latin for "impatient," referring to the quick seed release, and *noli-(me)-tangere* means "touch-me-not." The phrase "touch-me-not" was supposedly spoken by Christ to Mary Magdalene after his resurrection; why it has been applied to this plant is uncertain. ✿ The Blackfoot used spotted touch-me-not pulp to relieve rashes and eczema. American tribes used the watery juice to treat poison ivy itchiness, bruises, warts and jaundice. The young shoots can be cooked and eaten. ✿ Scientists have isolated a fungicide from this plant. ✿ There are 400 species of *Impatiens* in the world, mainly in India, with a few in temperate and tropical regions of the Americas. Showy members of *Impatiens* are cultivated as ornamental plants. The other Alberta species, spotted touch-me-not (*I. capensis*), has bright-orange to yellow flowers that are usually more densely spotted, a broader, more pouch-like spur that is abruptly bent back parallel with the sac, and more shallowly and distantly toothed leaves.

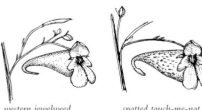

western jewelweed   *spotted touch-me-not*   *spotted touch-me-not* (DJ)

mountain hollyhock, wild hollyhock, globe-mallow, streambank rose mallow

Iliamna rivularis (Dougl. ex Hook.) Greene

MONTANE, SUBALPINE

HABITAT AND RANGE: Moist slopes, stream banks, meadows, roadsides; in the Waterton Lakes National Park-Crowsnest Pass area.

FLOWERS: On short, thick stalks in long, interrupted clusters. **Petals 5, purplish pink to whitish, about 2 cm long.** Club-shaped stigma surrounded by stamens that are united at base. Calyx of 5 united sepals, 3 to 5 mm long, surrounded by 3 bracts. July to August.

FRUIT: Segmented, each segment rounded at tip, covered with long, rigid, star-shaped hairs and containing 2 to 3 centrally attached seeds.

LEAVES: Alternate, simple. **Each leaf**

mountain hollyhock (CWE)

heart to kidney-shaped, 4 to 7-lobed; the lobes irregularly toothed and with star-shaped hairs that are visible under a microscope. Leaves somewhat resembling maple or grape leaves, 5 to 15 cm broad, decreasing in size upward.

GROWTH HABIT: Robust, branched perennial, 0.5 to 2 m tall with sparse, star-shaped hairs.

The origin of *Iliamna* is unknown, although some suggest it honours the mother of Romulus and Remus in Roman legend. *Rivularis* means "of the brook," a reference to the stream bank habitat. ✐ There are 7 *Iliamna* species, mainly of western North America. Only this species is found in Alberta, where it is considered rare. It is similar to the familiar hollyhock grown as an ornamental. Mountain hollyhock appears quickly after fires.

mountain hollyhock (CWE)

scarlet mallow, scarlet globe-mallow, apricot mallow
Sphaeralcea coccinea (Nutt.) Rydb.

PRAIRIE, ASPEN PARKLAND

scarlet mallow (CWA)

HABITAT AND RANGE: Grasslands, badlands, dry hillsides, roadsides, gravelly disturbed places; often on exposed, sandy soil. In the southern half of the province and in the Peace River country.

FLOWERS: Several, terminal. **Petals 5, pale orange to brick-red (paler at base)**, notched at tip, separate, 10 to 20 mm long. Style yellow, elongated. Calyx of 5 sepals, each broadly triangular, woolly, joined at base, 5 mm long. No bracts at base of calyx. June to July.

FRUIT: Round, hairy capsule with 10 compartments. Seeds black, veiny, kidney-shaped, 1 to 2 mm long.

LEAVES: Alternate, long-stalked, in 3 to 5 divisions, lobed at tips. **Hairy with star-shaped clusters of hairs.** Up to 4 cm long.

GROWTH HABIT: Perennial up to 20 cm tall from branched, long, scaly, thick, woody rootstock. **Appears grayish because of dense, white, star-shaped hairs.** May occur singly or form large colonies.

Mallow comes from a Greek word meaning soft, because many of the species have soft, downy leaves or because of the soothing properties of the roots. *Sphaeralcea* is from the Greek *sphaera* (a sphere), referring to the round fruits, and *alcea* is an ancient name of a plant of the mallow family. *Coccinea* is Latin for "scarlet." ✐ The Blackfoot chewed scarlet mallow and applied the mucilaginous paste to scalds, sores and burns as a cooling agent. It also acted as protection against scalding. ✐ This species is not very palatable to domestic livestock but has excellent forage value for deer. ✐ There are more than 200 species of *Sphaeralcea*, in Africa and the western hemisphere. There are 3 in Alberta, the other 2 only recently discovered and likely introduced. Gooseberry-leaved globe-mallow (*S. grossulariaefolia)* has wider-lobed leaves (resembling those of gooseberries) and a calyx with 3 small bracts at base. Munro's globe-mallow (*S. munroana*) has less deeply divided leaf lobes than the other 2 species. Both gooseberry-leaved and Munro's globe-mallow are known only from a few locations near the Oldman River.

scarlet mallow

Munro's globe-mallow

gooseberry-leaved globe-mallow

early blue violet, western long-spurred violet
Viola adunca J.E. Smith

PRAIRIE, ASPEN PARKLAND, BOREAL FOREST, MONTANE

HABITAT AND RANGE: Grassland, open woods, slopes; often on gravelly soil. Widespread in Alberta.

FLOWERS: Several, irregular, 5-petalled, each 10 to 15 mm long, from upper leaf axils. **Purple and white petals with darker guidelines. Largest petal with hooked spur half as long as the lowest petal. Side petals white-bearded.** Sepals and stamens 5. Style hairy. May to June.

FRUIT: Capsule 4 to 5 mm long, with 3 valves. Seeds numerous, dark brown, mucilaginous.

LEAVES: Mostly basal. Basal leaves long-stalked, sometimes hairy. **Oval with heart-shaped base, 1 to**

early blue violet   (CWE)

3 cm wide, margins with round teeth. Stem leaves with shorter stalks. Stipules narrow, spiny-toothed or entire, 3 to 10 mm long.

GROWTH HABIT: **Tufted, branched and leafy**, herbaceous perennial, 5 to 30 cm tall from woody, scaly rootstock.

*V*iola is from the Latin name for various sweet-scented flowers. *Adunca* means "hooked," because of the hook on the spur. An uncus was a hook used by the Romans to drag executed bodies away. ✒ Violets have been used as food back to early Greek and Roman times. They are still cultivated for food in some areas of Europe. Young leaves and flower buds may be used raw in salads or boiled as a pot-herb in soups and stews. Violet leaves are high in Vitamins C and A and can be used to make a bland tea. In the southern United States violets are called wild okra and are often used to thicken soups; the **seeds and rhizomes should not be eaten**, however. ✒ There are about 300 species of *Viola* in all continents of the world, mainly in cool and damp locations; 14 species occur in Alberta. Bog violet (*V. nephrophylla*) has leaves and flower stalks arising from the base of the plant; oval to kidney-shaped, smooth leaves that are scalloped on the margins and 3 to 5 cm wide; and dark-purple flowers, each with a spur 2 to 3 mm long. It has been collected from moist meadows, banks and woods in the southern half of the province and in the extreme northeast.

bog violet   (CWA)

western Canada violet
Viola canadensis L. var. *rugulosa* (Greene) C.L. Hitchc.
PRAIRIE, ASPEN PARKLAND, BOREAL FOREST, MONTANE

western Canada violet   (CWE)

HABITAT AND RANGE: Shaded woods, moist meadows. Widespread in Alberta.

FLOWERS: Irregular, from the axils of the upper leaves. Petals in 5s, **whitish or pinkish with purple guidelines, lavender-tinged at the edge and underneath, yellow at base**, to 1 cm long. **Lateral petals bearded, lower petal with a long spur.** Stamens 5. Sepals 5, dark green, pointed, about 6 mm long. May to September.

FRUIT: Spiny, oval capsule, about 8 mm long, with 3 valves. Capsule pops open when ripe to release numerous brown, mucilaginous seeds, 1.5 to 2 mm long.

LEAVES: **Stem leaves alternate**, simple, heart-shaped to oval, somewhat **wrinkled**, sharp-pointed at the tip, **with round-toothed margins**. Roughened, shiny on top, bright green above, lighter below, prominently veined. Basal leaves longer, long-stalked. **Stipules papery, translucent, 1 to 2 cm long.**

GROWTH HABIT: Few-leaved, erect perennial, 20 to 40 cm tall. Often occurs in clumps from numerous above-ground prostrate stems. This plant is highly variable in appearance.

*C*anadensis is Latin for "of Canada." *Rugulosa* means "wrinkled," referring to the leaves. ✿ Violet flowers have been used as a poultice for swellings, as a laxative for children and to treat respiratory problems. ✿ Sweet blue violets of Europe are grown commercially for bouquets and for their essential oils, which are used in perfumes and flavouring. ✿ Yellow prairie violet (*V. nuttallii*) has bright-yellow, purple-veined flowers, leafy stems and lance-shaped to oval, tapering leaves. It is widespread in the southern half of the province.

western Canada violet   (BA)

yellow prairie violet   (CWA)

sand-lily, evening star

Mentzelia decapetala (Sims) Urban & Gilg

PRAIRIE

HABITAT AND RANGE: Exposed clay hillsides, roadsides; **often in eroded areas and badlands.** Found in the southern quarter of the province.

FLOWERS: Terminal at ends of branches. Showy, with **10 white to pale-yellow, pointed petals** (inner 5 are actually *staminodia* or sterile stamens), **5.5 to 8 cm long, surrounded by rough-hairy, pale orange, broadly triangular bracts, about 3 cm long, joined at base.** Stamens yellow, numerous. **Flowers open in evening.** July to August.

FRUIT: Rough-hairy, oblong capsules, 3 to 4.5 cm long, opening at the top to release many thin-winged, grayish seeds, each 3 to 3.5 mm long.

sand-lily   (CWA)

LEAVES: Alternate, prominently veined; sharply, sometimes doubly toothed, 5 to 15 cm long. **Strongly roughened with thick, whitish, spine-like hairs.** Upper stalkless, lower stalked.

GROWTH HABIT: Grayish green, stiffly hairy, pleasant-smelling, stout, leafy, branched biennial, up to 1 m tall from a deep, thick tap root. **Forms a flat rosette of basal leaves the first year and 1 or more flowers on a stem the second year.**

The flowers open in the evening, hence the name "evening star." *Mentzelia* honours 17th-century German botanist C. Mentzel, while *decapetala* refers to the 10 petals. *◢* The Northern Cheyenne of Montana called related giant blazing-star (*M. laevicaulis*) "white-medicine" and used it in treating fevers and other ailments.

The Tewa tribe of the U.S. rubbed rough-leaved stickleaf (*M. multiflora*) on young boys' skin to help them cling to their horses when riding. *◢* There are 50 species of *Mentzelia*, chiefly in deserts and drier tropical regions of North and South America. Only this species is found in Alberta.

sand-lily   (BA)

cushion cactus, ball cactus
Coryphantha vivipara (Nutt.) Britt. & Rose
PRAIRIE

cushion cactus (CWa)

HABITAT AND RANGE: Dry, often eroded, sandy or rocky soil in grasslands and badlands; often on south-facing slopes. Restricted in Alberta to the southeastern part of the province.

FLOWERS: With many lance-shaped, **deep-pink or reddish purple petals**, each up to 15 mm long. Sepals numerous, thick, greenish, overlapping. Stigma large, many-lobed. Stamens numerous, yellow. Flowers last only 1 to 2 days. June to August.

FRUIT: Fleshy, greenish red, edible berry, 1 to 2 cm long, containing many light-brown seeds, 1 to 2 mm long.

LEAVES: The **inflated, succulent stems** take on the function of leaves, and the leaves are modified into sharp reddish and whitish spines. Stems long, oblong, **composed of tubercles with spines radiating outwards in clusters**. 3 to 5 main spines, up to 2 cm long, and 10 to 20 smaller, slender, marginal spines per cluster.

GROWTH HABIT: Squat, low-growing (3 to 6 cm) perennial from branching tap root. Grows singly or in clumps.

*C*oryphantha originates from the Greek *koryphe* (a cluster) and *anthos* (flower). *Vivipara* means "live-bearing," possibly because the plant can be propagated easily from the buds. ✐ The berries are edible and taste like gooseberries. They can be made into a jam and are also browsed by wildlife such as antelope. Unlike prickly-pears, the fruits of cushion cactus are not spiny. ✐ There are 35 species of *Coryphantha* in the world, all in North America. Only this species occurs in Alberta.

prickly-pear, plains prickly pear
Opuntia polyacantha Haw.
<small>PRAIRIE, ASPEN PARKLAND</small>

HABITAT AND RANGE: Dry, exposed slopes and plains, badlands, eroded areas; often on rocky or sandy ground. Found in the southeastern quarter of the province.

FLOWERS: Large, showy. **Petals numerous, predominantly yellow, waxy, up to 3.5 cm long. Conspicuous, large, green stigma** and numerous yellow to orange stamens. Sepals numerous, thick, reddish, up to 12 mm long, in several rows. June to July.

FRUIT: Reddish, soft, spiny, edible berry up to 3.5 cm long. Seeds large, whitish, flattened, up to 5 mm in diameter.

LEAVES: Reduced to clusters of **narrow, sharp spines, up to 3.5 cm long, often with tuft of barbed bristles at base.** These bristles can work into the skin and cause pain when brushed against.

prickly-pear   (JH)

GROWTH HABIT: Succulent and prostrate, mat-forming perennial. **Stems flattened into circular pads up to 12 cm wide and 15 cm tall,** turning reddish and wrinkled in winter.

*O*puntia originates from the Greek name for a different plant which grew around the ancient town of Opus in Greece. *Polyacantha* is from the Greek *poly* (many) and *acantha* (a thorn), or possibly *canthus* (wheel), likely referring to the spines which radiate outward. ✎ The flowers appear very attractive to bees, and the fruit is eaten by antelope and sheep. Spineless varieties of prickly-pear have been cultivated for animal feed. Prickly-pear was eaten roasted (with thorns and the outer layer removed) in times of famine, and the juice inside the stems used as an emergency water source. Cactus flesh was also cooked in soups or mixed with deer fat and berries by the B.C. Okanagan and Thompson tribes. Cactus is high in calcium, phosphorus and Vitamin C and is said to taste like raw cucumber or green beans. The ripe fruit is sold as a candy or jelly in some places, and the dried seeds can be ground into flour or used as a thickener. ✎ There are about 250 species of *Opuntia*, all native to North and South America; 2 occur in Alberta. Brittle prickly-pear (*O. fragilis*) has smaller stem segments with round, rather than flat, joints between them; it has a wider range, occurring in both central and Peace River aspen parkland.

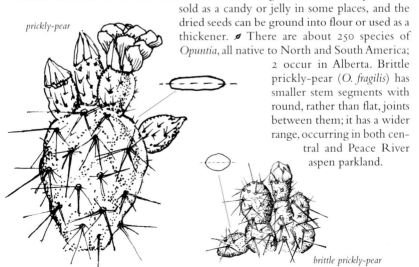

prickly-pear

brittle prickly-pear

purple loosestrife
Lythrum salicaria L.

<small>PRAIRIE, ASPEN PARKLAND, BOREAL FOREST, MONTANE</small>

purple loosestrife (DJ)

HABITAT AND RANGE: Wet meadows, along streams, rivers, marshes. Introduced from Eurasia and of sporadic occurrence in Alberta.

FLOWERS: Showy, **clustered in leaf axils to form long, interrupted spikes. Petals 4 to 7, reddish purple, 7 to 10 mm long.** Calyx long-tubular with short lobes at tip. Stamens 8 to 10, of 3 different lengths.

FRUIT: Round, 2-compartmented capsule, about 3 mm long, with persistent style. Seeds numerous, dark brown, angled, about 1 mm long.

LEAVES: Opposite, some alternate or whorled in 3s. Lance-shaped, stalkless, roughened to soft-hairy. Tapered to tip, rounded to heart-shaped at base, 3 to 10 cm long.

GROWTH HABIT: White-hairy perennial, 0.5 to 1.5 m tall from rhizomes. Stems simple to branched above, **angled**.

The common name loosestrife originates from *lysimachia* (to deliver from strife). *Lythrum* is from the Greek *luthron* (blood), in reference either to the plant's ability to produce a red dye or to the flower colour; *salicaria* is from the Latin *salicinus* (willow-like). ✿ There are 30 species of *Lythrum* in the world, chiefly of wetlands in the northern hemisphere. There is only this species in Alberta. ✿ Despite their attractiveness, **varieties of loosestrife have no place in Alberta gardens.** This fast-spreading weed chokes out the native vegetation of wetlands, drastically reducing food for wildlife and crucial shoreline nesting areas for birds. Garden escapes are at present responsible for most of our infestations.

Evening-primrose Family (Onagraceae)

A small family of annuals, biennials and perennials, the evening-primroses are characterized by erect stems, opposite or alternate leaves and flower-parts generally in 4s (occasionally 2s): 4 sepals, 4 petals and 8 stamens. The stigma is often 4-lobed, and the fruit may be a many-seeded capsule or 1-seeded and nut-like. Flowers of most species open in the late afternoon or early evening (hence the common name) and are mostly solitary in the leaf axils or numerous in terminal clusters. Cultivated varieties of evening-primrose (*Oenothera* species) may be purchased to grow in Alberta gardens.

enchanter's nightshade, small enchanter's nightshade
Circaea alpina L.
ASPEN PARKLAND, BOREAL FOREST, MONTANE

enchanter's nightshade   (JH)

HABITAT AND RANGE: Moist woodlands and willow thickets, mainly in boreal forest and aspen parkland. Widespread in Alberta.

FLOWERS: In terminal clusters. **Petals 2, small, notched, white, 1 to 2 mm long.** Stamens and sepals 2. Sepals reflexed, 1 to 2 mm long. Flower stalks erect to spreading, sometimes reflexed in fruit.

FRUIT: **Teardrop-shaped capsule, 2 to 3 mm long, covered with hooked white hairs.** 1 or 2 seeds.

LEAVES: Opposite, **oval to heart-shaped at base**, thin, coarsely toothed or entire, 2 to 6 cm long. Tapered to a pointed tip.

GROWTH HABIT: Simple or branched, slender perennial, 5 to 50 cm tall from thick rootstock.

Despite the name, this plant is not particularly attractive and is not similar in appearance to the nightshades (*Solanum* genus). *Circaea* is from the Greek goddess Circe who attempted to enchant Ulysses; *alpina* means "alpine" in Latin. ✎ This plant has a strong tendency to become weedy. ✎ There are 7 species of *Circaea* in North America and Eurasia, including this species in Alberta. There are 2 subspecies of *C. alpina* in Alberta. Subspecies *alpina*, which is widespread, has heart-shaped, toothed leaves and an upper stem without straight, appressed hairs. Subspecies *pacifica*, found in Waterton Lakes National Park, has rounded, entire leaves and an upper stem with appressed, straight hairs.

common fireweed, willow-herb

Epilobium angustifolium L.

PRAIRIE, ASPEN PARKLAND, BOREAL FOREST, MONTANE, SUBALPINE, ALPINE

HABITAT AND RANGE: Disturbed areas, clearings, roadsides, shaded riverine woods. Often occurs after a fire. Widespread in Alberta and Canada.

FLOWERS: In long terminal clusters. **Petals 4, deep pink to whitish, up to 2 cm long, with narrow bases. Bracts between petals are narrow.** Styles white, curved. Stigma 4-lobed, white. Sepals 8 to 16 mm long. **Flowers bloom from bottom of cluster first.** June to August.

FRUIT: Narrow capsule, 5 to 10 cm long. Seeds 1 to 1.3 mm long **with tuft of whitish hairs**.

LEAVES: Alternate, appearing whorled, up to 20 cm long. Longest leaves in middle of plant. Dark green with whitish midrib, lighter underneath, prominently veined, lance-shaped. Leaves have distinctive **lateral veins running beside entire to toothed leaf margins**.

GROWTH HABIT: Erect, robust perennial 1 to 3 m tall. May spread by long-lived rhizomes and is often found in colonies.

common fireweed (CB)

The common name fireweed originates from the plant's tendency to spring up from seeds and rhizomes on burned-over lands. The leaves resemble willow leaves, hence the alternate name willow-herb. *Epilobium* is derived from the Greek *epi* (upon) and *lobos* (a pod), which refers to the position of the petals and sepals on top of the seed pod. *Angustifolium* means "narrow-leaved." ✿ The sticky, sweet pith was eaten fresh or cooked by British Columbia natives, and the young leaves and new shoots were boiled. The inner pith can be used to flavour and thicken soups and

broad-leaved fireweed (BA)

broad-leaved fireweed (CWE)

Hornemann's willow-herb (JP)

stews, and the young flower stalks and leaves have been used in salads. Fireweed was called *asperge* and was highly prized by French Canadians of the Gaspé peninsula. The flower buds are edible and add colour to meals but are **slightly laxative** so should be eaten in moderation. Fireweed is very high in Vitamins C and A, and fireweed honey is prized. ✐ The cottony seed fluff was mixed with other fibres, such as dog hair, and used for spinning and weaving by coastal tribes of British Columbia and Washington. The Blackfoot rubbed fireweed flowers on articles to waterproof them. The inner pith was dried, powdered and used to prevent chapped skin. The Haida used the outer stem-fibres to make twine and fishnets. The green or dried leaves can be used for tea. ✐ Fireweed is the floral emblem of the Yukon. ✐ There are 150 species of *Epilobium*, widespread throughout the world; 17 of these occur in Alberta, with 9 currently classified as provincially rare. Broad-leaved fireweed or river beauty (*E. latifolium*) is particularly attractive, with its pink, broad-bracted flowers, 1 to 3 cm long petals and bluish green leaves often covered with a whitish bloom. It is common on gravel bars and stream edges in the mountains and foothills. Hornemann's willow-herb (*E. hornemannii*) is a much smaller plant than either of the above and has dark-pink to white flowers, with petals 3 to 9 mm long. It occurs in the foothills, Rockies and Cypress Hills.

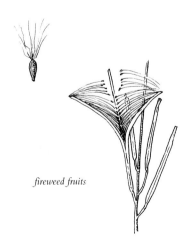

fireweed fruits

scarlet butterflyweed, scarlet gaura
Gaura coccinea Pursh
PRAIRIE, ASPEN PARKLAND

HABITAT AND RANGE: Grassland, dry south-facing hillsides, roadsides; often on sandy soil. Common in the southern half of the province.

FLOWERS: Petals whitish, **becoming scarlet, orange-red or shell-pink with age**; spoon-shaped, unequal, not united at base, 4 to 7 mm long. Sepals 4, reddish, reflexed, 1 cm long. Stamens 8, **red-tipped, protruding and conspicuous**. Flowers open fully only at night. June to August.

FRUIT: Nut-like, finely hairy, 4-angled capsule, about 6 mm long with 1 to 4 seeds.

LEAVES: Numerous, alternate, stalkless, oblong to linear, 1 to 3 cm long. Entire or with shallow teeth, **bluish green or gray-green**, short-hairy, prominently veined.

GROWTH HABIT: Erect or spreading, usually finely hairy, branched perennial herb up to 40 cm tall.

scarlet butterflyweed (BA)

The butterfly-shaped flowers give the plant its common name. *Gaura* is from the Greek *gauros* (superb or proud), because of the "proud" erect flowers, while *coccinea* means "scarlet," referring to the flower colour. ✐ Because the flowers are small and open only 1 or 2 at a time, this plant is not particularly showy. ✐ There are 18 species of *Gaura* in tropical and temperate North America. Only this species occurs in Alberta.

scarlet butterflyweed (CWa)

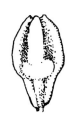

fruit of scarlet butterfly-weed (magnified 4.5 times)

yellow evening-primrose, common evening-primrose
Oenothera biennis L.

yellow evening-primrose   (CWa)

HABITAT AND RANGE: Sandy river and stream banks, meadows; from plains to low elevations in the mountains. Often on lighter, well-drained soils and disturbed ground. Widespread in the southern two-thirds of the province and also found in the extreme northeastern corner.

FLOWERS: Numerous, in **dense, long, leafy clusters**. Petals 4, yellow, rounded, notched at tip, 1 to 2 cm long. Sepals 4, bent backward, soft-hairy, 2 cm long. **Large, bright yellow-orange, cross-shaped stigma** and numerous yellow stamens. Flower stalks widened and **purple-spotted at base**, about 4.5 cm long. Flower usually opens in the evening and fades in the morning. July to August.

FRUIT: **Rough-hairy, sometimes purple-spotted, long-cylindric capsules, 2.5 to 4 cm long.** Capsules contain many small seeds.

LEAVES: Soft-hairy above and below, narrowly elliptic, toothed. Midvein prominent, whitish, thickened. Basal rosette leaves stalked, stem leaves nearly stalkless, alternate. Middle leaves to about 4.5 cm long, becoming smaller at the top of the plant. Numerous leaf-like stipules.

GROWTH HABIT: Erect, leafy, robust biennial or short-lived perennial with **solitary, stout, reddish, rough-hairy, spiny stems. Forms rosette the first year and a tall, leafy stem the second year.** Grows to 180 cm tall from a tap root.

yellow evening-primrose   (CB)

The plant gets its common name because it blooms at dusk to attract moths for pollination. *Oenothera* is a Greek word meaning "wine-scented," from *oinos* (wine) and *thera* (to induce wine drinking). ✐ Although the leaves are edible when cooked, it is usually the roots of the first-year plant (prior to flowering) that are gathered in the fall and then eaten boiled, in soups or stews, or dried for winter use. They are said to be nutritious and have a nut-like flavour. Some *Oenothera* species have edible seed pods, and in many species both young stems and leaves are edible. The young leaves may be cooked like dandelion greens, and both young leaves and shoots have been used in salads. ✐ Medicinally, yellow evening primrose has been used to alleviate colds and to treat skin conditions. Seed oil from common evening-primrose is currently being used on an experimental basis to treat such conditions as eczema, migraines, arthritis and alcoholism. ✐ The plant is sometimes used in roadside plantings to control erosion. ✐ There are 90 species of *Oenothera*, all but 1 in North or South America; 8 species occur in Alberta. White evening-primrose (*O. nuttallii*) has white to pinkish flowers and whitish, shredding stems; it is found in dry, sandy habitats. Butte-primrose *(O. caespitosa)* is described on page 146.

white evening-primrose   (CWₐ)

butte-primrose, gumbo evening-primrose, rock rose, tufted evening-primrose

Oenothera caespitosa Nutt.

PRAIRIE

butte-primrose (SR)

HABITAT AND RANGE: Heavy, often clayish, eroded prairie soils, dry roadcuts and slopes. Widespread in the southern quarter of the province.

FLOWERS: Showy, **white (aging to bright pink), with 4 large, shallowly lobed petals, each up to 4 cm long.** Sepals 4, reflexed, pale pink, up to 3 cm long. Cross-shaped yellow stigma and 8 long, yellow-tipped stamens. Sweet-scented. The **flowers open in the early morning and close at night.** June to August.

FRUIT: In cluster from the base of the plant. **Woody, oblong, angled capsules, up to 4 cm long, with lines of short white hairs.**

LEAVES: Basal, entire, **spoon-shaped to lance-shaped**, wavy-margined to irregularly toothed. Dark green, sometimes reddish-tinged, up to 20 cm long. Leaf stalks yellow to reddish, winged at base.

GROWTH HABIT: **Tufted**, smooth to hairy perennial with **rosette of basal leaves**. Flower stalk up to 10 cm tall from thick, woody root.

The common names reflect the plant's habit and habitat. The derivation of *Oenothera* is explained on page 145, and *caespitosa* refers to the tufted or clumped growth habit. ◢ The Blackfoot pounded the roots and used them on sores and to reduce inflammation. ◢ Attractive ornamental species in this genus are available from garden centres in Alberta.

wild sarsaparilla, wild ginseng

Aralia nudicaulis L.

ASPEN PARKLAND, BOREAL FOREST

HABITAT AND RANGE: Dry to moist shaded woods and thickets. Primarily occurs from the Bow River north, but also found in the Cypress Hills.

FLOWERS: In 2 to 7 **umbrella-shaped clusters**, 2 to 5 cm across, on a flower stalk that is **shorter than the leaves**. Flowers greenish or whitish, inconspicuous, 3 to 5 mm in diameter. Sepals and petals 5. June to July.

FRUIT: Hard, valved, berry-like; 6 to 8 mm long, with flat seeds. Initially green or white, becoming **purplish black** when mature. Although the berries are supposedly edible, they are not recommended because eating them has caused cases of **severe illness**.

wild sarsaparilla (CWE)

LEAVES: Usually a single, **pale-green compound leaf on a long stalk**. Leaflets oval to lance-shaped with toothed margins, 3 to 6 cm long. Tapered abruptly to a sharp point.

GROWTH HABIT: Stemless perennial with flower stalk reaching more than 30 cm tall, from a long, branching rootstock.

The root of this plant was once used as a substitute for sarsaparilla, a drink made from a tropical vine that grows in Mexico and the Caribbean. *Aralia* is the Latinized form of the French *aralie*, the Quebec Habitant name for the plant. *Nudicaulis* means "bare stem" and applies to the leafless flower or fruit stalk. ✿ The fragrant roots have been eaten as a famine food and boiled to make a tea drunk as a cough remedy. They were also made into a compress for cuts and wounds by the Cree, and, mixed with Labrador tea, were used to increase appetite, treat venereal disease and act as a poultice. ✿ The plant was used as a stimulant and to produce a

wild sarsaparilla (BA)

sweat by some American peoples. The Plains tribes used wild sarsaparilla as a diuretic, and the Blackfoot used it as a tonic and purgative. ✿ The related spikenard (*A. racemosa*) of eastern North America was used by the Micmac to make salve to treat wounds and cuts. Various North American natives have used it as a sedative and to treat backache, coughs, and rheumatism. ✿ There are 25 species of *Aralia* in the world, all in North America, Asia and Australia. Only this species occurs in Alberta.

Carrot Family (Apiaceae or Umbelliferae)

3,000 species (possibly more) occur in this family that supplies us with many valuable food and spice plants, such as carrot, parsnip, celery, dill, anise, caraway and fennel, but also contains water-hemlock, probably the most poisonous native plant in the province. Carrot family members are characterized by simple or compound, umbrella-like inflorescences called *umbels*, and often have much-divided, compound (occasionally simple) leaves that are sheathing at the base. Frequently the plants have a large pith that shrivels at maturity, leaving a hollow stem. Each flower has 5 petals, 5 stamens, and 1 pistil with 2 styles often enlarged to form a *stylopodium* (for example in sweet cicely, shown on page 156). *(See key for this family beginning page 308.)*

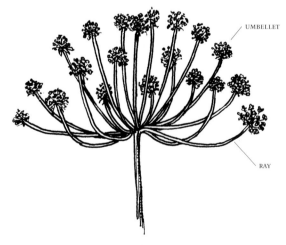

UMBELLET

RAY

compound umbel

yellow angelica

Angelica dawsonii S. Wats.

MONTANE, SUBALPINE

HABITAT AND RANGE: Moist banks, slopes and lakeshores at low to middle elevations in the southwestern Rockies.

FLOWERS: **Tiny, greenish yellow flower heads in a compound umbel, usually surrounded at base by several large, toothed, leafy bracts.** Petals notched, rounded. Rays of umbel 2 to 4 cm long. June to August.

FRUIT: Oblong, **flattened, winged fruit, 4 to 7 mm long.**

LEAVES: **Long-sheathing and inflated at base. Compound, with leaflets opposite.** Upper leaves lobed and irregularly toothed. Terminal leaflets to 5.5 cm, lateral leaflets to 3 cm long. Basal leaves large, long-stalked. Stem leaves few and short-stalked.

GROWTH HABIT: Stems robust, reddish at base, glaucous at top. Perennial up to 1 m tall from thick rootstock.

yellow angelica (IM)

*A*ngelica is from the Latin *angelus* (angel), referring to the supposed medicinal properties of some members of the genus, or to the plant's flowering at the time of the feast of St. Michael the Archangel. *Dawsonii* honours Sir John Dawson, a 19th-century Canadian geologist and ethnobotanist. ✎ Some North American natives mixed the dried roots of yellow angelica into a form of tobacco. The fresh roots, which are **poisonous**, were used by members of some tribes to commit suicide. ✎ In ancient times the related European *A. sylvestris* was taken medicinally for "tremblings and passions of the heart" and "to abate the rage of lust in young persons" (Parkinson 1629). ✎ There are about 50 species of *Angelica*, circumboreal in distribution; 3 occur in Alberta. White or sharptooth angelica (*A. arguta*) usually has white (sometimes pinkish) flowers and lacks the bracts at the base of the umbel. It also is found in the southwestern Rockies. Kneeling angelica (*A. genuflexa*) also has white flowers and, as the common and species name suggest, has a reflexed main leaf stalk and sharply drooping leaflets. It occurs in north-central Alberta, along the Athabasca River and west to the Peace River country.

white angelica (CWE)

water-hemlock, spotted water-hemlock
Cicuta maculata L. var. *angustifolia* Hook.

water-hemlock (JH)

HABITAT AND RANGE: Marshes, river and stream banks, ditches; low, wet areas from prairie to montane elevations. Widespread in Alberta.

FLOWERS: Several in **umbrella-like clusters (compound umbels)**. Rays of umbels 6 to 20 cm long. Petals white, numerous, 2 mm in diameter. **Narrow bracts at base of umbellets but not at the base of the umbel.** June to July.

FRUIT: Yellow to brownish, round, ribbed, nut-like, 2 to 4 mm long. Usually longer than broad.

LEAVES: Alternate, with many **bipinnate and tripinnate** basal and stem leaves. **Leaflets lance-shaped**, toothed, 3 to 20 cm long.

GROWTH HABIT: Robust, branching perennial 30 to 180 cm tall, from thickened, partitioned base (when viewed in cross-section). Stem often purplish, noticeably ribbed.

*C*icuta is from the ancient Latin name of some poisonous member of the carrot family. *Maculata* means "spotted," likely in reference to the blotches on the stem, while *angustifolia* indicates narrow leaves. ✐ This genus is considered by some to be **the most poisonous in North America. All parts of the plant are toxic**, especially the roots. Some American common names express the plant's deadly nature: children's bane, beaver poison, death-of-man. Eating just the basal parts of a single plant is enough to kill a cow.

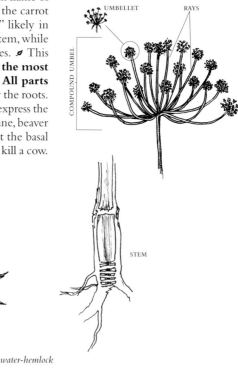

water-hemlock

The root was chewed by Cherokee women to induce permanent sterility, but too much was known to be deadly. In Oregon, the Klamath made poison-tipped arrows from rotted deer's liver, rattlesnake venom and the juice of water-hemlock. The Okanagan of British Columbia also used the powdered root as a poison for their arrows. The Blackfoot split the roots and applied them to rattlesnake bites to draw out the poison. They also occasionally chewed the roots to commit suicide. Some Montana tribes used small amounts of water-hemlock to induce vomiting and to make medicine to treat sores. ✍ There are 8 species of *Cicuta* in the world, mainly in North America. Of these, 3 occur in Alberta. Bulb-bearing water-hemlock (*C. bulbifera*) is readily distinguished from water-hemlock by its narrow, linear leaflets and small "bulbs" in the axils of the leaves. Narrow-leaved or European water-hemlock (*C. virosa*) is similar to water-hemlock but usually has 50 or more rays in the umbellets, as opposed to 12 to 25, and fruit that is as broad as or broader than it is long. ✍ Water-hemlock is similar in appearance to water parsnip (*Sium suave*). Water parsnip has bracts at the base of the umbel, narrower, mainly singly pinnate leaves and a non-partitioned base. It is not as toxic as *Cicuta* species.

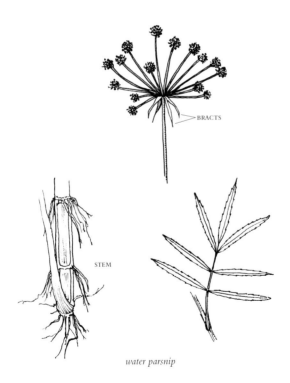

BRACTS

STEM

water parsnip

cow parsnip, wild rhubarb
Heracleum lanatum Michx.

<small>PRAIRIE, ASPEN PARKLAND, BOREAL FOREST, MONTANE, SUBALPINE</small>

cow parsnip   (BA)

HABITAT AND RANGE: Riverine shaded prairie, stream banks, clearings and moist, open aspen woods. Widespread in Alberta.

FLOWERS: In large, **compound, umbrella-shaped clusters (umbels), 20 cm or more across.** Umbels composed of numerous white flowers with white petals in 5s; central flowers smaller, outer large with petals notched, up to 8 mm long. June to July.

FRUIT: Pale greenish, **flattened, ribbed, nut-like, 8 to 12 mm long,** with fine hairs. **Dark oil tubes extend downward from the tip.** Pleasant smelling.

LEAVES: **Compound in 3s, very large (to more than 30 cm long),** softly hairy, paler underneath, sharply lobed, toothed along margins. Leaf stalks have large enclosing sheaths at base. Stipules pale brownish, pointed.

GROWTH HABIT: Tall **(to more than 2 m),** robust, strong-smelling perennial. **Stems ribbed, stout, hollow;** usually with stiff, white hairs in lines.

*H*eracleum refers to Hercules, likely because of the plant's large size; *lanatum* means "woolly." ✒ The roots were cooked and eaten by some native tribes, but some sources say they are **poisonous.** The Cree and Blackfoot crushed and boiled the root to poultice bruises and swellings. The Blackfoot also used the root to treat arthritis and rheumatism. Some tribes blew ground root into the throat to treat diptheria, and pieces of raw root were stuffed into cavities to alleviate toothache. The Blood applied cow parsnip to warts to dry them up. ✒ The young, tender leaf and flower stalks were eaten raw by some North American natives. The Blackfoot roasted the young spring stalks on hot coals and ate them. They also used the stalks in their Sun Dance ceremony. The stems (which must be peeled because of **skin irritants** in the outer layer) are said to be very nutritious and high in protein, and the base of the plant is said to have been used as a salt substitute. ✒ There are 60 species of *Heracleum*, but only this species is native to North America.

long-fruited wild parsley, white prairie parsley

Lomatium macrocarpum (Hook. & Arn.) Coult. & Rose

PRAIRIE, MONTANE, SUBALPINE

HABITAT AND RANGE: Dry, open slopes, rocky plains, ridges and coulees. Widespread in the prairies from the Red Deer River south to the Montana border.

FLOWERS: Small, white or purplish (sometimes yellow) flowers in **umbrella-like clusters**, often obscured by the **narrow bracts. Rays of umbel unequal**, up to 6 cm long. May to June.

FRUIT: **Flattened**, usually smooth **fruits with narrow to broadly winged, white edges, 9 to 20 mm long**. Fruits occur in dense clusters.

LEAVES: Clustered near base of plant. **Finely dissected** (similar to parsley), bluish green or light-green leaf blades, sparsely to densely hairy, 3 to 12 cm long, on long stalks. Leaf stalks have long, whitish or purplish sheaths to about the middle.

GROWTH HABIT: **Densely gray-hairy** (becoming smoother with age), branched perennial up to 25 cm tall from **thick tap root. Purplish near base.**

long-fruited wild parsley　(CWE)

*L*omatium is from the Greek *loma* (border), in reference to the winged fruit. *Macrocarpum* comes from the Greek *karpos* (fruit) and *macro* (large) and alludes to the large size of the fruits. ✎ The plant was known as Indian carrot or Indian sweet potato, as the long tap roots of non-flowering plants were gathered in the spring and eaten raw or roasted by many native North Americans. They are said to be peppery and taste like celery leaves. Indian celery tea was made from related species and drunk by B.C. tribes to treat sore throats and colds. The leaves of some of wild parsley species were used by the Thompson people as a perfume and as padding on child carriers to help the child sleep well. Western wild parsley (*L. triternatum*) seeds were used by the Blackfoot in tanning hides, and the roots were used to induce abortions and stop nosebleed. The roots of biscuit-root (*L. cous*) were often ground into flour. The Blackfeet of Montana made a tea from the roots when feeling debilitated and made horses inhale the smoke from the burning root to treat horse distemper. ✎ There are 75 species of *Lomatium* in western and central North America; 6 of these are found in Alberta. Western wild parsley has leaves divided into a few, long segments, as opposed to the dissected leaves of long-fruited wild parsley.

western wild parsley　(BA)

fruit of long-fruited wild parsley
(magnified 2.5 times)

153

leafy musineon

Musineon divaricatum (Pursh) Nutt.

PRAIRIE, MONTANE, SUBALPINE, ALPINE

leafy musineon (CWA)

HABITAT AND RANGE: Dry grassland, exposed hillsides, rocky slopes; often on south and west exposures. Alkali tolerant. From the Red Deer River south to the Montana border.

FLOWERS: **Yellow** with 5 rounded petals, each about 1 mm long, in a **compound, umbrella-like cluster,** 5 to 7 cm across. Flower stalks and calyx **roughened-glandular,** especially just below the inflorescence. April to June.

FRUIT: Narrowly oval, rounded, **prominently ribbed** fruits, 3 to 5 mm long, with **roughened projections** on the surface.

LEAVES: Oblong, **smooth,** flattened, bright green, parsley-like, with many dissected leaflets. Lower leaves inflated at the base, often purplish. Leaflets sometimes spiny-tipped.

GROWTH HABIT: Spreading or erect low-growing perennial, 10 to 20 cm tall from thick, swollen tap root. Usually rough to the touch, particularly on the upper stem below the flowers. Stems are often curved at the base.

*M*usineon is derived from the Greek name for some member of the carrot family. *Divaricatum* likely refers to the divergent rays of the flower and fruit clusters. ⌀ There are 4 species of *Musineon* in the world, mainly in western North America. Only this species occurs in Alberta. Leafy musineon is similar in appearance to hairy-fruited wild parsley (*Lomatium foeniculaceum*) but musineon is smooth rather than hairy, has greener, less finely dissected leaves and its fruit is not winged.

fruit of hairy-fruited parsley (magnified 3 times)

fruit of leaf musineon (magnified 8 times)

hairy-fruited wild parsley (CWA)

spreading sweet cicely
Osmorhiza depauperata Philippi
ASPEN PARKLAND, BOREAL FOREST, MONTANE, SUBALPINE

HABITAT AND RANGE: Partly shaded moist meadows and woodlands to moderate elevations. Widespread except in the prairies and the northern third of the province.

FLOWERS: Small, **white to greenish white, in spreading or reflexed umbrella-shaped clusters**.

FRUIT: **Fruits long-stalked, black with bristly white hairs. Narrowly club-shaped, 10 to 15 mm long, with slender, raised ribs.** Seeds can stick to clothing and fur.

LEAVES: Compound, with oval, coarsely toothed leaflets, 2 to 7 cm long. Basal leaves long-stemmed.

GROWTH HABIT: Stiff-hairy to smooth perennial herb, up to 1 m tall from well-developed, aromatic tap root.

spreading sweet cicely   (BA)

Cicely derives from *seseli*, an ancient Greek name for some sweet-scented plant. *Osmorhiza* is from the Greek *osme* (odour) and *rhiza* (root), referring to the pleasant smell of some of the species. *Depauperata* means "dwarfed or starved," derivation unknown. ✿ The Blood treated sores, chest pains, stomach aches and hemmorhages with sweet cicely; they made a love potion from the roots. It was believed that when a piece of the root was held in the mouth, a person could not tell lies. Sweet cicely was also believed to make things

western sweet cicely   (CWA)

sacred; ordinary people were not allowed to touch it. A charm made from the plant was tied onto horses to help them win races, and the leaves were made into a decoration to encourage babies to be born quickly. The Blackfoot fed the roots to pregnant mares to improve their condition for foaling; they also made flour from the ground root. The roots of related blunt-fruited sweet cicely (*O. chilensis*) were dug and eaten cooked by some interior B.C. tribes. Sweet cicely root flour can be used to add a licorice flavour to cookies. The seeds have been dried and used as a seasoning. ✐ There are 11 species of *Osmorhiza* in North America, the Andes of South America and east Asia. Spreading sweet cicely is the most common *Osmorhiza* of the 5 species occurring in the province. Western sweet cicely (*O. occidentalis*) is the only Alberta species with a smooth, non-tapered fruit and pale-yellow flowers. It is restricted to forests in the southwestern quarter of the province.

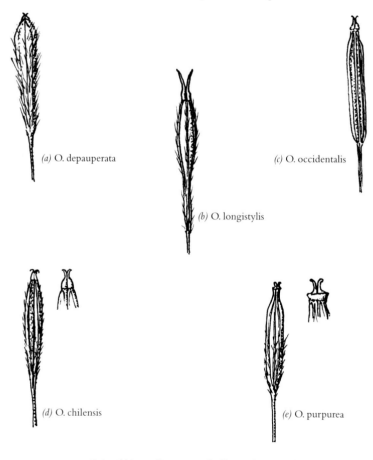

(a) O. depauperata

(c) O. occidentalis

(b) O. longistylis

(d) O. chilensis

(e) O. purpurea

Fruits of (a) spreading sweet cicely, (b) smooth sweet cicely,
(c) western sweet cicely, (d) blunt-fruited sweet cicely,
(e) purple sweet cicely

yampa, squawroot, wild caraway, Gairdner's yampa, Indian carrot, Indian turnip

Perideridia gairdneri (Hook. & Arn.)
(Mathias ssp. *borealis* Chuang & Constance in Moss 1983)
PRAIRIE, MONTANE

yampa (BA)

HABITAT AND RANGE: Dry woods and dry-to-moist meadows in the southern half of the province.

FLOWERS: **In compound umbels** to about 6 cm long. Flowers white or pinkish, very small, rays 8 to 20. Calyx-teeth conspicuous. **No involucral bracts.** July to August.

FRUIT: Brown, flattened, ribbed, capsule-like, about 2 mm long; splits into segments at maturity.

LEAVES: Few, **pinnate or occasionally bipinnate, with 3 to 7 linear or lance-shaped, erect leaflets, 4 to 12 cm long.** Leaf stalks not much inflated or sheathing. **Leaves often shrivelled by the time flowers appear.**

GROWTH HABIT: Smooth, usually unbranched, **aromatic perennial**, 30 to 60 cm tall **with 1 or more tapered, spindle-shaped, tuberous roots**.

Yampa is named after the Yampa River area in northwestern Colorado where the plant is abundant. The name yampa is also applied to the root. *Perideridia* may be from the Greek *peri* (around) and *derris* (leather coat), in reference to the tough "skin" around the root. *Gairdneri* honours Meredith Gairdner, an early 19th-century Hudson's Bay Company surgeon and plant collector. ❧ The roots, which are high in sugars, Vitamins A and C, and potassium and which are said to have a sweet, nutty, parsnip-like flavour, were a favourite food of various native peoples. The women gathered the roots and placed them in baskets in running water, then walked over them with bare feet to remove the skins. British Columbia tribes dug the roots in May and June and stored them in pits lined with pine needles. ❧ Alberta Blackfoot ate the roots raw or boiled. They chewed the roots and used the resulting liquid to relieve sore throats; they also used the roots to poultice swellings. The Blood used the roots to treat coughs, sore throats and liver trouble. ❧ Yampa seeds have been used as seasoning. ❧ There are 9 species of *Perideridia*, all in North America. Only this species occurs in Alberta. Yampa is somewhat similar to western wild parsley (*Lomatium triternatum*), but the latter has flowers in dense, round, bright-yellow compound umbels, and has much larger, broadly winged fruit (see illustration on page 153); yampa is usually also considerably taller.

snakeroot, black sanicle

Sanicula marilandica L.

MONTANE, SUBALPINE, ASPEN PARKLAND, BOREAL FOREST

snakeroot (DJ)

HABITAT AND RANGE: Moist woods, thickets. Scattered throughout all but extreme northern Alberta and the prairies.

FLOWERS: **Greenish white, in ball-like umbels about 1 cm wide. Some flowers perfect (with stamens and pistil), others only staminate.** Staminate flowers on stalks. Calyx of narrow, long-tapered sepals, each 1 to 1.5 mm long. June.

FRUIT: Oval, 4 to 6 mm long, narrowed to the leaf stalk, **covered with long, curved prickles that are thicker at the base.** Fruit splits into separate segments at maturity.

LEAVES: Basal and lower stem leaves long-stalked, palmately compound with 5 to 7 broadly lance-shaped, toothed segments that are wedge-shaped at base, often split at the tip. **Marginal teeth have long spines.** Upper leaves short-stalked or stalkless.

GROWTH HABIT: Fibrous-rooted, smooth perennial 30 to 60 cm tall. Stem solitary.

Native North Americans pounded the root into a poultice to treat snakebite, hence the common name. *Sanicula* is from the Latin *sanare* (to heal) or *sanus* (whole or sound), as the plant was believed to have medicinal qualities. *Marilandica* means "of Maryland." ✍ Members of this genus give a bad taste to milk of dairy cows that graze it. ✍ There are 40 species of *Sanicula*, widely distributed, although mainly in temperate regions and mountainous parts of the tropics. Only this species is native to Alberta.

heart-leaved alexanders, meadow parsnip
Zizia aptera (A. Gray) Fern.
PRAIRIE, ASPEN PARKLAND, BOREAL FOREST, MONTANE, SUBALPINE, ALPINE

HABITAT AND RANGE: Riverine prairie, moist meadows, open woods, shrubby slopes, wetland margins, stream banks. Widespread except in the northern third of the province.

FLOWERS: Numerous, **in compound, flat-topped cluster** up to 4 cm wide. Flowers small, **petals 0.5 to 1 mm long, bright yellow.** May to July.

FRUIT: Flattened, oblong, narrowly ribbed, nut-like, 2 to 4 mm long with green to brown, 5-ribbed seeds.

LEAVES: Leathery, dark green. **Lower heart-shaped and long-stalked, sheathing.** Upper short-stalked or stalkless. **Toothed or scalloped along the margin.**

GROWTH HABIT: Erect, hollow-stemmed, smooth perennial up to 60 cm tall, occurring singly or in clumps.

The origin of the name alexanders is unknown. *Zizia* is from Johann Baptist Ziz, an early German botanist. *Aptera* means "wingless," perhaps because in contrast to many other members of the carrot family, the fruit lacks winged margins. ✐ There are 4 species of *Zizia* in North America, but only this species is native to Alberta.

heart-leaved alexanders   (BA)

bunchberry, dwarf cornel, dwarf dogwood, pigeonberry

Cornus canadensis L.

ASPEN PARKLAND, BOREAL FOREST, MONTANE, SUBALPINE

bunchberry (CWE)

HABITAT AND RANGE: Moist coniferous, mixedwood or occasionally poplar forest; often on stumps or rotting logs. Widespread in Alberta and across Canada.

FLOWERS: Cluster of inconspicuous, greenish white flowers, each 1 mm long. **Bracts showy, petal-like, white, greenish or pinkish white**; broadly oval, 1 to 2.5 cm long. June to August.

FRUIT: **Berry-like, bright red, 5 to 8 mm long.**

LEAVES: **In a terminal whorl of 4 to 7. Prominently veined**, up to 8 cm long. Dark green above, lighter underneath, turning purplish red in the fall. Leathery, sometimes finely hairy, elliptic, tapered to base.

GROWTH HABIT: Low-growing perennial with reddish stem, up to 20 cm tall from creeping rootstock. Often forms a dense ground cover.

*C*ornus is from the Latin for "horn" or "antler," referring to the hard wood of some of the species; or possibly may be derived from the resemblance of the inflorescence to the cornus pieces or knobs on cylinders used for rolling up manuscripts. *Canadensis* means "of Canada": the species is widely distributed in boreal forest across the country. ✐ The berries are considered sweet and flavourful by some, or dry and insipid according to others; flavour and juiciness likely depend on habitat and climatic conditions. They were eaten raw by certain B.C. tribes, and the Inuit preserved them for winter use. They are also a source of food for deer, grouse and songbirds. ✐ The roots and bark have been used as a cold remedy, and the bark as a laxative. ✐ Nootka legend says that bunchberries arose from the blood of a native woman marooned above the ground in a cedar tree by her jealous husband. ✐ There are 30 species of *Cornus*, mainly in northern temperate regions; 2 are found in Alberta, the other being the common red-barked shrub, red-osier dogwood (*C. stolonifera*). Bunchberry is related and similar in appearance to Pacific dogwood (*C. nuttallii*), the provincial floral emblem of B.C.

The heaths are usually dwarf shrubs but can range in size from the tiny bearberry to a giant species of rhododendron reaching 25 m in height. Economically valuable heaths include ornamental rhododendrons and azaleas, and the edible blueberries, cranberries and huckleberries. Because the plants often occur in acidic, boggy environments where root development is restricted due to low oxygen and available nutrient levels in the soil, the simple leaves are often leathery and evergreen to preserve water and nutrients. The corolla is 4 to 5-lobed and often urn-shaped, and the stamens are usually twice as numerous as the corolla-lobes. Sepals number 4 to 5, and fruits may be capsules, drupes or berries. *(See key for this family beginning page 309.)*

bog rosemary, moorwort
Andromeda polifolia L.
BOREAL FOREST

bog rosemary   (JH)

HABITAT AND RANGE: **Peat bogs, fens** in northern half of Alberta. Range does not extend much south of the North Saskatchewan River.

FLOWERS: 2 to 6 in loose, terminal clusters. **Urn-shaped, pinkish, 5-lobed, 5 to 8 mm long, on curved flower stalks.** Anther has 2 horns at the top. Calyx deeply lobed, each lobe about 1 mm long. Stamens 10, with hairy filaments. June to July.

FRUIT: Round, 5-valved smooth capsule, 4 to 6 mm thick, with many shiny, round, tan seeds, each about 1 mm long.

LEAVES: Alternate, **leathery**, entire, **persistent**. Narrowly lance-shaped to oblong, 1.5 to 4 cm long, with pointed tip. Upper surface dull green with noticeable veins; lower surface has whitish coating. **Margins strongly inrolled.**

GROWTH HABIT: Dainty, **low-spreading evergreen shrub** with erect stems, 10 to 150 cm tall, from creeping rootstock.

Rosemary comes from *rosmarinus* or *ros maris*, meaning "dew of the sea," a name applied to a Mediterranean plant because of its maritime habitat or smell of the sea. Andromeda, in Greek legend, was chained to a rock in the sea by the sea god Poseidon and later rescued by the god Perseus, son of Jupiter. Bog rosemary is similarly perched on hummocks in bogs, hence the origin of the genus name. *Polifolia* means "many-leaved." ✿ Bog rosemary contains a **poisonous alkaloid**, *andromedotoxin*, that is poisonous to livestock, especially sheep. The toxin lowers blood pressure and causes loss of energy, respiratory distress and paralysis leading to death. ✿ The leaves and twigs of bog rosemary were used for tanning in Russia. ✿ There are 1 or 2 species of *Andromeda* in the boreal northern hemisphere. Only this species is found in Alberta.

common bearberry, kinnikinnick

Arctostaphylos uva-ursi (L). Spreng.

Aspen Parkland, Boreal Forest, Montane, Subalpine, Alpine

HABITAT AND RANGE: Rocky outcrops, dry open woods, eroded slopes, well-drained sandy or gravelly soils. Widespread except in the prairie grasslands.

FLOWERS: 3 to 10 **bell-shaped, drooping flowers, pale pink or whitish with darker-pink tips**. Corolla 4 to 5-lobed, 4 to 8 mm long. May to July.

FRUIT: **Bright-red, large-seeded "berry,"** 6 to 8 mm in diameter. Edible but mealy and dry.

LEAVES: Alternate, **leathery; shiny bright green on the upper surface, lighter underneath.** Older leaves may be orange or reddish. Entire, 1 to 3 cm long, rounded at the tips.

common bearberry (CWa)

GROWTH HABIT: **Evergreen**, trailing, **mat-forming** perennial shrub with reddish, scaly bark. Plant can root from the prostrate branches.

*A*rktos is Greek for "bear," *staphyle* means "bunch of grapes" and *uva-ursi* is Latin for "bear's grape." As the common and scientific names suggest, this plant is a staple food for bears. Kinnikinnick is believed to be of Algonquin origin, in reference to the plant's use in tobacco mixtures. *ø* Although the berries are dry, mealy and flat-tasting, they are edible and have been used in teas, fried, boiled and made into pemmican. They are said to suppress the appetite and are an excellent survival food because they are high in carbohydrates and remain on the plant over winter. The Blackfoot believed that a heavy berry crop meant a severe winter was on the way. *ø* The leaves contain glycosides and have been grown commercially in Spain,

common bearberry (CWa)

alpine bearberry   (CWA)

Canada and the U.S. for use as diuretics and astringents. Herbalists use them to treat
kidney and bladder problems. ✿ The leaves were smoked by several native tribes
and may be used to tan hides, produce a yellow-gray dye and make Christmas
decorations. The leaves can also be brewed into a tea, but be cautioned: the tea is
diuretic and can produce **digestive upset** due to its high tannin content. ✿ There
are about 45 species of *Arctostaphylos* known, mainly from the west coast of North
America. The only other Alberta species, alpine bearberry (*A. rubra*), has deciduous
leaves that are scalloped on the margins, smoother branches and a juicy "berry." It is
less common, restricted to the north-central Rockies and the extreme northern boreal
forest.

western mountain-heather, mountain-heather
Cassiope mertensiana (Bong.) D. Don
SUBALPINE, ALPINE

HABITAT AND RANGE: Open subalpine forests and moist alpine areas in the northern and central Rockies.

FLOWERS: Several, near ends of branches. **Bell-shaped**, nodding, **white**, 5-lobed; 4 to 8 mm long on short stalks. Sepals oval, **reddish**, 2 to 3 mm long. June to August.

FRUIT: Dry, brownish, compartmented capsule, 2 to 3 mm long, with attached thick beak. Capsule contains many tiny, tan seeds.

LEAVES: **Opposite, evergreen. Pressed closely to the stem and overlapping**; narrow, short, somewhat needle-like, 2 to 5 mm long. In distinct rows.

western mountain-heather (CWE)

GROWTH HABIT: Small (5 to 30 cm tall), **branched, mat-forming shrub**.

*C*assiope was the mother of Andromeda in Greek mythology. *Mertensiana* honours F.C. Mertens, an early German botanist. ✐ Western mountain-heather has a high resin content and can be used to fuel fires. The branches are said to produce a golden-brown dye. ✐ There are 12 species of *Cassiope* in north temperate and arctic regions, including 2 species native to Alberta. White mountain-heather (*C. tetragona*) has a long groove on the underside of the leaf and often occurs in more extensive patches in somewhat drier habitats than western mountain-heather. The famous heather of Scotland belongs to the *Calluna* and, to a lesser extent, *Erica* genera.

leaves of western mountain-heather

white mountain-heather (CWE)

leaves of white mountain-heather

prince's-pine, pipsissewa

Chimaphila umbellata (L.) Bart. ssp. *occidentalis* (Rydb.) Hult.

BOREAL FOREST, MONTANE, SUBALPINE

prince's-pine   (TC)

HABITAT AND RANGE: Shaded, dry montane and subalpine coniferous woods, mainly in the Rocky Mountains and Cypress Hills.

FLOWERS: Several in loose, terminal clusters. Petals 5, **waxy, pale pinkish white, darker at base**, rounded, 4 to 7 mm long. Stamens 10, **purple-tipped. Ovary pale green, ringed with purple, topped by round, shiny, 5-lobed green stigma.** Flower stalks spreading to reflexed, pinkish. Calyx dark red at base with 5 tiny, whitish, rounded lobes. Pleasant-smelling. July to August.

FRUIT: Dry, brown, round capsule, 5 to 7 mm wide with many seeds.

LEAVES: In 1 or 2 whorls. Dark green above and paler beneath, evergreen, wedge-shaped at base. **Shiny, leathery, thick**; 2 to 8 cm long on short stalks. Margins with **widely spread teeth that have tiny spines**.

GROWTH HABIT: Creeping, somewhat woody perennial plant, to 30 cm tall or more, with a tough, curved, greenish stem.

Pipsissewa is from the Cree name for the plant, *pipsisikweu*, meaning "it breaks into small pieces," as it was believed that juice from the plant would break down kidney and gallstones. *Chimaphila* originates from the Greek *cheima* (winter) and *philos* (loving), because of this species' evergreen habit. *Umbellata* alludes to the umbel type of inflorescence, while *occidentalis* means "of the west." ✿ Some American natives steeped prince's-pine in water and applied the liquid to blisters. The Thompson of British Columbia pounded the plant to a pulp, which they applied to leg and foot swellings; they also boiled the leaves, stems and root to make a tea. The plant was used by some tribes and early European settlers to promote sweating and to treat rheumatism, sore eyes, gonorrhea sores, colds, sore throats and backache. ✿ Prince's-pine was listed in the United States Pharmacopoeia until 1916 as an astringent, and medical journals report that it increases urine flow and disinfects the kidneys. Many native peoples were aware of the plant's medicinal properties and drank a tea brewed from it for kidney trouble. ✿ There are 6 species of *Chimaphila* in North America and Asia; only this species occurs in Alberta. *Chimaphila* is placed in the wintergreen (Pyrolaceae) family by some taxonomists.

bog laurel, northern laurel, pale laurel, swamp laurel

Kalmia polifolia Wang.

BOREAL FOREST

HABITAT AND RANGE: Sphagnum bogs of the northeastern boreal forest.

FLOWERS: Showy, **rosy-pink to purplish, on reddish stalks**, in clusters from upper leaf axils and at the top of the plant. Bowl-shaped, 6 to 15 mm broad, composed of **5-lobed, united petals**. Calyx deeply 5-lobed. **Stamens 10, purple-tipped, protruding from pouches on each petal.** June to July.

FRUIT: Oval, partitioned capsule, about 6 mm long, with persistent appendage (style). Seeds numerous.

LEAVES: Opposite, simple, **evergreen, leathery**, 2 to 4 cm long. **Shiny dark green above, light beneath, with prominent veins.** Narrowly lance-shaped, often curled under at margins. Short-stalked.

bog laurel   (CWE)

GROWTH HABIT: **Erect or matted, branched shrubs**, up to 60 cm tall. Branches 2-angled; bark somewhat flaky. Plant spreads by layering and by short rhizomes.

Kalmia honours Peter Kalm, an 18th-century student of the famed botanist Linnaeus. *Polifolia* is from the Latin *polio* (to whiten) and *folium* (a leaf), in reference to the pale leaf underside. ✿ The 10 anthers of bog laurel are inserted into corresponding openings on the petals. When the petals or filaments are touched by an insect, the anthers are quickly released and coat the insect with pollen. ✿ Gray and yellow dyes can be produced from the leaves. The leaves and flowers contain alkaloids such as *andromedotoxin*, which may cause **lowering of blood pressure, respiratory paralysis and death** in people and livestock. ✿ There are about 6 species of *Kalmia* in North America, only 2 of which occur in Alberta. Mountain laurel (*K. microphylla*), found primarily in wet meadows and bogs of the northern Rockies, is a smaller plant (usually 10 to 20 cm tall), with shorter leaves (1 to 2 cm) than bog laurel.

mountain laurel   (BG)

one-flowered wintergreen, single delight, wood nymph

Moneses uniflora (L.) A. Gray

ASPEN PARKLAND, BOREAL FOREST, MONTANE, SUBALPINE, ALPINE

one-flowered wintergreen   (BA)

HABITAT AND RANGE: Shaded, moist woods and alpine meadows. **Often found on rotting wood.** Found throughout the province except on the prairies.

FLOWERS: **Solitary, nodding on stem,** fragrant. Petals 5, white with darker guidelines, **wavy-margined**, grooved in centre, 8 mm long. Sepals usually bent backward, with jagged edges. Stamens 10, brownish, conspicuous. **Stigma large, bright green, with 5-lobed tip. Ovary conspicuous, green, 5-grooved.** July.

FRUIT: Nearly round, brown capsule up to 7 mm thick, on an upright stalk. Capsule contains numerous tiny seeds.

LEAVES: Several basal, roughly oval, somewhat leathery, scalloped, evergreen leaves, 1 to 2.5 cm long. Leaf stalks half as long, to nearly equal in length to leaf. Stem leaf single, tiny, curved, bract-like.

GROWTH HABIT: Delicate, **evergreen,** nearly stemless perennial, 3 to 15 cm tall from creeping rootstock.

The common and species name originate from the solitary flower and the tendency of the leaves to remain green throughout the winter. *Moneses* is from the Greek *monos* (single) and *hesis* (delight). ✐ The Haida made a weak tea from one-flowered wintergreen to treat diarrhea, cancer and smallpox, and also to bring good luck. ✐ This plant is often included by taxonomists in the genus *Pyrola*; however, it differs from our *Pyrola* species in that it has only a single flower per plant. Both *Pyrola* and *Moneses* are considered by some taxonomists to belong in the wintergreen family (Pyrolaceae). There is only this *Moneses* species in Alberta and Canada, ranging from Alaska and the Yukon to the maritimes and south to California and New England. This species is also found in Eurasia.

Indian-pipe, ghost plant
Monotropa uniflora L.
ASPEN PARKLAND, BOREAL FOREST

HABITAT AND RANGE: Shaded, moist poplar woods on rich soil. Uncommon in Alberta.

FLOWERS: Nodding, **solitary, 14 to 20 mm long**. Petals usually 5, oblong, broadened above, sac-like at base, **turning black with age**. Stamens 10 to 12, brownish yellow; anthers have 2 conspicuous slits. Stigma large, 5-lobed, yellowish. July to August.

FRUIT: Brown, nearly round capsule, about 6 mm long, with many seeds.

LEAVES: Thick, **short (to 1 cm long or less), whitish scales that turn black-tipped with age**.

GROWTH HABIT: **White or occasionally pinkish (turning brown to black on drying), waxy plant** to 25 cm tall. Grows in clumps or solitary from the dense root system. This plant contains no chlorophyll and is *saprophytic*, meaning it obtains its nutrients from dead and decaying plant or animal matter.

Indian-pipe   (JH)

The name Indian-pipe is derived from the pipe-like appearance of the nodding flowers on a thick, nearly leafless stem. *Monotropa* is from *monos* (one) and *tropos* (direction), because the flowers are turned to one side. *Uniflora* means "one flower."
 ◿ A clear fluid from the stems was used to treat sore eyes and inflamed eyelids.
 ◿ There are about 3 species of *Monotropa* in the world, occurring in North America and Asia. They are considered to be in the Indian-pipe family (Monotropaceae) by some taxonomists. Another closely related plant is found (rarely) in Alberta: fringed pinesap (*Hypopitys monotropa*; *Monotropa hypopitys* in Moss 1983) is yellow, pink or reddish, has more than a single flower per flower stalk, and the flowers are less than 14 mm long. The Blackfoot used fringed pinesap to treat wounds.

fringed pinesap   (CWE)

one-sided wintergreen

Orthilia secunda (L.) House

<small>Aspen Parkland, Boreal Forest, Montane, Subalpine, Alpine</small>

one-sided wintergreen (BA)

HABITAT AND RANGE: Moist, mossy, usually coniferous, but sometimes deciduous or mixed woods. Widespread in the Rocky Mountains and in the northern two-thirds of the province.

FLOWERS: 6 to 20, **bell-shaped, in 1-sided**, sometimes curved, clusters on short stalks, each stalk 3 to 8 mm long, with **leaf-like bract at base. Petals greenish white**, overlapping, 4 to 5 mm long. Stigmas protruding, on **straight styles**, each style 3 to 6 mm long. Flower stem straightens as fruit matures. June to August.

FRUIT: Rounded capsule, about 5 mm across, with many sutures. Contains numerous tiny, orange-coloured seeds.

LEAVES: Alternate. Stem leaves few, tiny, scale-like. Basal leaves rounded to pointed, to 6 cm long. **Shiny green above and below, oblong, with tiny teeth at vein tips.** Evergreen.

GROWTH HABIT: **Creeping**, reddish-stemmed perennial up to 20 cm tall from rhizomes. Often forms dense clumps.

The origin of *Orthilia* is unknown; however, *orth* is from the Greek for "straight," so it may refer to the straight style. *Secunda* means "to one side," in reference to the flower cluster. ✿ One-sided wintergreen is included with the other wintergreens (*Pyrola* genus, Pyrolaceae) by some taxonomists; recent texts, however, tend to split the groups, with *Orthilia* having a 1-sided inflorescence of bell-shaped, somewhat closed flowers and *Pyrola* lacking a 1-sided inflorescence and bell-shaped flowers. This is the only species in the genus and it is found mainly in the Rocky Mountains of North America and in Eurasia.

red heather, purple heather, purple mountain-heather
Phyllodoce empetriformis (Sw.) D. Don
SUBALPINE, ALPINE

HABITAT AND RANGE: Alpine and subalpine meadows and glades in coniferous woods in the Rocky Mountains.

FLOWERS: Clustered at the top of the stem. **Erect to nodding, deep-pink to reddish purple, bell-shaped flowers, 5 to 8 mm long, on slender, reddish, glandular-hairy flower stalks.** Sepals lacking glands, joined to form 5-lobed, reddish cup. Pleasant-scented. June to August.

FRUIT: Small, round, glandular capsule, about 2 mm long, with many tiny seeds.

LEAVES: Stiff, dark green, **narrow and almost needle-like, 5 to 12 mm long**. Persistent, blunt-tipped, broadly grooved beneath and narrowly grooved above.

red heather (LK)

GROWTH HABIT: **Dwarf (to 30 cm tall), evergreen, mat-forming shrub.**

Heath is from the Anglo-Saxon *haeth*, meaning "wasteland." Originally, heather meant a plant that grew on a heath. *Phyllodoce* was a sea-nymph in early Greek mythology and *empetriformis* means the leaves resemble crowberry (*Empetrum nigrum*). ✎ There are 7 species of *Phyllodoce*, in North America and Eurasia, of which 2 occur in Alberta. Yellow heather (*P. glanduliflora*) has yellow-green flowers, glandular-hairy sepals and shorter, broader leaves. The 2 species interbreed to produce pink heather (*P. x intermedia*), a plant intermediate in characteristics, with a whitish to pink flower. The true Scottish heathers belong to the *Calluna* and *Erica* genera. ✎ Red and purple heather have less closely appressed leaves than mountain-heathers (*Cassiope* species), and the mountain-heathers have white flowers. Red heather leaves are similar to those of crowberry (*Empetrum nigrum*, page 129), but crowberry has leaves in whorls, with a narrow groove beneath and none above.

yellow heather (CWE)

pink heather (CWE)

pine-drops, woodland pine-drops
Pterospora andromedea Nutt.
MONTANE

pine-drops   (CWA)

HABITAT AND RANGE: In deep humus of coniferous and mixed woods. Found only in the Waterton Lakes-Crowsnest Pass area and the Cypress Hills. Rare in Alberta.

FLOWERS: Many, nodding on stalks **in long cluster**. Flowers **cream-coloured, each 5 to 8 mm long, urn-shaped**, with 5 small spreading lobes. Calyx 5-lobed, glandular-hairy. Stamens 10, with 2 awns per stamen. July.

FRUIT: Yellow to pink or brown, round, indented, capsule, 8 to 12 mm broad, with numerous, winged seeds.

LEAVES: Mostly near the stem base. Brownish, scale-like, lance-shaped, thick, 1 to 3.5 cm long.

GROWTH HABIT: **Purple or reddish brown** *saprophyte* (a plant that obtains its nutrients from decaying plant or animal matter), up to 1 m tall or more, from enlarged bulbous base. **Very sticky throughout from glandular hairs.**

The name pine-drops may be derived from pine woods, a common habitat of this plant. *Pterospora* is from the Greek *pteron* (wing) and *sporos* (seed), because the seeds have a broad, winged appendage at 1 end. *Andromedea* refers to Andromeda of Greek legend, who was chained to a rock in the sea as a sacrifice to a sea-monster and rescued by Perseus, son of Jupiter. ✐ The Flathead of Montana boiled this plant with blue clematis to make a shampoo. The Cheyenne mixed the ground-up stem and berries in boiling water. It was called "nosebleed medicine" and was also drunk for bleeding of the lungs. ✐ There is only this species of *Pterospora* in North America.

common pink wintergreen
Pyrola asarifolia Michx.

PRAIRIE, ASPEN PARKLAND, BOREAL FOREST, MONTANE, SUBALPINE, ALPINE

HABITAT AND RANGE: Moist to dry coniferous and mixed forests, riverine forest in prairie. Very common.

FLOWERS: Several in a long cluster, each flower on a short stalk. **Petals 5, pinkish white, waxy, up to 7 mm long. Style long, curved, attached to the prominent ovary.** Sepals 5, joined at bases. Stamens 10. June to August.

FRUIT: Dry, round, brownish, valved capsule, about 5 mm wide, with many small seeds.

LEAVES: **In basal rosette. Leathery, dark green, shiny, rounded at tip,** up to 7 cm long. Edges wavy, with **tiny teeth where veins meet leaf margin. Leaf stalks are usually as long as leaf blade or longer.** Often 1 or 2 small, scaly leaves below inflorescence.

GROWTH HABIT: Erect perennial, up to 20 cm or more, from long, trailing rootstock.

common pink wintergreen (BA)

The genus name *Pyrola* is derived from the resemblance of the leaves of some species to those of the pear tree (*Pyrus*). *Asarifolia* means "leaves similar to those of wild ginger" (*Asarum*). The leaves survive the winter (but are replaced the following growing season), hence the name wintergreen. ✍ Common pink wintergreen, also known as liverleaf wintergreen or rheumatismweed, was used medicinally by some native peoples to treat rheumatism. ✍ This plant should not be transplanted because its roots require a specific fungus. ✍ Our Alberta wintergreens do not produce oil of wintergreen; it is derived from false wintergreen (*Gaultheria procumbens*), found in northeastern North America. ✍ There are 15 species of *Pyrola*, mainly in North America and Eurasia. There are 7 species in Alberta, *P. asarifolia* being the most common. Greenish-flowered wintergreen (*P. chlorantha*) has greenish white flowers and nearly round leaves; it occupies many of the same habitats as common pink wintergreen.

greenish-flowered wintergreen (LA)

common blueberry, velvet-leaf blueberry, Canada blueberry, sour-top blueberry

Vaccinium myrtilloides Michx.

BOREAL FOREST

common blueberry (BA)

HABITAT AND RANGE: Dry muskegs, shaded pine and mixed woods, wooded rocky areas, often on acidic soil or sandy ground. Widespread in the boreal forest from Newfoundland to British Columbia.

FLOWERS: Bell-shaped, in short clusters. **Greenish white, tinged with pink**, 4 mm long. Sepals joined, with 5 lobes. June to July.

FRUIT: **Light-blue berries with a whitish film**, 4 to 7 mm in diameter. Edible and tasty.

LEAVES: Alternate, **oval, thin, softly hairy (especially underneath)**, up to 40 mm long. Tapered at both ends, short-stalked.

GROWTH HABIT: Low, deciduous, much-branched shrub up to 40 cm tall. Twigs hairy, stems often shredding. Grows in dense clumps.

Vaccinium is of Latin origin, perhaps for a shrub grazed by cows, as *vacca* means "cow." *Myrtilloides* is Latin for "like those of the myrtle plant," describing the leaf characteristics. ✍ Blueberries can be eaten fresh or made into pies, syrups, jams and jellies. They were dried, mashed into cakes and made into pemmican by native peoples and European settlers. The berries are also a food source for bears, grouse, songbirds, deer, moose and caribou. The leaves and fruits can be made into a tea that has diuretic effects and is also used as a remedy for diarrhea. The dried berries are supposed to make better tea than the leaves. Blueberry leaf tea is also said to be a blood tonic. The berries are also reputed to decrease vomiting and cure coughs, respiratory disease and ulcers. Mashed berries can be used to make a purple dye. ✍ There are 150 species of *Vaccinium*, primarily in cold and mountainous areas of all continents except Australia. 8 species, all low shrubs, occur in Alberta. Low or dwarf bilberry (*V. myrtillus*) has smooth to sparsely hairy leaves, 10 to 30 mm long, a dark-red to bluish berry and greenish, angled, immature branches. It occurs in montane to alpine habitats in the mountains. Low bilberry may be confused with grouseberry (*V. scoparium*); however, the latter has smaller leaves (8 to 15 mm), a branchy growth habit and bright red berries. Bog cranberry (*V. vitis-idaea*) is illustrated on page 175.

low bilberry (BA)

small bog cranberry

Vaccinium oxycoccos L.
(*Oxycoccus microcarpus* Turcz. in Moss 1983)
BOREAL FOREST, SUBALPINE, ALPINE

HABITAT AND RANGE: **In wet sphagnum moss** in northern and mountain bogs.

FLOWERS: 1 to 3, nodding, terminal
flowers per plant on slender, reddish
stalks with 2 reddish scales near the
middle. **Flowers deeply 4-lobed,
5 to 7 mm long, pinkish. Petals
slender, curved backward.** Stamens
8, protruding, bright yellow June to
July.

FRUIT: Round berry, **reddish
(sometimes with darker spots),
5 to 10 mm in diameter. Looks
oversize on delicate stem.** Edible.

LEAVES: Alternate, thick, leathery, 2 to
8 mm long; widely spaced on the

small bog cranberry   (CWE)

stem. **Dark green above, whitish-spotted and lighter underneath; evergreen. Narrow
(1.5 to 2 mm wide),** oblong, pointed at the tip, with the margins curled under.

GROWTH HABIT: **Trailing, delicate,** somewhat woody plant with slender, flexible, white-hairy
stems.

Cranberry comes from the old German *Kranbere* or *Craneberry*, and was applied
to this plant because the long stamens resemble a crane's bill. The genus name
is the Latin name for blueberry, and the species name is from the Greek *oxys* (acid,
sharp or bitter) and *kokkos* (round berry). ✎ The berries are rather sour but high in
Vitamin C. They can be frozen, dried or stored covered in the fridge, and were eaten
raw, dried or boiled with meat by British Columbia natives. A related eastern species
is cultivated to produce the familiar cranberries used at Thanksgiving and Christmas. Cranberries are also a favourite food of bears and grouse. ✎ The leaves, which
are diuretic, are said to be useful in treating kidney disorders. ✎ Another plant known
as bog cranberry in Alberta (*Vaccinium vitis-idaea*) is also a dwarf shrub but is much
more robust, with larger (6 to 15 mm long), leathery, rounded leaves and an urn-
shaped flower.

small bog cranberry   (JH)

bog cranberry   (JH)

The primrose family, chiefly comprised of annual or perennial herbs, mainly occupies north temperate and arctic zones. Flowers are regular, with the petals joined together in a wheel, bell or funnel shape. The flower parts are usually in 5s around a single style and typically club-shaped stigma. The simple, mostly entire leaves are often opposite but may be alternate, whorled or basal. The number of stamens is the same as the number of corolla-lobes, and the stamens are usually inserted on the corolla-tube. The fruits are generally capsules. Cultivated varieties of primroses and shooting stars, particularly well suited to rock gardens, are available in Alberta. *(See key for this family beginning page 311.)*

sweet-flowered androsace, rock jasmine, sweet-flowered fairy candelabra

Androsace chamaejasme Wulfen

MONTANE, SUBALPINE, ALPINE

HABITAT AND RANGE: Open slopes, gravelly and rocky banks, screes, open woods, disturbed areas; often on sandy soils. Mainly in the mountains.

FLOWERS: Terminal cluster of 2 to 8 pleasantly scented flowers on short stalks. Delicate, **white to cream-coloured, with yellow, orange or pinkish centre**, 5 to 10 mm across. Calyx 5-lobed. May to August.

FRUIT: Small capsule, about 4 mm long. Seeds few, reddish brown, glandular, about 2 mm long.

LEAVES: In a dense **basal rosette**. Narrow, hairy (especially on the margin), lance-shaped, 4 to 10 mm long.

GROWTH HABIT: Small (2 to 10 cm tall), attractive, **tufted perennial** that may form mats from creeping stems. Leafless stem has long, white hairs.

sweet-flowered androsace   (CWA)

The genus name is from *androsakes*, the Greek name for a marine plant, while *chamaejasme* is derived from the Greek *chamae* (ground) and *jasme* (possibly jasmine). ✒ The hairiness and reduced size of this delicate plant are typical adaptations to the cold, dry alpine environment. Bright light and low temperatures lower green chlorophyll pigments and allow anthocyanin pigments to build up in leaves and young stems, producing a reddish colour in many alpine plants, especially just after snowmelt and at the end of the growing season. These anthocyanins filter the strong, damaging ultraviolet rays of the sun. ✒ There are approximately 100 species of *Androsace* in the world, mainly in north temperate and arctic areas; 3 of these occur in Alberta. Northern fairy candelabra or northern pygmy flower (*A. septentrionalis*) and western fairy candelabra (*A. occidentalis*) are annuals found on dry soil. They have tiny white or pinkish flowers in an umbrella-like inflorescence. Western fairy candelabra is much shorter (2 to 5 cm tall) than northern pygmy flower (5 to 25 cm tall) and has elliptic to oval, rather than narrowly lance-shaped, bracts below the flower cluster.

northern fairy candelabra   (LK)

saline shooting star, western shooting star

Dodecatheon pulchellum (Raf.) Merr.

PRAIRIE, ASPEN PARKLAND, BOREAL FOREST, MONTANE, SUBALPINE, ALPINE

saline shooting star (JH)

HABITAT AND RANGE: Open moist grassland, mountain meadows and banks, wet, often saline areas, lakeshores, moist woods. Widespread in the southern half of the province.

FLOWERS: Corolla to about 20 mm long. Petals 5, dark purple to whitish, united at base in a **purple-ringed, yellowish collar. Petal lobes curved backwards** to reveal the **yellow to purplish stamens,** which are united into a **yellow to orange, smooth or vertically wrinkled tube.** May to September.

FRUIT: Oval or cylindric, green to reddish brown capsule up to 15 mm long with persistent style. **Capsule with pointed teeth at tip.** Numerous seeds, 2 to 3 mm long.

LEAVES: **In a basal rosette.** Simple, gray-green, somewhat fleshy, 4 to 15 cm long (including leaf stalk). Smooth or slightly glandular-hairy, oval to narrowly lance-shaped, rounded at tip and tapering to a flattened leaf stalk.

GROWTH HABIT: Showy, smooth to glandular-hairy perennial herb, 10 to 50 cm tall. Flower nodding initially but becoming erect in fruit. Often grows in dense colonies.

The reflexed flower structure (similar to that of the related ornamental cyclamen) suggests a shooting star, hence the common name. *Dodecatheon* is taken from the Greek *dodeka* (twelve) and *theos* (god). This plant either was thought to be protected by Greek gods or the cluster of flowers suggested a grouping of gods. *Pulchellum* is from the Latin for "beautiful." ◢ The Okanagan peoples mashed the flowers to make a pink dye for their arrows. ◢ There are 13 species of *Dodecatheon*, all in North America, including 2 in Alberta. Mountain shooting star (*D. conjugens*) often has glandular-hairy leaves; the tube-like base for the anthers is horizontally wrinkled as opposed to smooth or vertically wrinkled, and the capsule teeth are squared off, not pointed at the tip. White forms sometimes occur.

(a)   *(b)*

capsules of (a) saline shooting star and (b) mountain shooting star

white form of saline shooting star (CB)

sea milkwort
Glaux maritima L.
<small>PRAIRIE, ASPEN PARKLAND, BOREAL FOREST</small>

HABITAT AND RANGE: Edges of saline marshes, lakeshores, meadows; in muddy to sandy soil. Throughout the province except in the mountains.

FLOWERS: No petals. **Sepals tiny, petal-like, white to pinkish, cup-shaped, 5-lobed, 3 to 4 mm long.** Stamens 5. May to July.

FRUIT: Small, round capsule, 2 to 3 mm long, 5-valved at top, with attached, persistent style. Seeds 2 to 5.

LEAVES: **Opposite, light green, fleshy, stalkless.** Oval to narrowly oblong, 3 to 12 mm long. Several brownish scales near the base of the plant.

GROWTH HABIT: Erect, **leafy-stemmed**, short (to about 15 cm tall) succulent, much-branched perennial from creeping rootstock. Lower stem has prominent horizontal ridges.

sea milkwort   (CWE)

G*laux* is from the Greek *glaukos* (bluish green) and *maritima* (of the sea), referring to the plant's coastal tideland habitat. ✎ Some coastal tribes ate the rootstocks of a subspecies of this plant to induce sleepiness. Eating too many, however, caused sickness. ✎ This is the only species in this genus. It is found from the arctic through temperate North America and in Eurasia.

fringed loosestrife
Lysimachia ciliata L.
PRAIRIE, ASPEN PARKLAND, MONTANE

fringed loosestrife (BA)

HABITAT AND RANGE: Aspen woods, damp meadows, thickets, banks. Widespread in the southern half of the province on rich, organic soils.

FLOWERS: **On long stalks from upper leaf axils. Petals 5, yellow, veiny**, about 12 mm long, united, with fringed edges; sometimes with an abruptly pointed tip. Functional stamens 5, sometimes interspersed with additional sterile stamens. June to August.

FRUIT: Oval, valved capsule, about 6 mm long, with many 3-angled seeds.

LEAVES: Opposite, **oval to broadly lance-shaped, rounded at base**, tapered to a pointed tip. Leaf blade up to 10 cm long and **3 to 5 cm wide**, smooth except for tough, hairy margins. Prominently veined, bright green, lighter underneath; with **hairy-margined leaf stalks, 5 to 20 mm long.**

GROWTH HABIT: Leafy perennial, up to 1 m tall from creeping rootstock.

The common name loosestrife is derived from the scientific name. The genus name comes from the Greek *lysis* (to release) and *mache* (strife). One story of the origin of the name explains that King Lysimachos of Thrace (in the Balkan peninsula) pacified an angry bull using loosestrife. *Ciliata* refers to the fringe of hairs on the leaf stalks or the fringed petals. ❧ The scent of loosestrife is said to keep snakes away. ❧ There are 100 species of *Lysimachia* worldwide, mainly in the north temperate zone; 3 of these occur in Alberta. Tufted loosestrife (*L. thyrsiflora*) has flowers in dense, bottle-brush-like clusters in the leaf axils and glandular-dotted leaves that are tapered to the base. Provincially rare lance-leaved loosestrife (*L. lanceolata*) has narrow (to 2 cm wide), gradually tapered leaves with leaf stalks that sometimes have long marginal hairs, but only on the lower half of the leaf stalks.

tufted loosestrife (DJ)

mealy primrose
Primula incana M.E. Jones
PRAIRIE, ASPEN PARKLAND, BOREAL FOREST

HABITAT AND RANGE: In moist, saline meadows, open moist slopes, slough margins, stream and river banks, mud flats, calcareous springs. Mostly known from the central part of the province.

FLOWERS: Borne in a cluster at the top of a leafless stem. **Pale purple with yellow centre**, 6 to 11 mm across. Petals 5, **deeply notched**. Calyx tubular, 5-lobed, **mealy, striped**. Stamens 5. Flower cluster surrounded at base by flat, narrow, lance-shaped, green bracts, 5 to 10 mm long.

FRUIT: Short, valved capsule, 2.5 to 5 mm in diameter, often covered by dry sepals. Seeds numerous, angular, roughened.

LEAVES: Basal, simple, oval, blunt-tipped, 2 to 10 cm long. Green above; **whitish to yellowish and mealy underneath**. Leaves broadest at tip, shallowly toothed, **veiny**.

mealy primrose (CWA)

GROWTH HABIT: Low (40 cm tall) perennial with basal rosette of leaves.

The common name describes the cream-coloured, mealy scales on the leaf undersides. *Primula* is from the Latin *primus* (first), because of the early flowering of many of the species, while *incana* is Latin for "pale gray or hoary." ✒ There are 200 *Primula* species in the world, mainly in boreal and mountainous areas; 4 species occur in Alberta. Greenland primrose (*P. egaliksensis*) has entire or wavy-margined leaves that are not mealy, and is known to occur only in the northern Rockies. Dwarf Canadian or Mistassini primrose (*P. mistassinica*) is a shorter plant (rarely more than 12 cm tall) that is not mealy (or is only slightly so) and frequently has toothed leaves. Erect primrose (*P. stricta*) has awl-shaped, rather than flat, bracts at the base of the flower cluster, and its leaves are less toothed and less mealy than mealy primrose; it occurs on alpine slopes. Both the latter species occur sparsely in the northern and north-central Rocky Mountains and in extreme northeastern Alberta. Greenland primrose and erect primrose are classified as provincially rare.

dwarf Canadian primrose (CWE)

prairie gentian, oblong-leaved gentian, large gentian
Gentiana affinis Griseb.
PRAIRIE, ASPEN PARKLAND, MONTANE

prairie gentian   (OD)

HABITAT AND RANGE: Moist prairie, open woods, slough margins, wet meadows, river banks; often on sandy or saline soils. Widespread from the Red Deer River south to the Montana border, from prairie to low-elevation mountain locations.

FLOWERS: 1 or more per plant, terminal and from upper leaf axils. **Corolla 20 to 30 mm long, dark blue or purplish, funnel-shaped, often marked with green.** Calyx greenish to blue-tinged, with unequal lobes. Stamens attached to middle of corolla. July to September.

FRUIT: Oblong, brownish, usually 2-valved capsule, with flattened, dark, finely veined seeds.

LEAVES: **Opposite, simple, up to 4 cm long. Oblong or lance-shaped**, pointed to somewhat rounded at tip. Lower leaves reduced in size and somewhat sheathing.

GROWTH HABIT: Tufted, smooth, leafy perennial up to 30 cm tall from thick, fleshy roots. Often forms small colonies.

Gentiana is named for Gentius, a king of Ilyria (a coastal region of the Adriatic Sea) who recognized the medicinal properties of this plant, curing a fever that was affecting his army. *Affinis* means "related," but its derivation is unknown. ◢ European gentian species were used as a gastric stimulant, and American species have been used to treat backache. Many North American natives use gentians in tonics. ◢ There are 300 species of *Gentiana* in the world, mainly in temperate and arctic regions. There are 4 other species in Alberta, mainly subalpine to alpine. The dwarf moss gentian (*G. prostrata*) has a sprawling growth form, azure flowers and tiny leaves (3 to 5 mm) with broad, white margins. Mountain gentian (*G. calycosa*) is similar to prairie gentian but has a larger, solitary flower (30 to 40 cm long) and broader, round-tipped leaves; in Alberta it is found only in subalpine to alpine habitats of Waterton Lakes National Park. Provincially rare alpine gentian (*G. glauca*), another subalpine to alpine species, has a shorter (12 to 18 mm), greenish blue flower and occurs in the northern Rockies. Marsh gentian (*G. aquatica*), also rare, occurs in marshes and has white-margined leaves less than 6 mm long, with small (5 to 8 mm), solitary, purplish green flowers.

mountain gentian   (CWE)

felwort, northern gentian

Gentianella amarella (L.) Börner ssp. *acuta* (Michx.) Gillett.

ASPEN PARKLAND, BOREAL FOREST, MONTANE, SUBALPINE

HABITAT AND RANGE: Moist places in meadows, moist woods, ditches, along stream banks. The most widespread of all Alberta gentians, found throughout the province except on the prairies.

FLOWERS: 10 to 20 mm long, **pale pinkish or purplish to greenish yellow, solitary or in clusters in the upper leaf axils. Corolla-tube slender and divided into 4 or 5 spreading lobes that are entire or have few teeth. Inner surface of lobes fringed with hairs.** Calyx 4 to 5-cleft nearly to base, with narrow, sharply pointed, unequal lobes. Stamens 5, attached to lower part of corolla tube. June to September.

FRUIT: Capsule to 12 mm long, with round, yellow to brown seeds.

LEAVES: Oval to narrowly lance-shaped opposite leaves. Basal leaves sometimes with marginal hairs. Lower leaves blunt at tip, upper pointed.

GROWTH HABIT: Single-stemmed or branched annual or biennial, 15 to 40 cm tall. Stem slightly ridged. Often occurs in large colonies.

felwort (BA)

The origin of the word gentian is explained on page 182. *Amarella* is from the Latin *amarus* (bitter), because of the bitter alkaloids in the plant's juices, and *ella* means "the diminutive of." *Acuta* means "sharp-pointed," in reference to the leaves. ✿ *Gentianella* is considered by some taxonomists to be part of genus *Gentiana*; however, they differ in that there are no folds between the corolla lobes of *Gentianella,* while there are folds between the lobes of *Gentiana*; and the lobes are 5 to 9-veined in *Gentianella*, 3-veined in *Gentiana*. ✿ There are 3 other species of *Gentianella* in Alberta. The others have longer flowers (more than 2 cm) or lack fringed hairs on the corolla. ✿ Another less common member of the gentian family, marsh felwort (*Lomatogonium rotatum*), is similar to felwort but has a wheel-shaped, rather than tubular, corolla and has its stamens inserted at the base of the corolla, rather than attached to the corolla-tube.

corolla of prairie gentian

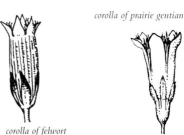

corolla of felwort

marsh felwort (DJ)

bog-bean, buck-bean

Menyanthes trifoliata L.

<small>ASPEN PARKLAND, BOREAL FOREST, MONTANE</small>

bog-bean (CWE)

HABITAT AND RANGE: Wet bogs, marshes, ditches, lake and pond margins, primarily in the boreal forest. Found in the northern two-thirds of the province and the Waterton Lakes area.

FLOWERS: In crowded clusters at the end of long, leafless stems. Corolla 10 to 15 mm long, funnel-shaped and divided into 5 lobes, white (pink-tinged on the outside), with a **dense inner fringe of soft, white, curly hairs**. Stamens 5, red or purple-tipped, attached to the corolla-tube. Calyx 5 to 6-lobed, half as long as the corolla. June.

FRUIT: Brownish, oval, thick-walled capsules to 10 mm long, with a persistent style and with numerous shiny, smooth, yellowish brown seeds, each about 2 mm long.

LEAVES: Alternate, **thick**, shiny, entire to wavy, oval leaves, 3 to 10 cm long. Mostly from near the base, **3-parted on long, clasping leaf-stalks**.

GROWTH HABIT: **Aquatic to semi-aquatic** perennial, 10 to 30 cm tall from thick, scaly, creeping rootstocks. Stems trailing with flower branches erect.

The names bog-bean and buck-bean may be derived from the similarity of the leaves to those of broad beans. *Menyanthes* is from the Greek *men* (month) and *anthos* (flower), either because the bloom lasts about one month or because the plant was used to induce menstruation. *Trifoliata* refers to the 3-parted leaves. ⚘ Northern peoples have used the rhizomes as a famine food and the leaves to produce a purging tonic. Bog-bean tea has been drunk to treat migraines, fevers, indigestion and parasites and has been applied externally to ulcers. ⚘ There is only this species of *Menyanthes* in the world.

bog-bean (CB)

spreading dogbane, flytrap dogbane

Apocynum androsaemifolium L.

PRAIRIE, ASPEN PARKLAND, BOREAL FOREST, MONTANE

HABITAT AND RANGE: Sandy areas on slopes, coulee gullies, dry wooded areas, hillsides, roadsides and riverine prairie. Widespread.

FLOWERS: Fragrant, in clusters at the ends of the branches and in leaf axils. 5 **pinkish white (often with darker-pink stripes) petals**, 6 to 9 mm long, joined at the base and **often flared or curved backwards to produce a bell shape.** Stamens 5. Stigma yellow, grooved. **Calyx usually less than half as long as the corolla;** composed of reddish, rounded, lobed sepals, 2 mm long. June to August.

FRUIT: **Drooping,** narrow, round, **reddish, paired, many-seeded pods,** 2 to 12 cm long. **Seeds have tufts of long, silky hairs.**

LEAVES: Opposite, oval to oblong, 2 to 7.5 cm long, pointed and reddish at the tip, finely hairy beneath. Bright green, lighter underneath, turning yellow or red in the fall. Short-stalked. Leaves often **noticeably droopy in hot weather.**

spreading dogbane (JH)

GROWTH HABIT: Leafy, spreading perennial shrub-like herb up to 150 cm tall, with smooth, **forked, reddish branches**. Stems contain an acrid, milky juice.

Flies and small moths searching for nectar may become trapped in the V-shaped nectaries, hence the name flytrap dogbane. The genus name is taken from the Greek *apo* (against) and *kyon* (dog) and is echoed in the common name dogbane. Perhaps the plant's poisonous pods were used to kill unwanted dogs! *Androsaemifolium* means "leaves like the androsaemum plant." ✒ All dogbanes are **poisonous** and have caused death in livestock, although the taste of the resins and glycosides generally repels grazing animals. Spreading dogbane contains a chemical related to digitalis and was used in the United States at one time as a digitalis substitute; however, harmful side effects were noticed. The green seeds were boiled to make a heart and kidney medicine by some native tribes. The roots have laxative properties and were believed to reduce fever, prevent hair loss and induce vomiting by the Blackfoot. The roots were also boiled in water and the resulting liquid drunk as a contraceptive. ✒ The Blackfoot wove cord made from dogbane stems into fishing lines and nets. The fibres keep for years and do not shrink in water. ✒ There are 5 species of *Apocynum* in North America, including 3 in Alberta. Indian hemp (*A. cannabinum*) has erect or spreading (not drooping), stalked leaves on the main stem and greenish white flowers. Ranges of the 2 species overlap, and they are capable of interbreeding to produce an intermediate species called western dogbane (*A. medium*) that has a pointed, lobed calyx, no more than half as long as the corolla.

Indian hemp (CWA)

showy milkweed

Asclepias speciosa Torr.

PRAIRIE, ASPEN PARKLAND

showy milkweed   (CWA)

HABITAT AND RANGE: Moist grassland, roadsides, thickets, and along creeks and rivers; often growing in sandy or loamy soil. From the Red Deer River south to the Montana border.

FLOWERS: Numerous, strong-smelling, in large, umbrella-shaped clusters. Flowers 8 to 10 mm long, **purple or pink, with incurved "horns" at the top.** Corolla 5-parted, with reddish and reflexed lobes. **Sepals green with reddish tinge.** Stamens 5, united at base. Flower stalks covered with white hairs. June to July.

FRUIT: Large (7 to 11 cm long), **soft, narrowly oval pod with tiny projections**; on recurved stalk. Seeds numerous, broad, wrinkled, about 8 mm long, with **tuft of long, white hairs**.

LEAVES: Opposite, short-stalked. **Oblong or oval**, rounded or heart-shaped at the base, 10 to 20 cm long. Thick and prominently veined with unbranched veins. Rounded leaf tip sometimes has a sharp spine.

GROWTH HABIT: Softly hairy to smooth perennial growing to more than 1 m tall from thick, creeping rootstocks. Often grows in clumps.

The genus name honours Asklepios, Greek god of medicine, and suggests the plant's medicinal properties. *Speciosa* means "showy" in Latin. The milky latex that oozes from cut stems gives the plant its common name. This latex, after it is allowed to harden, may be chewed as gum and has been used as an emergency substitute for rubber. ⌀ Many species of milkweed are **poisonous** if eaten in large amounts. Showy milkweed contains alkaloids and resins, especially in the stems and leaves, and can poison livestock, although they tend to avoid it. Monarch butterfly larvae feed on milkweed and accumulate toxic glucosides in their bodies as a defence mechanism. ⌀ The young leaves, young shoots and immature seedpods are said to be edible when cooked, particularly if the water is changed a number of times during

showy milkweed   (BA)

low milkweed (CWE)

cooking. The Crow people of Montana boiled and ate the flowers and immature seeds. The flowers contain a chemical that can act as a meat tenderizer. ❧ The plant has been used medicinally by North American natives to treat warts and ringworm and to heal cuts and infections. The Cheyenne made an eye medicine from boiled showy milkweed, while the Flathead made tea from the boiled roots to treat stomach aches. Alberta's Blood tribe used an extract from the plant as a poultice on swellings. ❧ The fibres from mature stems were used in making twine and fishnets, and the fluffy seeds can be used as a pillow stuffing. ❧ There are 100 species of *Asclepias* in the world, mainly in Africa and the Americas. There are 2 other species of milkweed in Alberta, both rare. Low or oval-leaved milkweed (*A. ovalifolia*), found occasionally in east-central Alberta and the Peace River country, is smaller than showy milkweed and has leaves that taper at the base, greenish white flowers and a pod without projections. Green milkweed (*A. viridiflora*), occurring in extreme southeastern Alberta, has a white, greenish or yellow-green flower and leathery, wavy-margined leaves.

green milkweed (CWA)

collomia, narrow-leaved collomia
Collomia linearis Nutt.
PRAIRIE, ASPEN PARKLAND, BOREAL FOREST, MONTANE

collomia   (DJ)

HABITAT AND RANGE: Dry to moist open areas, slopes, roadsides; often on disturbed sites. Widespread throughout Alberta

FLOWERS: **In terminal, leafy-bracted clusters. Corolla pinkish (occasionally purplish or white), funnel-shaped, 10 to 15 mm long,** 5-lobed. Calyx papery, 5-lobed; lobes narrowly triangular, 1.5 to 3 mm long, often glandular-hairy. Stamens 5. June to August.

FRUIT: Capsule with short (3 mm long), brown, bumpy seeds that are sticky when wet.

LEAVES: Simple, entire, alternate. Narrowly lance-shaped, 2 to 5 cm long, roughened to short-hairy. **Leaves surrounding flower cluster have broad, paler base, abruptly tapered to long, slender tip.** Stalkless.

GROWTH HABIT: Simple or branched, leafy annual, 10 to 40 cm tall. Smooth to hairy and glandular above.

The name *Collomia* is derived from the Greek *kolla* (glue), describing the moistened seeds. *Linearis* describes the linear leaves. ✿ There are 13 species of *Collomia* in the world, native to temperate North and South America, mainly in the western United States. Only this species occurs in Alberta.

moss phlox, Hood's phlox
Phlox hoodii Richards.
<small>PRAIRIE, ASPEN PARKLAND, MONTANE</small>

HABITAT AND RANGE: Dry, exposed hillsides, eroded slopes, roadsides. Widespread in the foothills and prairies in the southern part of Alberta.

FLOWERS: Solitary (sometimes 2 or 3), terminal, up to 1 cm across. **5 whitish (occasionally pale-purple) petals, 5 mm long, united into a tube below.** Stamens 5, orange. Calyx 5-lobed, hairy, sometimes with glands. May to June.

FRUIT: Dry, oval, 3-valved wrinkly capsule, 2 to 3 mm long, with small, brownish, wrinkly seeds. Capsule enclosed by dry, hairy sepals.

LEAVES: **Awl-shaped with spiny tips, tiny (3 to 8 mm long), overlapping. Gray-green, woolly-hairy at base.**

moss phlox (CWA)

GROWTH HABIT: Prostrate, **tufted, mat-forming** perennial with leafy stems. 3 to 5 cm tall from tap root.

*P*hlox is the Greek for "flame," descriptive of some of the reddish-flowered species. *Hoodii* honours Robert Hood, a midshipman on one of Sir John Franklin's expeditions. ✿ The Blood people may have used the flowers for a dye. ✿ There are 50 to 60 species of *Phlox* in the world, native to North America and northern Asia; 2 species are found in Alberta. Blue phlox (*P. alyssifolia*) is much less common, occurring from the Oldman River region south to the Montana border. It has larger, white to pinkish flowers that become bluish on drying, and wider, hairy-margined leaves. Low whitlow-wort (*Paronychia sessiliflora*) is similar in appearance to moss phlox when not in flower, but has inconspicuous, star-shaped sepals (no petals), each 2 to 3 mm long, and conspicuous papery bracts and stipules.

blue phlox (JH)

low whitlow-wort (CWE)

showy Jacob's-ladder
Polemonium pulcherrimum Hook.
Montane, Subalpine, Alpine

showy Jacob's-ladder (CWa)

HABITAT AND RANGE: Dry, open, often rocky slopes and alpine ridges; often on gravelly soil. To high elevations in the Rocky Mountains.

FLOWERS: Attractive, **bell-shaped, pale to dark-blue flowers with yellowish bases, 5 to 15 mm long**. Calyx cup-shaped, 4 to 8 mm long, with wide, triangular lobes. **Stigma with 3 long, curly prongs at tip. Stamens 5, inserted on corolla tube.** Flower stalks long and slender, with thick, white hairs. May to August.

FRUIT: 3-valved capsule with several, brown, spindle-shaped seeds, each about 2 mm long. Seeds become sticky when wet.

LEAVES: Alternate, pinnately compound, **unpleasant-smelling**; most densely clustered from the base. **Leaflets 11 to 25, round to elliptic, nearly opposite**, often sparsely glandular-hairy (at least when young). Stem leaves more or less reduced.

GROWTH HABIT: Tufted, short (10 to 35 cm) perennial from tap root. Glandular, especially in the inflorescence.

The plant is called Jacob's-ladder because of its ladder-like leaf arrangement, resembling Jacob's ladder to heaven in the Bible story. *Polemonium* is named after Polemon, a Greek philosopher, or may be derived from the Greek *polemos* (strife), because a dispute about the discovery of this plant or its qualities triggered a war between 2 kings. *Pulcherrimum* is from the Latin *pulcher* (beautiful). ✒ There are 20 species of *Polemonium* in North America, South America and Eurasia; 3 of these occur in Alberta. Tall Jacob's-ladder (*P. caeruleum*; *P. acutiflorum* in Moss 1983) is taller (40 to 100 cm), more robust and found primarily in wetlands in the northern half of the province. Skunkweed or sky pilot (*P. viscosum*), which occurs mainly in the Waterton-Crowsnest Pass area, has a flower that appears disproportionately large in relation to the leaves and glandular-sticky, skunky-smelling, whorled leaflets.

tall Jacob's-ladder (CWe)

silky scorpionweed, mountain phacelia
Phacelia sericea (Graham) A. Gray
MONTANE, SUBALPINE, ALPINE

HABITAT AND RANGE: Gravelly roadsides, rocky meadows, rock crevices, slopes, open woods, disturbed areas. In the mountains and foothills.

FLOWERS: In dense terminal clusters to 20 cm long. Corolla tubular, with **5 dark-blue or purple lobes**, each about 3 mm long. **Stamens yellow-tipped, protruding.** Styles cleft nearly to the middle. Calyx 5-lobed. June to August.

FRUIT: Capsule, 4 to 6 mm long containing dark-brown, veiny, pitted seeds.

LEAVES: Alternate, prominently veined, **silvery soft-hairy when young**. Oval, **deeply incised**, up to 3 cm long. Reduced upwards. Lower leaves with leaf stalks, upper stalkless.

GROWTH HABIT: Tufted, leafy, sometimes reddish-stemmed perennial, 10 to 40 cm tall. **Thinly hairy to densely woolly, giving a silvery colour.**

silky scorpionweed   (OP)

*P*hacelia is from the Greek *phakelos* (bundle), referring to the dense flower cluster. *Sericea* means "silky." ✍ There are approximately 150 species of *Phacelia*, primarily in the United States and northern Mexico; 4 other species occur in Alberta, of which 2 are provincially rare. ✍ Silver-leaved scorpionweed or silverleaf phacelia (*P. hastata*) is fairly common within its southwestern Alberta range. It has entire, lance-shaped, prominently veined, grayish-hairy leaves and a white (occasionally pinkish or bluish) flower. Rare linear-leaved or thread-leaved scorpionweed (*P. linearis*) is an annual and is the only other Alberta species with mainly entire (sometimes with narrow lobes), rather than divided, leaves. It has bright-blue (rarely white) flowers and much narrower leaves than silver-leaved scorpionweed. It is confined to dry slopes and grassland in southwestern Alberta.

linear-leaved scorpionweed

silver-leaved scorpionweed   (EJ)

Sitka romanzoffia, mist maiden, cliff romanzoffia
Romanzoffia sitchensis Bong.
SUBALPINE, ALPINE

Sitka romanzoffia (JP)

HABITAT AND RANGE: Moist, rocky cliffs and ledges. Of scattered occurrence in the Rocky Mountains.

FLOWERS: Several, in loose, elongated cluster. Each flower 6 to 9 mm long. **Petals 5, united, with round lobes at tips; white to cream-coloured, with yellow bases. Stamens 5, of unequal length, inserted near the base of the corolla and alternate with the petals.** Sepals 5, brownish green, narrowly oblong, united at base. June to August.

FRUIT: Oblong, 2-valved **capsule** with many seeds.

LEAVES: **Blades kidney-shaped, 0.8 to 3 cm broad, with 3 to 7 large lobes.** Mostly basal on long, overlapping, hairy-margined, **inflated stalks** that are much longer than the blades. Stem leaves few or none.

GROWTH HABIT: Dainty, smooth, tufted perennial, 10 to 30 cm tall from **a bulbous base formed by the swollen bases of the leaf stalks.** Sometimes glandular-hairy in the inflorescence.

*R*omanzoffia honours Count Nikolai Romanzoff (1754-1826), a Russian patron of botany. *Sitchensis* is Latin for "of Sitka Sound" in southeastern Alaska, where the plant was discovered on an expedition sponsored by Romanzoff. ✍ There are 4 species of *Romanzoffia* in the world, all in western North America, but only this species occurs, rarely, in Alberta. Sitka romanzoffia can be confused with saxifrages as its growth habit is similar; however, this plant has 5 petals united to form a tube, and the fruit is a capsule. Saxifrage petals are not united at the base, and the fruit consists of 2 "pods" that open along 1 side.

This large family of annual and perennial herbs is characterized by coarsely hairy stems and leaves and often by beautiful blue flowers, frequently in tight, 1-sided clusters that uncoil as they open. The flowers have a 5-parted calyx and petals united at the base to form a tube. The 5 stamens are attached to the corolla-tube and alternate with the corolla-lobes. The 5 sepals may be distinct or united, the leaves are simple and usually alternate, and the fruit typically consists of 4 hairy to smooth nutlets. Familiar garden members of the borages include forget-me-nots and lungworts; blueweed and bluebur are commonly encountered weeds. *(See key for this family beginning page 313.)*

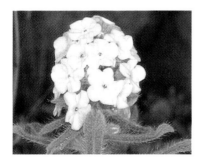

Macoun's cryptanthe
Cryptantha macounii (Eastw.) Payson
PRAIRIE

HABITAT AND RANGE: Dry grasslands, slopes; often on sandy soil. In the southern part of the province from the Oldman/South Saskatchewan River to the Montana border.

FLOWERS: In long, clustered inflorescence. **Corolla narrowly funnel-shaped, white, 6 to 8 mm broad.** May to July.

FRUIT: Nutlets 4, wrinkled above, 2.5 to 3 mm long, with a single seed per nutlet.

LEAVES: Alternate, entire, narrow, 1.5 to 5 cm long, with **short, white and longer, bristly hairs.** Basal leaves densely tufted, broadly lance-shaped. Stems leaves reduced in size.

Macoun's cryptanthe (CWA)

GROWTH HABIT: Tufted, bristly-hairy, solitary or several-stemmed perennial, 10 to 20 cm tall from thin tap root.

The name *Cryptantha* is from the Greek *kryptos* (hidden) and *anthos* (flower), as many members of this genus have flowers that never open and are thus difficult to see. The species name *macounii* commemorates John Macoun, famous for his botanical expeditions throughout the Canadian West in the late 1800s. ✍ There are 150 species of *Cryptantha* in the world, native to western North and South America; 5 other cryptanthes occur in Alberta. Uncommon Fendler's cryptanthe (*C. fendleri*) and rare small cryptanthe (*C. minima*) are annuals with corollas less than 2 mm wide. Clustered oreocarya (*C. nubigena*) has a large corolla, 7 to 11 mm long, and broader, often spoon-shaped basal leaves.

clustered oreocarya (CWA)

blueweed, viper's-bugloss, blue devil,
Echium vulgare L.

PRAIRIE, ASPEN PARKLAND, MONTANE

HABITAT AND RANGE: Roadsides, pastures, disturbed sites throughout Alberta. Often found on dry, shallow soils over limestone. This European invader is becoming a problem weed in the Crowsnest Pass area.

FLOWERS: Numerous, attractive, **hairy, in bracted clusters**. Each flower **bright blue (sometimes pinkish or white), 15 to 20 mm long, funnel-shaped with unequal lobes, upper side longer**. Calyx bristly-hairy, deeply divided into 5 lobes. Stamens unequal, 4 of the 5 protruding. Style hairy, divided at the tip. June to September.

FRUIT: Nutlets 4, pitted, ridged, attached at base.

LEAVES: Alternate, simple, bristly-hairy with prominent midvein. Basal leaves broadly lance-shaped, 6 to 25 cm long, 0.5 to 3 cm wide. Stem leaves narrowly lance-shaped, reduced upwards, becoming stalkless.

GROWTH HABIT: Erect, bristly-hairy biennial, 30 to 80 cm tall from a black tap root. **Bristles of different lengths, often with dark-coloured pustules at base. Plant forms flat rosette of leaves in first year and sends up a flower stalk in the second year.**

blueweed   (JH)

This plant was thought to be useful in curing snakebite, and the seed is shaped like the head of a viper, hence viper's-bugloss. Bugloss may come from the Greek *bous* (ox) and *glossa* (tongue), since the leaves are rough and resemble an ox's tongue. *Echium* originates from the Greek *echion*, the name for various members of the borage family; *echion* is from *echis* (viper). *Vulgare* means common. ✿ This plant is found across Canada. ✿ The bristly hairs on the stem and leaves can produce **severe skin irritation**. ✿ There are 50 species of *Echium*, in Europe, the Mediterranean, the Atlantic Islands and South Africa. Only this species now occurs in Alberta.

large-flowered stickseed, many-flowered stickseed

Hackelia floribunda (Lehm.) I.M. Johnston

PRAIRIE, ASPEN PARKLAND, MONTANE, SUBALPINE

large-flowered stickseed (JH)

HABITAT AND RANGE: Moist woods, thickets, seepage areas, avalanche slopes, meadows, stream and river banks; in the southern half of Alberta.

FLOWERS: Long, narrow inflorescence with ascending branches. **Flower pale blue to whitish, with yellow centre; 4 to 8 mm wide**, tubular, abruptly expanding into 5 flat lobes. Style much shorter than sepals. Stamens 5. June to August.

FRUIT: **Nutlets 4, more or less keeled down the middle**, attached to a pyramid-shaped base. Nutlets 3 to 5 mm long, with a row of flat, hooked prickles along the margin that are often joined at the base. A single seed per nutlet.

LEAVES: Simple, alternate, entire, hairy. Lower leaves to 18 cm long or more, narrowly lance-shaped, **broadest at the tip and tapering into leaf stalks**. Middle and upper leaves oblong to lance-shaped with a broad base, erect or ascending, stalkless.

GROWTH HABIT: Rough-hairy, robust, few-stemmed or solitary biennial or short-lived perennial, 50 to 100 cm tall from tap root.

The prickles on the nutlets cling to fur and clothing as a mechanism for seed dispersal, hence the name stickseed. *Hackelia* commemorates Czech botanist Joseph Hackel (1783-1869), and *floribunda* is Latin for "profusely flowering." ✐ This plant is sometimes grown as an ornamental. ✐ There are 30 species of *Hackelia*, widely distributed, mainly in western North America. There are 2 other *Hackelia* species in Alberta. Nodding stickseed (*H. deflexa* ssp. *americana*; *H. americana* in Moss 1983) has leaves that are pointed at both ends (not round at the base) and a smaller flower (about 2 mm wide). Jessica's or blue stickseed (*H. micrantha*; *H. jessicae* in Moss 1983) has a style about as long as the sepals and nutlets that are not keeled, with hooked prickles not restricted to the margins. *Hackelia* is sometimes included in the genus *Lappula*.

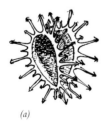

(a)

(b)

fruit of (a) large-flowered stickseed, (b) Jessica's stickseed

narrow-leaved puccoon, long-flowered stoneseed,
yellow stoneseed
Lithospermum incisum Lehm.
PRAIRIE, ASPEN PARKLAND, MONTANE

HABITAT AND RANGE: Dry hillsides, grasslands, foothills, gravelly railway rights-of-way; often on sandy soil and exposed sites. Widespread in the southern half of Alberta.

FLOWERS: **1 to 3 cm long**, occurring in clusters at the top of the plant. **Petals are bright yellow (occasionally orange)**, sweet-smelling, funnel-shaped, with **fringed or toothed lobes. Corolla-tube much longer than 5-lobed calyx.** Mid-May to August.

FRUIT: Oval, **cream to gray-coloured, shiny, somewhat pitted nutlets, 3 to 4 mm long. The nutlets resemble pointed teeth.**

narrow-leaved puccoon (CWE)

LEAVES: Numerous, alternate, gray-green, stalkless, narrowly lance-shaped, up to 6 cm long. **Rough-textured with short, stiff hairs.**

GROWTH HABIT: Coarse perennial herb, erect or branched from the base, **appressed-hairy or with short stiff hairs.** 1 to 50 cm tall from a woody tap root.

Puccoon is a native name for plants with yellow flowers, or it may come from the Algonquin term for plants used for staining and dyeing. *Lithospermum* refers to the hard, stony nutlets, from the Greek *lithos* (stone) and *sperma* (seed). *Incisum* likely derives from "incised" and may allude to the fringed, lobed flowers or the narrow leaves. ✐ The thick, reddish brown roots produce a red dye, used by the Plains peoples to colour animal skins. The Navajo chewed the roots to treat coughs and colds, and other tribes cooked them as food. ✐ There are 75 species of *Lithospermum* in the world, mainly in temperate or mountain regions; 2 occur in Alberta. Woolly gromwell (*L. ruderale*) is found in habitats similar to long-flowered stoneseed but can be distinguished by its shorter corolla (less than 10 mm long), which is not much longer than the sepals, its yellowish green, unfringed flowers and its longer nutlets (4 to 6 mm long). It is also a much more robust plant, growing in large clumps. ✐ An extract of woolly gromwell was taken by some native tribes for birth control because it contains natural estrogens. The Blackfoot burned the tops of these plants in ceremonies. They pounded the root into a flour or used it to make a purplish dye for

decorating animal skins, bows and faces. Okanagan children used nutlets of woolly gromwell as beads. Fluid from the stems was used to make poison for arrow tips by the Shuswap, who also made a tea from the roots to perk up the appetite.

woolly gromwell (CWA)

tall lungwort

Mertensia paniculata (Ait.) G. Don.

ASPEN PARKLAND, BOREAL FOREST, MONTANE, SUBALPINE

HABITAT AND RANGE: Moist woods, meadows, stream banks. Widespread except in prairie and alpine habitats.

FLOWERS: **Branched** and usually **drooping flowers** in open clusters. Corolla **pink when in bud, but blue, often with pinkish tinge**, at maturity. Corolla **tubular, abruptly enlarged near the middle**, shallowly 5-lobed at the tip, 8 to 16 mm long. Calyx hairy, deeply incised. **Flower stalks densely white-hairy.** June to July.

FRUIT: Tight cluster of 4 erect, usually wrinkled nutlets, surrounded by calyx.

tall lungwort (CWE)

LEAVES: Thin, stiff, 5 to 12 cm long, **prominently veined**, dark green, white-hairy on both sides (particularly below). **Basal leaves large, long-stalked, usually heart-shaped at base.** Stem leaves stalkless or short-stalked, rounded at base, tapered to the pointed tip.

GROWTH HABIT: Tall, usually hairy perennial with 1 to many stems, 20 to 80 cm tall from a woody rootstock.

*M*ertensia honours F.C. Mertens (1764-1831), an early German botanist. *Paniculata* likely refers to the panicled inflorescence. At one time the genus *Mertensia* was included in *Pulmonaria* (lungworts), plants with white-spotted leaves which were thought to be a useful treatment for lung diseases. ✿ Dried tall lungwort leaves can be made into tea, and fresh leaves can be added to soups and stews. ✿ There are 35 to 40 species of *Mertensia* in Eurasia and North America, 3 occurring in Alberta. Large-flowered lungwort (*M. longiflora*) and prairie or lance-leaved lungwort (*M. lanceolata*), both provincially rare and found only in the extreme southwest, are shorter (usually less than 40 cm tall) and lack prominent leaf veins. Large-flowered lungwort has a corolla-tube at least twice as long as the upper lobes, while prairie lungwort has a corolla-tube only slightly (if at all) longer than the upper lobes.

prairie lungwort (CWE)

large-flowered lungwort (BA)

alpine forget-me-not

Myosotis alpestris Schmidt ssp. *asiatica* Vestergr.

MONTANE, SUBALPINE, ALPINE

HABITAT AND RANGE: Moist meadows and slopes from low to high elevations in the foothills and Rocky Mountains.

FLOWERS: **Densely clustered**, fragrant and showy; clusters (*racemes*) elongating with age. Corolla 4 to 8 mm broad, composed of **5 united, deep-blue, occasionally whitish or pinkish, round petals on a short tube, surrounding a yellow centre**. Calyx white-hairy, 3 to 5 mm long, with 5 long lobes. June to August.

FRUIT: 4 blackish, smooth, small nutlets.

LEAVES: Alternate, simple, narrowly oblong, with **stiff, white to tan hairs**. Basal leaves up to 13 cm long. Numerous stem leaves, usually less than 6 cm long.

alpine forget-me-not (JH)

GROWTH HABIT: Erect, short-hairy perennial, 5 to 40 cm tall from a short, branched rootstock. Plant usually has dark-coloured, papery sheaths at base.

A number of legends are associated with the common name. The most famous is of a couple strolling along the Danube. The lady noticed a clump of beautiful blue flowers on the steep bank and her lover tried to pick some for her. He slipped and fell into a deep pool but managed to toss the flowers to her and call with his dying breath, "Forget me not!" (as quoted in Durant 1976). *Myosotis* is from the Greek *mus* (mouse) and *otis* (ear), as leaves of some species resemble a mouse's ear. *Alpestris* means "of the lower mountains," while *asiatica* means "of Asia." ✍ Alpine forget-me-not is the state flower of Alaska. ✍ There are 30 or 40 species of *Myosotis* in the world, widely distributed in temperate and boreal regions. There are 3 other *Myosotis* species in Alberta, all introduced and uncommon as garden escapes.

Borage Family (Boraginaceae)

western false gromwell

Onosmodium molle Michx. var. *occidentale* (Mack.) Johnston
PRAIRIE

western false gromwell   (BG)

HABITAT AND RANGE: Gravelly banks, dry open woods, slopes, thickets; in the southwestern part of the province from the Bow River south to the Oldman River.

FLOWERS: Greenish to yellowish white, in leafy, curved clusters. **Corolla tubular, silky-hairy, 12 to 20 mm long.** Corolla lobes 3 to 4 mm long, triangular, narrow, erect. Styles extend beyond the flower. Stamens 5. June to July.

FRUIT: **Nutlets shiny, creamy-white**, broadly oval, **smooth or pitted**, 3.5 to 5 mm long.

LEAVES: Upper leaves numerous, stalkless, oval to lance-shaped, 4 to 10 cm long, **prominently veined and very stiff-hairy. Lower leaves fewer, deciduous.**

GROWTH HABIT: **Rough-hairy**, branched, **grayish green**, leafy perennial, 40 to 80 cm tall from a woody root.

O*nosmodium* is from a resemblance to *Onosma*, a genus in the same family. *Molle* is Latin for "soft," probably applied to the fuzzy-hairy leaves, and *occidentale* means "western." ✿ There are 5 species of *Onosmodium*, all in North America. Only this species is found in Alberta; it is classified as provincially rare.

Mint Family (Lamiaceae or Labiatae)

The mints are annual or perennial herbs, oft[...]minty odour and usually 4-angled stems. The leaves are oppos[...]toothed and often glandular-dotted (the glands contain volatile [...] ostly irregular, often in terminal or axillary clusters. The calyx [...] aped and the corollas are mainly 2-lipped and 5-lobed. The 2 [...] re attached to the corolla-tube, and the style is divided in 2 at the top [...] ts consist of 4 small nutlets, each containing a single seed. Although the mint family is a source of many herbs (peppermint, spearmint, rosemary, basil, savory) and ornamentals (creeping thyme, bee balm and salvia), many Alberta species are weedy in moist locations. *(See key for this family beginning page 314.)*

A 2-lipped corolla and square stem are characteristics of many members of the mint family.

giant hyssop
Agastache foeniculum (Pursh) Ktze.
PRAIRIE, ASPEN PARKLAND, BOREAL FOREST

giant hyssop   (LA)

HABITAT AND RANGE: Common in thickets and along riverbanks and roadsides in the aspen parkland and prairies of the central part of the province; also in the boreal forest.

FLOWERS: **Dense, often interrupted, spike of blue-purple flowers,** each 6 to 12 mm long. Corolla tubular and 2-lipped, hairy. **Calyx cup-shaped, bluish, ribbed, white-hairy, with long teeth at the tip. Stamens 4, paired, with the upper pair longer than the lower.** Each stamen purple-tipped, protruding from the flower. July to August.

FRUIT: 4 small, beige, 1-seeded nutlets, each about 2 mm long, enclosed in a cup-like calyx.

LEAVES: Opposite, short-stalked. Oval or triangular-oval, 2 to 7 cm long, coarsely toothed and pointed at the tip. Dark green above, paler and hairy below.

GROWTH HABIT: Erect, tall (30 to 100 cm), branched perennial with creeping rootstocks. The square stems (in cross section) are typical of the mint family.

*A*gastache is from the Greek *agan* (much) and *stachys* (spike), which refers to the inflorescence type. *Foeniculum* means "scent like fennel." ☙ Montana natives used the leaves (which have a licorice scent when bruised) in tea and as a flavouring. The flowers were often collected by the Cree for medicine bundles and eaten in salads or boiled as pot herbs. The seeds were ground into meal. The leaves of giant hyssop are now occasionally made into a tea to treat coughs, colds and fevers. ☙ There is only this species of *Agastache* in Alberta; there are 20 worldwide, mainly in North America and southeastern Asia.

giant hyssop

hemp-nettle
Galeopsis tetrahit L.
ASPEN PARKLAND, BOREAL FOREST

HABITAT AND RANGE: Meadows, margins of wetlands, moist woods, pastures, roadsides, disturbed areas. Introduced from Europe. Mainly in central and northern Alberta.

FLOWERS: **Terminal in spikes and in clusters where leaves join stem.** Corolla purple to pinkish (occasionally white), from 15 to 23 mm long. **Corolla 2-lipped, lower spreading and 3-lobed; upper arching. Calyx spiny, hairy, 5-ribbed, lobed with unequal teeth.** Stamens 4, lower pair longer. July to August.

FRUIT: Composed of 4 smooth nutlets, 3 to 4 mm long, with gray-brown, oval seeds.

LEAVES: Opposite, stalked. Blade diamond-shaped to oval, coarsely toothed and hairy, 3 to 10 cm long.

GROWTH HABIT: Weedy, branched annual, 15 to 100 cm tall. **Bristly-hairy with downward-pointing, thick, white hairs. Stem square, swollen at the nodes.**

hemp-nettle   (BA)

Galeopsis is Latin for a plant with a 2-lobed corolla. *Tetrahit* refers to the 4-sided stem, from *tetra* meaning "four." ✐ Hemp-nettle is an agricultural pest because of its competitive ability. It is a prolific seed producer, and its seeds can remain dormant for many years until conditions are favourable for germination; it is also resistant to 2,4-D-based herbicides. ✐ There are 6 *Galeopsis* species native to Europe and Asia. Introduced yellow-flowered hemp-nettle (*G. speciosa*) is also found occasionally in Alberta.

western water-horehound, rough water-horehound

Lycopus asper Greene

western water-horehound (CWA)

HABITAT AND RANGE: Shores, marshes, wet meadows; sometimes in somewhat alkaline areas. Scattered throughout Alberta.

FLOWERS: In dense, stalkless clusters from the leaf axils. Corolla 4-lobed, white, 3 to 5 mm long, with short tube that is hairy in the throat. Calyx cup-shaped, with narrowly lance-shaped lobes, usually 1 to 2 mm long. Calyx lobes 1 to 2 mm long, longer than the nutlets at maturity. June to August.

FRUIT: **3-angled, light green, wedge-shaped nutlets, about 2 mm long; squared off and sometimes wavy at the tip.**

LEAVES: Opposite, **glandular-dotted,** smooth to hairy, 3 to 10 cm long. Leaves usually ascending, lance-shaped to somewhat oblong, little reduced upward. **Lower and middle leaves toothed, stalkless or nearly so.**

GROWTH HABIT: Erect, leafy perennial, 20 to 80 cm tall from enlarged rootstock. **Stem sometimes reddish, with spreading hairs on angles above or throughout.**

The origin of the common name horehound is obscure. *Lycopus* is from the Greek *lykos* (wolf) and *pous* (foot), because of a resemblance of some of the species' leaves to a wolf's foot. *Asper* is Latin for "rough." ◿ The Blackfoot used water-horehound species, mixed with other plants, to treat children's colds. Fleshy tubers of northern water-horehound (also called bugleweed) were eaten after steam-cooking by the Thompson, Shuswap and Okanagan peoples. ◿ There are 12 species of *Lycopus*, most native to northern temperate regions (1 in Australia); 2 other species occur in Alberta. Rare cut-leaved or American water-horehound (*L. americanus*), which occurs in the southern half of the province, often has stalked lower and middle leaves, always deeply incised; its nutlets have a rounded, entire margin. Northern water-horehound (*L. uniflorus*), of northern and central Alberta, has shorter (less than 1 mm long), broader calyx-lobes that are shorter than or equal in length to the nutlets at maturity. Western water-horehound looks much like wild mint (see page 205), except that it has white flowers and lacks the mint odour.

(a)

(b)

leaves and nutlets of (a) western water-horehound and (b) cut-leaved water-horehound

wild mint, Canada mint, field mint
Mentha arvensis L.

PRAIRIE, ASPEN PARKLAND, BOREAL FOREST, MONTANE, SUBALPINE

HABITAT AND RANGE: Wetland margins, moist woods, banks and shores, bogs. Sometimes in shallow water. Widespread throughout Alberta.

FLOWERS: **Crowded in dense clusters in upper leaf axils.** Corolla 4 to 5-lobed and tubular, purplish to pinkish or bluish, occasionally white, about 8 mm long. Upper flower lobe cleft and broader than others. Calyx tubular, hairy, 2 to 3 mm long. Stamens 4. June to August.

FRUIT: 4 tan, oval nutlets, about 1 mm long, with a single seed per nutlet.

LEAVES: Opposite, prominently veined, short-stalked. Bright green, smooth to roughened, toothed, glandular-dotted on both surfaces. Oval to lance-shaped, 1 to 8 cm long.

GROWTH HABIT: Erect, **square-stemmed** perennial, 10 to 50 cm tall from creeping rootstocks. **Stems hairy on angles**, simple or sparsely branched. **Strong-smelling (particularly if leaves are rubbed),** from glands containing volatile oils.

wild mint (BA)

Mentha is from the Greek *Minthe*, a mythological nymph loved by Pluto. Jealous Proserpine changed the nymph into a mint plant. *Arvensis* means "growing in fields." ❧ The strong, distinctive taste of mint plants is due to their volatile oils. The leaves have long been used fresh, dried or frozen as a flavouring or tea. The Blackfoot used the leaves to flavour meat and pemmican, and lined dried meat containers with them prior to winter storage. Dried leaves were also used to treat heart disease, chest pain, rheumatism and arthritis. They are often added to salads or made into jelly. ❧ Strong mint teas were brewed to treat colds, coughs and fever, and both natives and early European settlers drank mint tea to alleviate vomiting. The Montana Flathead used the plant as a tonic and to pack around tooth cavities, while the Cheyenne chewed the leaves and rubbed them on their bodies to improve their love lives. Mint was used as a scent by the Thompson, Shuswap and Montana Flathead. The Cree used the plant in a medicine to treat stomach upset and as a tonic. Traps were boiled with mint to cover the smell of humans. ❧ There are 25 to 200 species of *Mentha* in the world, depending on which taxonomy is used; 2 occur in Alberta. Spearmint (*M. spicata*) has flowers in terminal clusters rather than in leaf axils and is introduced, not native.

western wild bergamot, horsemint, bee balm

Monarda fistulosa L. var. *menthaefolia* (Grah.) Fern.

<small>Prairie, Aspen Parkland, Boreal Forest, Montane, Subalpine</small>

western wild bergamot (SR)

HABITAT AND RANGE: Semi-shaded woods, moist meadows, ditches, thickets, coulee slopes, floodplains. Common in the southern half of the province and in the Peace River country.

FLOWERS: Numerous, in dense, showy, round cluster of softly hairy, irregularly shaped, purple to rose-coloured (occasionally whitish) flowers. Each **flower long-tubular, with long (12 mm) upper lip bearded at the tip, lower curved lip with 3 lobes.** Calyx tubular, ribbed, glandular, with 5 tiny, narrow, purplish lobes. **Stamens 2, protruding, pale green with purplish tips.** Flower cluster surrounded by circle of green, leafy bracts. June to September.

FRUIT: 4 smooth, brown, oblong nutlets, about 2 mm long, with a single seed per nutlet.

LEAVES: Opposite, 2.5 to 8 cm long, sometimes with pairs of smaller leaves in axils. Broadly lance-shaped, truncate at base, toothed, prominently veined underneath. Gray-green, velvety-hairy. Short-stalked or stalkless. **Leaves have minty smell when crushed.**

GROWTH HABIT: Tall (30 to 100 cm), erect stem, often reddish to purplish and square in cross-section. **Strong-smelling**, leafy perennial from spreading rootstocks. Often occurs in colonies.

*M*onarda honours an early Spanish physician and author of books on New World plants, Nicolas Monardez, who described many North American plants. *Fistulosa* means tubular, alluding to the flower shape, while *menthaefolia* means leaves like mint. ✑ Horsemint leaves contain thymol, which has been used as a stimulant, to relieve gas and to kill worms, fungi and bacteria. The Blackfoot boiled the leaves and applied them to pimples, made a tea from the blossoms as an eyewash and made a tea from leaves and flowers combined to soothe stomach pains (although too much could cause stomach upset). The leaves were also boiled and eaten with meat by some tribes. ✑ The Blood used an extract of the plant for birth control, to treat sores and galls, and, combined with cherry willow bark, to make a potion to relieve an infected uterus. ✑ The Montana Flathead used horsemint to treat colds, fever, flu and pneumonia. The patient drank a tea brewed from the plant and then was covered with blankets to sweat. Horsemint was also used in treating gas and kidney conditions and to treat toothache. It was used by various tribes as a perfume, meat preservative and insect repellent, and the Kutenai used it to produce a pleasant smell in sweat houses. ✑ There are about 15 species of *Monarda*, all native to North America. Only this species occurs in Alberta.

heal-all, self-heal
Prunella vulgaris L. ssp. *lanceolata* (Bart.) Hult.
MONTANE, PRAIRIE, BOREAL FOREST

HABITAT AND RANGE: Moist woods, fields, stream banks, lakeshores, roadsides. A single collection from the Peace River country, the remainder from west and west-central Alberta.

FLOWERS: In dense, terminal clusters, 2 to 5 cm long, usually surrounded by the upper leaves. **Bracts kidney-shaped to oval, with spines at the tips and often hairy along the margins. Corolla purplish to pink or white (fringed with hairs), 10 to 15 mm long. Corolla 2-lipped, upper helmet-shaped, entire; lower 3-lobed, with middle lobe the largest.** Stamens 4, filament jointed near the tip, with anther on the lower fork. **Calyx 7 to 10 mm long, purplish green, 2-lipped; upper broad, shallowly 3-toothed, lower with 2 sharp, narrow teeth.** May to September.

FRUIT: 4 smooth nutlets.

LEAVES: Few, opposite, stalked, smooth to sparsely hairy. Basal and stem or only stem leaves present. Oval to lance-shaped, 2 to 9 cm long, wedge-shaped to rounded at base, entire or slightly toothed. Lower leaves broader than upper.

GROWTH HABIT: Small (10 to 30 cm tall), sprawling or erect, **square-stemmed** perennial with fibrous roots. Solitary or in colonies.

heal-all   (BA)

The name *Prunella* is likely derived from the earlier *Brunella*, from the German for "quinsy," an abscess of the tonsils that this plant supposedly cured. Some authors, however, suggest that *Prunella* may be from the Latin *prunum* (purple), describing the flower colour. *Vulgaris* means "common," and *lanceolata* means "lance-shaped," describing the leaves. ❧ Various parts of this plant have been used to relieve boils, cuts, bruises, internal bleeding and swellings, hence the origin of the common name. Because it was used to treat wounds caused by sharp objects, the plant was also known as hook-heal or carpenter's herb. ❧ The leaves can be chopped and brewed into a drink. The Alberta Cree treated sore throats with heal-all, and the Blackfoot used it as an eyewash and to treat horses' saddle sores and sore backs. ❧ There are about 6 species of *Prunella* in the world, this species widespread, the others native to Europe, Africa and Asia.

marsh skullcap, common skullcap

Scutellaria galericulata L.

PRAIRIE, ASPEN PARKLAND, BOREAL FOREST, MONTANE

marsh skullcap   (DJ)

HABITAT AND RANGE: Wet meadows, stream banks, lake shores, shallow marshes; sometimes in slightly saline habitats. Mainly found in the northern half of the province.

FLOWERS: **In pairs, or occasionally solitary, from leaf axils**; on stalks about 2 mm long. **Corolla 12 to 25 mm long, tubular, dark blue on the outside, pale blue on the inside, expanded at the throat. Corolla 2-lipped, upper lip hood-like.** Calyx cup-shaped, reddish-tinged, 3.5 to 4.5 mm long, 2-lipped, with a distinctive bump on the upper surface. **Lips more or less equal, entire, upper with a pouch.** Stamens 4, lower pair longer; anthers hairy. June to August.

FRUIT: Nutlets 4, dark-coloured, bumpy, with a single seed per nutlet.

LEAVES: **Opposite**, hairy (particularly underneath), darker above, conspicuously veined. Oblong to lance-shaped, rounded at base, **irregularly scalloped along margins**, 2 to 5 cm long. Lower leaves stalked, upper stalkless.

GROWTH HABIT: Slender, erect or ascending, simple or branched, smooth to hairy (especially on stem angles), occasionally glandular perennial, 10 to 80 cm tall from creeping rootstock. Can spread to form colonies.

Skullcap describes the hood-like appearance of the upper lip of the corolla. *Scutellaria* is from the Latin *scutella* (tray or small dish), referring to the pouch-like calyx, and *galericulata* means "helmet-shaped." ✍ The Ojibwa used marsh skullcap as a heart tonic, and the American Cherokee used related blue skullcap or mad-dog weed (*S. lateriflora*) to treat chest pain and diarrhea. Various skullcap species have also been used to treat rabies and as a sedative and antispasmodic. ✍ There are 113 species of *Scutellaria*, widespread in the New World. Only this species occurs in Alberta.

marsh skullcap

marsh hedge-nettle, hemp-nettle
Stachys palustris L. ssp. *pilosa* (Nutt.) Epling
PRAIRIE, ASPEN PARKLAND, BOREAL FOREST

HABITAT AND RANGE: Wetland margins, wet ditches, shores and banks, thickets, moist disturbed areas. Common throughout the province.

FLOWERS: **In interrupted spike at top of plant** and also often in axils of stem leaves. Each flower is 10 to 25 mm long, **pale purple to whitish with darker mottling; 2-lipped, with erect upper lip and 3-lobed lower lip.** Stamens 4. **Calyx funnel-shaped, with long, white hairs, 5-lobed with pointed tips.** June to August.

FRUIT: 4 small brown nutlets, 2 mm long, contained in calyx. Single seed per nutlet.

LEAVES: Opposite, simple, 2.5 to 12.5 cm long, short-stalked or stalkless. Light green, hairy, lance-shaped to oval, scalloped to toothed on margins. Lowest leaves smaller and deciduous.

GROWTH HABIT: Hairy, simple or branched perennial, erect or occasionally curved at base, usually 30 to 40 cm tall from creeping rootstocks. **Square-stemmed, often reddish at base,** sometimes glandular. Has typical mint odour. May form large colonies.

*S*tachys is Greek for "spike," referring to the inflorescence type. *Palustris* is Latin for "of wet places," and *pilosa* refers to the fine hairs on the leaves and stems. ✐ There are approximately 200 species of *Stachys*, in North America, South America and South Africa. Only this species is found in Alberta.

marsh hedge-nettle   (BA)

marsh hedge-nettle   (CWA)

Figwort Family (Scrophulariaceae)

The figworts are a large family, containing mostly herbs, with some partially parasitic members, like the paintbrushes and louseworts, and several valued ornamentals, like snapdragons and penstemons. The flowers are typically irregular, with a tubular 2-lipped corolla (upper lip 2-lobed and bottom 3-lobed) and the stamens (usually 4 but may be anywhere from 2 to 5) attached to the corolla-tube. The fruit is a many-seeded (usually 2-valved) capsule, and the leaves are generally opposite, although sometimes alternate or whorled. *(See key for this family beginning page 315.)*

kittentails

Besseya wyomingensis (A. Nels.) Rydb.

PRAIRIE, MONTANE, SUBALPINE, ALPINE

HABITAT AND RANGE: Dry, open rocky slopes, fescue prairie; in the Cypress Hills and southern Rocky Mountains.

FLOWERS: Several in dense, narrow, bracted cluster. No corolla. Calyx 2-lobed, pink to purplish, hairy. **Stamens 2, protruding, with purplish filaments.** April to June.

FRUIT: Many-seeded, broadly oval, hairy capsule. Seeds light brown, disk-shaped, veiny, 1 to 2 mm long.

LEAVES: Mainly basal, long-stalked, oval to oblong, **heart-shaped to squared-off at base, 2 to 5 cm long. Scalloped or toothed on margins. Grayish; basal leaves and stalks often reddish-tinged.** Stem leaves small, stalkless.

GROWTH HABIT: Grayish-hairy perennial, 15 to 30 cm tall, from fibrous roots.

The cluster of long, protruding, purple stamens gives the plant the name kittentails. *Besseya* honours Charles E. Bessey (1845-1915), an American botanist, and *wyomingensis* means "of Wyoming." ✍ There are 7 species, mainly in the Rocky Mountains of the United States and Canada. Only this species is found in Alberta.

kittentails   (CWA)

common red paintbrush
Castilleja miniata Dougl. ex Hook.
Aspen Parkland, Montane, Subalpine

common red paintbrush (CWA)

HABITAT AND RANGE: Alpine meadows, well-drained slopes, open subalpine forests, moist banks, open woods in the foothills. Widespread in central and southern Alberta.

FLOWERS: Variable in colour. In the mountains and foothills, the irregularly lobed bracts are scarlet to reddish orange (occasionally yellow), while in the aspen parkland they are pink or rose-coloured. Corolla 2-lipped, 2 to 3.5 cm long. **Upper lip (*galea*) arched and long, forming a hood. Lower lip short, 3-lobed or toothed**, dark green, thickened. Stamens 4, in pairs, protruding from the flower. Calyx tubular, 4-lobed. June to September.

FRUIT: Dry capsule, 2 cm long, with many seeds.

LEAVES: Alternate, simple. Parallel-veined, smooth to hairy, **narrowly linear to lance-shaped**, 3-nerved, up to 7 cm long. Entire to 3-lobed above. Stalkless.

GROWTH HABIT: Erect, smooth to hairy, often branched perennial, up to 75 cm tall from a woody rootstock. Stem often reddish.

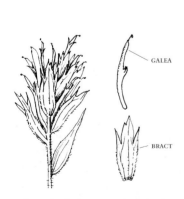

GALEA

BRACT

flower detail of common red paintbrush

alpine red paintbrush (CWA)

Castilleja commemorates Domingo Castillejo, an 18th-century Spanish botanist. *Miniata* is from *minium*, the scarlet oxide of lead. ✐ The blossoms of some paintbrushes were mixed with beard-tongues, steeped in water and the liquid applied to centipede bites. ✐ Although beautiful, this plant should not be transplanted as it is partly parasitic and does not survive transplanting well. ✐ There are 150 to 200 species of *Castilleja*, mostly in western North America; 9 are found in Alberta, chiefly in the Rocky Mountains. Another reddish-flowered species, alpine red paintbrush (*C. rhexifolia*), has dark-red to purplish flowers but appears to interbreed with common red paintbrush. Cusick's yellow paintbrush (*C. cusickii*) and stiff yellow paintbrush (*C. lutescens*), both yellow-flowered species, are much less common. The former usually has simple, leafy, hairy stems and is found only in extreme southwestern Alberta. The latter usually has

Cusick's yellow paintbrush (CWₐ)

a branched stem, spreading leaves and shorter hairs. It occurs in southwestern Alberta from the Red Deer River to the Montana border.

stiff yellow paintbrush (CWₑ)

blue-eyed mary
Collinsia parviflora Lindl.
MONTANE, SUBALPINE

blue-eyed mary (BA)

HABITAT AND RANGE: Moist, open woods, open grassy slopes, gravel flats, ridges; in the Rocky Mountains and Cypress Hills.

FLOWERS: On short stalks, solitary or 2 to 6 in clusters, surrounded at base by upper leaves. **Corolla 4 to 6 mm long, 2-lipped; upper lip 2-cleft, blue to whitish; lower lip purplish, 3-lobed, forming a pouch** that encloses 4 fertile stamens. Calyx 3 to 6 mm long, with 5 unequal, narrowly triangular lobes. May to July.

FRUIT: Capsules bumpy, 3 to 5 mm long with 2 to 4 seeds. Each seed about 2 mm long, smooth, reddish brown, with thickened, inrolled margin.

LEAVES: Middle to upper leaves simple, opposite (often in clusters), mostly stalkless, oval to narrowly lance-shaped, narrowed to the base, 1 to 2.5 cm long. Entire, smooth to short-hairy. Lower leaves stalked, spoon-shaped to round, usually deciduous.

GROWTH HABIT: Tiny (10 to 30 cm tall), **delicate, erect or trailing annual** with simple or branched stem. Hairy or smooth, sometimes glandular above. **Leaves and stem often purplish.**

In the United States this plant is sometimes called maiden blue-eyed mary of the west or blue-lips. While the blue in blue-eyed mary stems from the dark-blue flowers, the origin of the Mary is unknown; perhaps it honours Mary, mother of Jesus. *Collinsia* takes its name from the American botanist Zacheus Collins (1764-1831) of Philadelphia, and *parviflora* means small-flowered. ✍ Several species of *Collinsia* are often included in commercial wildflower mixes. ✍ There are 17 species of *Collinsia*, all in temperate North America. Only this species is native to Alberta.

toadflax, butter-and-eggs
Linaria vulgaris P. Mill
PRAIRIE, ASPEN PARKLAND, MONTANE

HABITAT AND RANGE: Roadsides, railroad rights-of-way, ditches, fields, disturbed areas. Common in Alberta.

FLOWERS: In dense, terminal clusters that elongate with age. **Flowers bright yellow with orange throats, 20 to 30 mm long. Corolla spurred at the base, 2-lipped; upper lip 2-lobed, lower 3-lobed** (very similar to the snapdragon, which belongs in the same family). Calyx of 5 distinct sepals, 3 to 4 mm long. Stamens 4. June to September.

FRUIT: Oval, 2-compartmented capsule, 8 to 12 mm long with many flattened, blackish, veiny, winged seeds.

LEAVES: Many alternate, **narrow,** somewhat fleshy, dark-green leaves, up to 10 cm long and **1 to 5 mm wide.**

GROWTH HABIT: Leafy, tall (20 to 80 cm), unpleasant-smelling, branched perennial, from creeping rootstocks. Forms dense colonies.

toadflax (BA)

*T*oad in early English meant "useless"; therefore toadflax meant "useless flax." The name may also refer to the flowers, which open like a toad's mouth (similar to a snapdragon). The name butter-and-eggs is derived from the bright-yellow and orange colour of the flowers. The origin of *Linaria* is the Latin *linum* (flax), because of the similarity of the non-flowering parts of some *Linaria* species to flax plants. *Vulgaris* means "common." ⌀ Toadflax was introduced to Canada from Europe as a garden plant but is now considered a noxious weed here. It was used in early Europe to treat jaundice, piles and eye infections, and was also boiled in milk to make a fly poison. ⌀ There are more than 100 species of *Linaria* in the world, 2 in North America, the others in Eurasia; 3 have been introduced to Alberta. Broad-leaved toadflax (*L. genistifolia* ssp. *dalmatica*; *L. dalmatica* in Moss 1983) is similar to toadflax but has clasping, broadly oval (10 to 20 mm wide) leaves and larger (30 to 40 mm long) flowers. Field or blue toadflax (*L. canadensis* var. *texana*) has light-blue flowers and a rosette of prostrate, leafy stems at the base of the erect flowering stem.

yellow monkeyflower, common monkeyflower
Mimulus guttatus Fisch. ex DC.
SUBALPINE, ALPINE

yellow monkeyflower (CWE)

HABITAT AND RANGE: Moist meadows, seepage springs and stream banks of extreme southern Alberta.

FLOWERS: **Usually in clusters of 5 or more**, or solitary. Striking 2-lipped yellow flower, dotted with red or purple, 1.5 to 2 (occasionally 4) cm long. Lobes of upper lip erect or bent backwards, lower lip lobes spreading. **Throat with 2 longitudinal hairy ridges.** Stamens 4, in pairs. Calyx 1 to 2 cm long, tubular, angled, becoming swollen as seeds ripen. **Calyx lobes unequal, upper usually much larger.** June to July.

FRUIT: Capsule enclosed by calyx. Capsule 2-valved, with persistent style, containing many tiny, brownish seeds.

LEAVES: Opposite, smooth or softly hairy, broadly oval to round, coarsely and irregularly toothed. Blade to 5 cm long. Upper leaves stalkless, somewhat clasping; lower stalked.

GROWTH HABIT: Erect or trailing, smooth to somewhat hairy annual or perennial with **succulent, hollow, nearly square stems.** Perennials may have creeping stems (*stolons*). Greatly variable in height (5 to 60 cm) and form.

yellow monkeyflower (LF)

*M*imulus is from the Latin *mimus* (mimic or actor), supposedly because of the "grinning face" of the flower. *Guttatus* means "spotted" or "speckled," referring to the flower's red spots. This species is grown in wet soils as an ornamental and has been introduced to Europe for this purpose. ✍ There are over 100 species of *Mimulus* in the world, primarily in western North America. Of the 6 species found in Alberta, all but red monkeyflower are classified as provincially rare. ✍ Red monkeyflower (*M. lewisii*), the only red-flowered Alberta species, is known only from the Waterton Lakes-Crowsnest Pass area and a couple of locations in the northern Rockies. Small yellow or purple-stemmed monkeyflower (*M. floribundus*) has smaller (less than 1.5 cm long) flowers than yellow monkeyflower and more or less equal calyx lobes. A recent addition to Alberta's known flora is smooth or Fremont's monkeyflower (*M. glabratus*), found at the

red monkeyflower   (LF)

edge of a wet pond in one location in the aspen parkland. It has a small flower (1 to 2 cm long), sometimes marked with red, and weak stems that are curved at the base and sometimes creeping to floating. Mountain or large monkeyflower (*M. tilingii*) may occur in the southwestern corner of the province. It usually has 1 to 5 yellow flowers with corollas 2 to 4 cm long; the upper calyx teeth are larger than the others.

smooth monkeyflower   (CWᴀ)

owl-clover
Orthocarpus luteus Nutt.

PRAIRIE, ASPEN PARKLAND, BOREAL FOREST, MONTANE

owl-clover   (CWA)

HABITAT AND RANGE: Dry grassy areas, slopes, river terraces; often on gravelly soils. Widespread.

FLOWERS: In a **terminal, leafy spike** at the top of an erect stem. **Bright yellow, hairy, 2-lipped**, 10 to 15 mm long. Upper lip beak-like with united lobes. Calyx unequally 4-cleft, with white hairs; margins of sepals lighter-coloured. Stamens 4, glandular-hairy. June to August.

FRUIT: Flattened, oblong, brown capsules, 5 to 7 mm long, with numerous brown, papery-winged seeds, 1 to 1.5 mm long.

LEAVES: Numerous, alternate, stalkless, hairy, linear or narrowly lance-shaped, 1 to 4 cm long. Mostly entire, some lobed; ascending. Uppermost leaves are actually bracts.

GROWTH HABIT: Erect, **glandular-hairy, leafy annual**, 10 to 40 cm tall. Simple or with a few branches. Parasitic, forming small sucker-like attachments to other plants' roots.

Orthocarpus is from *orthos* (straight) and *karpos* (fruit), referring to the capsule. *Luteus* means "golden," from the Latin *lutea*, describing the flower colour. ✎ This plant was used by some native peoples as a source of red dye, and the Alberta Blackfoot used it to colour small animal skins, horsehair and feathers. ✎ There are 25 species of *Orthocarpus*, mostly in the western United States. Only this species is found in Alberta.

elephant's-head, little red elephant,
elephant's-head lousewort
Pedicularis groenlandica Retz.

<small>BOREAL FOREST, MONTANE, SUBALPINE, ALPINE</small>

HABITAT AND RANGE: Wet meadows, stream banks, wetland margins, spruce-fir forests, primarily in the mountains and Cypress Hills.

FLOWERS: In dense cluster to 15 cm long. Each flower **reddish purple or pinkish, resembling an elephant's head, with a curved trunk and flared ears** (the trunk is the upper lip (*galea*) and the lobes of the lower lip form the ears). Stamens 4, in 2 pairs, 1 pair longer than the other. Calyx with 5 united lobes, with hairy-margined tips and hairy inside. June to August.

FRUIT: Flattened capsule up to 12 mm long, with appendage at tip. Contains many rough seeds.

LEAVES: **Compound, finely divided.** Lower stalked, upper sometimes stalkless, 5 to 20 cm long. **Often dark red to purple.**

GROWTH HABIT: **Purplish,** smooth perennial, 30 to 70 cm tall. Often grows in clumps.

*P*edicularis means "louse" in Latin, referring to the belief that cattle eating the plant were more likely to be affected by lice. *Groenlandica* means "of Greenland," although the first specimens were more likely seen in Labrador.

elephant's-head (CWA)

elephant's-head (BA)

western lousewort   (JH)

The roots (and tender young stems before flowering) may be eaten raw or cooked, and the Inuit still dig the roots of this species for a vegetable. Inuit children liked to suck nectar from the base of the flowers of closely related species. The leaves of related woolly lousewort (*P. lanata*) have been used to make tea. ✐ Although many louseworts are attractive plants, most can't be readily transplanted because they are semiparasitic on the roots of other plants. ✐ There are several hundred *Pedicularis* species in the world, chiefly in the northern temperate and boreal regions. There are 12 species in Alberta, of which 5 are rare. Western or bracted lousewort (*P. bracteosa*) has a yellowish (often red or purple-tinged) flower. The white or yellowish flower of coil-beaked or contorted lousewort (*P. contorta*) has a distinctive curved beak on the upper lip.

coil-beaked lousewort   (CWₐ)

yellow beardtongue, yellow penstemon

Penstemon confertus Dougl.

PRAIRIE, MONTANE, SUBALPINE, ALPINE

HABITAT AND RANGE: Moist to dry meadows, open woodlands, stream banks, dry hillsides, thickets. Mainly in the southern third of the province, particularly in the mountains.

FLOWERS: **In compact, interrupted clusters. Each flower pale yellow, 2-lipped,** 8 to 15 mm long. Upper lip 2-lobed, lower 3-lobed. **Bearded at throat.** Stamens 4, plus hairy, sterile stamen (*staminode*). Calyx 5-lobed, 5 mm long, with whitish, ragged margins. June to August.

FRUIT: Oval, light-brown, veiny, compartmented capsule, 4 to 5 mm long, with many seeds.

LEAVES: Entire, opposite. Lower stalked, upper attached directly to stem. Upper lance-shaped to nearly oval, to 10 cm long. Occasional plant has basal rosette.

GROWTH HABIT: Tufted, spreading or ascending perennial, 10 to 50 cm tall from woody rootstock. Smooth to occasionally finely hairy on stem.

yellow beardtongue   (BA)

The name beardtongue describes the hairy, tongue-like staminode in the throat of the flower. *Penstemon* originates from the Greek *pente* (five) and *stemon* (stamen), in reference to the number of stamens (4 fertile and 1 sterile). *Confertus* means crowded, likely referring to the flower clusters. ✍ The Okanagan peoples boiled the flowers and rubbed them on arrows and other items to dye them. They used the mashed leaves of shrubby beardtongue (*P. fruticosus* var. *scouleri*) to line moccasins. ✍ Several species of *Penstemon* are selenium absorbers and may cause problems for grazing livestock. ✍ There are 225 species of *Penstemon* in the world, 10 in Alberta; however, this is the only species in the province with yellow flowers. ✍ Crested beardtongue (*P. eriantherus*) has a purplish flower, 2 to 4 cm or longer, that has a very hairy throat and a conspicuous sterile stamen with long, yellow hairs. The stem is glandular near the top. Provincially rare shrubby beardtongue has very woolly anthers but a less hairy sterile stamen than crested beardtongue, large (3.5 to 4.5 cm long), pale-purple flowers, narrow (2 to 5 mm) and often toothed leaves; it is branched and woody at the base. Both species grow in southwestern Alberta; however, shrubby beardtongue's range also extends to the northern Rockies.

shrubby beardtongue   (DJ)

crested beardtongue   (TC)

smooth blue beardtongue, shining penstemon

Penstemon nitidus Dougl. ex Benth.

PRAIRIE, ASPEN PARKLAND, MONTANE

HABITAT AND RANGE: Dry, well-drained grassy or rocky slopes, sandy, exposed ridges. Common in the southern third of the province.

FLOWERS: Numerous, in dense clusters from leaf axils at the top of the plant. **Flowers tube-shaped, up to 20 mm long, purplish at base, becoming bright blue at the tip with purplish nectar guides. Flower 2-lipped, lower 3-lobed with soft, smooth hairs, upper 2-lobed.** Stigma yellowish (occasionally pink or purple), furry at tip. 4 fertile stamens and 1 sterile bearded stamen (staminode). May to June.

FRUIT: Pale brown, round, inflated capsule to about 14 mm long, with 2 sutures. Seeds numerous, wrinkly, brown, 3 to 4 mm long.

LEAVES: Opposite, uppermost united. **Thick, fleshy, pale green, covered with grayish bloom. Oval to lance-shaped.** Basal leaves to 10 cm long, upper leaves smaller.

GROWTH HABIT: Erect, often branched, usually several-stemmed perennial to 30 cm tall. Often grows in clumps.

smooth blue beardtongue (LF)

slender blue beardtongue (BA)

The common name is explained on page 221. *Nitidus* is Latin for "shiny, smooth, clear." ⌀ The Navajo treated rattlesnake bites with the pounded wet leaves of some *Penstemon* species. ⌀ Another blue-flowered species, with a range extending as far north as the Peace River country, is slender blue beardtongue (*P. procerus*). This species has much smaller (6 to 10 mm long), darker-blue flowers, and the flowers occur in a dense, sometimes interrupted spike. White beardtongue (*P. albidus*), as the name suggests, has white, broadly funnel-shaped, larger flowers enclosed by a glandular-hairy calyx. It is common on the southeastern prairies. Lilac-flowered beardtongue (*P. gracilis*) has a beautiful, light-mauve flower, 1.5 to 2.5 cm long, and a glandular-hairy inflorescence. Its range extends from the Montana border to the Peace River country.

white beardtongue   (LF)

lilac-flowered beardtongue   (CWA)

yellow rattle
Rhinanthus minor L.
PRAIRIE, ASPEN PARKLAND, BOREAL FOREST, MONTANE, SUBALPINE

yellow rattle   (BA)

HABITAT AND RANGE: Moist meadows, grassland, open woods, edges of thickets, avalanche slopes. Very common in the mountains and the boreal forest.

FLOWERS: Numerous in **leafy, terminal cluster, with each flower protruding from its encasing calyx. Flowers bright yellow, 2-lipped, 1 to 2 cm long.** Upper corolla lip hooded, 2-lobed, lower 3-lobed. **Calyx tubular, inflated in fruit, 4-toothed, yellowish green, sac-like,** veiny, noticeably hairy on margins. Stamens 4. July to August.

FRUIT: Nearly circular, flat, shiny capsule, 10 to 15 mm long, encased by calyx. Seeds large (up to 6 mm long), flattened, light brown, with prominent wings.

LEAVES: Opposite, simple, stalkless. **Lance-shaped with toothed or scalloped margins, prominently veined, stiff white-hairy above,** 2.5 to 5 cm long.

GROWTH HABIT: Erect, simple or sparsely branched, smooth to somewhat hairy annual, 15 to 60 cm tall.

The plant is known by its common name because the mature seeds rattle within their capsule if shaken. Other names less commonly applied to this plant include money-grass, rattlebag, shepherd's-coffin and yellow cockscomb. ✐ *Rhinanthus* is from the Greek *rhinos* (snout) and *anthos* (flower), referring to the unusual shape of the flowers; *minor* means "smaller." ✐ There are 2 species of *Rhinanthus* in the world. Only this species occurs in Alberta.

common mullein, flannel mullein
Verbascum thapsus L.
<small>PRAIRIE, ASPEN PARKLAND, MONTANE</small>

HABITAT AND RANGE: Roadsides, dry slopes, disturbed, often gravelly areas. Introduced from the Mediterranean region of Europe and common in southern Alberta.

FLOWERS: **Small, bright yellow (rarely whitish).** Each flower 5-lobed, 20 to 25 mm across, **maturing at intervals along a dense spike, 10 to 50 cm long.** Unlike other members of the figwort family, this plant has **nearly regular 5-lobed flowers** (not 2-lipped). Stamens 5, orange-tipped; **yellow to white-hairy on the filaments**; lower 2 smooth. Calyx 5-lobed. Flower has pleasant aroma. June to September.

FRUIT: Numerous, hairy, oblong to rounded capsules, 7 to 10 mm long, in long spike. Seeds numerous, tiny, brown, cylindrical, ridged.

LEAVES: **Basal rosette of grayish green, fuzzy-hairy, lance-shaped leaves appears in the first year.** Stem leaves alternate, numerous, 10 to 40 cm long, becoming smaller and clasping near the top.

GROWTH HABIT: Densely hairy biennial from tap root. **Leafy rosette appears in the first year, followed in the second year by a tall (more than 2 m), straight spike that remains standing for a year or longer after the plant dies.**

common mullein (BA)

The name flannel mullein is derived from the softly hairy leaves. Mullein is from the Latin *mollis,* meaning "soft." *Verbascum* is thought to be derived from *barbascum*, meaning "bearded," perhaps alluding to the hairy bases of the stamens or to the hairy leaves of some species. *Thapsus* is derived from the ancient town of Thapsus in Sicily. ✿ The plant was long used medicinally in Europe and has been used in North America to treat respiratory conditions such as coughs and asthma. Some North American tribes smoked the dried leaves (the plant is sometimes called Indian tobacco) to alleviate asthma, but too much is said to be dangerous. The leaves were also crushed into poultices and applied to swellings and wounds because the chemicals in the plant soothe irritated tissues and act as a sedative. The Kootenay made horses with colds inhale the smoke of burning mullein to help them breathe easier. ✿ Flannel mullein is often indicative of poor soil or overgrazing. ✿ There are 200 *Verbascum* species, all native to Eurasia. Of the 3 that occur in Alberta, this species is most common. Black mullein (*V. nigrum*) has purplish, rather than white or yellow, hairs on the stamen filaments. Woolly mullein (*V. phlomoides*) is a smaller plant (30 to 120 cm) with wider (20 to 50 mm) flowers.

common mullein (BA)

alpine speedwell

Veronica wormskjoldii Roemer & Schultes var. *wormskjoldii*
(*Veronica alpina* L. in Moss 1983)

HABITAT AND RANGE: Moist subalpine and alpine meadows, stream banks and river flats in the Rocky Mountains and along the Athabasca River.

FLOWERS: Several, 4 to 5 mm across, **in terminal, hairy cluster.** Corolla of **4 united, deep-blue petals with darker veins.** Stamens 2. **Calyx deeply incised into 4 white-hairy lobes. Flower stalks are glandular-hairy and sticky.** July to August.

FRUIT: Flattened, **slightly notched, glandular-hairy capsule,** 5 to 8 mm long, with numerous seeds.

LEAVES: Opposite, simple, dark green, **stalkless.** Oval, rounded at tip, entire or slightly scalloped, smooth to hairy, 15 to 35 mm long.

GROWTH HABIT: Erect perennial, 5 to 30 cm tall.

alpine speedwell (LA)

Speedwell is an old English blessing similar to "god speed," but why it was applied to this plant is unknown. Perhaps it was due to its alleged healing qualities. *Veronica* may derive from St. Veronica, who is said to have wiped Christ's face as he carried the cross to Calvary; *wormskjoldii* honours Lt. Morton Wormskjold (1783–1845), a Dane who travelled with Kotzebue to the Kamchatka peninsula and Kodiak Island. ✿ Canada's *Veronica* species are all edible. The young leaves and stems have a peppery flavour and can be eaten raw in salads or cooked as a vegetable. Closely related plants were used to prevent scurvy, and the leaves were occasionally used to produce a vitamin-rich tea. Herbalists use some speedwell species to treat urinary and kidney complaints and as a blood purifier. ✿ There are over 200 species of *Veronica* in the world, mainly in the north temperate zone. There are 10 species in Alberta, half of which are introduced. Another common species, American brooklime (*V. americana*), has flower clusters in the axils and short-stalked leaves. It is found in wet areas throughout the province, except for the prairies and the extreme northeast.

American brooklime (JH)

clustered broom-rape
Orobanche fasciculata Nutt.
PRAIRIE, MONTANE

HABITAT AND RANGE: Open slopes, grassland; often on dry, sandy soils. Mainly in the southern third of the province.

FLOWERS: **3 to 10 on long, thin, glandular-hairy stalks.** Corolla purplish or yellowish, 2 to 3 cm long, 5-lobed. Lobes rounded or with a sharp point at the end. Calyx cup-shaped, glandular-hairy, with narrow lobes equal to or shorter than the tube. Stamens 4. May to July.

FRUIT: Valved capsule with numerous, small seeds.

LEAVES: Alternate, scale-like, glandular-hairy, with short (less than 2 cm) blade. Yellow due to the absence of chlorophyll.

GROWTH HABIT: **Fleshy, dark-brown, yellowish or purple-tinged, scaly-stemmed, glandular-hairy perennial,** 3 to 20 cm tall from thick, **hard base.** Stems solitary or clustered. **Parasitic, usually on roots of sageworts and other composites.**

clustered broom-rape (LF)

The name broom-rape comes from a re-lated British species that is parasitic on scotch broom. *Orobanche* is from the Greek *orobos* (clinging plant) and *ancho* (to stran-gle), because of the plant's parasitic habit. *Fasciculata* means "fascicled" and refers to the bunched flowers. ✐ There are about 99 spe-cies of *Orobanche*, widespread in the world; 2 other *Orobanche* species are found in Alberta, both rare. Louisiana broom-rape (*O. ludoviciana*) has nearly stalkless flowers in a dense cluster. One-flowered cancer-root (*O. uniflora*) has a single flower (some-times 2 or 3) from each branch and a soft, rather than hard, woody base. ✐ Blackfoot medicine men applied chewed Louisiana broom-rape to wounds.

Louisiana broom-rape (CWA)

one-flowered cancer-root

common butterwort

Pinguicula vulgaris L.

BOREAL FOREST, MONTANE, SUBALPINE, ALPINE

common butterwort (LA)

HABITAT AND RANGE: Bogs, seeps, springs, calcareous wetlands, river banks, lakeshores; from the foothills to the Rocky Mountains and in the boreal forest.

FLOWERS: **Pale to dark purple (occasionally whitish), solitary at top of leafless stalk. Corolla 2-lipped, 1 to 2 cm long,** with slender nectar spur and broad, rounded lobes. Corolla tube whitish, with hairy opening. Calyx about 3 mm long, divided into 3 upper and 2 lower lobes. June to August.

FRUIT: Round, 2-valved capsule with many seeds.

LEAVES: **Basal, in short-stalked rosette.** Entire, elliptical, **pale yellow-green,** 2 to 5 cm long. **Greasy-feeling because of the glandular hairs on the upper surface.** The sticky, inward-curling leaves trap insects and then digestive enzymes break them down to provide nitrogen for the plant.

GROWTH HABIT: Carnivorous plant with a **glandular-hairy stem,** 4 to 15 cm tall from fibrous roots.

Butterwort describes the buttery feel of the sticky leaves. The plant supposedly had a beneficial effect on cows' milk (and butter) production. *Wort* is middle English for "plant." *Pinguicula* is from the Latin *pinguis* (fat), also attributed to the greasy appearance and feel of the leaves, and *vulgaris* means "common." ✿ Common butterwort has developed its carnivorous habit to supplement the low nitrogen content of its nutrient-poor habitats. ✿ There are 30 species of *Pinguicula*, primarily of the northern hemisphere and the South American Andes; 2 species occur in Alberta. The other, small butterwort (*P. villosa*), is smaller than common butterwort and has a smooth flower stalk and a corolla less than 10 mm long. It is rare in Alberta and is known only from the northeastern corner of the province.

common bladderwort

Utricularia vulgaris L. ssp. *macrorhiza* (Le Conte) Clausen

PRAIRIE, ASPEN PARKLAND, BOREAL FOREST, MONTANE, SUBALPINE

HABITAT AND RANGE: In slow-moving water of wetlands, lakes, creeks and ditches. Widespread throughout Alberta.

FLOWERS: 6 or more on short stalks that extend above the water. **Corolla 2-lipped, 14 to 20 mm long, bright yellow with brown stripes on the throat.** Upper and lower lips 1 to 2 cm long. **Floral tube extended into a short, spur-like sac at base.** Calyx 2 to 5-parted, about 5 mm long, consisting of pale-greenish, prominently veined sepals. June to July.

FRUIT: 2-valved, round, beaked capsule, about 5 mm long on curved stalks. Seeds numerous.

LEAVES: Numerous, alternate, brownish green, submerged, **round, hair-like, forked or incised leaves, 1 to 5 cm long, with many bladders on the same branch**, each bladder 3 to 5 mm long and 1 to 3 mm wide. **Leaves mostly divided into 2 segments near base, then further divided.**

GROWTH HABIT: **Aquatic**, carnivorous, **submersed**, free-floating perennial that traps prey in its many bladders. When small aquatic insects swim into the bladders, they trip guard hairs and the bladders shut. The insects are then digested by the plant and provide a source of nitrogen. The plant produces buds that fall to the bottom of the water and grow into new plants the following spring.

common bladderwort　　(BA)

*U*tricularia is from the Latin *utriculus* (small bottle), referring to the bladders. *Vulgaris* means "common" and *macrorhiza*, "long or large-rooted." ✿ There are 300 species of *Utricularia* in the world, mainly in the tropics; 4 species are found in Alberta. Horned bladderwort (*U. cornuta*) has small, simple, inconspicuous leaves, is terrestrial and is known only from extreme northeastern Alberta. Flat-leaved bladderwort (*U. intermedia*) has leaves and bladders borne on separate branches. Small bladderwort (*U. minor*) is much less robust than common bladderwort and has flattened leaves and smaller flowers (4 to 8 mm long).

northern bedstraw
Galium boreale L.

northern bedstraw (DJ)

HABITAT AND RANGE: Shaded riverine or moist prairie, open woods, roadsides, thickets. Common and widespread in Alberta.

FLOWERS: Numerous, fragrant, in short-stemmed, terminal clusters. Petals with white to cream-coloured lobes, pointed at the tips, 2 mm long. No calyx. Stamens 4, tiny, yellow. June to August.

FRUIT: **Pair of round, brown to black nutlets,** 1 to 2 mm long, with short white hairs or occasionally smooth.

LEAVES: Simple, entire, stalkless; **in whorls of 4. Dark green, prominently 3-veined, narrow, tapered at both ends,** 1.5 to 5 cm long.

GROWTH HABIT: Leafy, erect perennial up to 80 cm tall from creeping, brown rootstocks. **Stems 4-sided,** often short-hairy just below the nodes.

The dried plants were once used to stuff mattresses, hence the common name bedstraw. *Galium* is derived from the Greek *gala* (milk), for another species which was used to curdle milk. *Boreale* originates from *Boreas*, the Greek god of the north wind, in reference to this plant's northern distribution (circumpolar from sea level to treeline). ✍ The immature plant can be cooked as a vegetable or added to soups and stews. The roasted seeds are similar to coffee in flavour and aroma, and are said to make the best substitute for coffee in Canada. True coffee plants are in the same family. ✍ The Cree used the roots to make a red dye. Early Romans believed that the juice of bedstraw could combat bites from venomous spiders and snakes. ✍ There are 300 species of *Galium*, mainly in temperate zones of the world; 8 of these occur in Alberta. Cleavers (*G. aparine*) is a delicate, trailing annual with square stems roughened by tiny, backward-pointing spines, leaves in whorls of 6 to 8 and tiny (about 2 mm across) greenish white flowers. It is an introduced, troublesome weed in moist soils of cultivated fields, gardens and wooded areas of the province; however, the leaves and stems are edible when cooked, and the fruits of the plant may be dried and roasted into a coffee substitute. Another common species, sweet-scented bedstraw (*G. triflorum*), has broader leaves in whorls of 5 to 6 instead of in 4s, and has a more spreading form (due to weak stems) than northern bedstraw.

sweet-scented bedstraw (JH)

cleavers (BA)

twinflower
Linnaea borealis L.

ASPEN PARKLAND, BOREAL FOREST, MONTANE, SUBALPINE

HABITAT AND RANGE: Moist or dry, shady, coniferous, deciduous and mixed woods, bogs. Common.

FLOWERS: Short (about 1 cm) glandular-hairy, **paired flower stalks** with tiny, pointed bracts at the base, support **drooping pale-pink, bell-shaped flowers that are whitish and 5-lobed at the tips.** Flowers darker pink and woolly-hairy inside, sweet-scented, 8 to 16 mm long. Stamens 4, 2 long and 2 short. June to July.

FRUIT: 1-seeded capsule, 2 mm long, enclosed by glandular-hairy bractlets.

LEAVES: Opposite, evergreen, oval to spoon-shaped, usually with a few rounded teeth on the end, lighter and shiny underneath, to about 2 cm long. **Abruptly narrowed to a short stalk.**

GROWTH HABIT: **Trailing, delicate leafy perennial**, woody at base, with flower stems 5 to 10 cm tall. **Forms large mats.**

twinflower   (CWA)

This plant was much loved by Linnaeus, the prominent Swedish botanist who developed our system for naming plants, and was named after him. *Borealis* refers to its northern distribution. ✍ The Kootenay made a tea from the leaves of this plant. ✍ There is only this species in the genus, circumpolar in distribution.

twining honeysuckle

Lonicera dioica L. var. *glaucescens* (Rydb.) Butters.

PRAIRIE, ASPEN PARKLAND, BOREAL FOREST, MONTANE, SUBALPINE

twining honeysuckle (BA)

HABITAT AND RANGE: Shaded prairie riverine forest, coulees, moist woods, rocky slopes, gravelly banks. Widespread in Alberta.

FLOWERS: **Yellow at base, orange to occasionally reddish at the top, paired flowers** in terminal clusters. Each flower to about 25 mm long, **funnel-shaped**, indistinctly 2-lipped, with 5 reflexed lobes at the top and a **swollen nectary at the base**. Stamens 5, hairy, yellow, protruding. July to August.

FRUIT: Berries in clusters at the top of the plant. Each berry red to orange, up to 1 cm in diameter, containing many seeds.

LEAVES: **Opposite, upper pair joined to form bowl-shaped "bract" at base of inflorescence. Pale green with whitish bloom** and occasionally short hairs underneath, smooth, oval, somewhat fleshy, up to 8 cm long. Short-stalked to nearly stalkless.

GROWTH HABIT: **Twining** perennial vine, older stems **woody**, with **hollow twigs** and somewhat **shreddy bark**.

Honeysuckle likely describes the sweet-tasting nectar, while *Lonicera* honours Adam Lonitzer, a 16th-century German botanist and physician. *Dioica* is from the Greek *di* (two) and *oikos* (dwelling), perhaps in reference to the frequently paired flowers. *Glaucescens* means "becoming glaucous." ✐ Berries of several species have caused illness in Europe and are therefore **not recommended for consumption**. The Lillooet children of British Columbia sucked nectar from the flowers of related species. ✐ Stem fibres of various honeysuckles were woven into mats, bags and blankets, and the woody stems were used to construct suspension bridges over the Fraser and Thompson Rivers in British Columbia. The Montana Flathead boiled the stems to produce a shampoo which was said to make the hair grow longer. ✐ There are about 150 species of *Lonicera* in the world, in temperate and subtropical regions of the northern hemisphere. There are 5 species in Alberta, of which the other 4 are erect shrubs.

Sitka valerian, mountain valerian, wild heliotrope, mountain heliotrope

Valeriana sitchensis Bong.

SUBALPINE, ALPINE

HABITAT AND RANGE: Moist subalpine and alpine meadows, stream banks and upper elevation open woodlands of the Rocky Mountains.

FLOWERS: Small, **in open, rounded to nearly flat-topped clusters. Often pinkish to lavender early in the season, turning whitish with age. Corolla funnel-shaped**, 5-lobed, **6 to 8 mm long**. Stamens 3. June to August.

FRUIT: Small, flat achenes with bristles (the remains of the calyx).

LEAVES: Opposite, dark green, segmented, 10 to 15 cm long. **Basal leaves stalked, mostly divided into 3 to 5 segments.** Stem leaves 2 to 4 pairs, on short leaf stalks or attached directly to the stem. **Terminal lobes largest.** Leaf edges smooth or slightly toothed.

GROWTH HABIT: Strong-smelling, erect perennial with squarish, leafy stems; 40 to 80 cm tall from a thick rootstock. Becomes stronger-smelling after a frost.

Sitka valerian (LA)

*V*alerian is from the Latin *valere* (to be in health or be strong) and alludes to the medicinal properties of the plant. *Sitchensis* is from Sitka Sound in southeast Alaska, where the species was first collected. ✍ The cooked roots of some valerians have been eaten but are considered by some to be **poisonous**. The Plains peoples are believed to have used the rootstocks to treat stomach ailments. The Thompson of British Columbia applied powdered roots to wounds to act as an antiseptic; they mixed dried, powdered roots and leaves together to flavour tobacco. Fresh roots have also been mashed and applied to injured areas, and fresh leaves chewed and placed on wounds. The Blackfoot ate the roots raw or dried and used them to treat indigestion and stomach complaints. The plant should be considered a famine food and is not recommended for consumption. ✍ The Shuswap used the plant as a perfume and disinfectant and to bathe race horses. Valerian species were also used as perfume and spice by Persians and Egyptians. Cats treat it like catnip and it was once called cat's fancy. ✍ There are about 200 species of *Valeriana* in the world, widely distributed; 2 species are native to Alberta. Northern valerian (*V. dioica*) has smaller flowers (corolla 1 to 3 mm long), undivided basal leaves and stem leaves with 9 to 15 segments.

Sitka valerian (LK)

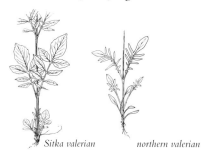

Sitka valerian   *northern valerian*

harebell, bluebell

Campanula rotundifolia L.

harebell (JH)

HABITAT AND RANGE: Moist to dry grassland, rocky hillsides, open woods, thickets. Widespread in Alberta.

FLOWERS: 1 to 5 per plant. Petals are joined to form a **5-lobed, bell-shaped corolla**, 1.5 to 2.5 cm long. Petals **purplish blue** (rarely white), prominently veined. The flower tends to be a darker-blue in shady locations. Stigma pale green, 3-lobed. Calyx **shiny**, bright green with long, narrow sepals, united at base. Stamens 5. June to September.

FRUIT: Short, papery, grooved capsule, 1 cm long, with pores that open to release the many brown, shiny seeds.

LEAVES: Numerous, alternate, narrow, **linear to lance-shaped** stem leaves, 1 to 5 cm long. Short-lived basal leaves are round to heart-shaped, to 2.5 cm long on long stalks.

GROWTH HABIT: Solitary, showy, slender, single-stemmed perennial with milky juice. Up to 45 cm tall from slender rootstocks.

This is the famous bluebell of Scotland. The name harebell is said to be from an old custom of naming plants for animals; or it may be a contraction of "heatherbell." *Campanula* is from the Latin *campana* (bell), and *rotundifolia* refers to the round, basal leaves. ✎ The leaves contain alkaloids and are avoided by grazing animals. ✎ The Cree chopped and dried the roots to make them into compresses to stop bleeding and reduce swelling of cuts and other wounds. The young shoots and leaves of garden bluebell (*C. rapunculoides*), which is introduced in Alberta, can be eaten raw in salads or cooked. The boiled roots are said to have a nut-like taste. ✎ There are 300 species of *Campanula*, mainly in temperate and arctic regions; 4 are found in Alberta. Besides garden bluebell, we also have the native Alaska harebell (*C. lasiocarpa*) and alpine harebell (*C. uniflora*), both of which are confined to alpine scree slopes and have hairy calyces and solitary flowers.

alpine harebell (JH)

Alaska harebell (JH)

Kalm's lobelia, brook lobelia

Lobelia kalmii L.

HABITAT AND RANGE: Calcareous bogs and meadows, shores, ditches, stream banks. Of scattered occurrence, mainly in central Alberta.

FLOWERS: Few, **on slender, spreading stalks in open, sometimes 1-sided cluster. Corolla of 5 united petals, light blue or purplish with white or yellow centre (occasionally white throughout), 8 to 15 mm long. 2-lipped; upper lip has 2 small lobes bent backwards, 3 lobes of lower lip bend abruptly down.** Sepals 5, about 3 mm long, united at base, **with narrowly triangular, reddish-tinged lobes.** July to August.

FRUIT: Pod-like capsule, 4 to 8 mm long, with many roughened seeds that are pointed at both ends and less than 1 mm long.

LEAVES: Simple, alternate, bluish green. Basal leaves spoon-shaped or broadly oval, stalked, usually hairy, 1 to 3 cm long, often early deciduous. **Stem leaves narrow, linear to lance-shaped,** mostly 1 to 7 cm long.

GROWTH HABIT: Leafy-stemmed, delicate, smooth or hairy biennial or perennial, 10 to 30 cm tall from fibrous roots. Simple or branched below. Leafy rosette forms in the first year, then the flower stalk appears. Often forms clumps.

Kalm's lobelia (CWA)

*L*obelia commemorates the French physician turned botanist, Matthias de L'Obel (1538-1616). *Kalmii* is named for Pehr Kalm, the 18th-century student of Linnaeus who discovered this plant. ❧ The Cree are said to have used lobelia species to induce vomiting. Several species are known to have caused sickness and death when used for medicinal purposes by early European settlers. ❧ There are more than 300 species of *Lobelia* in the world, widely distributed; 2 other *Lobelia* species occur in central to northern Alberta, but both are rare. Water lobelia (*L. dortmanna*) is aquatic, has no stem leaves and has round, hollow leaves in a basal rosette. Spiked lobelia (*L. spicata*) has flowers in a dense, stalkless cluster and leaves usually more than 10 mm wide.

Aster or Composite Family
(Asteraceae or Compositae)

This widespread, very large plant family (vying with orchids for possessing the most species in the world) is also the largest plant family in Alberta, with approximately 250 species in 67 genera occurring here.

The composites are the most highly developed of all plant groups and consist of annual, biennial or perennial herbs and some shrubs and trees. Each flower head is actually composed of several ray florets and/or disk florets attached to a common base called a *receptacle*. The ray florets are strap-shaped, often conspicuous, and act as banners to attract insects, while the disk florets are tubular and 5-lobed at the tip. A large number of composite flowers are yellow, as this colour is reputed to be the most attractive to the required insect pollinators.

The fruit is an achene, often topped with a pappus of hairs, scales or bristles. The flower head is surrounded by sepal-like bracts, which may be sticky or have spines to discourage predation. Food plants, such as sunflowers and lettuce, and many troublesome weeds, such as thistles, dandelions, ragweeds, burdocks and knapweeds, are well-known members, as are such colourful ornamentals as daisies, asters, zinnias, dahlias and marigolds. The composite family also supplies us with dyes, poisons and medicines. *(See key for this family beginning page 318)*

PAPPUS

BEAK

achene

an Erigeron *flower*

DISK FLORET   RAY FLORET

INVOLUCRE OF BRACTS

an Aster *flower*

common yarrow, milfoil
Achillea millefolium L.

PRAIRIE, ASPEN PARKLAND, BOREAL FOREST, MONTANE, SUBALPINE

HABITAT AND RANGE: Occurs in dry to moist grasslands, open riverine forest, aspen woods, low to moderate elevations in the mountains and disturbed areas. Widespread and very common throughout Alberta

FLOWERS: Individual flower heads to 5 mm across in a **dense, flat-topped or rounded terminal cluster, to 4 cm or wider**. Ray florets 5 to 12, light-cream to white (occasionally pinkish) and notched at the tip. Central disk florets straw-coloured to gray. June to August.

FRUIT: Head composed of small achenes. Each achene gray, oblong, flattened, about 2 mm long. No pappus.

LEAVES: Soft, **woolly, grayish to blue-green**, 3 to 15 cm long. Alternate, **finely divided and fern-like** in appearance. Lower leaves on stalks; upper attached directly to stem.

GROWTH HABIT: Erect perennial, 15 to 70 cm tall, with several very woolly-hairy stems, from a branched rootstock. Aromatic.

common yarrow (BA)

The common name yarrow is derived from the name of a Scottish parish. The genus name honours the legendary Greek warrior Achilles, who supposedly made an ointment from the plant's juice to heal the wounds of his soldiers in the battle of Troy. *Millefolium* means "thousand leaves," in reference to the many finely divided leaf segments. ✍ Yarrow contains an alkaloid, now called *achillein*, that reduces the clotting time of blood. Montana's Flathead and Kutenai peoples were aware of this characteristic and made a mash of the crushed leaves to wrap around wounds. Early Europeans also made use of the plant's medicinal qualities and called it soldier's wound wort. ✍ Alberta's Blackfoot drank tea obtained from the entire plant as a laxative. A tea made from the leaves and flowers only was used in the treatment of consumption (tuberculosis), stomach trouble and headache, and as a lotion for sore eyes. The Blood tribe used an extract from the stems to treat liver ailments, sore throats, horses' sore eyes, and to reduce pain in childbirth. ✍ There are 75 species of *Achillea* in the world, all in the northern hemisphere, including 3 species in Alberta. Introduced sneezewort or sneezeweed (*A. ptarmica*) has slightly toothed leaves, and native many-flowered yarrow (*A. sibirica*) has incised leaves, compared to the bipinnately dissected leaves of common yarrow.

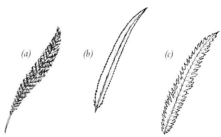

leaf of (a) common yarrow, (b) sneezewort, (c) many-flowered yarrow

yellow false dandelion, false dandelion,
large-flowered false dandelion, pale agoseris
Agoseris glauca (Pursh) Raf.

<small>PRAIRIE, ASPEN PARKLAND, MONTANE, SUBALPINE, ALPINE</small>

yellow false dandelion   (BA)

HABITAT AND RANGE: Dry to moist grassland, open woods, meadows, ditches and disturbed areas from low to high elevations. Widespread in the southern half of the province; also found in the Peace River country. The densely hairy var. *dasycephala* is primarily found at high elevations in the mountains.

FLOWERS: Usually a **single flower head per plant on a leafless stem (*scape*).** Flower heads bright yellow, drying to pale yellow or pink, 2.5 to 5 cm in diameter. Petals (ray florets) fringed at their tips. **Bracts in several series, hairy along the margins, and sometimes purple-spotted.** July to August.

FRUIT: Dry, striped, **thick-beaked achene, 5 to 12 mm long**, with white bristles (pappus) at the base.

LEAVES: Bluish green, lance-shaped, 4 to 20 cm long, in a **basal rosette**. Hairy, or sometimes smooth, often slightly toothed, with a **prominent whitish midvein**.

GROWTH HABIT: Erect perennial up to 40 cm tall, with a leafy rosette at the base and a long tap root. Flower stalk reddish; **exuding a sticky, milky juice when cut.**

*A*goseris is from the Greek *aix* (goat) and *seris* (chicory), for reasons unknown; *glauca* derives from the Greek *glaukos* (bluish), describing the bloom on the leaves and stem. The flower head is similar to that of the common dandelion, but this plant is taller and has nearly toothless leaves. ✍ The Thompson people chewed

pink false dandelion   (JH)

orange false dandelion   (CWₑ)

the leaves and the milky sap when it had hardened on exposure to air. The dried leaves were also chewed like bubblegum by the Spokane. The Okanagan peoples used the powdered root, mixed with a robin's heart and tongue, in a potion applied to the face to cast a spell on a loved one. ✍ There are 9 species of *Agoseris* in the world, of which 8 are found in North America; 3 occur in Alberta. Orange false dandelion (*A. aurantiaca*) has orange ray florets and achenes with slender beaks, while the recently discovered pink false dandelion (*A. lackschewitzii*) has pink ray florets and is restricted to subalpine and alpine meadows. The beaks of the achenes of the latter are less abruptly narrowed than those of orange false dandelion.

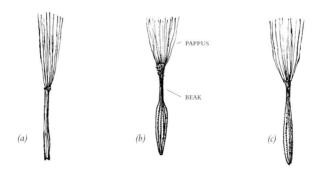

PAPPUS

BEAK

(a)   *(b)*   *(c)*

achenes of (a) yellow false dandelion, (b) orange false dandelion, (c) pink false dandelion

pearly everlasting

Anaphalis margaritacea (L.) Benth. & Hook.

BOREAL FOREST, MONTANE, SUBALPINE

pearly everlasting   (CWE)

HABITAT AND RANGE: Gravelly open woods in the foothills, pine and spruce-fir forests, subalpine meadows. Chiefly in the Rocky Mountains and Cypress Hills.

FLOWERS: In dense, rounded terminal clusters. **Male and female flowers on separate plants. Disk florets yellowish, white or pale brownish. No ray florets. Bracts spreading, white-papery, each often with brown spot at base.** July to August.

FRUIT: Dry, irregular, bumpy achene.

LEAVES: **Numerous** stem leaves, alternate, attached directly to stem (stalkless). Lance-shaped or oblong, light green above, lighter beneath, up to 10 cm long. Basal leaves small, usually withered by flowering time. **Very soft-fuzzy with white or light-tan hairs.** Prominent midvein and 2 less pronounced ones. Margins frequently turned under.

GROWTH HABIT: Can be solitary but usually grows in colonies. Leafy, soft-hairy, robust rhizomatous perennial to more than 80 cm tall.

This plant is called everlasting because, like strawflowers, the dry flowers last for a long time. The derivation of *Anaphalis* is obscure but seems to be from the Greek name of some similar plant. *Margaritacea* means "of pearls" and refers to the appearance of the flowers or whitish bracts. Other common names for this plant include life everlasting, none so pretty, moonshine, Indian posy and ladies' tobacco. Pearly everlasting was used to treat colds, coughs, diarrhea, bruises, sprains and sheep diseases   the 1800s. The smoke from crushed, burned petals was inhaled by the Ojibwa   dy for paralysis. Prior to battle, the Cheyenne chewed the plant and rubb   bodies to give strength and protection from enemies, while dried   re placed on horses' hooves and blown between their ears to s   t. The Thompson stuffed pillows with the dried flower   *naphalis* in the world's north temperate zones, mainly   Alberta. Pearly everlasting looks somewhat like   asting (*Antennaria* spp.); however, it is leafier and   from the base to the top of the plant, as they are in

broad-leaved everlasting, broad-leaved pussy-toes

Antennaria neglecta Greene

PRAIRIE, ASPEN PARKLAND, BOREAL FOREST, MONTANE, SUBALPINE

HABITAT AND RANGE: Prairie and open woods, grassy slopes. Widespread in Alberta.

FLOWERS: Heads in a dense to slightly open cluster. Disk florets up to 12 mm long, **white to cream-coloured**; surrounded by narrow, **tan to whitish-tipped bracts. Female and male flowers on different plants.** June to July.

FRUIT: Dry, brown achene, 1 to 1.5 mm long, with white bristles (pappus).

LEAVES: Stem leaves slender, short, linear. **Basal leaves elliptical or spoon-shaped, 1 to 4 cm long, mainly green above and white-woolly below.**

GROWTH HABIT: **Mat-forming perennial,** 10 to 40 cm tall, **with creeping above-ground stems** (*stolons*).

broad-leaved everlasting (LK)

The cluster of soft, fuzzy flower heads gives the plant the common name pussy-toes. *Antennaria* is from the Latin *antenna* (a feeler), because the pappus hairs of the male flowers have swollen tips resembling butterfly antennae. *Neglecta* means "neglected" or "overlooked," likely in reference to the plant's inconspicuous growth habit. ✿ There are 25 to 30 species of *Antennaria* in the world, mainly throughout North America, in South America and circumpolar in the North. There are about 15 species in Alberta. This species has noticeably wider, greener leaves than most of our other *Antennaria* species. ✿ Small-leaved everlasting (*A. microphylla; A. parviflora* in Moss 1983), which is found on dry slopes, open woods and grasslands, is shorter (10 to 25 cm tall) and grayish in colour, with smaller (1 to 2 cm) gray leaves that are white-woolly on both sides. Showy everlasting (*A. pulcherrima*) has well-developed stem leaves, long, broadly lance-shaped, prominently 3-ribbed basal leaves, 5 to 15 cm long, and white or tawny-tipped bracts, each with a dark spot at the base. ✿ The leaves of the related rosy everlasting or pink pussy-toes (*A. rosea*), a species with pinkish-tinged bracts, were sometimes chewed by Blackfoot children and used in tobacco mixtures.

showy everlasting (LK)

small-leaved everlasting (LF)

rosy everlasting (BA)

common burdock, lesser burdock, wild rhubarb, beggar's buttons

Arctium minus (Hill) Bernh.

PRAIRIE, ASPEN PARKLAND, BOREAL FOREST, MONTANE

common burdock   (CWA)

HABITAT AND RANGE: Found in pastures, fence rows, roadsides and disturbed sites. Introduced from Eurasia. Established through most of North America.

FLOWERS: Scattered at the ends of ascending to spreading branches, in stalkless or short-stalked heads 2 to 2.5 cm thick. **Disk florets only, narrow, tubular, purplish to pink or white.** Heads surrounded by several series of hairless involucral bracts (sometimes white-woolly near the base). **Outer bracts hooked, forming a ball** that sticks to hair, fur and clothing for seed dispersal. July to September.

FRUIT: Oblong, ribbed achenes that are squared off at the tip. Pappus of many, short, stiff, yellowish bristles.

LEAVES: White, woolly-hairy below when immature, usually almost hairless when mature. Triangular, sometimes heart-shaped at base; margins coarsely toothed or wavy. **Lower leaves mostly hollow-stalked. First-year leaves similar in appearance to rhubarb leaves, forming basal rosette.** Basal leaves to 30 cm long, stem leaves smaller, alternate.

GROWTH HABIT: Erect, branched biennial to more than 1 m tall from a thick, fleshy tap root. Basal leaves form a rosette in the first year, flowering stalk develops in second year. Stem grooved, rough, sometimes purplish.

*A*rctium is likely from the Greek *arktos* (bear), referring to the hairy, unkempt, fur-like appearance of the bracts of great burdock. *Minus* means "lesser." ø Burdock species have been cultivated for food in Europe and Japan. The young

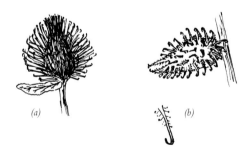

bracts of (a) common burdock, (b) cocklebur

leaves and shoots (if peeled) can be eaten raw or as a potherb. Young roots can be also be boiled and eaten, or roasted and ground as a coffee substitute. In Japan, the edible roots are called *gobo*. ✍ The efficiency of the hooked tips of the involucral bracts inspired the development of velcro. ✍ There are 4 species of *Arctium* in the world. *Arctium* species are native to and widespread in Eurasia, weedy elsewhere; 3 occur in Alberta. Great burdock (*A. lappa*) has long, solid leaf stalks, larger (to 50 cm long) leaves and larger (3 to 4.5 cm wide) heads in a mounded, not elongated, cluster (as in common burdock). Woolly burdock (*A. tomentosum*) has a tangled-woolly involucre. Cocklebur (*Xanthium strumarium*) is another weedy member of the composite family with a "burr." The burr of cocklebur, however, has much tougher, more hooked prickles and cannot be compressed between the fingers like the burr of burdocks.

common burdock   (BA)

heart–leaved arnica
Arnica cordifolia Hook.

BOREAL FOREST, MONTANE, SUBALPINE, ALPINE

heart-leaved arnica (BA)

HABITAT AND RANGE: Moist and dry wooded areas in the Rockies, foothills and boreal forest. Mainly in the western half of the province but also occurs in the Cypress and Hand Hills.

FLOWERS: Heads 1 to 3. **Petals (ray florets) 10 to 15, bright yellow, up to 3 cm long. Central, tightly bunched disk florets also bright yellow.** Bracts joined, pointed at the tips, up to 22 mm long; with white, spreading hairs and often glandular. June to August.

FRUIT: Short-hairy and/or glandular, ribbed, narrow achenes, about 7 mm long, with a pappus of barbed, **whitish** hairs.

LEAVES: Basal and in **2 to 4 pairs** along the stem. Dark green above, paler below; prominently veined, entire to deeply toothed, with fuzzy hairs on upper and lower surfaces. **Basal leaves long-stalked** and usually somewhat **heart-shaped**. Stem leaves more squared-off at the base, up to 10 cm long.

GROWTH HABIT: Hairy-stemmed, often glandular, solitary to few-stemmed perennial up to 60 cm tall.

*A*rnica is said to originate from the Greek *arnakis* (lamb's skin), because of the woolly bracts and leaf texture of some of the species. *Cordifolia* refers to the heart-shaped leaves. ✐ This species is the most common *Arnica* of the Alberta Rocky Mountains. Parts of the plant have been used medicinally to treat back pain, bruises and sprains; however, it is said to be **dangerous, possibly fatal, if taken internally.** ✐ There are 30 species of *Arnica* in the world, chiefly in boreal and mountainous regions; 15 species are found in Alberta. Broad-leaved or mountain arnica (*A. latifolia*) is similar to heart-leaved arnica and is found in the same habitats. The lower leaves of the former are usually squared-off rather than heart-shaped at the base; the bases of the involucres are sparsely hairy, and the achenes are smooth (especially below), not hairy throughout. Another mountain species, cordilleran arnica (*A. mollis*), has a straw-coloured pappus and lance-shaped to oval leaves that are tapered to the base.

cordilleran arnica (JP)

shining arnica
Arnica fulgens Pursh
PRAIRIE, ASPEN PARKLAND, MONTANE

HABITAT AND RANGE: Open mesic to moist grasslands to low elevations in the mountains. Occurs from the Montana border to the aspen parkland of the Peace River country.

FLOWERS: Heads usually solitary but there may be up to 4 per plant. Petals (ray florets) yellow, up to 2.5 cm long. **Disk florets glandular, with spreading, white hairs.** Bracts tapered, purplish on margins, glandular-hairy. May to June.

FRUIT: Hairy, tan to black achene, 4 to 6 mm long, **with barbed, white to brownish pappus**.

LEAVES: Entire, gray-green. Mostly basal; lance-shaped, strongly tapering to base, 5 to 15 cm long, stalked. **Stem leaves smaller, in pairs, lance-shaped or linear, nearly or completely stalkless.**

GROWTH HABIT: Erect perennial, up to 60 cm tall from short, scaly rhizomes. **Basal leaves and old leaf remnants with tufts of brown "wool" between the leaf stalk and the stem.** Stems thick, with stalked glands, and often hairy, especially towards the top of the plant.

The derivation of the genus name is explained on page 244. *Fulgens* means shining, perhaps in reference to the bright-yellow flowers. This species can be distinguished from our other arnicas by the tufts of brown hair between basal leaf stalks and stem.

shining arnica   (BA)

TUFTS OF BROWN HAIR

shining arnica

pasture sagewort, pasture sage, fringed sage,
pasture wormwood
Artemisia frigida Willd.

pasture sagewort (BA)

HABITAT AND RANGE: Dry grassland, open slopes, disturbed sites. Common in the province, especially on sandy or gravelly soils.

FLOWERS: Numerous, **yellowish, inconspicuous disk florets, 2 to 3 mm long, in terminal, leafy clusters.** Bracts small, hairy, 2 to 4 mm long. July to September.

FRUIT: Smooth, yellow to brownish achenes to 1 mm long, narrowed at base.

LEAVES: Alternate and aromatic. Soft, **silvery, silky-hairy, deeply dissected,** 1 to 4 cm long.

GROWTH HABIT: **Grayish, fragrant** perennial up to 40 cm tall from a woody crown and tap root. Young branches often hairy. Frequently mat-forming.

*A*rtemis was the Greek name for Diana, the goddess of the hunt, but why this plant should be named for her is unclear. The specific name *frigida* is apt, as this plant is found as far north as Alaska and Siberia. The Blackfoot burned branches of pasture sagewort so that the smoke would repel biting insects, and branches were sometimes also placed under bedding to deter bedbugs,

long-leaved sagewort

fleas and lice. They also crushed the leaves and mixed them with meat to help preserve it, and used various plant parts to treat fever, heartburn and colds. Alberta Cree used the plant in bathing, while the Blood formed the leaves into mats, fans to keep away flies and bandages for cuts; they also applied them as a cleanser after childbirth. In British Columbia, the Shuswap covered sweat house floors with pasture sagewort and boughs of Douglas-fir, while the Thompson used the plant for smoking hides. ⍟ Pasture sagewort is relatively unpalatable to livestock and tends to increase as range becomes heavily grazed. It is eaten by pronghorn antelope, however. ⍟ The true sages (*Salvia* spp.) used in seasonings are actually members of the mint family.

pasture sagewort (BA)

⍟ There are over 100 species of *Artemisia* in the world, primarily in the northern hemisphere and South America; 15 species occur in Alberta, of which 2 are shrubs. If you suspect a plant may be a sagewort, rub the leaves and check for the characteristic sage aroma. Pasture sagewort can be distinguished from our other sageworts by its very finely dissected, soft grayish leaves and small size (usually less than 40 cm tall). Look for long-leaved sagewort (*A. longifolia*) with long, narrow, inrolled leaves that are gray to green and sparsely hairy above, white-woolly below, on eroded slopes and saline plains in grasslands of southeastern Alberta.

prairie sagewort, prairie sage, western mugwort, white sage, mugweed, cudweed sagewort, white mugwort

Artemisia ludoviciana (Nutt.) T. & G.

PRAIRIE, ASPEN PARKLAND, BOREAL FOREST, MONTANE, SUBALPINE

prairie sagewort (BA)

HABITAT AND RANGE: Mesic grasslands, disturbed areas, roadsides. Widespread south of the North Saskatchewan River and of scattered occurrence farther north.

FLOWERS: Numerous small heads in narrow cluster. **Brownish disk florets only, no ray florets.** Bracts very hairy. June to August.

FRUIT: Small, smooth, dark-gray to brown achenes 1 to 2 mm long.

LEAVES: Alternate, simple, aromatic; lance-shaped to occasionally deeply lobed. **Pale gray-green, usually with tiny brown tip. Felty whitish-hairy or nearly smooth above.** Margins entire to slightly toothed. Upper leaves shorter and narrower than lower. Variable in width and shape, depending on variety.

GROWTH HABIT: Perennial up to 60 cm tall from creeping, woody rootstock. Can form large colonies.

The origin of *Artemisia* is described on page 246. *Ludoviciana* means "of Louisiana." ✐ The Blackfoot used prairie sagewort (which they called man sage) in the ritual cleansing portion of sweat lodge ceremonies. ✐ The Alberta Blackfoot and the Okanagan and Shuswap of British Columbia placed these plants under their bedding to repel bedbugs, fleas and lice. The Blackfoot used it as a personal deodorant and in saddles, pillows, hide bags and moccasins, as well as to treat coughs, hemmorhoids, stomach and liver complaints. The Montana Flathead used the leaves and Douglas-fir boughs in their sweat houses as incense. They also brewed a tea from the leaves as a cold remedy, and mixed them into a concoction to treat bruises and itchiness. The Crow and Cheyenne had numerous medicinal uses for the plant, from deodorants to treatment of eczema. The Alberta Stoney used prairie sagewort in sweat lodges and as medicine, while the Cree lit it as incense, treated headaches with it and chewed it before religious ceremonies. ✐ Certain sagewort species are known to cause **rashes** in susceptible individuals.

showy aster

Aster conspicuus Lindl.

<small>ASPEN PARKLAND, BOREAL FOREST, MONTANE, SUBALPINE</small>

HABITAT AND RANGE: Open woodlands at low elevations in the mountains, foothills, aspen parkland and boreal forest. Widespread in Alberta.

FLOWERS: **Ray florets blue-purple, 10 to 15 mm long.** Disk florets brownish yellow. Bracts overlapping, glandular, broad and papery at their bases, with green tips. July to August.

FRUIT: Achene, 3 mm long, with white hairs.

LEAVES: Alternate, **large (to 18 cm long), wide (2 to 8 cm), rough to the the touch, toothed.** Hairy beneath and short-stalked or stalkless. Lower leaves soon deciduous.

GROWTH HABIT: Erect perennial up to 1 m tall, with leaves rough to the touch and a thick stem. The plant is **glandular toward the top**.

*A*ster is from the Latin for "star," referring to the flower shape, while *conspicuus* means "conspicuous," perhaps because of the showy flowers. ✿ The Okanagan soaked the root in water and used the resulting liquid to treat boils, sores and gonorrhea. The leaves were applied to boils as a poultice. ✿ Most of the 250 species of *Aster* in the world are found in North America; 19 species occur in Alberta, of which 3 are discussed in detail

showy aster   (EJ)

in this book. Western willow aster (*A. hesperius*), a widespread species of moist areas, has narrow (5 to 25 mm wide), willow-like leaves and usually more than 10 heads per plant. Another wet habitat species, usually of cold bogs, rush aster (*A. borealis*) has even narrower leaves (2 to 5 mm) and generally fewer than 10 heads per plant.

western willow aster   (CWA)

rush aster   (CWA)

creeping white prairie aster, little gray aster

Aster falcatus Lindl.

<small>PRAIRIE, ASPEN PARKLAND, BOREAL FOREST, MONTANE</small>

creeping white prairie aster   (JH)

HABITAT AND RANGE: Dry, open grassland areas, slopes, banks of rivers, roadsides. Widespread in Alberta.

FLOWERS: **Heads solitary or few at the ends of branches. Ray florets usually white, 22 to 35, mostly 7 mm long or longer.** Disk florets yellow. **Involucre 5 to 8 mm tall, composed of hairy bracts with spiny tips.**

FRUIT: Achene white-hairy, up to 2 mm long, with attached whitish pappus.

LEAVES: Linear, entire, short-hairy. Often **spiny at the tip**. Leafy, often with **tufts of shorter leaves in the leaf axils**.

GROWTH HABIT: Often branched perennial up to 50 cm tall or more from creeping rhizome. Sparsely to densely hairy with flattened, over-lapping or spreading hairs.

The derivation of *Aster* is explained on page 249. *Falcatus* means "falcate" or "sickle-shaped," in reference to the arching flower stalks. ✐ This species resembles tufted white prairie aster (*A. ericoides* ssp. *pansus*) and occurs in similar habitats; however, tufted aster has more flower heads, which appear 1-sided on the branch; smaller and fewer ray florets (10 to 20, usually less than 7 mm long); and a smaller involucre (2.5 to 4.5 mm long).

smooth blue aster, smooth aster

Aster laevis L.

HABITAT AND RANGE: Open wooded or grassy areas, coulees, ditches; often on gravelly soils. Found throughout Alberta.

FLOWERS: Heads few to many in loose clusters. Ray florets 20 or more, **pale to dark purple or bluish,** up to 1 cm long; surrounding **bright-yellow centres** composed of disk florets. Bracts 5 to 7 mm long, overlapping, **sharp-pointed with green tips and dark midribs.** July to September.

FRUIT: Ribbed, flattened, brownish achenes, 3 mm long, with many brownish bristles.

smooth blue aster   (CWE)

LEAVES: Alternate, **dark green to bluish green, often with a whitish bloom** but no hairs. Oval or oblong, entire or toothed, to about 15 cm long. Upper leaves somewhat **fleshy, often clasping the stem. Lower leaves with winged leaf stalks.**

GROWTH HABIT: Erect, robust, rhizomatous perennial up to 120 cm tall from a fibrous root system. Can form colonies.

The derivation of *Aster* is explained on page 249. *Laevis* means smooth and applies to the lack of hairs. ✎ Smooth blue aster is believed to be a selenium absorber and therefore may be dangerous to livestock in pastures or when present in hay. Some people may develop **rashes** from contact with asters. A smoke smudge of smooth blue aster was used by certain native tribes to revive the unconscious and in sweat baths. ✎ Lindley's aster (*A. ciliolatus*), common in Alberta except on the prairies, has overlapping, non-glandular bracts with a whitish margin, pale-blue ray florets and lower stem leaves that are heart-shaped and have long stalks with hairy margins. ✎ It can be difficult to tell the asters from the fleabanes (*Erigeron* spp., see pp 258-60), but the asters usually have wider, fewer ray florets and several series of thicker, stiffer bracts that are often white at the bottom with green tips. In general, asters are taller, leafier plants with more flower heads per stem.

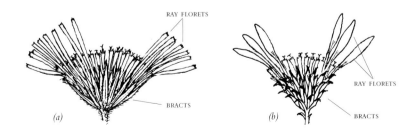

RAY FLORETS

BRACTS

(a)

RAY FLORETS

BRACTS

(b)

differences in flowers between (a) fleabanes and (b) asters

balsamroot, **arrowleaf balsamroot**, Oregon sunflower

Balsamorhiza sagittata (Pursh) Nutt.

<small>PRAIRIE, MONTANE, SUBALPINE</small>

balsamroot   (BA)

HABITAT AND RANGE: Dry, open, often south-facing hillsides in the foothills and grasslands of southwestern Alberta.

FLOWERS: **Large (to 10 cm across), showy, bright-yellow, solitary flower head on a long stalk.** Petals (ray florets) oval, 8 to 25 or more, up to 4 cm long. Disk florets yellow with dark styles. Bracts in 2 to 4-series, covered with tangled hairs, outer spreading, about 3 cm long, inner appressed. May to July.

FRUIT: Dry, smooth, 4-sided black achenes, 7 to 8 mm long.

LEAVES: Many, **large (to 30 cm long and 15 cm wide), basal, long-stalked, arrow or triangular-shaped, thick leaves with prominent veins. Blade gray-green** due to fine white hairs. Stem leaves thin, few.

GROWTH HABIT: Large, robust, hairy, spreading perennial plant with many basal leaves. Up to 80 cm tall from thick, odorous, woody tap root.

*B*alsamorhiza is from the Greek *balsamon* (balsam) and *rhiza* (root), referring to the resinous cover of the tap root. *Sagittata* (sagittate) describes the arrowhead-shaped leaves. ✿ The Thompson ate the ripe seeds, pounded them into a flour or thickener for soups, stews and desserts, and boiled them with deer fat. Various tribes ate the seeds alone or with berries or meat. In the United States "Mormon biscuits" were made with flour from the crushed seeds. The roots were cooked and eaten by the Blackfoot, Nez Perce and Salish. Alberta's Blood tribe burned the roots as a type of incense before battle to bring good luck. Roasted and ground, balsamroot roots also produce an acceptable coffee substitute. The Salish ate the tender, young emerging shoots raw and steamed the roots in the spring to eat as a vegetable or dessert. The Montana Flathead used the leaves to poultice burns and drank tea brewed from the roots to treat tuberculosis and whooping cough and as a cathartic. The Okanagan stuffed the leaves into their moccasins in winter to keep their feet warm. The stems of the flower buds can be peeled and the inner portion eaten (they are said to taste like green sunflower seeds); however, the mature leaves and flower heads are inedible. ✿ There are 12 species of balsamroot in the world, all of which occur in western North America. Only this species occurs in Alberta.

nodding beggarticks, bur–marigold

Bidens cernua L.

PRAIRIE, ASPEN PARKLAND, BOREAL FOREST

HABITAT AND RANGE: Edges of marshes, lakes, streams, ponds; ditches, willow thickets. Widespread in Alberta.

FLOWERS: Heads 12 to 25 mm wide, nodding with age. **Ray florets 6 to 8, yellow, up to 1.5 cm long. The flower head has a scruffy appearance: the ray florets are irregularly spaced and sometimes missing.** Disk florets numerous. Bracts in 2-series: outer large, unequal and leafy, often reflexed; inner membraneous, yellow (often with red or brown stripes). July to September.

FRUIT: Achenes tan-coloured, 5 to 7 mm long, wedge-shaped, with cartilaginous ribs. **Pappus of 4 (sometimes 2) awns, 2 to 3 mm long, with backward-pointing barbs** that stick to clothing and fur for seed dispersal.

LEAVES: Opposite, **stalkless**, sometimes clasping at base. **Narrowly lance-shaped, often wavy or coarsely toothed along the margin,** 5 to 15 cm long.

GROWTH HABIT: Simple or branched, smooth or rough annual with angled stems, 20 to 100 cm tall from fibrous roots.

nodding beggarticks (BA)

The name beggarticks refers to the prickly fruits that easily attach to people and animals. *Bidens* is from the Latin for "two teeth," in reference to the often 2-awned pappus of many of the species; *cernua* is from the Latin *cernuum* (drooping or nodding), likely referring to the nodding flower heads. ✐ There are about 200 species of *Bidens*, widely distributed in the world; 2 other species are found in Alberta. Common beggarticks (*B. frondosa*) is rare in Alberta, only occurring in the extreme southwest corner of the province. It has compound, 3 to 5-parted leaves that are mostly on stalks and absent or inconspicuous ray florets. Tall beggarticks (*B. tripartita*) usually has stalked, lobed leaves and lacks ray florets.

nodding beggarticks (BA)

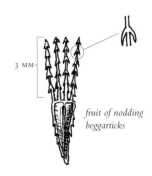

3 MM

fruit of nodding beggarticks

spotted knapweed

Centaurea maculosa Lam.

PRAIRIE, MONTANE

spotted knapweed (EJ)

HABITAT AND RANGE: Roadsides, disturbed ground. An introduced weed that is becoming a problem in the southern part of the province.

FLOWERS: Heads at the ends of branches. **Disk florets only, dark pink to purple or rarely white.** Involucre 10 to 13 mm tall with **ribbed, closely overlapping, pale-green bracts; middle and outer bracts fringed, black-tipped.** June to September.

FRUIT: Flattened achene with pappus up to 2 mm long, sometimes lacking.

LEAVES: Basal and lower leaves deeply incised and sometimes noticeably glandular-dotted. Upper leaves entire. Basal up to 8 cm long, or longer, including leaf stalk.

GROWTH HABIT: Biennial or short-lived perennial, 0.3 to 1.5 m tall, usually from tap root. Covered with thin, white-woolly, tangled hairs that disappear with age.

Knapweed is from the ancient English *knap*, meaning "knob" or "bump," referring to the bumps on the branches. *Centaurea* is from the Greek *kentaur* (centaur), a mythical creature believed to have healing powers. *Maculosa* means "spotted," describing the bracts. ✍ There are 400 species of *Centaurea* in the world, mainly in the Mediterranean region. Besides spotted knapweed, there are 4 other species (all introduced) in Alberta. Russian knapweed (*C. repens*) has entire, rounded, broad bracts with pointed tips, entire or somewhat lobed leaves and a long pappus (6 to 11 mm long). Diffuse knapweed (*C. diffusa*) has involucral bracts with central spines and has many branches. It has no pappus. Russian knapweed has deep rootstocks that can send up shoots from a level below which cultivator blades can reach, and small, cut-up pieces of root can establish new plants. The spines of diffuse knapweed can injure the mouths and digestive systems of livestock, and the roots of both diffuse and spotted knapweed produce chemicals that prevent the germination of other species nearby, allowing knapweed to increase. Understandably, prevention of the spread of these noxious weeds is a serious concern. Yellow star-thistle (*C. solstitialis*) has long spines (more than 10 mm) on the bracts and yellow flowers. It has caused poisoning in horses. The common ornamental bachelor's button or cornflower (*C. cyanus*) has long, bright-blue (occasionally pink or white) flowers and entire, often white-woolly leaves.

(a)

(b)

(c)

involucres of (a) spotted knapweed, (b)Russian knapweed, (c) diffuse knapweed

Canada thistle, field thistle, creeping thistle
Cirsium arvense (L.) Scop.

<small>Prairie, Aspen Parkland, Montane, Boreal Forest</small>

HABITAT AND RANGE: Cultivated fields, roadsides, disturbed areas. Originated in Eurasia but introduced all across Canada.

FLOWERS: In heads, 1 to 2.5 cm long, at the ends of branches. **Male (*staminate*) and female (*pistillate*) flowers usually occur on different plants. Disk florets mauve to pinkish, occasionally white.** No ray florets. Bracts occasionally purplish-tinged, may have prickles at the tips. July to September.

FRUIT: Whitish to dark brown, oblong, flattened, ribbed achene, 3 to 5 mm long, with a feathery, white, deciduous pappus.

LEAVES: Alternate, oblong to lance-shaped, somewhat clasping, stalkless. Smooth to white-hairy beneath, **wavy-margined, spiny-lobed**.

GROWTH HABIT: Much-branched leafy perennial up to 1.2 m tall from a thin, white, creeping rhizome. Often occurs in large colonies.

*C*irsium originates from the Greek *kirsos* (swollen vein), as thistles were supposed to remedy this problem. *Arvense* means "of cultivated fields," likely a reference to the plant's habitat. ✿ Various species of thistles have edible taproots that were eaten boiled or steamed by the B.C. Thompson, Shuswap and Flathead Salish. The root of wavy-leaved thistle (*C. undulatum*) was used to treat toothache by the Lillooet. White or Hooker's thistle (*C. hookerianum*) roots were eaten raw

Canada thistle   (BA)

wavy-leaved thistle   (DJ)

white thistle (BA)

or cooked with meat by Alberta Blackfoot. The young leaves and stems (peeled and with the prickles removed) may also be eaten raw or cooked. ✿ Over the years herbalists have prescribed thistles to treat ailments such as convulsions and nervous diseases. ✿ Canada thistle is a valuable nectar source for honey bees but the extensive creeping underground root system and many wind-blown seeds combine to make this a troublesome (and noxious) weed in Alberta. ✿ There are about 200 species of *Cirsium*, all native to the northern hemisphere. This is the most common of Alberta's 8 thistles. The others are native except for bull thistle (*C. vulgare*). ✿ Wavy-leaved thistle has a large head composed of light-purple or pinkish disk flowers, bracts with a sticky ridge on the back, the outer with spiny tips, long (5 to 7 mm) achenes and broadly lobed leaves. Hooker's thistle has a densely cobwebby involucre, whitish disk flowers and usually cobwebby to tangled-hairy leaves. Bull thistle has a large, attractive, dark-pink to rose-purple flower head, achenes less than 4 mm long, a spiny-bracted involucre to 4 cm long and spiny, rough-hairy leaves.

bull thistle (LF)

scapose hawk's-beard

Crepis runcinata (James) T. & G.

PRAIRIE, ASPEN PARKLAND, MONTANE, SUBALPINE

HABITAT AND RANGE: Moist open areas, saline meadows. Widespread in the southern half of the province.

FLOWERS: 3 to 15 flower heads per plant, all composed of **yellow ray florets, 9 to 18 mm long. Involucre 9 to 16 mm tall**, smooth to hairy, sometimes glandular. Involucral bracts in 1 to 2-series; outer smaller.

FRUIT: **Round, ribbed, brownish achenes, about 1 mm long, constricted at the apex or with a short beak.** Pappus of long, white bristles, about as long as the ray florets.

LEAVES: **Mostly basal in smooth to hairy rosette**, broadly lance-shaped to elliptic, entire to toothed or deeply divided. Stalkless or with winged stalks. Stem leaves few, alternate, narrower.

GROWTH HABIT: 1 to 3-stemmed perennial **with milky juice**, 20 to 70 cm tall from a tap root.

annual hawk's-beard (BA)

*C*repis is derived from the Greek *krepis* (boot or sandal) for unknown reasons. *Runcinata* is from *runcinate*, meaning "having large lobes or teeth pointing towards the base" (referring to the plant's leaves). ✐ There are 200 species of *Crepis* in the world, native to Eurasia, northern Africa and North America. There are 8 species in the province. Annual hawk's-beard (*C. tectorum*) is a weedy annual that lacks a basal rosette at flowering time and has a shorter involucre (6 to 9 mm tall). Alpine or dwarf hawk's-beard (*C. nana*) is a dwarf (2 to 8 cm tall), cushion plant that is found on rocky alpine slopes in the Rocky Mountains.

alpine hawk's-beard (JH)

scapose hawk's-beard

tufted fleabane, wild daisy

Erigeron caespitosus Nutt.

tufted fleabane   (JH)

HABITAT AND RANGE: Dry, open places, south-facing slopes, coulees and eroded badlands; often on rocky soils. Widespread in the southern half of the province and also occurs in the Peace River country.

FLOWERS: Heads **solitary to few per stem. Ray florets 30 to 100**, usually white but sometimes blue or pink, numerous, narrow, 5 to 15 mm long and 1 to 2.5 mm wide. Petals surround central yellow disk florets. Bracts white-hairy, glandular, thickened, overlapping, narrow, 4 to 7 mm long. June to August.

FRUIT: Hairy brown achenes, 1 to 2 mm long, with attached bristly pappus.

LEAVES: **Basal gray-green, short-hairy, lance-shaped to spoon-shaped**, 3-nerved (nerves sometimes obscure), up to 6 cm long, tapering to a leaf stalk. Stem leaves much smaller, stalkless.

GROWTH HABIT: Low growing, sparsely to densely hairy perennial from a **woody base** and deep tap root. Stems several, curved at base then erect, 10 to 30 cm tall. Often forms small clumps or tufts.

cut-leaved daisy   (BA)

In ancient times it was believed that bundles of related species would discourage fleas, hence the common name fleabane. ✎ *Erigeron* is from the Greek *eri* (spring) and *geron* (old man) and possibly refers to the hairy-tufted fruits or the overall hairiness of some of the species. *Caespitosus* means tufted and refers to the growth habit. ✎ Tufted fleabane contains a volatile turpentine-like oil, and the liquid from the boiled roots and leaves was used to treat many ailments such as rheumatism, hemorrhoids and gonorrhea. The Cree boiled the plant and drank the resulting tea as a diarrhea remedy. Various species were listed in the U.S. Pharmacopoeia for their stimulating properties. ✎ The smoke of burned plants is said to repel gnats and fleas. ✎ There are about 200 species of *Erigeron* in the world,

purple daisy   (LA)

many in western North America and some in South America, Europe and Asia. Approximately 23 species are found in Alberta. Cut-leaved daisy or compound-leaved fleabane (*E. compositus*) also has white, pink or blue flowers (sometimes the ray florets are absent) and is found in similar habitats, but may be distinguished by its finely dissected leaves. ✎ An attractive species of alpine sites, purple daisy (*E. humilis*) is a small plant with shorter, white to purplish ray florets (3 to 6 mm long) and stem; young leaves and involucre covered with long purple hairs. ✎ Fleabanes are difficult to tell apart and are sometimes hard to tell from asters; however, the species can be distinguished by several characteristics. Fleabanes generally have narrower, more numerous ray florets. The bracts on fleabanes usually lack the papery white bases and green tips seen in many asters; the bracts are often nearly equal in length and arranged in a single series (see page 236). In general, most fleabanes are shorter and have fewer leaves and fewer flower heads per stem than asters.

smooth fleabane, smooth daisy

Erigeron glabellus Nutt.

PRAIRIE, ASPEN PARKLAND, BOREAL FOREST, MONTANE, SUBALPINE

smooth fleabane (DJ)

HABITAT AND RANGE: Meadows, gravelly banks, roadsides, disturbed areas; moist open areas in grasslands, mountains and open woods. Common.

FLOWERS: Heads with **numerous (well over 100) bluish, pink or nearly white ray florets to 1 mm wide and 8 to 15 mm long.** Disk yellow, to 5.5 mm wide. Involucre 5 to 9 mm high, hairy. **Bracts narrow, with a noticeable green to brown midvein.** June to August.

FRUIT: Pale brown, flattened, 2-nerved achenes, 1 to 2 mm long. **Pappus of long, bristly hairs and short, thicker hairs.**

LEAVES: **Mainly basal.** Lowest leaves lance-shaped, up to 15 cm long, persistent. Stem leaves gradually reduced upwards. Dark green, smooth to short-hairy.

GROWTH HABIT: Erect biennial or perennial up to 60 cm tall with simple or branched stems. Stems curved from base, sparsely to very hairy. May form small clumps.

When burned or dried in bundles, fleabane smoke is said to repel insects, hence the common name. Despite the name smooth fleabane (*glabellus* means "smooth"), this plant is often hairy. The origin of the genus name *Erigeron* is explained on page 259. ⌀ This plant is similar to Philadelphia fleabane (*E. philadelphicus*); however, the leaves of Philadelphia fleabane are more clasping at the base and spoon-shaped. Philadelphia fleabane contains compounds that have been used to treat chronic diarrhea and hemmorhage in childbirth. Wandering daisy (*E. peregrinus* ssp. *callianthemus*), which is common in the mountains, has wider (2 to 4 mm), usually deep-pink to purplish (sometimes lighter or white) ray florets and leaves with sunken, usually hairy veins; it reaches 10 to 70 cm tall.

wandering daisy (CWA)

Philadelphia fleabane (EJ)

gaillardia, **brown-eyed susan**, blanket flower
Gaillardia aristata Pursh
<small>PRAIRIE, ASPEN PARKLAND, MONTANE</small>

HABITAT AND RANGE: Open grasslands, dry hillsides, roadsides, open woods. Widespread in the southern half of the province.

FLOWERS: 1 or more large, showy flower heads per plant, on long stalks. **Ray florets yellow, broad, often reddish or purplish at base,** 1 to 3 cm long with **3 small lobes at the tip. Central disk purplish or reddish, woolly-hairy,** 1.5 to 4 cm wide. Involucre 2 to 3 cm wide, composed of tapering, hairy, reflexed bracts.

FRUIT: Grayish to black achenes with long, stiff hairs and long pappus of **5 to 10 pointed, bristly scales.**

LEAVES: Numerous, alternate, lance-shaped; margins entire, coarsely toothed or lobed. Lower leaves 5 to 12 cm long, stalked; upper stalkless and smaller. **Grayish and rough due to short hairs.**

GROWTH HABIT: Attractive, somewhat hairy, erect, occasionally branched, perennial herb, 30 to 60 cm tall, from slender taproot.

gaillardia (BA)

This plant is named after a French botanist, Gaillard de Marentonneau. The species name *aristata* means "bristly" or "bearded," in reference to the bristles of the flower head. ✐ The Alberta Stoney drank a tea of gaillardia to relieve menstrual problems, and the Blackfoot used the root to treat human gastroenteritis and saddle sores in horses. The Okanagan steeped the whole plant in water to treat venereal diseases. ✐ There are 12 species of *Gaillardia* in the world, mainly in North America. Only this species is native to Alberta, although cultivars are grown here ornamentally.

gumweed, resin weed, gum plant, tarweed

Grindelia squarrosa (Pursh) Dunal

PRAIRIE, ASPEN PARKLAND, BOREAL FOREST, MONTANE

gumweed (CWE)

HABITAT AND RANGE: Dry, eroded slopes, dry grassland, roadsides, river flats, saline areas, disturbed sites. Often on sandy or gravelly soil. Common, particularly in the southern half of the province.

FLOWERS: Numerous heads per plant, composed of bright-yellow ray florets, 7 to 15 mm long, and central disk florets in a dense head, 1 to 2 cm wide. **Bracts numerous, sticky, shiny, narrow, overlapping; the lower usually reflexed.** July to September.

FRUIT: Ribbed, light-brown achenes, 2 to 4 mm long, with a 2 to 3-awned deciduous pappus.

LEAVES: Alternate, dark green, narrowly oblong, stiff, **glandular-sticky**, entire or slightly toothed, to 6 cm long. Upper stalkless and somewhat clasping, with short, pointed or rounded apex; lower leaves with long leaf stalks.

GROWTH HABIT: Red to purplish-stemmed, often wide-branched, **sticky perennial or biennial**, 30 to 100 cm tall from a tap root.

The common names allude to the sticky resins produced by the plant. The genus name commemorates David Grindel, an early Russian botanist, and *squarrosa* means "with parts spreading or recurved at ends," referring to the lower bracts. ✍ Gumweed was listed in the United States Pharmacopoeia until 1926, primarily as a sedative, antispasmodic and treatment for poison ivy rashes. It contains resins, tannic acid, volatile oils and an alkaloid. ✍ Some North American tribes made a tea from the flowers and leaves to treat poison ivy. The Blackfoot, Flathead and Crow drank a solution containing the leaves and flowers to treat bronchitis, asthma, pneumonia and colds, and to relieve muscle spasms. They also prepared a cough medicine from the sticky buds. The Blackfoot used the boiled roots to treat liver problems and drank a tea made from the plant to treat kidney disease and prevent syphilis. The Flathead rubbed the flower heads into horses' hooves to strengthen them. The Cree used the plant as a contraceptive and, combined with chamomile, to relieve kidney pain. Europeans and Americans used a gumweed extract to treat some bladder diseases. ✍ There are over 50 *Grindelia* species in the world, native to western North America and South America. Only this species is found in Alberta.

broomweed, **snakeweed**, broom snakeroot
Gutierrezia sarothrae (Pursh) Britt. & Rusby
PRAIRIE, ASPEN PARKLAND

HABITAT AND RANGE: Dry grasslands on clay or gravelly soils; dry, sandy, exposed slopes in the badlands. Often in disturbed areas. Widespread in the southern third of the province.

FLOWERS: Numerous small flower heads in flat-topped to slightly rounded terminal clusters. **Ray florets few, bright yellow, up to 7 mm long.** Disk florets yellow. **Bracts sticky-glandular, in overlapping series; lower narrow and greenish, upper straw-coloured, stiffer.** July to September.

FRUIT: Dry 5-angled achenes, 2 to 3 mm long, with scaly pappus.

broomweed (CWA)

LEAVES: Narrowly linear, gray-green, stalkless, somewhat clasping, **frequently glandular-dotted**. Some leaves entire, some divided, often slightly hairy, 1 to 4 cm long.

GROWTH HABIT: Low-growing, **tufted, much-branched perennial** up to 40 cm tall from deep tap root. Woody at base.

The common name broomweed comes from the numerous roughened stems. A tea made from the plant has been used to treat snake bite, which perhaps accounts for the name snakeweed. The genus name honors P. Gutierrez, an early Spanish botanist, and *sarothrae* is from the Greek for "broom, especially one made of twigs." ✍ The plant contains **poisonous** saponins which cause sheep and cattle to abort and may cause death. It is most toxic in the leaf-formation stage and when growing on sandy soils, especially when other grazing is scarce. ✍ Chewed broomweed was applied to insect stings and was occasionally used by some southern United States tribes as a tea to soothe gastric upset. Navajo women drank a tea of broomweed to promote expulsion of the placenta after birth. The plants boiled in water were used to treat malaria and rheumatism. The Blackfoot inhaled steam from the boiled roots as a treatment for respiratory ailments. ✍ There are 25 species of *Gutierrezia* in the world, native to western North America, Mexico and South America. Only this species occurs in Alberta.

spiny ironplant, ironweed

Haplopappus spinulosus (Pursh) DC.

PRAIRIE, ASPEN PARKLAND

spiny ironplant (CWᴇ)

HABITAT AND RANGE: Dry, saline flats, eroded slopes and roadsides (often on sandy soil) of the grasslands and foothills in the southern third of the province.

FLOWERS: Many heads per plant, each to 2 cm across. **Ray florets 15 to 50, yellow, 12 to 15 mm long. Central disk florets yellow**, disk to about 1.5 cm wide. **Involucres 5 to 8 mm tall**, composed of narrowly linear, overlapping, pointed or bristle-tipped bracts, in 4 to 6-series. **Bracts usually spreading or curved backwards with age.** July to September.

FRUIT: Achenes tan to white, 2 to 2.5 mm long; hairy with tuft of stiff, tan bristles (pappus).

LEAVES: Alternate, 1 to 4 cm long, **incised into narrow segments**. Grayish or bluish green, usually woolly-hairy, **usually with spiny teeth on the margins**.

GROWTH HABIT: Prostrate or erect, several-stemmed, branched perennial, to 40 cm tall from a woody base. Can spread rapidly in disturbed sites.

*H*aplopappus is from the Greek *haplous* (simple) and *pappus* (seed down). *Spinulosus* is in reference to the spiny leaves. ✒ Several species of *Haplopappus* are poisonous to horses, cattle and sheep. ✒ There are 150 species of *Haplopappus* in the world, mainly in North and South America; 4 of these occur in Alberta. This is the only Alberta species with deeply divided leaves; the leaves of the others have occasional teeth or are entire. Lyall's ironplant (*H. lyallii*) is a short (5 to 10 cm), glandular-hairy species of alpine slopes. It has spoon-shaped to broadly lance-shaped, somewhat glandular leaves. One-flowered ironplant (*H. uniflorus*) has a thickly hairy involucre and often hairy lower leaves; the heads are mostly solitary. It is generally found on open slopes at lower elevations.

Lyall's ironplant (CWᴀ)

one-flowered ironplant (CWᴇ)

sneezeweed
Helenium autumnale L.
PRAIRIE, BOREAL FOREST, ALPINE

HABITAT AND RANGE: Stream banks, ditches, river banks and other wet locations. Mainly in the southern half of the province but also reported from the boreal forest.

FLOWERS: Heads several at the ends of branches. **Ray florets 10 to 20, yellow to orange, hairy and often glandular, wedge-shaped, 3-lobed at the tip, often bent sharply downwards. Disk florets yellow, glandular, in round disk 8 to 20 mm wide. Involucral bracts narrow, reflexed, in 2 to 3-series.** July to September.

FRUIT: 4 to 5-angled, hairy, tan achenes. Pappus of several sharp, broad, white to brownish scales, each less than 2 mm long.

LEAVES: Alternate, numerous, short-hairy, **glandular-dotted**. Lance-shaped to oval, margins shallowly toothed to entire, 4 to 15 cm long. Stalkless or with short, winged stalks. Lowest leaves deciduous.

GROWTH HABIT: Sparsely hairy to smooth, glandular, leafy perennial, 30 to 100 cm tall, from fibrous roots.

sneezeweed   (CWA)

The Blackfoot crushed the flowers and inhaled them to treat hay fever (perhaps its use for this purpose gave the plant its common name sneezeweed). Others suggest that the name originates from the use of the dried flower heads as a source of snuff. *Helenium* honours Helen of Troy, while *autumnale* means "pertaining to autumn," a reference to the late flowering. This plant has apparently caused livestock poisoning. There are approximately 40 species of *Helenium*, native to North and South America. In Alberta we have 2 varieties of the species *autumnale*. Variety *montanum* (Nutt.) Fern. has ray florets 10 to 15 mm long, and variety *grandiflorum* (Nutt.) T. & G. has ray florets 15 to 25 mm long.

common annual sunflower

Helianthus annuus L. ssp. *lenticularis* (Lindl.) Cockerell

<small>Prairie, Aspen Parkland</small>

common annual sunflower (CB)

HABITAT AND RANGE: Disturbed roadsides, open areas, moist meadows, edges of marshes, dry, eroded slopes. Fairly common in southern Alberta, of scattered occurrence north of the Red Deer River.

FLOWERS: Several large, showy flower heads with numerous, **bright-yellow, pointed, grooved petals (ray florets), 40 to 45 mm long**. Disk florets reddish brown or purple, sometimes yellow, disk 2 to 4 cm wide. Bracts in 2 to 3-series, broadly oval, **abruptly tapered above middle**, darker at base, with stiff, spiny hairs, **long-hairy on the margins**. June to September.

FRUIT: Head of brown to black, slightly hairy, angled achenes, 4 to 5 mm long, with 2 deciduous awns.

LEAVES: Mainly **alternate**, stalked, usually toothed. Thick, prominently veined, **stiff-hairy with a rough surface**. Lower leaves sometimes heart-shaped, upper oval to somewhat triangular.

GROWTH HABIT: Bushy, robust, rough-hairy annual up to 120 cm tall. Stems stout, often mottled, with stiff, short hairs.

*H*elianthus is from the Greek *helios* (sun) and *anthos* (flower). *Annuus* refers to the annual nature of the plant, while *lenticularis* means "lens-shaped," perhaps in reference to the achenes. ✍ Some North American natives ate the seeds raw or cooked into a gruel. They are said to act as a diuretic and expectorant, and have been used to treat respiratory diseases and whooping cough. They may also be roasted and ground into a coffee and are a valuable emergency food, being high in protein, calcium and Vitamins A, B, D and E. In some regions of Germany, the leaves are dried and used as a tobacco substitute. Sunflowers should be used in moderation, however, as they are said to contain **toxic nitrates**. ✍ The pith from the stems has been used as a mounting medium for specimens to be studied under a microscope, the stem-fibres can be made into thread, and the inner stalk has been made into writing paper. ✍ Our cultivated sunflowers have been bred from this species. Common annual sunflower is the state flower of Texas. ✍ There are 60 species of *Helianthus*, chiefly in the New World; 5 occur in Alberta. The only other annual species, called Coupland's annual sunflower (*H. couplandii*), occurs in similar habitats. It has soft hairs, its lower leaves are wedge-shaped at the base and the involucral bracts lack long hairs on the margins. Rhombic-leaved sunflower (*H. rigidus* var. *subrhomboideus*; *H. subrhomboideus* in Moss 1983) and common tall or Nuttall's sunflower are pictured on page 267.

rhombic-leaved sunflower

Helianthus rigidus (Cass.) Desf. var.*subrhomboideus* (Rydb.) Cronq.
(*Helianthus subrhomboideus* Rydb. in Moss 1983)

PRAIRIE, ASPEN PARKLAND

HABITAT AND RANGE: Dry grassland, roadsides, dry, open areas, disturbed sites; often on light soils. Mostly in the southern half of the province but also in the Peace River country.

FLOWERS: Heads few or solitary. Ray florets 15 to 20, bright yellow, 1.5 to 4 cm long, surrounding a purple or reddish brown (occasionally yellow) central disk, **1 to 2 cm wide**. Bracts dark green, shining, overlapping, **broadly oval to lance-shaped**, with short-hairy margins. July to September.

FRUIT: Slightly hairy achenes, with **pappus of 2 long awns and some shorter scales**.

LEAVES: Mainly opposite, 3-nerved, 5 to 15 cm long, 1.5 to 6 cm wide,

rhombic-leaved sunflower (CWE)

obliquely 4-sided (hence the variety name). Lower spoon-shaped, upper lance-shaped. Entire or slightly toothed, thick, **tapering at both ends. Roughened or stiff-hairy on both sides** and minutely glandular-dotted.

GROWTH HABIT: Showy, erect, usually stiff-hairy perennial, up to 120 cm tall from a stout rootstock.

The genus name is from the Greek *helios* (sun) and *anthos* (flower). *Rigidus* means "rigid," possibly describing the robust stalk or short, stiff hairs, and *subrhomboideus* refers to the nearly rhomboid (diamond-shaped) leaves. ✿ The Alberta Blackfoot ate the seeds raw and used the oil from the seeds as a lotion for skin and hair. The seeds are also eaten by grouse and pheasant, songbirds and small mammals. Some native tribes boiled the seeds to release the oil, which then floated to the surface.

common tall sunflower (JH)

The oil was used for cooking. ✿ Sunflower oil was used for making soaps, candles and varnishes in Europe. ✿ Common tall or Nuttall's sunflower (*H. nuttallii*) is taller (up to 2 m), has a yellow or light-brown disk, narrow, tapering involucral bracts and narrower leaves (0.5 to 3 cm wide), and its stem is roughened below the inflorescence. Narrow-leaved sunflower (*H. maximiliani*) is a perennial with short, white, flat-lying hairs on the stem below the inflorescence and on the upper involucral bracts, mainly opposite (usually folded) leaves and a yellow or light-brown disk. ✿ Both narrow-leaved sunflower and related, cultivated Jerusalem artichoke (*H. tuberosus*) have edible tuberous roots.

golden aster, hairy golden aster
Heterotheca villosa (Pursh) Shinners
PRAIRIE, ASPEN PARKLAND, MONTANE

golden aster   (CWE)

HABITAT AND RANGE: Dry, open, sandy prairie and hillsides, often on southern exposures; river terraces, disturbed areas. Widespread in the southern half of the province.

FLOWERS: Heads 1 to many. Numerous, lance-shaped, **bright-yellow ray florets, 6 to 15 mm long, with yellow to brown central disk florets**, 6 to 9 mm long. Bracts white-hairy, pointed, overlapping, 5 to 10 mm long. July to September.

FRUIT: Head of flattened, pale-gray to light-brown, hairy achenes, 2 to 4 mm long, each with a **double row of tawny-white bristles** (pappus).

LEAVES: Numerous, alternate, stalkless or with short stalks. Gray-green, oblong or broadly lance-shaped, 2 to 5 cm long, sometimes covered with slightly sticky hairs. Entire or sometimes toothed, occasionally glandular. Leaves longest near the middle of the plant. Lower leaves deciduous.

GROWTH HABIT: Stiff-hairy, grayish green, sprawling or ascending perennial herb, mostly 10 to 60 cm tall, with **several rigid stems** from a woody tap root. May form large patches.

*H*eterotheca is from the Greek *heteros* (different) and *theca* (case or container) for unknown reasons, while the species name *villosa* means "soft-haired."

narrow-leaved hawkweed

Hieracium umbellatum L.

PRAIRIE, ASPEN PARKLAND, BOREAL FOREST, MONTANE, SUBALPINE, ALPINE

HABITAT AND RANGE: Open woods, grassy meadows, roadsides, clearings, disturbed areas. Common throughout Alberta.

FLOWERS: Heads 1 to many, on ascending stalks. Heads composed only of yellow ray florets, no disk florets present. **Involucres 8 to 12 mm tall, with blackish green, overlapping, smooth or slightly hairy bracts.** June to September.

FRUIT: Slender, ribbed, brown achene 3 mm long. **Pappus of rough, yellowish or brownish bristles.**

LEAVES: Middle leaves lance-shaped or oval, hairy to roughened or smooth, **distantly toothed** or entire. Upper leaves reduced, stalkless, sometimes clasping. Basal and lowest stem leaves soon deciduous.

GROWTH HABIT: Leafy perennial, 20 to 100 cm tall **with milky juice** and short, woody rootstock. Stems solitary or few, smooth or sparsely hairy with white and black hairs.

narrow-leaved hawkweed   (DJ)

*H*ieracium is from the Greek *hierax* (hawk), as it was once believed that eating these plants improved a hawk's vision. *Umbellatum* likely refers to the umbel shape of the flower clusters. ✿ When cut, the leaves, stems and roots exude a milky latex that was used as a chewing gum by British Columbia tribes. ✿ There are from 800 to 10,000 species of *Hieracium* (depending on the taxonomic authority) in the Old and New World. There are 5 *Hieracium* species in Alberta. Woolly hawkweed (*H. scouleri* var. *griseum*; *H. cynoglossoides* in Moss 1983) is extremely hairy with long, white to tan hairs. White hawkweed (*H. albiflorum*) has white flowers and a tufted habit; it is found on grassy slopes and river terraces to alpine elevations.

woolly hawkweed   (JH)

white hawkweed   (JP)

narrow-leaved hawkweed

tufted hymenopappus
Hymenopappus filifolius Hook.
PRAIRIE

tufted hymenopappus (CWA)

HABITAT AND RANGE: Dry hills, grasslands; often on sandy or gravelly soil. Restricted to the extreme south of the province.

FLOWERS: Few to many heads in an uneven cluster. Disk florets tubular, yellowish, glandular at base, about 7 mm long. **No ray florets. Involucres 5 to 9 mm tall, covered with soft, white, woolly hairs.** Bracts in 2 to 3-series; inner bract tips broad, rounded, and yellowish to greenish. June to July.

FRUIT: Narrow, wedge-shaped, ribbed, long, white, silky-hairy achenes with pappus of tiny scales.

LEAVES: Mostly basal, **deeply divided into narrow segments and white woolly-hairy when young,** becoming smooth with age. Lower leaves stalked and elongate; upper few, smaller, alternate.

GROWTH HABIT: Smooth to tangled-hairy, several-stemmed perennial, 20 to 40 cm tall, from tap root.

*H*ymenopappus is from the Greek *hymen* (membrane) and *pappos* (pappus); *filifolius* refers to the filiform (thread-like, long and slender) leaves. ✍ There are 12 species of *Hymenopappus*, all native to North America. Only this species occurs in Alberta.

butte marigold, stemless rubber-weed
Hymenoxys acaulis (Pursh) Parker
PRAIRIE

HABITAT AND RANGE: Dry, often sandy or rocky, exposed hillsides, grasslands, eroded slopes. Restricted to the southern quarter of the province.

FLOWERS: Bright-yellow, showy, **solitary heads on leafless stalks**. Ray florets 3-lobed, reflexed with age, up to 20 mm long; occasionally missing. Disk florets orange-yellow; disk to 3 cm wide. **Bracts white, hairy, linear to oblong, in 2 to 3-series, not united at base.** May to June.

FRUIT: Head of achenes. Each achene 2 to 3 mm long, white-hairy with **scaly pappus**.

LEAVES: **All basal, entire, narrowly lance-shaped to spoon-shaped**, up to 8 cm long, gray-green, soft-hairy. Often whitish-papery at base.

GROWTH HABIT: Creeping, tufted, hairy or smooth perennial, up to 30 cm tall from a woody rootstock. Spreads to form small colonies.

The roots ooze a milky, white sap when cut, likely the source of the name "rubber-weed." *Hymenoxys* is from the Greek *hymen* (membrane) and *oxys* (sharp), referring to the the pappus scales. *Acaulis* means "lacking a stem." ✿ This species is often recommended as an ornamental for rock gardens. ✿ There are 20 species of *Hymenoxys*, most in the interior of western North America but some in South America; 2 species occur in Alberta. Colorado rubber-plant (*H. richardsonii*), described on page 272, has narrower ray florets and linear leaves, usually with 2 to 3 divisions; its outer bracts are partly united.

butte marigold   (LF)

Colorado rubber-plant

Hymenoxys richardsonii (Hook.) Cockerell

PRAIRIE, ASPEN PARKLAND

Colorado rubber-plant (CWa)

HABITAT AND RANGE: Dry, often rocky or eroded slopes and grasslands; roadsides, badlands. Often on well-drained soil. Widespread in the southern half of the province.

FLOWERS: Flower heads few, sometimes solitary; 1.5 to 2 cm across **in flat-topped cluster.** Inflorescence hairy. Ray florets yellow, 3-lobed at tip, 7 to 15 mm long. Disk florets yellow, 3 to 5 mm long; disk 7 to 17 mm wide. Involucre 4 to 8 mm tall; **bracts in 2 series. Outer bracts partly united at base, hairy.** May to July.

FRUIT: Head of achenes. Each white-hairy achene is about 3 mm long and has 5 or 6 narrow, pointed, pale-coloured scales.

LEAVES: Alternate, **divided into 3 to 7 narrow segments.** Tufted, mostly basal, fleshy, to 10 cm long. Smooth or occasionally hairy, with glandular dots.

GROWTH HABIT: Perennial up to 30 cm tall from branched and woody rootstock. Often with dead leaves and tuft of white hairs at base of stem. May form small colonies.

The plant secretes a milky latex from the roots, which is likely the origin of the common name. The derivation of *Hymenoxys* is explained on page 271; *richardsonii* honours explorer John Richardson. ✦ The Blood used this plant to treat headaches, colds and liver ailments, to colour arrow shafts and to fix dyed materials. It can be poisonous to sheep, goats and cattle. ✦ The closely related butte marigold (*H. acaulis*), described on page 271, has hairy, undivided leaves that are all basal, compared to Colorado rubber-plant's divided, usually smooth leaves, wider flower heads (to 3 cm) and bracts that are not united at base.

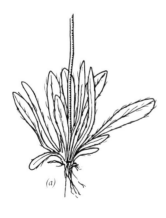

(a)   *(b)*

leaf differences between (a) butte marigold and (b) Colorado rubber-plant

common blue lettuce, wild blue lettuce

Lactuca tatarica (L.) C.A. Mey. ssp. *pulchella* (Pursh) Stebb.
(*Lactuca pulchella* (Pursh) DC. in Moss 1983)
PRAIRIE, ASPEN PARKLAND, BOREAL FOREST

HABITAT AND RANGE: Fields, roadsides, meadows, thickets, shores, stream banks, alkali flats; often on moist, heavy soil. Widespread in Alberta.

FLOWERS: Several heads per plant, each up to 2.5 cm across. **Pale to dark-blue ray florets, 17 to 22 mm long, toothed at tip**; no disk florets. **Involucral bracts overlapping, frequently reddish to purplish, with broad, white margins. Bracts form cylinder 15 to 20 mm long.** June to September.

FRUIT: Ridged achenes, 4 to 7 mm long, with short, thick beak and thick, soft, white pappus. Achenes red when immature, grayish with age. Beak equal in length or shorter than body of achene.

LEAVES: Alternate, **pale bluish green, with whitish bloom and prominent whitish midvein. Narrowly lance-shaped, often with backward-pointing lobes**, stalkless, 5 to 18 cm long. Lower leaves toothed, upper entire.

GROWTH HABIT: Branched, leafy perennial, 40 to 90 cm tall from spreading rhizome. **Stems and roots exude milky sap when cut.** Often occurs in colonies.

common blue lettuce   (BA)

*L*actuca is from the Latin *lac* (milk), referring to the milky sap. *Tatarica* refers to Asian origins, while *pulchella* is derived from the Latin *pulcher* (beautiful), describing the attractive flowers. The *Lactuca* genus is particularly enjoyed by horses, and the plants are sometimes called horseweeds. *L. sativa* is our common garden lettuce. ✐ There are 50 species of *Lactuca*, native to Eurasia, Africa and North America; 2 additional species are found in Alberta. Rare tall blue lettuce (*L. biennis*) has larger leaves (10 to 40 cm long) and its achene lacks a beak. Prickly lettuce (*L. serriola*) has yellow flowers and spiny leaves. The young leaves of prickly lettuce have been eaten raw, although they are said to be bitter and are believed to have caused cattle poisoning.

tall blue lettuce   (BA)

ox-eye daisy, white daisy, field daisy, marguerite, poverty weed, white-weed

Leucanthemum vulgare Lam.(*Chrysanthemum leucanthemum* L. in Moss 1983)

PRAIRIE, ASPEN PARKLAND, MONTANE, SUBALPINE

ox-eye daisy   (BA)

HABITAT AND RANGE: Introduced weed from Europe. Found in disturbed sites, roadsides and pastures.

FLOWERS: Heads terminal on long stalks. Flower head up to 5 cm across, composed of **white ray florets 1 to 2 cm long, surrounding yellow d⸱ ⸱rets. Bracts overlapping, narrow, ⸱nsparent at margin and tip, and ⸱brown tracing near margin.** June

⸱ownish, **white-ribbed** achenes,

⸱ooth to slightly hairy. Basal ⸱nce-shaped to spoon- ⸱ to lobed margins. Stem ⸱kless, smaller, somewhat clasp- ⸱wer and toothed near their bases.

⸱ABIT: Smooth to sparsely hairy peren- ⸱o 1 m tall from short rootstock. Can form ⸱rge patches.

D aisy is from the Anglo-Saxon *day's eye*, because the English daisy closes at night, opens at sun-up and thus is the "eye of the day." *Leucanthemum* comes from the Greek *leukos* (white) and *anthos* (flower), and *vulgare* means "common." ❧ The young leaves may be used in salads, although they are strongly flavoured. When eaten by dairy cattle, they give a bad taste to the milk. ❧ Ox-eye daisy was used in developing the ornamental Shasta daisy. Ox-eye daisy is similar to scentless chamomile (*Matricaria perforata*), but chamomile has narrow, finely dissected leaves.

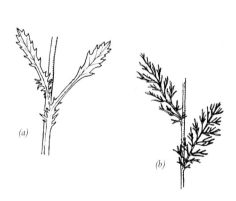

leaf differences between (a) ox-eye daisy and (b) scentless chamomile

ox-eye daisy   (BA)

dotted blazingstar, dotted gayfeather
Liatris punctata Hook.

HABITAT AND RANGE: Dry grassland and hillsides (often on southern exposures) and dry, sandy soils. Common in the southern third of the province.

FLOWERS: **Disk florets only, purple or rose-coloured**, crowded in stalkless, closely bunched clusters at the top of the stem. Flower heads about 12 mm across. Flowers long-tubular, 5-lobed. Stigmas 2-lobed, protruding, curved. Bracts in several series, broadly lance-shaped, hairy-margined, glandular-dotted. Late July to September.

FRUIT: Head of tapered, hairy, gray-black, 10-ribbed achenes with feathery bristles.

dotted blazingstar   (CWA)

LEAVES: Numerous, alternate, entire, gray-green with a whitish midvein, thick but narrow. Linear to lance-shaped, **2 to 4 mm wide** and 3 to 15 cm long, somewhat **dotted with translucent spots**, often hairy on thickened white margins. Basal leaves longest, upper leaves shorter.

GROWTH HABIT: Leafy, tufted, curved to erect perennial herb, 20 to 60 cm tall from a thickened root. Often forms clumps.

The derivation of *Liatris* is unknown but gayfeather and blazingstar suggest the bright, star-shaped flowers. *Punctata* refers to the glands on the leaves, which appear like dark puncture marks. ✿ The plant was called crow root by the Blackfoot because the root is said to be eaten in fall by crows and ravens. The Blackfoot ate the thickened root in spring, and also boiled it to treat swellings. A tea made from the root was drunk to remedy stomach aches. ✿ There are 30 species of *Liatris* in the world, most native to temperate North America; 2 occur in Alberta. Meadow blazingstar (*L. ligulistylis*) has larger (1 to 3 cm wide), rounder heads and wider (10 to 20 mm) lower leaves. It is usually found in moister habitats of the aspen parkland.

meadow blazingstar   (CWA)

skeletonweed, prairie pink, skeleton-plant, rush skeletonweed
Lygodesmia juncea (Pursh) D. Don
PRAIRIE, ASPEN PARKLAND

skeletonweed   (CWA)

HABITAT AND RANGE: Dry, often sandy grasslands, ridges, roadsides and eroded slopes. Found in the southern half of the province.

FLOWERS: Heads 1 to 1.5 cm in diameter, **solitary at the ends of upper branches**. Ray florets 5, pink, to about 2 cm long. No disk florets. Involucre 10 to 16 mm tall, usually composed of 5 narrow bracts. Late June to September.

FRUIT: Head of narrow achenes. Each achene 4 to 8-ribbed, 5 to 7 mm long, with soft, tan bristles.

LEAVES: **Small, linear, usually less than 5 cm long.** Upper reduced and scale-like.

GROWTH HABIT: Much-branched perennial, up to 40 cm tall from creeping root. Stems grooved, exuding a milky juice when broken. Often covered with round insect galls.

*L*ygodesmia comes from the Greek *lygos* (plant twig) and *desme* (bundle), referring to the appearance of the plant. *Juncea* means "rush-like." ∅ The Blackfoot and Sioux used a mixture containing the stems to treat sore eyes and made a tea from the leaves to increase milk flow in nursing mothers. Sap from broken stems was allowed to harden, then chewed like gum. The plant was also used in a mixture to ease heartburn. The Stoneys treated themselves with skeletonweed to relieve fever, and the Cree chopped the stems and brewed them into a tea to ease morning sickness. Using this plant medicinally is not recommended, however, as it **can contain nitrates in toxic levels**. ∅ There are 6 species of *Lygodesmia* in the world, mostly in the western United States and adjacent Mexico; 2 species occur in Alberta. The rare annual skeletonweed (*L. rostrata*) is an annual, has longer leaves (mostly more than 5 cm long), is usually taller (30 to 100 cm tall) and occurs on sandy banks and dunes in the southeastern and east-central parts of Alberta.

annual skeletonweed   (CWA)

hoary aster, canescent aster

Machaeranthera canescens (Pursh) A. Gray
PRAIRIE

HABITAT AND RANGE: Dry, open ground: roadsides, clay flats, sandy soils. In the southern third of the province.

FLOWERS: Many heads in an open cluster, often glandular in the inflorescence. **Ray florets relatively few, bluish purple, 5 to 12 mm long.** Involucre 6 to 10 mm tall, hairy, sometimes glandular. **Bracts overlapping, in several series, squared-off and green at the tips, lighter at the base, and often spreading or bent backwards.** June to September.

FRUIT: Hairy tan achenes, 3 to 4 mm long, each achene with a stiff, unequal, bristly pappus.

hoary aster (CWA)

LEAVES: **Entire to toothed with spiny tips.** Basal leaves broadly lance-shaped to spoon-shaped, sometimes deciduous. Stem leaves smaller and narrowly lance-shaped to linear.

GROWTH HABIT: Usually branched, several-stemmed biennial or short-lived perennial, 10 to 50 cm tall from tap root. **Hairy, particularly near the top, with short, whitish hairs, giving the plant a greyish appearance.**

*M*achaeranthera means "sickle-shaped anther." *Canescens* means "grayish-coloured due to the fine hairs." ✒ Tansy aster *(M. tanacetifolia)* may be differentiated from hoary aster by its dissected leaves. Toothed ironplant (*M. grindelioides*) also occurs in southern Alberta, but it lacks ray florets and therefore may be readily distinguished from hoary aster and tansy aster.

hoary aster (JH)

toothed ironplant (CWA)

pineappleweed, rayless chamomile, rayless mayweed
Matricaria discoidea DC.
(*Matricaria matricarioides* (Less.) Porter in Moss 1983)
PRAIRIE, ASPEN PARKLAND, MONTANE

HABITAT AND RANGE: Disturbed ground, roadsides. Introduced from Eurasia and now a common weed throughout the province.

FLOWERS: Heads several, **without petals (ray florets). Greenish yellow disk florets in compact cone-shaped head, up to 10 mm broad. Bracts with broad, whitish margins, prominent darker midvein**; in 2 to 3-series. July to August.

FRUIT: Ribbed, dry achenes at base of disk florets. Achenes 1.5 mm long, greenish with 1 red vein.

LEAVES: Alternate, leafy green, to 5 cm long. **Finely dissected with narrow (1 to 2 mm) segments.**

GROWTH HABIT: Branching annual, up to 40 cm tall from tap root.

pineappleweed (BA)

The crushed leaves and flowers of this plant produce a pineapple aroma, hence the name pineappleweed. Chamomile originates from the Greek *chamoi* (on the ground) and *melon* (an apple). *Matricaria* is from the Latin *mater* or *matrix* (mother) and *caria* (dear), arising from the plant's medicinal uses. *Discoidea* is sometimes used to refer to composites where the flowers are composed of disk florets only. ⊘ The Blackfoot used an extract of the entire plant to treat diarrhea and dried the flowers to make a perfume and insect repellent. The Alberta Cree used the flowers in an eye treatment. Kootenay children threaded the flower heads as beads, while adults used them to scent their homes and to stuff pillows. Okanagan children ate the flower heads, and the Crow used the dried, crushed plants to line baby cradles. The Flathead of Montana used pineappleweed as an insect repellent and meat preservative; they also brewed a medicinal tea from it to treat upset stomach and diarrhea and to aid in delivering the placenta after childbirth. ⊘ There are 40 species of *Matricaria* in the world, native to the northern hemisphere and southern Africa; 3 species occur in Alberta. Wild chamomile (*M. recutita*) has similar leaves to pineappleweed but has white ray florets 4 to 10 mm long and cone-shaped disks. Scentless chamomile (*M. perforata*), a very troublesome weed, lacks the scent of pineappleweed, has larger (8 to 16 mm) ray florets than wild chamomile and has a hemispherical disk.

scentless chamomile (CWE)

278

palmate-leaved coltsfoot

Petasites frigidus (L. Fries) var. *palmatus* (Ait.) Cronq.
(*Petasites palmatus* (Ait.) A. Gray in Moss 1983)
ASPEN PARKLAND, BOREAL FOREST, MONTANE, SUBALPINE

HABITAT AND RANGE: Moist woods, thickets, wet meadows, fens, swamps; often in disturbed areas such as roadsides, clearings and stream banks. Widespread across the province at low to moderate elevations.

FLOWERS: Numerous, small, whitish to pinkish flowers in few to numerous heads. Plants possess **mostly female or mostly male flowers**. Involucral bracts often reddish-tinged and up to 13 mm long on male heads and 10 mm long on female heads. **Flowers early in spring before leaves appear**.

FRUIT: Brown to gray achenes. Each achene up to 3.5 mm long, narrow, ribbed, with a **pappus of soft, white bristles at the apex that become elongated and very noticeable** when the plant has set seed.

LEAVES: **Stem leaves alternate and bract-like, sheathing, parallel-veined**, usually purplish; often tipped with a small, green, inflated blade resembling the basal leaves. **Basal leaves long-petioled; blades round to kidney-shaped, with 5 to 11 deeply cleft primary lobes of almost equal size**; lobes entire or toothed. Leaves sparsely hairy above, sparsely hairy to white-hairy below.

GROWTH HABIT: **Perennial**, up to 50 cm tall from a slender, creeping rhizome.

palmate-leaved coltsfoot (BA)

Coltsfoot describes the leaf shape of some *Petasites* species. *Petasites* is from the Greek *petasos* (a broad-brimmed hat); *frigidus* (cold) likely refers to the habitats of var. *frigidus*, and *palmatus* refers to the large, palmately lobed basal leaves. ✐ The leaves were used by the Cree to poultice infections and have been used to make an

palmate-leaved coltsfoot (BA)

arrow-leaved coltsfoot (JH)

ointment to treat insect bites, burns and inflammations. Some native peoples chewed the roots or brewed them into a tea to treat respiratory disorders, sore throats and rheumatism. The plant was used as a salt substitute, and the roots, leaves and young flower shoots may be eaten roasted or boiled. Coltsfoot should be used with **caution** as strong doses are said to induce abortion. ◢ *Petasites* is native to the temperate, subarctic and arctic zones of the northern hemisphere, and the number of species varies according to different taxonomic interpretations. Until recently, 4 or 5 species of *Petasites* were recognized in Alberta. However, recent research (Cherniawsky 1994, 1998) proposes that they all be considered varieties of *P. frigidus,* except grape-leaved coltsfoot (*P. frigidus* var. x *vitifolius*), which is a hybrid between arrow-leaved coltsfoot *(P. frigidus* var. *sagittatus)* and palmate-leaved coltsfoot. Arrow-leaved coltsfoot (*P. frigidus* var. *sagittatus*) has entire or toothed, rather than lobed, arrow-shaped leaves. Alpine coltsfoot (*P. frigidus* var. *frigidus,* including *P. frigidus* var. *nivalis*) has triangular leaves that are shallowly to deeply toothed and regularly or irregularly lobed. It occurs predominantly in moist subalpine to alpine habitats.

prairie coneflower, long-headed coneflower
Ratibida columnifera (Nutt.) Wooton & Standl.

PRAIRIE, ASPEN PARKLAND

HABITAT AND RANGE: Dry grassland, coulee bottoms, disturbed areas; often on gravelly soil. Common in the southern third of the province.

FLOWERS: Heads long-stalked. **Grayish to purple disk florets in a cylinder up to 4 cm long, surrounded at base by 3 to 7 oblong, bright-yellow or occasionally purplish or brownish petals** (ray florets). Each petal 1 to 3 cm long, deeply notched at tip or with 3 short lobes. Bracts narrow, leaf-like, hairy, in a single series. July to September.

FRUIT: **Cylindrical, dense head** of flattened, hairy, grayish to black achenes, each 2 mm long.

LEAVES: Alternate, grayish green, short-hairy, 3 to 10 cm long, mainly along the lower part of the stem. **Leaves deeply divided into somewhat thickened, oblong lobes, with terminal lobe the longest.**

GROWTH HABIT: Coarsely hairy, many-stemmed perennial, 30 to 60 cm tall from tap root. Stems slightly grooved.

prairie coneflower   (BA)

The origin of *Ratibida* is unknown. *Columnifera* refers to the cone-shaped flowers. ☙ The Blackfoot obtained a yellow or orange dye from the roots; the roots are also said to be mildly diuretic. The dried and nearly dry disk florets are edible and are said to taste like corn. Both disk florets and leaves were brewed into a tea by the Dakotas. ☙ There are 5 species of *Ratibida*, chiefly in the central United States. Only this species occurs in Alberta.

prairie coneflower   (JH)

black-eyed susan, coneflower

Rudbeckia hirta L.

black-eyed susan   (LF)

HABITAT AND RANGE: Roadsides, open meadows, disturbed areas, cultivated fields; usually where good moisture is available. Introduced.

FLOWERS: Heads mostly on long flower stalks. **Ray florets 8 to 20, orange to bright yellow, 2 to 4 cm long, sometimes toothed at the tip. Disk florets dark purple to brown, 1 to 2 cm wide.** Involucral bracts leafy, bristly-hairy, pointed, usually in 2-series; becoming backward-bent as flower head matures. July to September.

FRUIT: Smooth, blackish, 4-angled achenes, 2 to 3 mm long, with no pappus.

LEAVES: Alternate, **very rough-hairy, the leaf hairs often with bulbous green bases.** Lower leaves elliptic to broadly lance-shaped, entire to slightly toothed, long-stalked; upper narrowly lance-shaped to oval, shorter-stalked or stalkless.

GROWTH HABIT: Biennial to short-lived perennial, **usually rough-hairy throughout,** 30 to 100 cm tall. **Stems simple to branched, often purplish, or reddish-mottled.**

*R*udbeckia honours Uppsala botany professor Olaf Rudbeck, a mentor of Linnaeus. *Hirta* means "hairy." ✎ Livestock may be poisoned by eating large quantities of black-eyed susan. ✎ Black-eyed susan is similar to gaillardia (see page 261) in appearance; however, gaillardia has ray florets that are often reddish to purplish at base and more deeply 3-lobed at the tip, a hairy disk and a scaly pappus. ✎ There are about 24 species of *Rudbeckia*, all native to North America. Only this species is found in Alberta. It is native to the central United States and is introduced in our province.

dwarf saw-wort, purple hawkweed

Saussurea nuda Ledeb. ssp. *densa* (Hook.) G.W. Dougl.
(*Saussurea nuda* Ledeb. var. *densa* (Hook.) Hult. in Moss 1983)
ALPINE

HABITAT AND RANGE: Rocky slopes, scree, gravelly ridges and tundra, from moderate to high elevations throughout the Rocky Mountains.

FLOWERS: Heads crowded in dense cluster, about 6 cm wide, on the end of the stem. **Disk florets only, purple to pinkish, with slender tube and long, narrow lobes.** Involucres 10 to 15 mm tall, tangled-hairy. **Bracts in 4 to 5-series, narrow, tapered, some purplish-tipped. Outer bracts of the involucre as long as the inner.**

FRUIT: Oblong, angled, tan achenes, each about 3 mm long, with double pappus. **Outer pappus bristles short, stiff; inner longer and feathery.**

LEAVES: Alternate, crowded, lance-shaped, sharp-pointed, hairy, sometimes glandular-dotted. Wavy-margined, distantly toothed to entire. Lower leaves gradually tapered at base into winged stalk; upper stalkless.

GROWTH HABIT: Pleasant-smelling, leafy perennial, **10 to 20 cm tall** from woody base. Stems tangled-hairy to smooth. **Dense, thick head and tangled hairs give the plant a thistle-like appearance.**

dwarf saw-wort   (CWE)

Saussurea honours prominent Swiss naturalists Theodore and Horace Saussure. *Nuda* means "naked," perhaps in reference to the naked receptacle on which the disk flowers rest, and *densa* means "dense," applied to the dense cluster of flower heads. "Saw-wort" describes the toothed leaves. ✍ There are over 50 species of *Saussurea*, native to Eurasia and northern North America; 3 occur in Alberta. American saw-wort (*S. americana*) is much taller (30 to 120 cm), has triangular to heart-shaped leaves and is found only in moist meadows and slopes of Waterton Lakes National Park. Tall saw-wort (*S. glomerata*) is a lowland species that has the outer bracts of the involucre shorter than the inner. It is introduced rather than native.

prairie groundsel, silvery groundsel, woolly groundsel

Senecio canus Hook.

PRAIRIE, ASPEN PARKLAND, MONTANE, SUBALPINE, ALPINE

prairie groundsel   (BA)

HABITAT AND RANGE: Dry ground, sandy exposed hillsides, rocky ridges, open rocky cliffs. Widespread in the southern half of the province.

FLOWERS: Heads solitary to several, with 12 or more bright-yellow, notched ray florets, each up to 13 mm long, surrounding a cluster of disk florets to 12 mm across. Involucre 4 to 8 mm long, with **unequal bracts in 1 row.** May to July.

FRUIT: Head of achenes. Each achene brown, ribbed, oblong, 4 to 5 mm long. Pappus white, deciduous.

LEAVES: Both basal and stem leaves present. **Basal leaves spoon to lance-shaped**, up to 9 cm long on short stalks. Stem leaves alternate and reduced upwards, lobed to entire, attached directly to stem. **Gray-green with white, fuzzy covering of hair**; upper leaf surfaces sometimes smooth. Prominently veined.

GROWTH HABIT: Tufted, upright, single to many-stemmed perennial, up to 40 cm tall. **Usually grayish due to woolly hairs**, but often becomes less hairy with age.

The name groundsel may be derived from the Anglo-Saxon term for "ground-swallower," perhaps because of the weedy tendencies of some species, or "pus-swallower" because common groundsel (*S. vulgaris*) was used by early herbalists to treat eye discharges. *Senecio* is from *senex* (old man), either because the receptacle to which the flowers are attached is free of hairs like a bald head or because of the white-hairiness of some species. *Canus* means "ash-coloured, hoary," referring to the leaves. ✿ Many groundsels contain toxic alkaloids and are therefore **poisonous**. The chronic use of groundsels in herbal teas may lead to liver diseases such as cirrhosis. ✿ Some groundsels have been used by North American natives to ease the pain of childbirth and treat wounds. ✿ The genus *Senecio* is one of the largest in the world, with more than 1500 species, widely distributed; 18 species are found in Alberta, mostly in the mountains. Marsh ragwort (*S. congestus*) is a species of the marshes, ponds and wet areas, primarily of the aspen parkland and boreal forest. It is easy to distinguish from our other groundsels because of the combination of appearance (it is a thick, hollow-stemmed, hairy annual with a noticeably dense pappus) and distinctive habitat.

marsh ragwort   (BA)

brook ragwort, triangular-leaved ragwort, giant ragwort, spear-head senecio

Senecio triangularis Hook.

BOREAL FOREST, MONTANE, SUBALPINE, ALPINE

HABITAT AND RANGE: Moist subalpine woods to alpine meadows; stream banks, lake shores, moist slopes. Widespread in the mountains and of scattered occurrence in the boreal forest.

FLOWERS: In flat-topped cluster at top of plant. **Bright-yellow, linear to lance-shaped rays, up to 13 mm long. Disk of bright-yellow to orange florets. Involucre 6 to 10 mm long, composed of bright-green, dark-tipped bracts, smooth with ciliate edges.**

FRUIT: Dry, brownish, ribbed achene about 2 mm long, with dense white pappus up to 7 mm long.

LEAVES: Alternate, **truncate at base, triangular-shaped, sharply toothed nearly to the tip,** 5 to 15 cm long. Uppermost leaves short-stalked or attached directly to stem.

GROWTH HABIT: Leafy, tall (up to 1.5 m), smooth perennial from fibrous roots. Stems clustered, shiny; lower reddish.

brook ragwort (BA)

R̲agwort describes the ragged leaf margins of many members of this genus. The origin of *Senecio* is explained on page 284, and *triangularis* refers to the triangle-shaped leaves. Some brook ragworts on Vancouver Island have been measured at more than 2 m tall. ✿ Several groundsel species contain **toxic alkaloids** and are **poisonous** (but generally unpalatable) to livestock. People in African countries have been **poisoned** by eating flour contaminated with seeds of *Senecio* species. ✿ Another groundsel inhabiting moist subalpine and alpine slopes is black-tipped or entire-leaved groundsel (*S. lugens*). It differs from brook ragwort in having few small, narrow stem leaves. Cut-leaved ragwort (*S. eremophilus*) has deeply divided, often toothed leaves and is mainly a species of the aspen parkland and boreal forest.

cut-leaved ragwort (IM)

black-tipped groundsel

late goldenrod, tall smooth goldenrod, giant goldenrod

Solidago gigantea Ait. ssp.*serotina* (Ait.) McNeill
(*Solidago gigantea* Ait. var. *serotina* (Ait.) Cronq. in Moss 1983)
PRAIRIE, ASPEN PARKLAND, BOREAL FOREST, MONTANE

late goldenrod   (LF)

HABITAT AND RANGE: Moist woods and meadows, thickets, floodplains and lake shores. Sometimes on sandy or saline soils. Of scattered occurrence as far north as the Peace River country but most common in the southern half of the province.

FLOWERS: **Terminal, broadly pyramidal clusters of flower heads**, each head up to 7 mm across. **Ray and disk florets bright yellow.** Ray florets wide-spreading, about 5 mm long. **Involucre 3 to 5 mm tall, consisting of narrow, overlapping bracts with dark midvein.** Lower inflorescence branches often curved. July to September.

FRUIT: Small (about 1 mm long), white-hairy or occasionally smooth achenes, with whitish pappus about 3 mm long.

LEAVES: Numerous, alternate, thin. **Lance-shaped and toothed usually from above the middle, tapered at the base.** Up to about 12 cm long. Sometimes hairy on the veins below, but usually smooth above.

GROWTH HABIT: Tall, leafy, mostly smooth, thick-stemmed perennial up to 2 m tall, often in clumps.

*S*olidago is possibly from the Latin solidus (whole) and ago (to do or make), because of the plant's supposed healing qualities. *Gigantea* means "large," and *serotina* means "late," in reference to the late flowering. ✿ This is a noticeably showy goldenrod. Its flowers were ground into a lotion and applied to bee stings by the Meskwaki of Minnesota. ✿ This plant is very similar to Canada goldenrod (*S. canadensis*), but Canada goldenrod has leaves that are usually densely hairy above and below and stems that are hairy above the middle. Related velvety goldenrod (*S. mollis*) is known to have caused deaths in livestock and even small amounts are toxic to sheep. It has gray-green, velvety-hairy, oval to broadly lance-shaped, 3-veined, stalked, rigid lower leaves. It is found in dry grasslands, mainly south of the Oldman and South Saskatchewan rivers. ✿ There are approximately 100 species of goldenrod in the world, chiefly in North America; 9 species are found in Alberta.

alpine goldenrod, northern goldenrod
Solidago multiradiata Ait.
ASPEN PARKLAND, BOREAL FOREST, MONTANE, SUBALPINE, ALPINE

HABITAT AND RANGE: Dry open areas, often on sandy or gravelly soil. Widespread in the mountains and also occurs in the northern boreal forest and aspen parkland.

FLOWERS: **Heads in loose or dense, narrow, long clusters.** Ray florets yellow, 4 to 5.5 mm long. Disk florets yellow, usually 13 or more, each about 5 mm long. **Involucre 4 to 6 mm tall, of narrow, shiny, straw-coloured, hairy-margined bracts with greenish tips.** July to September.

FRUIT: White-hairy achene up to 1.5 mm long, with white pappus up to 4 mm long.

alpine goldenrod   (JH)

LEAVES: Alternate. Basal and lower stem leaves broadly lance or spoon-shaped, distantly toothed or entire, up to 10 cm long. **Margins of lower leaf stalks with noticeable long hairs.** Upper leaves few, reduced in size.

GROWTH HABIT: Tufted perennial, up to 50 cm tall, often with a reddish stem. May form clumps.

The origin of the genus name is explained on page 286. *Multiradiata* means "with numerous rays." ∅ The flowers produce a yellow dye. In 17th-century Europe, many goldenrod species were believed to stop the bleeding of ulcers and wounds. Related American species were used to treat a diversity of ailments including headaches, gas, nausea and stomach spasms. ∅ Alpine goldenrod may be distinguished from the similar mountain or dwarf goldenrod (*S. spathulata*) by its hairy-margined, basal leaf-stalks.

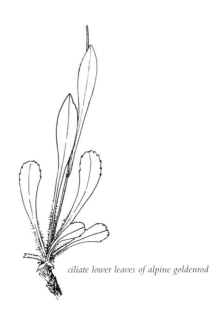

ciliate lower leaves of alpine goldenrod

perennial sow thistle, creeping sow thistle, field sow thistle

Sonchus arvensis L.

PRAIRIE, ASPEN PARKLAND, BOREAL FOREST, MONTANE

perennial sow thistle   (DJ)

HABITAT AND RANGE: Cultivated fields, roadsides, pastures, gardens. Prefers moist soils. Common throughout the province except at higher elevations in the mountains. Introduced and weedy.

FLOWERS: Heads several in open cluster, each head 3 to 5 cm wide. **Flowers look like dandelion flowers with large yellow ray florets, each up to 3 cm long**; no disk florets. **Involucre 14 to 24 mm tall. Involucral bracts glandular-dotted, sometimes with tufts of whitish hairs.** June to September.

FRUIT: **Ribbed, brownish, beakless, wrinkled achenes, 2.5 to 3.5 mm long.** Pappus of soft, white hairs.

LEAVES: Bluish green, alternate, 6 to 40 cm long. **Lobed, with small teeth and soft prickles along the margins.** Less lobed and more clasping toward the top. Midvein prominent.

GROWTH HABIT: **Perennial**, 0.4 to 2 m tall from long, creeping, rhizome-like roots. Branched near the top. **Stems secrete white milky juice when cut.**

Pigs like to eat this plant, hence the name "sow thistle." *Sonchus* is from the Greek *somphos* (spongy), referring to the porous stems. *Arvensis* means "of the fields," as the plant is a common invader in moist, cultivated fields. In addition to its deep root and long, creeping rootstocks, sow thistle produces large quantities of wind-borne seeds and is a formidable foe to farmers. ✐ There are 70 species of *Sonchus*, native to Eurasia and Africa. There are 4 species in Alberta, 2 perennials and 2 annuals, all introduced. Perennial sow thistle can be distinguished from smooth perennial sow thistle (*S. uliginosus*) because the latter lacks glandular hairs on the involucre and flower stalks. Prickly sow thistle (*S. asper*), an annual, is very prickly and has an involucre mainly 9 to 14 mm tall, upper leaves rounded at the base and 3-ribbed, non-wrinkled achenes. Annual sow thistle (*S. oleraceus*) has pointed, clasping leaves and its achenes have cross-wise wrinkles.

(a)   *(b)*   *(c)*

leaf and achene differences between (a) perennial sow thistle, (b) prickly sow thistle, (c) annual sow thistle

common tansy, golden-buttons
Tanacetum vulgare L.

HABITAT AND RANGE: Roadsides, embankments, pastures, fence rows, disturbed areas. Introduced and common in the province.

FLOWERS: Numerous, **flattened, yellow, button-like heads** that are indented in the middle, **5 to 10 mm wide**. Each head composed of many 5-lobed, tubular disk florets. Ray florets inconspicuous or none. Involucral bracts overlapping; tips and margins of inner bracts somewhat papery. Pappus short or none. July to September.

FRUIT: Ribbed, usually glandular, gray or brownish achene, about 1.5 mm long.

LEAVES: **Numerous, dark green, strong-smelling**, 10 to 20 cm long. **Finely dissected, fern-like, smooth**, glandular-dotted, often toothed. Short-stalked, stalks somewhat sheathing at base, or stalkless.

GROWTH HABIT: Perennial, 0.4 to 1.8 m tall from thick rhizome.

common tansy   (BA)

Tansy is from an old English name, *tanesy.* *Tanacetum* is from the Greek *athanatos* (long-lasting), possibly referring to the plant's use in medicine or to its long-lasting flowers. *Vulgare* means "common." ✐ In Britain, the juice of common tansy was used as a flavouring in Easter cakes. The plant was also placed in shrouds to repel insects and rodents from corpses. Tansy was originally cultivated in North America as a medicinal plant and gradually spread. It can cause abortion or death in livestock. Some native peoples made a tea from the plant to induce abortion, but the results were sometimes deadly to the mother as well. ✐ There are 50 species of *Tanacetum*, native to the northern hemisphere, mainly in the Old World; 2 species are found in Alberta. The rare Indian tansy (*T. bipinnatum* ssp. *huronense*; *T. huronense* Nutt. in Moss 1983) has leaves that are long-hairy when young and larger heads (disk 1 to 2 cm wide). It occurs on shores, sand dunes and gravel bars in the extreme northeast of the province.

Parry's townsendia
Townsendia parryi D.C. Eat.
PRAIRIE, ASPEN PARKLAND, MONTANE, SUBALPINE

Parry's townsendia (Ho)

HABITAT AND RANGE: Dry hills, river banks, roadsides, open rocky and grassy areas, dry gravelly slopes; from prairie to alpine elevations. Occurs in the mountains and foothills from the Red Deer River south; also in the Cypress Hills.

FLOWERS: Ray florets purplish to blue, about 3 mm wide, 1 to 2 cm long. **Disk to 4 cm wide, composed of yellow disk florets. Involucre 9 to 16 mm tall, of narrowly tapered, pointed, jagged bracts, translucent and hairy on the margins; often reddish at the tip.** May to September.

FRUIT: Head of achenes. Each achene flattened, 2-nerved, reddish brown, sometimes very hairy, about 5 mm long, with whitish, barbed pappus.

LEAVES: From base and along stem. Basal leaves spoon-shaped to broadly lance-shaped, to 6 cm long, often with pointed tip, hairy beneath and smooth above. Stem leaves few in number and reduced in size.

GROWTH HABIT: Thick, **reddish-stemmed** perennial to 25 cm tall from thick base and long tap root. A single to many flowering stems. **Stems, leaves and bracts white-hairy.**

The genus name honours David Townsend, an early American botanist from Pennsylvania, and *parryi* commemorates Charles Christopher Parry, a 19th-century American botanical explorer. ✿ The Blackfoot boiled the root of related low townsendia or Easter daisy (*T. exscapa*) and treated tired horses with the resulting liquid. ✿ There are 20 species of *Townsendia*, all native to western North America. There are 4 species in Alberta; however, this is the only one with a noticeable stem (the other three have a cushion-forming habit). Rare low townsendia differs from Hooker's townsendia (*T. hookeri*) in having a wider flower (8 to 10 mm wide as opposed to 5 mm) and lacking a tuft of tangled hairs at the tip of the involucral bracts. Alpine townsendia (*T. condensata*) has spoon-shaped leaves and densely tangled-hairy involucres. It is rare, restricted to the extreme southwestern corner of the province.

low townsendia (LA)

goat's-beard, yellow salsify
Tragopogon dubius Scop.

<small>PRAIRIE, ASPEN PARKLAND, MONTANE</small>

HABITAT AND RANGE: Grassland, roadsides, ditches, waste places, slopes, open, dry places. Introduced from Europe.

FLOWERS: **Heads solitary, large (may reach 6 cm across), surrounded by long, narrow, green, protruding bracts. Bright-yellow or greenish yellow ray florets,** toothed at ends, to 2 cm long. No disk florets. Flowers open on sunny mornings, close up around noon and stay closed on rainy or dull days. June to July.

LEAVES: Alternate, somewhat fleshy, **mostly narrow leaves but broad and clasping at base,** tapering to long, narrow tip, 5 to 30 cm long. Often with tufts of hair in axils. Leaves exude milky juice when cut.

FRUIT: Mass of narrow, ribbed, beaked achenes, each 25 to 35 mm long, with **pappus of plumed, whitish bristles, about 30 mm long.**

goat's-beard (BA)

GROWTH HABIT: Showy, solitary, erect, very leafy, hollow-stemmed, branched annual or biennial from long, fleshy tap root, 40 to 100 cm tall. **Stem swollen below flower head. Stems, leaves and roots produce a milky juice when cut.**

The common name goat's-beard likely refers to the mass of white achenes, which could be said to resemble a goat's beard. *Tragopogon* is derived from the Greek *tragos* (goat) and *pogon* (beard), which describes the seed and pappus. *Dubius* means "doubtful" but its application to this plant is unknown. ✐ The young leaves and roots from immature plants may be eaten, and the latex from the stem can be chewed, upon hardening. The fleshy roots can be cooked but are best prior to flowering. The milky stem juice was used by some native tribes to treat indigestion. ✐ There are 50 species of *Tragopogon* in the world, chiefly of Eurasia and northern Africa; 2 other species, also introduced, occur in Alberta. Meadow goat's-beard (*T. pratensis*) has yellow flowers but is not swollen below the flower head, while common salsify (*T. porrifolius*) has purple flowers. All 3 species can hybridize where their ranges overlap.

goat's-beard (BA)

LILIACEAE (see pp 14-33)

1A. Leaves lance-shaped or broader, less than 5 times as long as wide 2

  2A. Leaves mostly basal, stems leafless or with a few very small leaves 3

    3A. Flowers white, about 2 cm across, with spreading petals;
fruit a blue berry . . . . **Clintonia uniflora** *(p 18)*

    3B. Flowers yellow, 3 to 6 cm across, nodding, with petals bent
backward and up; fruit a 3-sided capsule . . . . **Erythronium grandiflorum** *(p 20)*

  2B. Leaves mostly on the flowering stems 4

    4A. Flowers usually more than 4, in clusters at stem tips; stems not branched 5

      5A. Plants robust, usually over 1 m tall, with large (to more than
30 cm long), strongly veined to pleated leaves; flowers green;
fruits capsules . . . . **Veratrum viride** *(p 29)*

      5B. Plants less than 1 m tall with smaller leaves; flowers whitish; fruits berries 6

        6A. Plants 20 to 100 cm tall, with 5 to 12 leaves 7

          7A. Flowers usually more than 20, in branched open clusters
5 to 15 cm long; stems 30 to 100 cm tall, slightly zig-zagged;
leaves 4 to 8 cm wide . . . . *Smilacina racemosa (p 25)*

          7B. Flowers usually less than 10, in elongated (rarely branched)
clusters 1.5 to 5 cm long; stems 20 to 60 cm tall;
leaves usually 1 to 5 cm wide . . . . **Smilacina stellata** *(p 24)*

        6B. Plants up to 20 cm tall, with 1 to 4 leaves 8

          8A. Petal-like segments 4; leaves heart-shaped . . **Maianthemum canadense** *(p 23)*

          8B. Petal-like segments 6; leaves more elongated,
tapered at base . . . . *Smilacina trifolia (p 25)*

    4B. Flowers single or in groups of 2 to 4; stems usually branched 9

      9A. Flowers in leaf axils 10

      10A. Plants 30 to 100 cm tall; stem joints hairless . . . . **Streptopus amplexifolius** *(p 27)*

      10B. Plants less than 30 cm tall; stem joints fringed with hairs 11

        11a. Flowers bell-shaped; petal-like segments 6 to 10 mm long;
leaves 3 to 10 cm long, 1 to 5 cm wide, toothless,
sometimes with scattered hairs along edges . . . . *Streptopus roseus (p 27)*

        11B. Flowers saucer-shaped; petal-like segments 2.5 to 4.5 mm
long; leaves 3 to 5 cm long, 1 to 2 cm wide, edged with tiny,
crowded teeth . . . . *Streptopus streptopoides (p 27)*

      9B. Flowers at stem tips 12

      12a. Fruits round, 8 to 10 mm long, velvety due to tiny bumps
(papillae) on surface; leaves hairless on upper surface and
with spreading hairs along edges . . . . **Disporum trachycarpum** *(p 19)*

      12B. Fruits ovate, 10 to 15 mm long, not velvety; leaves usually hairy
on upper surface and with hairs along edges pointing towards
the leaf tip . . . . *Disporum hookeri (p 19)*

1B. Leaves slender and linear to narrowly lance-shaped, more than 5 times as long as wide . 13

   13a. Leaves tough and fibrous, usually forming dense tufts 14

      14a. Leaves stiff, with firm, sharp points and whitish, fibrous edges;
      flowers 4 to 5 cm long . . . . **Yucca glauca** *(p 31)*

      14B. Leaves less stiff (more grass-like), with rough, saw-toothed edges;
      flowers 0.6 to 1 cm long . . . . **Xerophyllum tenax** *(p 30)*

   13B. Leaves softer, easily broken, not tufted 15

      15a. Leaves mostly on the flowering stem 16

         16a. Plants 10 to 35 cm tall; leaves usually less than 10, alternate;
         flowers yellow to orange, cup-shaped, 1.5 to 3.5 cm long,
         nodding . . . . **Fritillaria pudica** *(p 21)*

         16B. Plants 30 to 60 cm tall; leaves usually more than 10, alternate,
         whorled on upper stem; flowers orange to reddish, funnel-shaped,
         2.5 to 7 cm long, not nodding . . . . **Lilium philadelphicum** *(p 22)*

      15B. Leaves mainly basal, sometimes with a few small leaves on the flowering stem 17

         17a. Flowers 1 to 3; petals hairy on the inner surface and fringed
         at the margin . . . . **Calochortus apiculatus** *(p 16)*

         17B. Flowers in clusters of 4 or more; petals not hairy on the upper
         surface or fringed at the margin 18

            18a. Flowers in umbrella-shaped clusters (umbels) at tips of
            leafless stems; plants with an onion odour 19

               19a. Leaves round and hollow (at least near the base) . *Allium schoenoprasum (p 15)*

               19B. Leaves flat or channeled 20

                  20A. Flower cluster nodding . . . . **Allium cernuum** *(p 15)*

                  20B. Flower cluster erect to spreading, not nodding 21

                     21a. Leaves usually 3 or more; flowers usually pink,
                     6 to 8 mm long, often sterile and replaced by bulbils
                     at base of flower stalks . . . . *Allium geyeri (p 15)*

                     21B. Leaves usually 2; flowers usually white, 5 to 7 mm long,
                     fertile, not replaced by bulbils . . . . *Allium textile (p 15)*

           18B. Flowers in elongated clusters; plants lacking an onion-like odour 22

              22a. Leaves with their edges towards the stem (like iris leaves),
              in 2 vertical rows; plants from rhizomes 23

                 23a. Stems sticky near the top with gland-tipped hairs,
                 up to 50 cm tall . . . . **Tofieldia glutinosa** *(p 28)*

                 23B. Stems not sticky-hairy, usually less than 20 cm tall *Tofieldia pusilla (p 28)*

              22B. Leaves with their surfaces towards the stem, not in 2 vertical
              rows; plants from bulbs 24

                 24a. Flowers purplish blue, 3 to 6 cm across; leaves in
                 a basal whorl . . . . **Camassia quamash** *(p 17)*

                 24B. Flowers and leaves never as above 25

                   25a. Flowers narrowly bell-shaped, nodding,
                   greenish yellow to bronze . . . . **Stenanthium occidentale** *(p 26)*

                   25B. Flowers saucer-shaped, erect, whitish to greenish,
                   with a prominent gland at the base of each petal-like segment . . . 26

                     26a. Petal-like segments 8 to 11 mm long, with heart-shaped
                     glands at bases; leaves and stems with a bluish bloom
                     (glaucous), 20 to 60 cm tall . . . . **Zigadenus elegans** *(p 32)*

                     26B. Petal-like segments less than 7 mm long,
                       with an ovate gland at base; plants relatively
                     small and slender, 20 to 35 cm tall . . . . *Zigadenus venenosus (p 32)*

ORCHIDACEAE (see pp 35-45)

1A. Plants reddish brown to pale yellow, lacking green pigment (chlorophyll);
leaves scale-like 2

  2A. Stems slender (less than 3 mm wide), yellowish; flowers small,
with 1-nerved, 5 mm long petals and sepals . . . . ***Corallorhiza trifida*** *(p 38)*

  2B. Stems stout (over 3 mm wide), usually purplish; flowers larger,
with 3-nerved, 6 to 16 mm long petals and sepals 3

    3A. Flowers white with purplish spots; lip petal
with 2 lobes near base . . . . *Corallorhiza maculata (p 38)*

    3B. Flowers pink with reddish brown or purple stripes;
lip petal not lobed . . . . *Corallorhiza striata (p 38)*

1B. Plants green, with one or more well-developed leaves 4

  4A. Flowers with an inflated, pouch-like lower lip 5

    5A. Plants with a single, basal leaf, growing from a round corm . . . ***Calypso bulbosa*** *(p 37)*

    5B. Plants with 2 or more leaves, growing from rhizomes 6

      6A. Leaves 2, at the base of a leafless flowering stem;
flowers pink with red veins . . . . *Cypripedium acaule (p 40)*

      6B. Leaves 3 or more on the flowering stalk; flowers white to yellow 7

        7A. Flowers white, with a small (12 to 15 mm long),
white or pink lower lip and green, ovate sepals . . *Cypripedium passerinum (p 40)*

        7B. Flowers yellow to brownish and white, with a larger
(20 to 40 mm long) lower lip and long, slender,
purplish brown to greenish yellow sepals 8

          8A. Lip yellow (rarely white), often purple-dotted
around opening; flowers usually solitary . . . . . ***Cypripedium calceolus*** *(p 39)*

          8B. Lip white, often purple-tinged, not purple-dotted;
flowers usually in pairs . . . . *Cypripedium montanum (p 40)*

  4B. Flowers with a flat (not inflated) lower lip 9

    9A. Leaves in a single pair near mid-stem 10

      10A. Leaves heart-shaped; lower lip of flower split about
half way to base into 2 slender lobes . . . . *Listera cordata (p 42)*

      10B. Leaves broadly ovate to elliptic, rarely heart-shaped;
lower lip of flower rounded or notched at tip 11

        11a. Lip oblong, only slightly narrower at base than at tip,
abruptly notched at tip . . . . ***Listera borealis*** *(p 42)*

        11B. Lip wedge-shaped, much broader at tip than at base 12

          12a. Lip 8 to 10 mm long, held horizontally,
clearly notched at tip, abruptly narrowed at base,
fringed with tiny hairs . . . . *Listera convallarioides (p 42)*

          12B. Lip 5 mm long, held at an angle of about 45°,
rounded at tip, tapered to base, hairless on edges . . . . . . *Listera caurina (p 42)*

9B. Leaves otherwise 13

   13a. Leaf solitary (rarely 2 in *Platanthera obtusata*) and basal 14

      14a. Leaf elliptic to ovate, 3 to 9 cm long; flowers whitish to light pink;
           lip whitish to pinkish with reddish purple spots, 6 to 9 mm long,
           notched at tip and with 2 lobes at base . . . . ***Amerorchis rotundifolia*** *(p 36)*

      14B. Leaf ovate to lance-shaped, 4 to 12 cm long, flowers greenish
           white; lip slender, tapered to tip, 5 to 8 mm long . . . . *Platanthera obtusata* *(p 43)*

   13B. Leaves 2 or more 15

      15a. Flowers with a hollow appendage (spur) at base 16

         16a. Leaves basal, 2 to 4 17

            17a. Leaves 2 (rarely 3), broad, rarely more than twice
               as long as wide, lying on the ground; sepals 3-nerved;
               spur 15 to 30 mm long . . . . *Platanthera orbiculata* *(p 43)*

            17B. Leaves 1 to 4, lance-shaped, not lying on the ground;
               sepals 1-nerved; spur 3 to 5 mm long . . . . *Piperia unalascensis* *(p 44)*

         16B. Leaves spread along the stem, sometimes also clustered at the base 18

            18a. Flowers white to greenish white, fragrant;
               lip conspicuously broadened at the base and
               abruptly narrowed to a slender, tapered tip . ***Platanthera dilatata*** *(p 43)*

            18B. Flowers pale greenish, linear to lance-shaped,
               not abruptly narrowed from a broad base 19

               19a. Spur inconspicuous and sac-like, shorter
                  than the lip; lowermost leaves rounded to
                  blunt-tipped; flower clusters often loose,
                  with flowers widely separated
                  (at least near the base) . . . . *Platanthera stricta* *(p 44)*

               19B. Spur clearly visible, slender, as long as the lip;
                  lowermost leaves often with pointed tips;
                  flower clusters usually crowded . . . . *Platanthera hyperborea* *(p 43)*

   15B. Flowers lacking a basal spur 20

      20A. Leaves in a basal rosette, persistent, often dark green
           with white lines and blotches along veins;
            flowers in straight, spike-like clusters 21

         21a. Plants small and slender, 10 to 20 cm tall,
            with leaves 1 to 3 cm long and flower
            clusters 3 to 6 cm long . . . . *Goodyera repens* *(p 41)*

         21B. Plants more robust, up to 40 cm tall,
            with leaves 3 to 7 cm long and flowers
            clusters 5 to 10 cm long . . . . ***Goodyera oblongifolia*** *(p 41)*

      20B. Leaves not as above; flowers in spirally twisted, spike-like clusters 22

         22a. Flowers clusters dense, with flowers in
            2 to 3 vertically spiralling rows . . . . . . ***Spiranthes romanzoffiana*** *(p 45)*

         22B. Flowers clusters loose, with flowers in
            1 vertically spiralling row . . . . *Spiranthes lacera* *(p 45)*

POLYGONACEAE (see pp 49-55)

1A. Flowers in umbrella-shaped clusters (umbels) above a whorl of bracts 2

  2A. Bracts at the base of the involucre scale-like; flower clusters
    branched once (simple umbels), compact and head-like . . . . *Eriogonum ovalifolium (p 50)*

  2B. Bracts at the base of the involucre leaf-like; flower clusters branched more
    than once (compound umbels), forming flat-topped to rounded clusters 3

    3A. Leaves hairless above at maturity, white-woolly beneath;
      petal-like segments hairless . . . . *Eriogonum umbellatum (p 50)*

    3B. Leaves densely white hairy on both sides (sometimes greenish
      above with age); petal-like segments hairy at base . . . . **Eriogonum flavum** *(p 50)*

1B. Flower clusters not as above 4

  4A. Leaves heart- to kidney-shaped, rather fleshy, mainly basal . . . . . . **Oxyria digyna** *(p 51)*

  4B. Leaves not as above 5

    5A. Petal-like segments 5, not enlarging in fruit; fruits wingless;
      leaves often jointed at base 6

      6A. Leaves broadly arrowhead-shaped, with 2 lobes at base;
        stems trailing and twining . . . . *Polygonum convolvulus (p 53)*

      6B. Leaves lance-shaped to oval, tapered at base; stems erect or floating 7

        7A. Plants often aquatic and floating; leaves 5 to 15 cm long,
          somewhat leathery; flower clusters compact, pink to scarlet,
          showy, 1.5 cm thick . . . . **Polygonum amphibium** *(p 52)*

        7B. Plants terrestrial; leaves small and slender, firm but not
          leathery; flower clusters whitish, linear, 5 to 8 mm thick,
          often with bulb-like growths replacing flowers . . . . . *Polygonum viviparum (p 53)*

    5B. Petal-like segments 6, enlarging and often developing grain-like
      bumps in fruit; fruits winged; leaves never jointed at base 8

      8A. Plants with well-developed rhizomes, often growing in patches;
        flower clusters showy in fruit; seeds covered by veiny, rose-red
        enlarged sepals (valves) 1 to 3 cm wide . . . . *Rumex venosus (p 55)*

      8B. Plants with taproots, usually single; flower clusters various; valves smaller 9

        9A. Fruit valves 3 to 6 mm long, with well-developed, grain-like
          thickenings ½ to ⅔ as long as the valve; stems often
          branched from lower joints . . . . **Rumex salicifolius** *(p 54)*

        9B. Fruit valves 5 to 8 mm long, lacking grain-like thickenings;
          stems not branched below flower cluster . . . . *Rumex occidentalis (p 55)*

RANUNCULACEAE (see pp 62-76)

1A. Flowers 2-sided (irregular), purple to blue, showy 2

   2A. Petals inconspicuous, hidden by 5 petal-like sepals;
      upper sepal hooded, not spurred . . . . **Aconitum delphinifolium** (p 63)

   2B. Petals not hidden by sepals; upper sepal with a hollow
      extension (spur) projecting from its base 3

      3A. Stems usually hollow, 60 to 200 cm tall; flowers relatively small
         (about 1.5 to 2 cm across) but numerous and in large clusters
         usually over 15 cm long . . . . *Delphinium glaucum* (p 71)

      3B. Stems solid, 10 to 50 cm tall; flowers larger (about 4 cm across)
         but fewer and in smaller clusters usually less than 15 cm long 4

         4A. Lower 2 petals smooth-edged or notched less than ⅕ of the
            way to their base, deep blue to purple (like the sepals and
            upper petals); most leaves borne at the stem base . . . . . . **Delphinium bicolor** (p 71)

         4B. Lower 2 petals notched more than ⅕ of the way to their base,
            often pale blue to whitish (in contrast to the purple sepals
            and upper petals); most leaves borne on the stem . . . *Delphinium nuttallianum* (p 71)

1B. Flowers round (regular) 5

   5A. Flowers showy, with hollow spurs projecting back from the bases of their petals 6

      6A. Flowers yellow to red 7

         7A. Sepals yellow; petal blades 6 to 13 mm long, with an
            in-curved spur from each base . . . . *Aquilegia flavescens* (p 68)

         7B. Sepals orange to red; petal blades 2 to 6 mm long,
            with a straight spur from each base . . . . *Aquilegia formosa* (p 68)

      6B. Flowers blue or white 8

         8A. Plants small, less than 15 cm tall, with 1 flower
            and no stem leaves . . . . *Aquilegia jonesii* (p 68)

         8B. Plants larger, 20 to 80 cm tall, with few to several flowers
            and some stem leaves . . . . **Aquilegia brevistyla** (p 68)

   5B. Flowers lacking spurs 9

      9A. Plants usually 50 to 100 cm tall; leaves 2 to 3 times divided in 3s,
         with small, distinct leaflets; flowers numerous, less than 1 cm across 10

         10A. Leaflets pointed and sharply toothed; flowers with 1 pistil,
            3 to 5 petal-like sepals (soon falling) and 5 to 10 slender,
            white petals; fruits several-seeded, red or white berries . . . . . . **Actaea rubra** (p 64)

         10B. Leaflets blunt-tipped, with rounded lobes; flowers with
            several pistils (when present), 4 to 5 greenish sepals and
            no petals; fruits small, dry "seeds" (achenes) in compact clusters 11

            11a. Flowers with both male and female parts; anthers short,
               usually less than 1 mm long . . . . *Thalictrum sparsiflorum* (p 75)

            11B. Flowers usually either male or female; anthers usually
               more than 1 mm long 12

               12a. Plants large, over 1 m tall; leaflets dark green
                 and 3-lobed . . . . *Thalictrum dasycarpum* (p 75)

               12B. Plants usually less than 1 m tall; leaflets pale green, several-lobed 13

13a. Leaflets with conspicuously raised veins
on the lower side; achenes obliquely elliptic,
3 to 5 mm long, erect to ascending; filaments
3 to 5 mm long . . . . **Thalictrum venulosum** *(p 74)*

13B. Leaflets less conspicuously veined on lower surface;
achenes lance-shaped, 5 to 6 mm long, spreading or bent
backwards; filaments 5 to 10 mm long . . . . . *Thalictrum occidentale (p 75)*

9B. Plants not as above, usually less than 50 cm tall (except *Clematis*),
with entire or less divided leaves and fewer, larger flowers 14

14a. Plants woody, climbing vines; leaves opposite, divided into 3 to 7 leaflets 15

15a. Flowers small (1.5 to 2 cm across), whitish,
few to several in open clusters . . . . *Clematis ligusticifolia (p 70)*

15B. Flowers large (over 4 cm across), solitary 16

16a. Leaves divided into 3 leaflets; flowers blue to purple,
8 to 10 cm across . . . . **Clematis occidentalis** *(p 70)*

16B. Leaves divided into 5 leaflets; flowers yellow,
4 to 6 cm across . . . . *Clematis tangutica (p 70)*

14B. Plants herbaceous, not vine-like; leaves various 17

17a. Flowers with both petals and sepals; petals usually yellow 18

18a. Plants aquatic, usually with finely dissected submerged leaves 19

19a. Submerged leaves round to kidney-shaped,
divided into 3 to 5 slender lobes; flowers yellow;
achenes lacking horizontal ridges . . . . *Ranunculus gmelinii (p 72)*

19B. Submerged leaves kidney-shaped in outline;
repeatedly divided into thread-like segments;
flowers white; achenes with horizontal ridges 20

20A. Leaves with a slender stalk above their broadened
(stipular) bases, usually collapsing out of water;
achenes less than 30 per head . . . . *Ranunculus aquatilis (p 72)*

20B. Leaves lacking stalks above their broadened (stipular)
bases, not collapsing out of water;
achenes 30 to 80 per head . . . . *Ranunculus circinatus (p 72)*

18B. Plants terrestrial, though often in moist to wet habitats 21

21a. Leaves heart- to kidney-shaped, with rounded teeth;
stems trailing on the ground, rooting and producing
new plants at joints . . . . **Ranunculus cymbalaria** *(p 72)*

21B. Leaves deeply lobed or divided into leaflets 22

22a. Leaves divided into stalked leaflets; achenes
with stout, almost triangular beaks . . . . . *Ranunculus macounii (p 73)*

22B. Leaves shallowly to deeply lobed,
not divided into stalked leaflets; achenes
with slender, straight beaks . . . . **Ranunculus eschscholtzii** *(p 73)*

17B. Flowers lacking petals or with inconspicuous petals;
sepals showy and petal-like, usually white or pinkish 23

23a. Flowering stems with 2 to 5 opposite or whorled leaves;
fruits achenes, in compact heads 24

24a. Achenes with feathery, 2 to 4 cm long styles, forming
fluffy heads when mature; flowers usually over 5 cm across 25

25a. Flowers purplish to blue; basal leaves usually twice
divided, with smallest segments 3 to 4 mm wide;
plants of dry sites from prairies to middle
elevations in the mountains . . . . **Anemone patens** *(p 67)*

25B. Flowers white (sometimes purple-tinged);
leaves usually divided 3 to 4 times, with smallest
segments less than 2 mm wide; plants of moist
mountain slopes at high elevations . . . . ***Anemone occidentalis*** *(p 67)*

24B. Achenes with short (less than 1 cm) styles, forming compact
heads when mature; flowers usually less than 5 cm across 26

26a. Leaves 2 to 3 times divided into slender segments 27

27a. Stem leaves stalked; achenes woolly, in dense,
cylindrical, heads 2 to 4 cm long . . . . . . *Anemone cylindrica (p 66)*

27B. Stem leaves stalkless; achenes silky-hairy, in
rounded heads less than 2 cm long . . . ***Anemone multifida*** *(p 66)*

26B. Leaves cut into broad segments, variously toothed
or lobed, but not cut into slender segments 28

28a. Plants usually 30 to 70 cm tall; leaf segments
3 to 5, wedge-shaped, sharply toothed; achenes
hairless or with short, straight hairs . . ***Anemone canadensis*** *(p 65)*

28B. Plants usually 10 to 20 cm tall; leaf segments 3,
almost ovate, with small, rounded lobes;
achenes densely woolly . . . . *Anemone parviflora (p 65)*

23B. Flowering stems leafless or with alternate leaves; fruits
pod-like, several-seeded, splitting open down one side (follicles) 29

29a. Leaves deeply cut into 5 to 7 lobes or leaflets . . . . ***Trollius laxus*** *(p 76)*

29B. Leaves undivided, simply toothed along the edges 30

30A. Plants of wet, alpine meadows; stems erect, leafless
or with 1 leaf; flowers white to bluish . . . . . *Caltha leptosepala (p 69)*

30B. Plants of wetlands at low elevations, not in the
mountains; stems prostrate to ascending; flowers various 31

31a. Flowers bright yellow, 2 to 4 cm across; follicles
10 to 15 mm long, in clusters of 6 to 12;
stems ascending or prostrate . . . . ***Caltha palustris*** *(p 69)*

31B. Flowers white to pinkish, 1 cm across; follicles
5 mm long, in dense clusters of about 30;
plants floating or creeping along mud . . . . . *Caltha natans (p 69)*

BRASSICACEAE OR CRUCIFERAE (see pp 80-85)

1A. Pods round to ovate, usually inflated; plants tufted, usually
less than 25 cm tall; leaves in basal rosettes, covered with star-shaped hairs 2

2A. Pods elliptic to ovate, pointed at tip, flattened along
upper edges, borne on S-shaped stalks . . . . *Lesquerella alpina (p 84)*

2B. Pods round, borne on straight or slightly curved stalks 3

3A. Pods nodding on down-curved stalks; a plant of
dry, sandy southern plains . . . . ***Lesquerella arenosa*** *(p 84)*

3B. Pods erect to ascending on straight or slightly curved stalks; a plant
of dry northern slopes and ridges at higher elevations . . . . *Lesquerella arctica (p 84)*

1B. Pods linear to oblong, over 4 times as long as wide (siliques) 4

4A. At least some leaves deeply cut into many lobes or leaflets;
    flowers small, whitish to pinkish 5

  5A. Plants greyish with dense, branched hairs; lobe at leaf tip
    similar to lower lobes; stem leaves deeply lobed;
    pods 0.5 to 1.2 cm long and 1.5 mm wide or wider . . . . . **Smelowskia calycina** *(p 85)*

  5B. Plants not densely greyish-hairy; lobe at leaf tip
    clearly larger than lower lobes; stem leaves not deeply lobed;
    pods 1.5 to 4 cm long and usually less than 1.5 mm wide . . . . *Arabis lyrata (p 81)*

4B. Leaves undivided to shallowly lobed; flowers various 6

  6A. Flowers white to pinkish purple 7

    7A. Widespread plants at lower elevations, usually 20 to 70 cm
      tall; basal leaves densely hairy with branched hairs;
      flowers white to pale pink; pods gently curved
      downward or abruptly reflexed, 1 to 2 mm wide . . . . **Arabis holboellii** *(p 81)*

    7B. Alpine plants, usually less than 25 cm tall; leaves not as above;
      flowers deep pink to purplish; pods erect to divergent; 2 to 3 mm wide 8

      8A. Plants hairless or with a few variously branched hairs;
        pods 2 to 5 cm long; petals 6 to 10 mm long . . . . *Arabis lyallii (p 81)*

      8B. Plants with distinctive flat-lying, parallel hairs attached at the middle;
        pods 4 to 10 cm long; petals 10 to 16 mm long . . . . *Erysimum pallasii (p 83)*

  6B. Flowers yellow 9

    9A. Pods cylindrical, 4-angled, usually 2 to 10 cm long;
      some hairs attached at the middle, flat-lying and parallel,
      oriented with the axis of the leaf or stem 10

    10A. Flowers showy, with petals 15 to 25 mm long;
      pods usually 6 to 10 cm long . . . . **Erysimum asperum** *(p 83)*

    10B. Flowers small, with petals usually less than
      1 cm long; pods up to 5 cm long 11

      11a. Hairs on leaves mostly 3-branched; petals 2 to 5 mm long;
        pods 1 to 3 cm long; plants sparsely hairy . . . . *Erysimum cheiranthoides (p 83)*

      11B. Hairs on leaves mostly 2-branched; petals 6 to 12 mm long; pods
        2 to 5 cm long; plants densely greyish-hairy . . *Erysimum inconspicuum (p 83)*

    9B. Pods flattened, up to 2 cm long; hairs various, but not as above 12

    12a. Plants annual, with weak, slender taproots; leaves few,
      small, entire to slightly toothed; pods 3 to 10 mm long,
      with stalks usually 2 to 5 times as long as the fruit . . . . . . *Draba nemorosa (p 82)*

    12B. Plants perennial, with well-developed roots; basal leaves
      numerous, stem leaves various, usually not toothed;
      pods 6 to 20 mm long, with stalks less than twice as long as the fruit 13

      13a. Flowering stems with a single leaf or leafless . . . . *Draba incerta (p 82)*

      13B. Flowering stems with 3 or more leaves . . . . **Draba aurea** *(p 82)*

SAXIFRAGACEAE (see pp 89-95)

1A. Delicate, prostrate plants, usually with leafy stolons and small,
rounded to kidney-shaped leaves; flowers inconspicuous,
yellowish to green, 2 to 5 mm across, with 2 to 8 stamens, 4 sepals and no petals 2

  2A. Central flowers 2 to 3 mm wide, with 4 stamens;
sepals green, all similar . . . . *Chrysosplenium tetrandrum (p 90)*

  2B. Central flowers 3 to 5 mm wide, with 5 to 8 stamens; sepals
golden-yellow, the outer pair broader than the inner 2 . . . *Chrysosplenium iowense (p 90)*

1B. Plants not as above; flowers generally more conspicuous, of
various sizes and colours, with 5 or 10 stamens, 5 sepals, and (usually) 5 petals 3

  3A. Leaves roughly heart-shaped, toothed, lobed (occasionally divided into 3 leaflets) 4

    4A. Petals minutely feather-like, pinnately divided, with about 8 hair-like lobes 5

      5A. Flowers with 10 stamens; petals yellowish green, 4 mm long . . **Mitella nuda** *(p 92)*

      5B. Flowers with 5 stamens; petals green, 2 to 3 mm long . . . . . *Mitella pentandra (p 92)*

    4B. Petals not as above 6

      6A. Flowers with 5 stamens; capsules with 2 equal halves,
splitting open between 2 divergent beaks 7

        7A. Stamens projecting from the flowers, longer than the sepals 8

          8A. Petals white, twice as long as the sepals;
calyx 2 to 3.5 mm long; flowers in diffuse clusters
with slender, thread-like branches . . . . *Heuchera glabra (p 91)*

          8B. Petals pink, only slightly longer than the sepals;
calyx 5 to 10 mm long; flowers in branched
but less diffuse clusters . . . . **Heuchera richardsonii** *(p 91)*

        7B. Stamens hidden in the flowers, shorter than the sepals 9

          9A. Calyx 6 to 10 mm long; petals usually absent or
linear and less than half as long as the sepals;
flower clusters narrow and dense . . . . *Heuchera cylindrica (p 91)*

          9B. Calyx 2 to 3 mm long; petals tiny, ovate, 1.5 times as
long as the sepals; flower clusters elongating and
expanding with age . . . . *Heuchera parvifolia (p 91)*

      6B. Flowers with 10 stamens; capsules with 2 very unequal parts,
splitting lengthwise into 2, scoop-shaped parts 10

        10A. Leaves divided into 3 leaflets . . . . **Tiarella trifoliata** *(p 95)*

        10B. Leaves 3 to 5-lobed, not divided into leaflets . . . . *Tiarella unifoliata (p 95)*

  3B. Leaves variously shaped, but not as above 11

    11a. Leaves thick and stiff, densely overlapping,
at least on the lower portion of the stems 12

      12a. Leaves opposite in 4 vertical rows, 2 to 5 mm long;
flowers purplish pink . . . . **Saxifraga oppositifolia** *(p 94)*

      12B. Leaves alternate, on all sides of stems, 5 to 14 m long;
flowers white, usually with reddish or purplish spots 13

13a. Leaves tapered to a sharp point and
edged with tiny spines . . . . **Saxifraga bronchialis** *(p 93)*

13b. Leaves tipped with 3 sharp teeth . . . . *Saxifraga tricuspidata (p 93)*

11b. Leaves softer, more succulent, in basal rosettes and
more loosely arranged on stems 14

14a. Petals yellow; leaves mainly on the stem, succulent,
linear, 4 to 8 mm long . . . . *Saxifraga aizoides (p 93)*

14b. Petals white, sometimes with 2 greenish yellow blotches;
leaves in a basal rosette, wedge- to fan-shaped, with sharp,
coarse teeth on upper half . . . . *Saxifraga lyallii (p 94)*

ROSACEAE (see pp 97-107)

1A. Leaves simple, entire or shallowly toothed 2

2A. Flowers yellow, bell- or cup-shaped;
leaves wedge-shaped at base . . . . **Dryas drummondii** *(p 100)*

2B. Flowers white, saucer-shaped; leaves squared-off to heart-shaped at base 3

3A. Leaves with coarse, rounded teeth and a wrinkled surface; midvein
prominent and bearing yellowish brown glands beneath . . . . . *Dryas octopetala (p 100)*

3B. Leaves entire, toothless or with a few small teeth on the lower half;
midvein neither prominent nor glandular . . . . *Dryas integrifolia (p 100)*

1B. Leaves cut into slender lobes or divided into leaflets 4

4A. Leaves 2 to 3 times divided in 3s into small slender segments 5

5A. Plants erect, taprooted herbs; flowers in open, flat-topped clusters;
fruits dry, seed-like achenes, 5 to 20 per flower . . . . **Chamaerhodos erecta** *(p 99)*

5B. Plants prostrate, stoloniferous semi-shrubs; flowers in crowded, short clusters;
fruits 5-seeded capsules (follicles), 4 to 6 per flower . . . . . . **Luetkea pectinata** *(p 104)*

4b Leaves divided into broader (not linear) leaflets 6

6A. Leaves with 3 leaflets 7

7A. Leaflets squared and 3 to 5-toothed at tips; flowers about 7 mm wide,
with small yellow petals half as long as the sepals . . . **Sibbaldia procumbens** *(p 107)*

7B. Leaflets toothed for most of their length, rounded at tips;
flowers 1.5 to 2 cm wide with showy white petals 8

8A. Leaves yellowish green, edged with coarse teeth that point
outward, tipped with a tooth that extends beyond the rest;
flower clusters usually taller than the leaves . . . . *Fragaria vesca (p 101)*

8B. Leaves green to bluish green, edged with teeth that point forward,
tipped with a small tooth that is shorter than its 2 adjacent
teeth; flower clusters often lower than the leaves . . . **Fragaria virginiana** *(p 101)*

6B. Leaves with 4 or more leaflets 9

9A. Flowers yellow, about 7 to 8 mm across, in dense,
spike-like clusters; central part of flower (hypanthium)
tipped with many hooked bristles . . . . **Agrimonia striata** *(p 98)*

9B. Flower yellow, white or purplish, usually more than 1 cm wide
and in open clusters; hypanthium lacking hooked bristles 10

10A. Basal leaves with several smaller leaflets interspersed with
main leaflets along the central axis; leaflet at the tip larger
than lower leaflets; achenes hairy; styles persistent, long and
slender, feathery (at least near the tip when young) 11

11a. Flowers cup-shaped, with ascending, pinkish to
purplish sepals (and sometimes petals), nodding 12

12a. Flowering stems with several leaves; styles kinked
near the end, with a small feathery tip that breaks
off, leaving a stiff, hooked tip . . . . *Geum rivale (p 102)*

12B. Flowering stems with 1 pair of leaves; styles
feathery from base to tip, not kinked or
jointed near the end . . . . **Geum triflorum** *(p 103)*

11B. Flowers saucer-shaped, with spreading,
green sepals and yellow petals, erect 13

13a. Leaflets at tips of basal leaves much larger than
those below, heart- to kidney-shaped, with shallow,
rounded lobes; styles glandular-hairy . . . . . . *Geum macrophyllum (p 102)*

13B. Leaflets at tips of basal leaves similar to but somewhat
larger than those below, tapered to wedge-shaped
bases; styles not glandular . . . . **Geum aleppicum** *(p 102)*

10B. Basal leaves variously divided, but not as above; achenes hairless;
styles usually dropped at maturity, variously shaped but never feathery 14

14a. Leaflets in a finger-like (palmate) arrangement 15

15a. Plants usually less than 15 cm tall . . . . *Potentilla concinna (p 105)*

15B. Plants 30 to 70 cm tall . . . . **Potentilla gracilis** *(p 106)*

14B. Leaflets in a feather-like (pinnate) arrangement 16

16a. Plants of aquatic or marshy sites;
flowers reddish purple . . . . *Potentilla palustris (p 106)*

16B. Plants of drier sites; flowers yellow or white 17

17a. Flowers solitary, yellow; plants low and
spreading, rooting at the joints of
trailing stems (stolons) . . . . **Potentilla anserina** *(p 105)*

17B. Flowers more than 1, whitish to cream-coloured
(sometimes yellow in *P. arguta*), in flat-topped
clusters; plants taller, with erect stems 18

18a. Flowers in narrow compact clusters with erect
branches; petals equal to or only slightly longer
than sepals; stems stiff, 40 to 100 cm tall . . *Potentilla arguta (p 106)*

18B. Flowers in open to compact
clusters with spreading branches;
petals much longer than sepals;
stems slender, 15 to 30 cm tall . . . . . . *Potentilla glandulosa (p 106)*

FABACEAE OR LEGUMINOSAE (see pp 108-25)

1A. Leaves pinnately divided and tipped with a tendril (rather than a leaflet) 2

  2A. Styles slender, thread-like, hairy around the tip 3

    3A. Flower clusters dense, 15 to 40 flowers, turned to one side . . . . *Vicia cracca (p 125)*

    3B. Flower clusters loose, 2 to 9 flowers,
       pointing in all directions . . . . **Vicia americana** *(p 125)*

  2B. Styles flattened, hairy along one side 4

    4A. Leaves hairless, with 6 to 10 leaflets and 2 large,
       ovate to heart-shaped stipules that are up to
       ⅔ as large as the leaflets . . . . **Lathyrus ochroleucus** *(p 116)*

    4B. Leaves finely hairy on lower surface,
       with 8 to 12 leaflets and 2 small (less than ½ as
       long as the leaflets), lance-shaped stipules . . . . *Lathyrus venosus (p 116)*

1B. Leaves pinnately divided and tipped with a leaflet or with palmate (finger-like) leaflets . . 5

  5A. Leaves usually with 3 leaflets 6

    6A. Leaflets smooth-edged; flowers bright-yellow, 1.2 to
       2 cm long, in erect, showy clusters . . . . **Thermopsis rhombifolia** *(p 123)*

    6B. Leaflets edged with small teeth 7

      7A. Uppermost leaflet stalked, usually at least twice as long
        as wide; flowers in elongate clusters or in compact clusters
        with the lower flowers pointing upwards; petals withering at maturity 8

        8A. Leaflets usually toothed on upper half only; flowers in
          compact head-like clusters; pods curved or coiled . . . . . . *Medicago sativa (p 119)*

        8B. Leaflets usually toothed along entire length; flowers in
          long, slender clusters; pods elliptic to nearly round 9

          9A. Flowers yellow . . . . **Melilotus officinalis** *(p 119)*

          9B. Flowers white . . . . *Melilotus alba (p 119)*

      7B. Uppermost leaflet stalkless, usually only slightly longer than
        wide; flowers in dense, round heads; petals persisting in fruit 10

        10A. Plants annual, with weak roots and yellow
          flowers (brown with age) . . . . *Trifolium aureum (p 124)*

        10B. Plants biennial or perennial, often with leaf remnants
          from the preceding year; flowers white, pink or purple 11

          11a. Flower heads stalkless, immediately above 1 to 2
            short-stalked leaves; flowers usually over 1 cm long,
            dark pink to red (sometimes whitish), stalkless . . . . *Trifolium pratense (p 124)*

          11B. Flower heads on long, slender stalks, well above leaves;
            flowers usually less than 1 cm long, pale pink to white, short-stalked 12

            12a. Plants with creeping stems (stolons) rooting at joints;
              flowers white or slightly pinkish; leaflets 1 to 2.5 cm
              long, usually notched at tips . . . . **Trifolium repens** *(p 124)*

            12B. Plants more erect (though sometimes with stolons);
              flowers usually pink (sometimes white); leaflets 2 to 4 cm
              long, usually rounded at tips . . . . *Trifolium hybridum (p 124)*

28a. Leaflets densely silky, with 11 to 17 leaflets;
flowers 18 to 22 mm long, appearing in
May and early June . . . . **Oxytropis sericea** *(p 120)*

28b. Leaflets sparsely hairy, with 17 to 33 leaflets;
flowers 12 to 17 mm long, appearing in
mid-June to July . . . . *Oxytropis monticola (p 120)*

26b. Leaves mainly on stems; plants less tufted, more sprawling;
flower keel blunt-tipped 29

29a. Plants robust, clumped, with stems usually 5 to 10 mm
thick at base and most leaflets over 2 cm long 30

30a. Flowers reddish purple, 12 to 15 mm long;
plants 40 to 100 cm tall; leaflets 17 to 27,
1 to 3 cm long . . . . *Astragalus bisulcatus (p 112)*

30b. Flowers yellowish white, 20 mm long; plants 20 to 60 cm
tall; leaflets 9 to 17, 2 to 5 cm long . . . . . *Astragalus pectinatus (p 112)*

29b. Plants smaller and finer, with stems less than
5 mm thick and leaflets less than 2 cm long 31

31a. Plants low, often prostrate, usually less than 15 cm tall 32

32a. Flowers purple (sometimes white), 18 to 20 mm
long, in dense head-like clusters almost as wide as
long; pods oblong, 1 cm long, hairy . . . **Astragalus agrestis** *(p 111)*

32b. Flowers yellowish white, 20 to 25 mm long,
with a purple-tinged keel, in loose elongated
clusters; pods rounded, 2 cm across, hairless,
hard when mature . . . . *Astragalus crassicarpus (p 109)*

31b. Plants taller and more erect, over 20 cm tall
(*A. miser* sometimes smaller) 33

33a. Plants robust, 40 to 100 cm tall, clumped; flowers
reddish purple (rarely white) . . . . *Astragalus bisulcatus (p 112)*

33b. Plants smaller and finer, usually less than 50 cm tall;
flowers yellowish white to purplish 34

34a. Pods stalked (within the calyx), hanging,
flattened, hairless; flowers yellowish white,
7 to 9 mm long . . . . *Astragalus tenellus (p 109)*

34b. Pods stalkless (within the calyx), not strongly
flattened; flowers yellowish white, purple or
purple-tinged, 6 to 18 mm long 35

35a. Hairs attached by their middle, lying parallel
and flat against the surface; flowers
15 to 18 mm long; calyx 5 to 9 mm long;
pods oblong, 7 to 10 mm long, deeply
grooved along one side . . . . **Astragalus adsurgens** *(p 109)*

35b. Hairs all attached by their bases; flowers
6 to 14 mm long; calyx 3 to 4 mm long;
pods slender, 20 to 25 mm long . . *Astragalus miser (p 112)*

APIACEAE OR UMBELLIFERAE (see pp 148-59)

1A. Smallest leaf segments broad and well defined 2

  2A. Basal leaves simple, heart-shaped, toothed, long-stalked;
     stem leaves divided into leaflets, short-stalked or stalkless . . . . ***Zizia aptera*** *(p 159)*

  2B. All leaves deeply lobed or divided into leaflets 3

    3A. Plants robust, 1 to 2 m tall; leaves large, divided into
      3 broad leaflets, each 10 to 40 cm long and wide; flower
      clusters white, 10 to 30 cm wide . . . . ***Heracleum lanatum*** *(p 152)*

    3B. Plants less robust, usually less than 1 m tall; most leaves
      divided into more than 3 lobes or leaflets, and these less than 10 cm wide 4

      4A. Leaves deeply cut into finger-like (palmate) lobes or leaflets;
        fruits densely covered with hooked bristles . . . . ***Sanicula marilandica*** *(p 158)*

      4B. Leaves pinnate, with 5 or more leaflets; fruits lacking hooked bristles 5

        5A. Fruits linear to club-shaped, long-stalked, in open,
          widely spreading clusters; leaves divided in 3s, with
          well-defined, ovate to lance-shaped leaflets 6

          6A. Fruits 18 to 22 mm long, tipped with long (2 to 3 mm)
            styles; flower clusters with a whorl of small, persistent
            bracts at the base . . . . *Osmorhiza longistylis (p 156)*

          6B. Fruits 10 to 20 mm long, tipped with tiny (less than 0.5 mm)
            styles; flower clusters lacking bracts or bracts tiny and soon dropped 7

            7A. Fruits bristly, gradually tapered to a slender,
              wedge-shaped base; flowers whitish to purplish;
              stems usually solitary . . . . ***Osmorhiza depauperata*** *(p 155)*

            7B. Fruits hairless, rounded at base; flowers pale
              yellow; stems usually clumped . . . . *Osmorhiza occidentalis (p 156)*

        5B. Fruits oblong to almost round, usually less than 3 times
          as long as broad, in dense, flat-topped clusters; leaves not as above 8

        8A. Plants from clusters of fleshy, thickened, fibrous roots;
          fruits 2 to 4 mm long, with prominent thickened ribs 9

          9A. Leaves usually 2 to 3 times divided into lance-shaped
            leaflets; veins ending at notches between the teeth; stem
            base thickened, hollow with internal horizontal
            partitions, foul-smelling 10

          9B. Leaves once divided into linear to lance-shaped
            leaflets; veins not ending at notches between the teeth;
            stem base not as above . . . . *Sium suave (p 151)*

            10A. Flower clusters with 9 to 21 main branches and
              50 or more branches in the smaller clusters (umbellets);
              fruits 1.5 to 2.2 mm long, usually at least as wide as
              long, or wider . . . . *Cicuta virosa (p 151)*

            10B. Flower clusters with 18 to 28 main branches and
              12 to 25 branches in the umbellets; fruits 2 to 4 mm
              long, usually longer than wide . . . . ***Cicuta maculata*** *(p 150)*

        8B. Plants from taproots or vertical rhizomes;
          fruits 3 to 6 mm long, with winged ribs 11

11a. Flower clusters pale yellow (sometimes greenish-tinged),
with a whorl (involucre) of several large, leafy bracts
at the base . . . . **Angelica dawsonii** *(p 149)*

11b. Flower clusters white (sometimes pinkish-tinged),
with a few small bracts at the base or lacking bracts 12

12a. Leaves bent sharply backwards at the tip of the
main stalk, with the leaflets pointing downwards;
flower clusters with dense, short hairs . . . . . *Angelica genuflexa (p 149)*

12b. Leaves flat, not bent sharply backwards; flower
clusters hairless or with a few tiny bristles . . . . *Angelica arguta (p 149)*

1b. Smallest leaf segments tiny and/or very slender 13

13a. Leaves once or twice divided into slender, smooth-edged leaflets 14

14a. Leaves once (rarely twice) divided, with 3 to 7 linear leaflets;
fruits round, 2 mm long, not winged . . . . **Perideridia gairdneri** *(p 157)*

14b. Leaves 2 to 3 times divided, with numerous leaflets 15

15a. Plants with small, bulb-like growths replacing most of the
flowers; seeds round, 1.5 to 2 mm wide . . . . *Cicuta bulbifera (p 151)*

15b. Plants without bulb-like growths replacing the flowers;
seeds oblong, 3 to 6 mm wide, broadly winged, borne
in well-developed clusters . . . . *Lomatium triternatum (p 153)*

13b. Leaves 2 to 4 times divided into small, toothed leaflets, parsley-like 16

16a. Fruits only slightly flattened, almost round in cross-section,
3 to 5 mm long, with prominent, roughened ribs;
flowers yellow . . . . **Musineon divaricatum** *(p 154)*

16b. Fruits distinctly flattened, usually 5 to 20 mm long,
with well-developed wings on side ribs 17

17a. Mature fruits usually hairy; bracts at base of flower clusters
ovate, often with their bases fused into a cone . . . *Lomatium foeniculaceum (p 154)*

17b. Mature fruits hairless; bracts at base of flower clusters usually separate 18

18a. Stems hairy; fruits narrowly oblong, 9 to 20 mm long;
bractlets slender, tapered to tips, equalling or often
surpassing the enclosed flowers . . . . **Lomatium macrocarpum** *(p 153)*

18b. Stems hairless; fruits broadly elliptic, 5 to 12 mm long; bractlets ovate,
widest above middle, shorter than enclosed flowers . . . *Lomatium cous (p 153)*

ERICACEAE (see pp 161-75)

1a. Plants without green leaves 2

2a. Flowers urn-shaped, 5 to 8 mm long, more than 20, in narrow
elongated clusters; petals fused together . . . . **Pterospora andromedea** *(p 172)*

2b. Flowers bell-shaped, 10 to 20 mm long, nodding,
solitary or few in dense clusters; petals separate 3

3a. Plants waxy-white (blackened when dry), hairless;
flowers single, 14 to 20 mm long . . . . **Monotropa uniflora** *(p 169)*

3b. Plants yellowish to reddish, usually finely hairy;
flowers more than one, 10 to 12 mm long . . . . **Hypopitys monotropa** *(p 169)*

1b. Plants with green leaves 4

4A. Leaves thin, not leathery, withering, persistent or shed
at the end of each growing season 5

  5A. Fruits juicy red berries, 6 to 10 mm across, with
remnant dried sepals and petals at their bases;
leaves gradually tapered to a wedge-shaped base . . . . *Arctostaphylos rubra*

  5B. Fruits juicy red or blue berries, 3 to 8 mm across, tipped with
remnant dried sepals and petals; leaves usually rounded or squared at the bases 6

    6A. Branches round and brownish; leaves and young branches
soft-hairy; flowers numerous, densely clustered . . . . **Vaccinium myrtilloides** *(p 174)*

    6B. Branches angled and green (at least when young); leaves
and branches hairless or sparsely hairy; flowers in groups of 1 to 3 7

      7A. Branches erect, "broomy"; leaves 6 to 15 mm long (usually less
than 10 mm); berries bright red, 3 to 5 mm across . . *Vaccinium scoparium (p 174)*

      7B. Branches more widely spreading; leaves 10 to 30 mm long;
berries black, bluish or dark red, 5 to 8 mm across . . . *Vaccinium myrtillus (p 174)*

4B. Leaves thick and leathery, remaining green through the winter 8

  8A. Leaves scale-like, 2 to 5 mm long, arranged in 4 vertical rows;
flowers white, nodding bells with awned anthers 9

    9A. Leaves with a deep groove down the centre of the back . . *Cassiope tetragona (p 165)*

    9B. Leaves not grooved . . . . **Cassiope mertensiana** *(p 165)*

  8B. Leaves and flowers not as above 10

    10A. Leaves linear, needle-like, crowded, arranged like bristles on a bottle-brush 11

      11a. Flowers deep-pink, bell-shaped, with 5 reflexed lobes,
hairless; sepals ovate, less than half as long as petals,
hairless (except sometimes along edges) . . . . . . **Phyllodoce empetriformis** *(p 171)*

      11B. Flowers yellowish to greenish white, narrowly
urn-shaped, with 5 small, spreading lobes, usually
glandular-hairy; sepals lance-shaped, more than half as
long as petals, glandular-hairy . . . . *Phyllodoce glanduliflora (p 171)*

      11c. Flowers intermediate between the 2 preceding species,
pale pink, sparsely glandular-hairy . . . . *Phyllodoce* x *intermedia (p 171)*

    10B. Leaves broad to slender but not needle-like, less crowded on branches 12

      12a. Leaves tiny, 2 to 8 mm long, scattered along thread-like
trailing stems; flowers pinkish, with 4 petals bent
backwards, like tiny shootingstar flowers . . . . **Vaccinium oxycoccos** *(p 175)*

      12B. Leaves larger and more numerous; flowers urn- to saucer-shaped 13

        13a. Plants herbaceous, though often with woody bases;
flowers with separate petals 14

          14a. Leaves lance-shaped, broadest above middle, rounded
at tip, tapered to a wedge-shaped base, sharply toothed,
some borne in whorls of 3 to 8 . . . . **Chimaphila umbellata** *(p 166)*

          14B. Leaves round to ovate, with slender stalks, toothless
or with small, irregular teeth, borne in basal rosettes
or on the lower stem, not whorled 15

            15a. Flowers single . . . . **Moneses uniflora** *(p 168)*

            15B. Flowers more than 1, in elongated clusters 16

              16a. Flowers bell-shaped, all nodding to one side;
leaves borne on the lower third to half
of the stem . . . . **Orthilia secunda** *(p 170)*

              16B. Flowers more open, cupped to saucer-shaped, borne on
all sides of the cluster; leaves in more compact basal rosettes . . 17

17a. Flowers pink to purplish . . . . **Pyrola asarifolia** *(p 173)*

17b. Flowers greenish white . . . . *Pyrola chlorantha (p 173)*

13b. Plants low, woody shrubs; flowers with petals fused
into cupped or urn-shaped corollas 18

18a. Leaves broadly spatula-shaped, broadest above middle,
rounded at tip, tapered to a wedge-shaped base, edges flat
(not rolled under); branches trailing and rooting,
often forming mats . . . . **Arctostaphylos uva-ursi** *(p 163)*

18b. Leaves narrowly elliptic to oblong, edges
rolled under; branches various 19

19a. Plants with slender, creeping branches;
leaves 6 to 15 mm long, elliptic, glossy green
above, pale and dotted with scattered dark hairs beneath;
fruit a scarlet berry . . . . *Vaccinium vitis-idaea (p 175)*

19b. Plants with spreading to erect branches; leaves
10 to 40 mm long (occasionally longer), green
above, pale beneath but without dark hairs; fruit a dry capsule . . . 20

20a. Leaves linear to narrowly elliptic; flowers pink, urn-
shaped, 5 to 8 mm long, nodding . . **Andromeda polifolia** *(p 162)*

20b. Leaves oval to oblong-elliptic; flowers rose-pink,
saucer-shaped, 6 to 15 mm across, not nodding 21

21a. Plants small, 10 to 20 cm tall, with broad
leaves that are 1 to 2 cm long and
over half as wide . . . . *Kalmia microphylla (p 167)*

21b. Plants larger, usually over 30 cm tall, with
narrower leaves that are 2 to 4 cm long
and less than half as wide . . . . **Kalmia polifolia** *(p 167)*

PRIMULACEAE (see pp 176-81)

1a. Flowering stems leafy 2

2a. Plants fleshy, 5 to 15 cm tall, growing in saline or alkaline
habitats; flowers about 5 mm across, lacking petals . . . . **Glaux maritima** *(p 179)*

2b. Plants not distinctly fleshy, 20 to 100 cm tall, growing in
non-saline habitats; flowers larger, with petals 3

3a. Flowers about 6 mm across, in compact, stalked,
bottle-brush-like clusters in leaf axils; leaves tapered to base,
stalkless or very short-stalked . . . . *Lysimachia thyrsiflora (p 180)*

3b. Flowers 15 to 25 mm across, solitary in leaf axils, often forming
whorls; leaves (at least the lower ones) stalked 4

4a. Leaf stalks fringed with small hairs;
leaves at mid-stem lance-shaped to ovate,
2.5 to 6 cm wide; petal lobes up to 12 mm long . . . . **Lysimachia ciliata** *(p 180)*

4b. Leaf stalks fringed with hairs on lower half only; leaves at
mid-stem linear to narrowly lance-shaped, up to 2 cm wide;
petal lobes 6 to 9 mm long . . . . *Lysimachia lanceolata (p 180)*

1b. Flowering stems leafless; leaves in basal rosettes 5

5A. Flowers large and showy, rose to purple; petals 2 cm long, reflexed;
     stamens fused together, forming a conspicuous, narrow cone
     projecting from the flower centre 6

   6A. Leaves glandular-hairy (often sparsely so); fused filaments usually
     less than 1 mm long (up to 1.5 mm), with horizontal wrinkles;
     capsule teeth squared at tips . . . . *Dodecatheon conjugens (p 178)*

   6B. Leaves hairless; fused filaments usually over
     1.5 mm long, smooth or with lengthwise wrinkles;
     capsule teeth pointed at tips . . . . **Dodecatheon pulchellum** *(p 178)*

5B. Flowers smaller, white to pink or lilac; petals usually less than 1 cm
     long, spreading or ascending; stamens neither projecting nor forming a cone 7

  7A. Leaves essentially stalkless, usually less than 2 cm long;
     petals white, their fused tube usually shorter than the sepals 8

    8A. Plants perennial, with compact rosettes of leaves,
       spreading by trailing stems (stolons); often forming mats;
       flowers up to 12 mm wide, borne in compact clusters of
       4 to 8 flowers, with 1 flowering stalk per plant . . . . **Androsace chamaejasme** *(p 177)*

    8B. Plants annual, with rosettes of spreading leaves, from
       slender taproots; flowers less than 5 mm wide, in open,
       umbrella-like clusters of several flowers, often with
       several flowering stalks per plant 9

     9A. Bracts at the base of the flower cluster leaf-like,
         elliptic to ovate, usually about 3 mm long (occasionally
         longer); flowering stalks 2 to 5 cm tall . . . . *Androsace occidentalis (p 177)*

     9B. Bracts at the base of the flower cluster slender,
         lance- to awl-shaped, usually about 1 to 3 mm long;
         flower stalks 2 to 25 cm tall . . . . *Androsace septentrionalis (p 177)*

  7B. Leaves with winged stalks, usually over 2 cm long; petals pink
     to lilac, their fused tube longer than the sepals 10

    10A. Leaves smooth- or wavy-edged (not toothed), with blades
       equalling or shorter than their long, slender stalks,
       never mealy; capsules slender-cylindrical . . . . *Primula egaliksensis (p 181)*

    10B. Leaves usually toothed, with blades longer than their
       short, wide stalks, often mealy on lower surface; capsules
       thick-cylindrical to narrowly ovate 11

     11a. Flower cluster above a whorl of small (2 to 6 mm long)
         bracts at the tip of a slender, 5 to 12 cm tall stem;
         leaves rarely mealy; capsules 2 to 3 mm in diameter . . *Primula mistassinica (p 181)*

     11B. Flower cluster above a whorl of larger (3 to 14 mm long)
         bracts at the tip of a stout, 10 to 40 cm tall stem;
         leaves often mealy; capsules 2.5 to 5 mm in diameter 12

      12a. Leaves, calyxes and upper flower stalks green or
           slightly mealy; bracts at the base of the flower
           cluster awl-shaped . . . . *Primula stricta (p 181)*

      12B. Leaves (lower surface), calyxes and upper flower stalks
           densely mealy; bracts at the base of the flower cluster
           flat and lance-shaped to narrowly oblong . . . . **Primula incana** *(p 181)*

BORAGINACEAE (see pp 193-200)

1A. Nutlets armed with hooked bristles 2

  2A. Flowers 1.5 to 2 mm across; nutlet body
    2 to 3 mm long; stem leaves tapered to a stalk-like base . . . . *Hackelia deflexa (p 196)*

  2B. Flowers 4 to 8 mm across; nutlet body 3 to 4 mm long;
    stem leaves broad and rounded at the base 3

    3A. Plants with few stems (often 1) from a simple root crown;
      hooked prickles only on edges of nutlets;
      flowers 4 to 8 mm across . . . . **Hackelia floribunda** *(p 196)*

    3B. Plants with several stems from a branched root crown;
      hooked prickles often not restricted to edges of nutlets;
      flowers 7 to 11 mm across . . . . *Hackelia micrantha (p 196)*

1B. Nutlets smooth or roughened but lacking hooked bristles 4

  4A. Nutlets attached by a broad, low, spreading base; flowers in leafy clusters 5

    5A. Flowers blue; stamens conspicuous, projecting from
      the flowers; nutlets dark, bumpy . . . . **Echium vulgare** *(p 195)*

    5B. Flowers yellow or greenish white; stamens inconspicuous;
      nutlets white to pale brown, shiny, smooth or sparingly pitted 6

      6A. Flowers greenish white, tubular, with erect, pointed
        lobes, hairy on outer surface; styles conspicuously
        projecting from the flowers . . . . **Onosmodium molle** *(p 200)*

      6B. Flowers yellow, greenish yellow or orange, with rounded,
        spreading lobes, hairless on outer surface; styles not
        conspicuously projecting from the flowers 7

        7A. Flowers greenish to pale yellow, less than 1 cm long;
          nutlets 4 to 6 mm long . . . . *Lithospermum ruderale (p 197)*

        7B. Flowers bright yellow to orange, 1 cm long or longer;
          nutlets 3 to 4 mm long . . . . **Lithospermum incisum** *(p 197)*

  4B. Nutlets with a small point of attachment, lacking a broad,
    spreading base; flower clusters not leafy 8

    8A. Flowers blue to deep pink 9

      9A. Flowers less than 4 mm long and 4 to 8 mm wide, with
        flat-spreading lobes at the tip of a fused tube, borne in
        elongating, often 1-sided clusters . . . . **Myosotis alpestris** *(p 199)*

      9B. Flowers 10 to 20 mm long and less than half as wide, tubular
        to narrowly bell-shaped, often expanded at tip above a tubular
        base, nodding, borne in crowded (not elongated) clusters 10

        10A. Plants usually 40 to 80 cm tall; stems usually hairy; basal
          leaves heart-shaped to broadly lance-shaped, with strong,
          arching veins, stiff-hairy . . . . **Mertensia paniculata** *(p 198)*

        10B. Plants usually 10 to 40 cm tall; stems hairless; basal leaves
          linear-oblong to broadly lance-shaped, without strong, arching veins 11

11a. Basal leaves rarely seen on flowering plants;
flowers 15 to 20 mm long, with tubes at least twice
as long as the bells . . . . *Mertensia longiflora (p 198)*

11b. Basal leaves well developed at flowering time; flowers
about 10 mm long, with tubes equal to or slightly longer
than the bells . . . . *Mertensia lanceolata (p 198)*

8b. Flowers white 12

12a. Plants slender, annual, with few basal leaves; flowers
inconspicuous, less than 2 mm across 13

13a. Flower clusters with leafy bracts throughout . . . . *Cryptantha minima (p 194)*

13b. Flower clusters with leafy bracts below
lower flowers only . . . . *Cryptantha fendleri (p 194)*

12b. Plants relatively coarse, perennial, with a well-developed
tuft of basal leaves; flowers showy, 6 to 11 mm across 14

14a. Lower leaves 5 mm wide or narrower; flowers 6 to
8 mm across; nutlets 2 to 3 mm long . . . . **Cryptantha macounii** *(p 194)*

14b. Lower leaves 5 to 8 mm wide; flowers 7 to 11 mm
across; nutlets 3 to 4 mm long . . . . *Cryptantha nubigena (p 194)*

LAMIACEAE OR LABIATAE (see pp 201-09)

1A. Flowers borne in leaf axils, sometimes also numerous
and forming dense clusters at stem tips 2

2A. Flowers in the axils of normal stem leaves (except *Mentha spicata*) 3

3A. Flowers usually in pairs, tubular, 12 to 25 mm long,
clearly 2-lipped; calyx 2-lipped, with a distinctive
bump on the upper surface . . . . **Scutellaria galericulata** *(p 208)*

3B. Flowers in dense whorls, 2 to 6 mm long, not clearly 2-lipped;
calyx with 5, pointed lobes 4

4A. Plants aromatic, minty; flower clusters relatively showy,
usually pink to purplish (sometimes white); flowers 4 to 8 mm
long, with 4 fertile stamens . . . . **Mentha arvensis** *(p 205)*

4B. Plants odourless; flower clusters inconspicuous, usually white
(sometimes lavender); flowers 2 to 5 mm long, with 2 fertile stamens 5

5A. Calyx teeth broadly triangular to ovate, blunt or slightly
pointed, less than 1 mm long; leaves with inconspicuous,
shallow teeth . . . . *Lycopus uniflorus (p 204)*

5B. Calyx teeth narrowly triangular, tapered to a slender point,
1 to 2 mm long; leaves with conspicuous sharp teeth or lobes 6

6A. Lower to middle leaves edged with sharp, even teeth;
plants often growing on alkaline sites . . . . **Lycopus asper** *(p 204)*

6B. Lower and middle leaves cut into irregular, pointed
lobes; plants intolerant of alkali . . . . *Lycopus americanus (p 204)*

2B. Flowers in axils of stem leaves and also forming dense clusters
that are usually interspersed with much smaller leaves (bracts) at stem tips 7

7A. Plants with a strong, minty fragrance; flowers 2 to 4 mm
long, with 4 fertile stamens, borne in whorls in leafless
spikes at branch tips . . . . *Mentha spicata (p 205)*

7B. Plants and flowers not as above 8

    8A. Calyx teeth pointed but not tipped with spines;
       stems soft-hairy; flowers 10 to 25 mm long . . . . ***Stachys palustris*** *(p 209)*

    8B. Calyx teeth tipped with spines; stems bristly-hairy; flowers 15 to 30 mm long . . . 9

        9A. Flowers pink or purplish (sometimes white), 1.5 to
           2 cm long; calyx usually as long as the corolla tube . . ***Galeopsis tetrahit*** *(p 203)*

        9B. Flowers pale yellow with a purple spot on the lower lip, 3 cm
           long; calyx much shorter than the corolla tube . . . . *Galeopsis speciosa* *(p 203)*

1B. Flowers borne in dense, head-like clusters only 10

    10A. Flowers tubular, 20 to 35 mm long, with a slender, arching upper lip
       and 2 stamens; flower clusters short, usually wider than long . . ***Monarda fistulosa*** *(p 206)*

    10B. Flowers various, less than 20 mm long, with a broader
       upper lip and 4 stamens; flower clusters usually longer than wide 11

        11a. Plants 10 to 30 cm tall, with smooth-edged (sometimes obscurely
           toothed), oblong to lance-shaped leaves; calyx 2-lipped, with
           3 shallow teeth on the upper lip and 2 sharp, narrow teeth on
           the lower lip; flower clusters dense, 2 to 5 cm long . . . . ***Prunella vulgaris*** *(p 207)*

        11B. Plants 30 to 100 cm tall, with blunt-toothed, ovate to
           oblong leaves; calyx usually with 5 similar teeth,
           not 2-lipped; flower clusters usually over 5 cm long 12

           12a. Flowers 6 to 12 mm long, with conspicuous projecting
              stamens; lower lip of corolla small, poorly developed;
              leaves short-stalked, often squared at base, paler beneath
              with short, flat-lying hairs . . . . ***Agastache foeniculum*** *(p 202)*

           12B. Flowers 10 to 20 mm long, with inconspicuous stamens
              (not projecting beyond petals); lower lip of corolla broad,
              3-lobed; leaves short-stalked or stalkless, rounded at base,
              loosely silky-hairy beneath . . . . ***Stachys palustris*** *(p 209)*

SCROPHULARIACEAE (see pp 210-26)

1A. Leaves mostly alternate 2

    2A. Flowers with a hollow appendage (spur) projecting back from the base 3

        3A. Plants with a rosette of slender, prostrate, leafy stems at
           the base of the erect flowering stem; flowers light blue;
           capsules 2.5 to 4 mm long . . . . *Linaria canadensis* *(p 215)*

        3B. Plants lacking a basal rosette of stems; flowers yellow with
           orange on the lower lip; capsules 6 to 12 mm long 4

           4A. Leaves soft, slender, tapered to stalk-like bases;
              flowers 2 to 3 cm long, numerous in dense clusters . . . . . . ***Linaria vulgaris*** *(p 215)*

           4B. Leaves firm, ovate, pointed at tips, rounded and often
              clasping stems at bases; flowers 3 to 4 cm long,
              in loose, few-flowered clusters . . . . *Linaria genistifolia* *(p 215)*

    2B. Flowers lacking spurs 5

5A. Flowers forming dense, spike-like clusters, lacking petals
but with showy purple stamens projecting well
beyond the sepals . . . . **Besseya wyomingensis** *(p 211)*

5B. Flowers with petals; stamens and flower clusters not as above 6

  6A. Flowers yellow, with 5 equal, spreading lobes 7

    7A. Leaves green and thinly hairy on the upper surface, paler,
with dense, star-shaped hairs beneath; anther stalks
(filaments) with purple hairs . . . . *Verbascum nigrum (p 225)*

    7B. Leaves grey with dense woolly hairs on both sides;
filaments with white or yellowish hairs 8

      8A. Flowers clusters dense, spike-like; flowers 15 to 25 mm
across; upper leaves with edges extending down the
stem to the leaf below . . . . **Verbascum thapsus** *(p 225)*

      8B. Flower clusters loose, sometimes branched at base; flowers
20 to 55 mm across; upper leaves with edges not or
only slightly extending down the stem . . . . *Verbascum phlomoides (p 225)*

  6B. Flowers variously coloured, clearly 2-lipped 9

    9A. Plants annual, with slender stems from small taproots;
flowers yellow, with the upper lip equal to or only slightly
longer than the lower lip . . . . **Orthocarpus luteus** *(p 218)*

    9B. Plants perennial, with coarser stems from woody root
crowns; flowers variously coloured, with the upper lip
(a hood or beak) clearly longer than the lower lip 10

      10A. Flowers surrounded (and often hidden) by large, coloured bracts 11

        11a. Flower clusters pink, red or purple (occasionally
yellowish in *Castilleja miniata*) 12

          12a. Flower clusters pink to scarlet; lower lip of the
flower ⅕ as long as the upper lip or shorter;
plants usually over 30 cm tall . . . . **Castilleja miniata** *(p 212)*

          12B. Flower clusters purplish to crimson; lower lip of the
flower thickened, ⅕ to ⅓ as long as the upper lip;
plants usually less than 30 cm tall . . . . *Castilleja rhexifolia (p 213)*

        11B. Flower clusters yellow 13

          13a. Plants silky-hairy, unbranched; leaves ascending and
densely overlapping, often hiding the stem . . *Castilleja cusickii (p 213)*

          13B. Plants with short, fine hairs, usually branched;
leaves spreading, not hiding the stem . . . . . . *Castilleja lutescens (p 213)*

      10B. Flowers clearly visible above small green or purplish brown bracts 14

        14a. Plants robust, 30 to 100 cm tall; leaves mainly on the
stem; flowers yellow, often tinged purple, with the
upper lip rounded or very short-beaked . . . . *Pedicularis bracteosa (p 220)*

        14B. Plants usually less than 40 cm tall; leaves largest in the
basal rosette, smaller upwards on the stem; flowers variously
coloured, with the upper lip extended into a slender beak 15

          15a. Flowers white to yellowish, with the beak coiled
downwards and hidden between the lower lobes;
plants green . . . . *Pedicularis contorta (p 220)*

          15B. Flowers pink to reddish purple, with the beak
curved outward and up (like an elephant's
trunk) and the lower lobes spreading
(like an elephant's ears); plants often
reddish purple or purple-tinged . . . **Pedicularis groenlandica** *(p 219)*

1B. Leaves mostly opposite or whorled 16

  16a. Flowers blue or purplish, weakly 2-lipped, with 4 spreading lobes and 2 stamens 17

    17a. Leaves stalked; flowers in slender, spreading
    clusters from leaf axils . . . . *Veronica americana*

    17B. Leaves stalkless; flowers in dense clusters at stem tips . . . . **Veronica alpina** (p 226)

  16B. Flowers variously coloured, strongly 2-lipped, with 4 fertile stamens 18

    18a. Calyxes about 10 mm long in flower, inflated and
    enlarged to about 15 mm in fruit . . . . **Rhinanthus minor** (p 224)

    18B. Calyxes smaller, not inflated in fruit 19

      19a. Plants slender, 10 to 30 cm tall, annual, with weak taproots;
      leaves all on the stem 20

        20A. Leaves often whorled, toothless, 1 to 2.5 cm long, stalkless;
        flowers blue to purplish, 4 to 6 mm long . . . . **Collinsia parviflora** (p 214)

        20B. Leaves all opposite, toothed, 1 to 4 cm long, squared
        at base and stalked; flowers yellow, marked with red at
        the throat, 7 to 15 mm long . . . . *Mimulus floribundus* (p 217)

      19B. Plants coarser, usually perennial, with well-developed rootstocks;
      leaves often in basal clusters as well as on the stem 21

        21a. Flowers tubular, white, blue or purple (*P. confertus* sulphur-yellow),
        with 4 fertile stamens (2 long and 2 short) and 1 sterile stamen
        that is usually flattened and hairy at the tip 22

          22a. Flowers usually about 1 cm long, whorled in leaf axils and
          in dense spikes at stem tips 23

            23a. Flowers purplish blue
            (rarely pinkish or white) . . . . *Penstemon procerus* (p 223)

            23B. Flowers sulphur-yellow . . . . **Penstemon confertus** (p 221)

          22B. Flowers usually at least 1.5 cm long, less densely clustered 24

            24a. Plants shrubby; anthers densely woolly; leaves linear
            to lance-shaped, about 2 to 5 mm wide . . . . *Penstemon fruticosus* (p 221)

            24B. Plants herbaceous (not woody); fertile anthers
            hairless; leaves usually wider 25

              25a. Plants hairless, bluish green (glaucous);
              lower bracts broad, ovate to almost round or
              sometimes lance-shaped . . . . **Penstemon nitidus** (p 222)

              25B. Plants usually glandular-hairy in flower cluster,
              not glaucous; lower bracts slender, lance-shaped 26

                26a. Flowers white (sometimes tinged violet),
                about 2 cm long, glandular-hairy within the
                flower and on the calyx . . . . *Penstemon albidus* (p 223)

                26B. Flowers blue to purplish (occasionally white),
                not glandular-hairy within 27

                  27a. Flowers purplish, 25 to 40 mm long,
                  widely inflated at the mouth,
                  hairy within; ovary and capsules
                  glandular-hairy near tip . . . . *Penstemon eriantherus* (p 221)

                  27B. Flowers 18 to 20 mm long (occasionally
                  longer), relatively slender and pale, light mauve
                  or white and less conspicuously hairy within;
                  ovary and capsules usually hairless . . *Penstemon gracilis* (p 223)

        21B. Flowers broadly 2-lipped, red or yellow,
        with 4 stamens (2 long and 2 short) 28

28a. Flowers red to pinkish purple, marked with
yellow, 3 to 5 cm long . . . . *Mimulus lewisii (p 217)*

28B. Flowers yellow, often marked with red, 1 to 4 cm long 29

29a. Flowers 1 to 2 cm long, with few or no red dots,
open in the throat; lower and side calyx lobes
blunt-tipped . . . . *Mimulus glabratus (p 217)*

29B. Flowers 2 to 4 cm long; lower lip well developed
and strongly red-dotted, almost closing the throat;
lower and side calyx lobes pointed 30

30A. Plants usually less than 20 cm tall, spreading by
creeping rooting stems (rhizomes) to form thick mats,
often also with trailing stems that root at joints
only (stolons); flowers few, usually 1 to 5,
each 2 to 4 cm long . . . . *Mimulus tilingii (p 217)*

30B. Plants highly variable, ranging from small and prostrate
(5 cm tall) to erect and 60 cm tall, spreading by stolons
but lacking sod-forming rhizomes; flowers often in
clusters of more than 5, usually less than 2 cm long
when solitary or few . . . . **Mimulus guttatus** *(p 216)*

ASTERACEAE OR COMPOSITAE (see pp 236–91)

1A. Flower heads with ray florets only; plants with milky juice . . . . **Group 1**

1B. Flower heads with some disk florets; plants with watery juice 2

2A. Flower heads with disk florets only . . . . **Group 2**

2B. Flower heads with ray florets around a central cluster of disk florets 3

3A. Ray florets yellow or orange . . . . **Group 3**

3B. Ray florets white, pink or blue . . . . **Group 4**

GROUP 1 (RAY FLORETS ONLY; MILKY JUICE)

1A. Leaves all or mainly basal 2

2A. Plants tiny, 2 to 8 cm tall, growing on rocky alpine slopes, with dense,
rounded clumps of spatula-shaped basal leaves; flower heads small
(about 1 cm), yellow, interspersed among the basal leaves . . . . *Crepis nana (p 257)*

2B. Plants larger, 10 to 70 cm tall, with fewer, longer basal leaves;
flower heads larger, borne on long stalks well above the leaves 3

3A. Flowering stems usually with at least a few leaves;
flower heads few to several; involucral bracts in 1 to 2 rows,
with the outer row smaller . . . . **Crepis runcinata** *(p 257)*

3B. Flowering stems leafless; flower heads usually solitary;
involucral bracts in several overlapping rows 4

    4A. Flowers pinkish . . . . *Agoseris lackschewitzii (p 239)*

    4B. Flowers yellow or orange 5

        5A. Flowers yellow; achenes clearly ribbed, tipped with
a stout beak up to half as long as the body . . . . **Agoseris glauca** *(p 238)*

        5B. Flowers orange; achenes obscurely ribbed, tipped with a
long, slender beak over half as long as the body . . . . . *Agoseris aurantiaca (p 239)*

1B. Leaves all or mainly on the stem 6

  6A. Leaves coarsely toothed or lobed 7

    7A. Flowers blue or white 8

        8A. Plants robust, 50 to 200 cm tall, annual or biennial from
taproots; flower heads relatively small, with involucres
10 to 14 mm high . . . . *Lactuca biennis (p 273)*

        8B. Plants usually 30 to 60 cm tall, occasionally up to 90 cm,
perennial from spreading rhizomes; flower heads large and
showy, with involucres 15 to 20 mm high . . . . **Lactuca tatarica** *(p 273)*

    7B. Flowers yellow 9

        9A. Flower heads about 3 to 5 cm wide, with broadly
cupped 14 to 24 mm high involucres and usually over
100 florets; achenes beakless . . . . **Sonchus arvensis** *(p 288)*

        9B. Flower heads smaller, with involucres 10 mm high or
smaller, and fewer than 75 florets; achenes various 10

          10A. Involucres tubular, 10 mm high, hairless;
flower heads with 13 to 27 florets; achenes tapered
to a slender beak as long as or longer than the body . . . . . *Lactuca serriola (p 273)*

          10B. Involucres narrowly funnel-shaped, 6 to 9 mm high, hairy,
sometimes also glandular; flower heads with 30 to 70 flowers;
achenes spindle-shaped, not distinctly beaked . . . . *Crepis tectorum (p 257)*

  6B. Leaves smooth-edged or with a few small teeth 11

    11a. Plants much branched, with small, linear (often scale-like) leaves
scattered on branches; flowers pink (rarely white) 12

        12a. Plants 10 to 40 cm tall, perennial, from long rhizomes;
lower leaves usually less than 5 cm long; involucres
with about 5 long bracts . . . . **Lygodesmia juncea** *(p 276)*

        12B. Plants 30 to 100 cm tall, annual, from taproots;
lower leaves usually 5 to 20 cm long;
involucres with 7 to 9 long bracts . . . . *Lygodesmia rostrata (p 276)*

    11B. Plants less branched; leaves larger and more conspicuous;
flowers yellow or white 13

        13a. Pappus of long, feathery, inter-webbed hairs, forming
conspicuous fruiting heads up to 10 cm in diameter;
flower heads about 5 to 6 cm across . . . . **Tragopogon dubius** *(p 291)*

        13B. Pappus of small, simple hairs, forming fruiting heads
less than 2 cm in diameter; flower heads about 1 to 3 cm across 14

          14a. Plants with taproots, hairless or short-hairy on
lower stem and leaves; lower leaves stalked, toothed to
deeply lobed; upper leaves slender, stalkless, with basal
lobes clasping stems; pappus white . . . . *Crepis tectorum (p 257)*

          14B. Plants with fibrous roots and rhizomes, usually long-hairy on
lower stem and leaves; leaves edged with tiny, widely spaced
teeth or toothless; pappus dirty-white or brownish 15

15a. Leaves stalkless, largest at mid stem; lower leaves
usually withered by flowering time . . . . **Hieracium umbellatum** *(p 269)*

15b. Basal leaves stalked and largest, persisting at flowering time 16

16a. Flower white; plants lacking star-shaped
hairs on the involucres . . . . *Hieracium albiflorum (p 269)*

16b. Flowers yellow; plants with some star-shaped
hairs on leaves and/or involucres . . . . *Hieracium scouleri (p 269)*

GROUP 2 (DISK FLORETS ONLY)

1a. Pappus a tuft of hair-like or feathery bristles 2

2a. Leaves with spine-tipped teeth 3

3a. Plants 10 to 30 cm tall; leaves thick, greyish green, lance- to
spatula-shaped, 1 to 3 cm long, edged with spiny teeth,
not lobed; flower heads yellow, about 1 cm across . . *Machaeranthera grindelioides (p 319)*

3b. Plants 30 to 120 cm tall; leaves larger and lobed; flower
heads purplish pink to cream-coloured 4

4a. Stems growing from creeping rhizomes; flower heads less than
2.5 cm high, pinkish purple; involucres 1 to 2 cm high . . . **Cirsium arvense** *(p 255)*

4b. Stems growing from the centre of last year's rosette; flower heads larger 5

5a. Upper leaf surface with small, flat-lying spines, rough to
touch; flowers rose-purple (rarely white) . . . . *Cirsium vulgare (p 256)*

5b. Upper leaf surface spineless, not rough to touch;
flowers whitish to light pink-purple 6

6a. Involucral bracts up to 2 mm wide at base,
covered with dense, cobwebby hairs; flowers
cream-coloured to dirty white . . . . *Cirsium hookerianum (p 255)*

6b. Outer involucral bracts over 2 mm wide at base,
lacking cobwebby hairs; flowers pink-purple . . . . *Cirsium undulatum (p 255)*

2b. Leaves not spiny 7

7a. Leaves all or mainly basal or opposite 8

8a. Main leaves divided into 3 to 5 stalked leaflets . . . . *Bidens frondosa (p 253)*

8b. Main leaves not divided into leaflets, sometimes deeply cut into 3 to 5 lobes 9

9a. Leaves stalkless, simple (not lobed); flower heads usually
with conspicuous ray florets but sometimes without . . . . **Bidens cernua** *(p 253)*

9b. Leaves stalked, some deeply 3-lobed; flower heads
usually lacking ray florets . . . . *Bidens tripartita (p 253)*

7b. Leaves all or mainly alternate and borne on stem 10

10a. Tips of involucral bracts spiny or darkened and
fringed with a row of stiff bristles 11

11a. Involucral bracts tipped with spines 12

12a. Stems not winged; flowers creamy to purple-tinged;
involucral spines about 1.5 to 4 mm long . . . . *Centaurea diffusa (p 254)*

12b. Stems winged by extended leaf bases; flowers yellow;
involucral spines 10 to 30 mm long . . . . *Centaurea solstitialis (p 254)*

11B. Involucral bracts with dark tips fringed with short, stiff bristles 13

    13a. Lower leaves deeply cut into slender lobes; plant biennial
       or short-lived perennial, from strong taproots . .   ***Centaurea maculosa*** *(p 254)*

    13B. Lower leaves usually toothed (sometimes with a few
       narrow lobes); plant annual, weakly rooted . . . . *Centaurea cyanus (p 254)*

10B. Tips of involucral bracts not as above 14

    14a. Some or all leaves distinctly toothed or lobed 15

       15a. Outer involucral bracts round to ovate with wide,
          abruptly pointed, nearly transparent tips . . . . *Centaurea repens (p 254)*

       15B. Involucral bracts lance-shaped, more gradually tapered at tips 16

          16a. Some or all leaves usually deeply cut into slender
             lobes, hairless or sparsely hairy; involucral bracts
             hairless, in 1 main row (with a few shorter bracts at
             the base), at least some black-tipped; pappus of
             simple hairs; plants annual weeds . . . . *Senecio vulgaris (p 284)*

          16B. Some or all leaves coarsely toothed (sometimes toothless
             or lobed), usually cobwebby-hairy on the lower
             surface; involucral bracts sometimes cobwebby, in
             several overlapping rows; pappus usually of feathery bristles 17

             17a. Plants 30 to 100 cm tall; lower leaves triangular,
                squared or notched at base, with blades up to
                15 cm long and 8 cm wide . . . . *Saussurea americana (p 283)*

             17B. Plants 10 to 30 cm tall; lower leaves lance-shaped,
                with blades up to 12 cm long and 2 cm wide 18

                18a. Plants growing on rocky alpine slopes; outer involucral
                   bracts as long as the inner bracts . . . . ***Saussurea nuda*** *(p 283)*

                18B. Plants growing in disturbed areas, escaped
                   from cultivation; outer involucral bracts
                   shorter than the inner ones . . . . *Saussurea glomerata (p 283)*

  14B. Leaves smooth-edged, neither toothed nor lobed 19

    19a. Flower heads purple to rose-coloured, about 15 mm
       high, with thread-like appendages creating a feathery
       appearance, forming dense, spike-like clusters 5 to 15 cm
       long; florets with both male and female parts 20

       20A. Lower leaves firm, linear, 2 to 4 mm wide, dotted
          with translucent spots, thickened, white and fringed
          with hairs along edges . . . . ***Liatris punctata*** *(p 275)*

       20B. Lower leaves narrowly lance-shaped, broadest above
          middle, 10 to 20 mm wide, somewhat hairy (especially
          along edges), tapered to a winged stalk . . . . . . *Liatris ligulistylis (p 275)*

    19B. Flower heads white to pale pink or yellowish, less than
       10 mm high, in open, usually flat-topped clusters less
       than 5 cm long; florets either male or female 21

       21a. Basal leaves small, usually withered by flowering
          time; flower heads showy, with broad, spreading,
          pearly-white involucral bracts around the small
          cluster of yellow to white florets . . . . . . ***Anaphalis margaritacea*** *(p 240)*

       21B. Basal leaves well developed, often forming a tuft,
          present at flowering time; flower heads relatively
          inconspicuous, with less showy, more erect involucral bracts 22

          22a. Plants 20 to 50 cm tall; basal leaves prominently
             3-ribbed, 5 to 15 cm long, loosely woolly;
             stem leaves well developed . . . . *Antennaria pulcherrima (p 241)*

22B. Plants usually less than 25 cm tall; basal leaves not
3-ribbed, 1 to 5 cm long, mainly in basal rosettes;
stem leaves slender, usually much smaller than basal leaves 23

23a. Leaves green and hairless or thinly hairy on the
upper surface, white-woolly beneath, ovate, 1 to 4 cm
long and up to 1.5 cm wide . . . . . . ***Antennaria neglecta*** *(p 241)*

23B. Leaves densely white-woolly on both surfaces, narrowly
spatula-shaped, 1 to 2 cm long . . . *Antennaria microphylla (p 241)*

1B. Pappus composed of a few scales or stiff bristles, sometimes lacking 24

24a. Involucral bracts tipped with hooked spines, forming
bur-like heads; leaves simple (undivided), heart-shaped, with
blades up to 50 cm long and 50 cm wide 25

25a. Involucral bracts fused into a bony covering, transforming the mature
flower head into a hard, nut-like body covered with hooked prickles;
flower heads with either male or female florets . . . . *Xanthium strumarium (p 243)*

25B. Involucral bracts remaining separate; florets with both male and female parts 26

26a. Flower heads stalkless or short-stalked, borne in
elongated clusters (raceme-like); larger leaves with
pointed tips and slightly angled stalks . . . . ***Arctium minus*** *(p 242)*

26B. Flower heads usually long-stalked, borne in spreading
clusters; larger leaves with rounded tips and strongly angled stalks 27

27a. Leaf stalks usually solid; flower heads 3 to 4.5 cm wide,
with hairless involucres; corolla not glandular . . . . *Arctium lappa (p 243)*

27B. Leaf stalks usually hollow; flower heads 2 to 2.5 cm wide,
with dense cobwebby hairs on the involucres;
corolla glandular . . . . *Arctium tomentosum (p 243)*

24B. Involucral bracts lacking hooked bristles, not forming bur-like
heads; leaves divided into slender leaflets or simple and lance-shaped 28

28a. Disks strongly cone-shaped; leaves feathery, 1 to 3-times
divided into short, thread-like segments; crushed plants
with a pineapple-like fragrance . . . . ***Matricaria discoidea*** *(p 278)*

28B. Disks flat or slightly rounded, never cone-shaped;
leaves not as above; plants not smelling of pineapple 29

29a. Flower heads bright yellow, 5 to 15 mm across, in broad, flat-topped clusters . . . 30

30A. Leaves divided to the midrib into widely spaced,
thread-like segments; plants from stout taproots,
not aromatic; flower heads few to many . . . . . . ***Hymenopappus filifolius*** *(p 270)*

30B. Leaves divided 2 to 3 times into fine segments, but these
neither widely spaced nor thread-like; plants from stout
spreading rhizomes, aromatic; flower heads 20 to 200 ***Tanacetum vulgare*** *(p 289)*

29B. Flower heads pale yellow, less than 5 mm across, in elongated clusters 31

31a. Leaves twice divided into linear segments 1 mm
wide, densely white-woolly on both surfaces;
plants 10 to 40 cm tall, silvery-grey . . . . ***Artemisia frigida*** *(p 246)*

31B. Leaves linear to lance-shaped, toothless or slightly
toothed but not otherwise divided, with or without
woolly hairs; plants 30 to 120 cm tall, greyish to green 32

32a. Leaves white-woolly on both surfaces to nearly
smooth above, usually lance-shaped; involucres
3 to 4 mm high . . . . ***Artemisia ludoviciana*** *(p 248)*

32B. Leaves green to greyish on upper surface, white-woolly
on lower surface, linear, rolled under along edges;
involucres 4 to 5 mm high; plants 30 to 120 cm tall
with a shrubby appearance . . . . *Artemisia longifolia (p 247)*

GROUP 3 (DISK FLORETS PLUS YELLOW OR ORANGE RAY FLORETS)

1A. Pappus a tuft of hair-like or feathery bristles 2

  2A. Leaves opposite 3

    3A. Pappus of brownish yellow, feathery hairs . . . . *Arnica mollis (p 244)*

    3B. Pappus of white (sometimes brownish), simple hairs 4

      4A. Basal leaves lance-shaped, 10 to 30 mm wide, usually
        widest above middle, tapered to slender stalks; stems with
        tufts of brown hairs at the bases . . . . **Arnica fulgens** *(p 245)*

      4B. Basal leaves not as above, ovate to heart-shaped 5

        5A. Basal leaves usually heart-shaped and larger than the
          middle leaves; flower heads 1 to 3, silky-hairy at base of
          involucre; achenes uniformly hairy and/or glandular . . **Arnica cordifolia** *(p 244)*

        5B. Basal leaves usually ovate (occasionally heart-shaped) and smaller
          than the middle leaves; flower heads 1 to several, sparsely hairy
          at base of involucre; achenes hairless, at least near base . . . *Arnica latifolia (p 244)*

  2B. Leaves alternate 6

    6A. Pappus of 2 whorls of bristles, a short outer row
      and a longer inner row . . . . **Heterotheca villosa** *(p 268)*

    6B. Pappus of bristles of roughly equal length 7

      7A. Involucral bracts in 2 to several overlapping rows 8

        8A. Flower heads relatively large, 1 to several; involucres usually
          over 7 mm high; plants relatively small, usually less than 30 cm
          tall, with taproots; leaves or leaf teeth often tipped with small spines 9

          9A. Leaves grey or bluish green, woolly,
            deeply cut into slender lobes;
            involucral bracts spine-tipped . . . . **Haplopappus spinulosus** *(p 264)*

          9B. Leaves green, not woolly, toothless or obscurely toothed
            but not lobed; involucral bracts not spine-tipped 10

            10A. Plants 3 to 15 cm tall, glandular-hairy, densely tufted
              from much-branched root crowns, often forming cushions
              or mats, growing on dry alpine slopes . . . . . . *Haplopappus lyallii (p 264)*

            10B. Plants 10 to 30 cm tall, not glandular-hairy, in single
              clumps from simple root crowns, growing on open
              slopes at lower elevations . . . . *Haplopappus uniflorus (p 264)*

        8B. Flower heads small and numerous; involucres 3 to 6 mm high;
          plants relatively large, often well over 30 cm tall, with fibrous
          roots; leaves lacking spines 11

          11a. Basal leaves well developed, often in small clusters,
            clearly larger than the stem leaves; plants 5 to 40 cm tall 12

            12a. Stalks of basal leaves fringed with hairs, otherwise
              essentially hairless; flower heads usually in loose,
              relatively few-flowered clusters . . . . **Solidago multiradiata** *(p 287)*

            12B. Leaf stalks not as above; flower heads in compact,
              cylindrical to ovate clusters 13

13a. Leaves velvety-hairy, conspicuously 3-nerved . *Solidago mollis (p 286)*

13B. Leaves hairless or slightly hairy on the upper
surface, 1-nerved . . . . *Solidago spathulata (p 287)*

11B. Basal leaves poorly developed, never in clusters, clearly
smaller than the stem leaves; plants 30 to 200 cm tall 14

14a. Stems densely hairy below the flower cluster; leaves
usually densely hairy on both surfaces (sometimes
hairless on the upper side) . . . . *Solidago canadensis (p 286)*

14B. Stems hairless or only slightly hairy below the flower
cluster; leaves hairless (occasionally a few hairs on
the veins below) . . . . **Solidago gigantea** *(p 286)*

7B. Involucral bracts in one main row, sometimes with a
few, much smaller bracts at the base 15

15a. Plants relatively small, usually 10 to 30 cm tall, with
well-developed, often tufted, basal leaves and a few small,
clasping stem leaves, white-woolly throughout, growing in
dry, often rocky sites . . . . **Senecio canus** *(p 284)*

15B. Plants robust, 20 to 150 cm tall, with well-developed stem
leaves, hairless or silky hairy (not woolly), growing in moist to wet sites 16

16a. Leaves lance-shaped to linear, wavy along edges, stalkless and
clasping on upper stem, silky-hairy; plants annual, usually in
or by water; stems stout, hollow, 20 to 80 cm tall; flower heads
usually numerous, in open or congested clusters . . . . *Senecio congestus (p 284)*

16B. Plants not as above 17

17a. Plants with slender, well-developed basal leaves and only
a few, small stem leaves upwards on the stem . . . . . *Senecio lugens (p 285)*

17B. Plants with small basal leaves and large,
well-developed stem leaves 18

18a. Leaf blades elongate-triangular, coarsely
toothed along edges . . . . **Senecio triangularis** *(p 285)*

18B. Leaf blades tapered at the base (not triangular), deeply
cut into narrow teeth or toothed lobes . . . *Senecio eremophilus (p 285)*

1B. Pappus composed of a few scales or stiff bristles or lacking 19

19a. Leaves mainly opposite or basal 20

20A. Leaves mainly basal 21

21a. Leaves triangular to heart-shaped, 20 to 30 cm long,
with 2 backward-pointing basal lobes, long-stalked,
grey-woolly to silvery-silky; flower heads solitary,
5 to 11 cm across . . . . **Balsamorhiza sagittata** *(p 252)*

21B. Leaves narrowly lance-shaped, broadest above middle,
2 to 10 cm long, silky-hairy, dotted with resinous glands;
flower heads 1 to few, less than 5 cm across 22

22a. Leaves undivided, all basal; involucral bracts
all similar, in 2 to 3 overlapping rows;
ray florets 6 to 20 mm long . . . . **Hymenoxys acaulis** *(p 271)*

22B. Leaves deeply cut into 3 to 7 slender, linear segments,
both basal and on stem; involucral bracts in 2 distinct rows:
an outer row joined at the base, and an inner row
separate at the base and roughly fringed at the tips;
ray florets 7 to 15 mm long . . . . **Hymenoxys richardsonii** *(p 272)*

20B. Leaves mainly opposite 23

23a. Involucral bracts in 2 distinct rows, the outer row
broad and leaf-like; leaves simple and divided 24

24a. Main leaves divided into 3 to 5 stalked leaflets . . . . *Bidens frondosa (p 253)*

24b. Main leaves undivided (sometimes deeply cut into 3 to 5 lobes) 25

 25a. Leaves stalkless, simple (not lobed); flower heads usually
  with conspicuous ray florets but sometimes without . . **Bidens cernua** *(p 253)*

 25b. Leaves stalked, some deeply 3-lobed; flower
  heads usually lacking ray florets . . . . *Bidens tripartita (p 253)*

23b. Involucral bracts usually all green and leaf-like; leaves all simple 26

 26a. Involucral bracts broad, ovate, firm, pressed to flower
  head in several strongly overlapping rows;
  disk florets red, purple or dark brown . . . . **Helianthus rigidus** *(p 267)*

 26b. Involucral bracts narrow, lance-shaped, with loose,
  slender tips, in 1 main row; disk florets yellow . . . . . . *Helianthus nuttallii (p 267)*

19b. Leaves mainly alternate 27

27a. Upper plants and flower heads gummy with resin;
 leaves dotted with translucent glands; involucral bracts
 with slender tips curled out and reflexed . . . . **Grindelia squarrosa** *(p 262)*

27b. Plants not gummy with resin; involucral bracts not reflexed 28

 28a. Plants semi-shrubby from woody bases; leaves linear,
  1 to 3 mm wide, often dotted with translucent glands;
  flower heads small, usually less than 5 mm across, numerous,
  in flat-topped clusters . . . . **Gutierrezia sarothrae** *(p 263)*

 28b. Plants herbaceous; leaves not as above; flower heads 1 to few,
  large, 1 to 3 cm across or larger, showy 29

  29a. Involucral bracts in 2 distinct rows, outer row joined at
   the base, inner row separate at base and roughly fringed
   at tips; leaves deeply cut into 3 to 7 slender,
   linear segments . . . . **Hymenoxys richardsonii** *(p 272)*

  29b. Involucral bracts all similar, in 1 to several rows; leaves various 30

   30a. Ray florets distinctly 3-lobed at tips 31

    31a. Disk yellow, hemispherical or rounded, 8 to 20 mm
     across; rays yellow or orange, 8 to 20 mm long,
     eventually bent sharply downwards . . . . . **Helenium autumnale** *(p 265)*

    31b. Disk purplish, hemispherical, 15 to 40 mm across;
     rays yellow, usually purplish at base, 10 to 30 mm
     long, spreading, not bent sharply back . . . . . **Gaillardia aristata** *(p 261)*

   30b. Ray florets not distinctly 3-lobed at tips;
    disk florets mainly brown or purplish 32

    32a. Leaves pinnately divided into 5 to 9 slender lobes; disk
     cylindrical, 1 to 4 cm tall, grey to yellow when
     young, purplish brown when mature . . . . . **Ratibida columnifera** *(p 281)*

    32b. Leaves somewhat toothed or toothless, not lobed;
     disk flat to rounded or cone-shaped 33

     33a. Ray florets orange to bright yellow;
      disk hemispherical to cone-shaped, 1 to 3 cm
      wide; leaves slender, linear-elliptic to lance-shaped;
      plants perennial, from rhizomes 34

      34a. Leaves folded, narrowed to a short, winged
       leaf stalk; disk 2 to 3 cm wide . . . *Helianthus maximilianii (p 267)*

      34b. Leaves not folded; leaf stalk not winged;
       disk 1 to 2 cm wide . . . . *Rudbeckia hirta (p 282)*

     33b. Ray florets bright yellow; disk flat, button-like,
      1 to 4 cm wide; leaves broad, ovate to
      heart-shaped; plants annuals, weakly rooted 35

35a. Lower leaves mostly heart-shaped, with notched bases; involucral bracts broad, ovate, each abruptly narrowed to a slender point, fringed with conspicuous stiff hairs; disk 2 to 4 cm wide . . . . *Helianthus annuus (p 266)*

35b. Lower leaves mostly tapered to wedge-shaped bases; involucral bracts lance-shaped, each gradually narrowed to a point, not fringed with hairs; disks generally 1 to 2 cm wide . . . . *Helianthus couplandii (p 266)*

GROUP 4 (DISK FLORETS PLUS WHITE, PINK, BLUE OR PURPLE RAY FLORETS)

1a. Leaves compound 2

   2a. Leaves once or twice divided in 3s or dissected; stems 5 to 15 cm tall; flower heads 1 to 2 cm across, white, bluish or pink with yellow centres . . . . *Erigeron compositus (p 259)*

   2b. Leaves 1 to 3 times divided along a main axis (pinnate); stems usually more than 15 cm tall 3

      3a. Leaves once divided, sometimes simply toothed; flower heads white with yellow centres, solitary, 4 to 5 cm across . . . . **Leucanthemum vulgare** *(p 274)*

      3b. Leaves finely 2 to 3 times divided, feathery; flower heads more numerous and smaller 4

         4a. Flower heads small, about 5 mm across, with 5 to 12 ray florets . . . . **Achillea millefolium** *(p 237)*

         4b. Flower heads larger, 20 to 40 mm across, with 12 or more ray florets 5

            5a. Flower heads usually less than 10, in open, flat-topped clusters; ray florets whitish or blue; pappus of white, hair-like bristles . . . . *Machaeranthera tanacetifolia*

            5b. Flower heads usually more than 10, in dense, round or flat-topped clusters; ray florets white; pappus reduced to a short crown of scales or none 6

               6a. Plants with a pineapple-like fragrance; heads cone-shaped . . . . *Matricaria recutita (p 278)*

               6b. Plants odourless; heads hemisperical . . . . *Matricaria perforata (p 278)*

1b. Leaves simple 7

   7a. Leaves mostly along the stem; basal leaves usually withered by flowering time 8

      8a. Flower heads white, usually less than 1 cm across, with 6 to 12 ray florets, borne in flat-topped clusters; pappus lacking 9

         9a. Leaves finely toothed (sometimes almost toothless); ray florets showy, 4 to 5 mm long and nearly as broad; growing in disturbed areas . . . . *Achillea ptarmica (p 237)*

         9b. Leave coarsely sharp-toothed; ray florets not showy, 2 to 3 mm long; growing along stream banks and in moist thickets and forests . . . . *Achillea sibirica (p 237)*

      8b. Flower heads blue, purple, pink or white, usually more than 1 cm across with more than 12 ray florets; if smaller, borne in elongated (not flat-topped) clusters; pappus a tuft of white hairs 10

10A. Plants ash-coloured, covered with short, fine hairs;
biennial from taproots; involucral bracts gray-hairy,
spreading or bent backwards at their tips . . . . . . **Machaeranthera canescens** *(p 277)*

10B. Plants not ash-coloured, not covered with fine hairs; perennial
from fibrous roots and often rhizomes; involucral bracts not as above 11

11a. Leaves usually 3 to 8 cm wide, often clasping the stem,
firm, coarsely sharp-toothed, rough to the touch;
flower stalks and involucres glandular; flower heads
blue to purplish, 2 to 4 cm across . . . . **Aster conspicuus** *(p 249)*

11B. Leaves smaller and usually narrower; leaves may or may not
clasp the stem, toothed, untoothed or spine-tipped;
flower stalks and involucres not glandular; flower
heads variously coloured, usually smaller 12

12a. Involucral bracts tipped with small spines;
ray florets white; leaves not clasping 13

13a. Stems clustered; flower heads small, along
branches, tending to occur on one side;
involucres mostly 3 to 4 mm high . . . . **Aster ericoides** *(p 250)*

13B. Stems scattered along creeping rhizomes; flower
heads larger, often solitary at branch tips, not occurring
on one side only; involucres 5 to 8 mm high . . . . **Aster falcatus** *(p 250)*

12B. Involucral bracts not tipped with spines; ray florets
white, pink or bluish; upper leaves clasping 14

14a Stems hairless; lower leaves with winged petioles;
upper leaf bases clasping the stem . . . . **Aster laevis** *(p 251)*

14B. Stems often with lines of fine hairs extending down
from the leaf bases; leaves may or may not clasp stem 15

15a. Plants very slender, usually growing in wetlands
or on lake margins; leaves linear, 2 to 5 mm wide,
harshly stiff-hairy along edges, upper leaves
slightly clasping stem; flower heads 1 to 10 . . . . *Aster borealis* *(p 249)*

15B. Plants more robust, usually growing in moist regions
(such as woodlands, stream banks, edges of marshes,
clearings, ditches); leaves usually broader, hairless or hairy,
leaves not clasping the stem; flower heads few to many 16

16a. Lower leaves often heart-shaped, toothed,
abruptly narrowed to long, winged petioles,
present at time of flowering . . . . *Aster ciliolatus* *(p 251)*

16B. Lower leaves linear to lance-shaped, toothless
or irregularly toothed, gradually tapered to the
base, often fallen by flowering time . . . . . . *Aster hesperius* *(p 249)*

7B. Leaves mostly at the base of the stem; stem leaves reduced 17

17a. Basal leaves large, long-petioled, round,
triangular or heart-, arrow- or kidney-shaped;
stem leaves bract-like and sheathing . . . . **Petasites frigidus** *(p 279)*

17B. Basal leaves small, with short or long petioles, spatula-shaped, linear
or linear-lance-shaped; stem leaves not bract-like and sheathing 18

18a. Leaves long-petioled, broadly spatula-shaped, coarsely toothed
to deeply broad-lobed; flower heads about 4 cm across with
showy white ray florets around bright-yellow disk florets;
pappus lacking . . . . **Leucanthemum vulgare** *(p 274)*

18B. Leaves short-petioled or lacking petiole, narrowly spatula-shaped,
linear to linear-lance-shaped, toothless or obscurely toothed;
flower heads smaller with white, pink, blue or purple ray florets
around yellow disk florets; pappus a tuft of hairs 19

19a. Basal leaves forming dense rosettes from well-developed
taproots; flowers heads stalkless and nestled among the leaves,
or solitary on short stalks 20

  20A. Flower heads stalked; plants 5 to 25 cm tall . . . . . ***Townsendia parryi*** *(p 290)*

  20B. Flower heads stalkless, nestled among the leaves;
usually less than 5 cm tall 21

    21a. Leaves spatula-shaped; involucral bracts
densely silky-woolly . . . . *Townsendia condensata* *(p 290)*

    21B. Leaves linear to linear-lance-shaped, sometimes widest
above the middle; involucral bracts not densely silky-woolly 22

      22a. Flower heads usually more than 2 cm wide;
corolla of disk florets 8 to 10 mm long;
ray florets 12 to 22 mm long;
involucres 20 to 25 mm wide,
bracts usually lacking tangled hairs
at their tips . . . . *Townsendia exscapa* *(p 290)*

      22B. Flower heads usually less than 2 cm wide;
corollas of disk florets about 5 mm long;
ray florets 8 to 14 mm long; involucres
about 15 mm wide, bracts usually tipped
with a tuft of tangled hairs . . . . *Townsendia hookeri* *(p 290)*

19B. Basal leaves less densely tufted, usually with a single
flowering stem; flower heads usually less than 5 cm wide,
usually more than 1 per stem 23

  23a. Plants usually less than 25 cm tall; flower heads solitary;
ray florets white or purplish-tinged, inconspicuous;
involucres densely woolly, hairs with conspicuous
purple cross-walls . . . . *Erigeron humilis* *(p 259)*

  23B. Plants usually taller; flower heads 1 to several;
ray florets white, rose-pink, purple or blue, conspicuous;
involucres not densely woolly, hairs lack purple cross-walls 24

    24a. Stem leaves broad-based and clasping the stem;
flower heads 12 to 25 mm across
with 150 to 400 thread-like, rosy-pink to
purplish or white ray florets . . . . *Erigeron philadelphicus* *(p 260)*

    24B. Stem leaves not broad-based and clasping; flower
heads various with 175 or fewer ray florets 25

      25a. Ray florets 30 to 80, broad and showy,
8 to 25 mm long and 2 to 4 mm wide,
rose-purple (sometimes pale to white);
veins of leaves often depressed and
hairy; flower heads usually solitary,
2 to 6 cm across . . . . *Erigeron peregrinus* *(p 260)*

      25B. Ray florets 30 to 175, narrow, less showy, 5 to 15 mm
long and 1 to 2 mm wide; veins of leaves not
depressed and hairy; flower heads 1 to 10, generally smaller 26

        26a. Basal leaves 3-nerved; flower heads
usually solitary (occasionally a few
per stem), with 30 to 100 ray
florets, usually white . . . . **Erigeron caespitosus** *(p 258)*

        26B. Basal leaves not 3-nerved or only
very faintly so; flowerheads 1 to 10,
with 125 to 175 ray florets,
usually blue or pink . . . . **Erigeron glabellus** *(p 260)*

A comparison of scientific names used in this books with those in *Flora of Alberta* (Moss 1983).

NEW TAXONOMY	OLD TAXONOMY
Amerorchis rotundifolia	*Orchis rotundifolia*
Antennaria microphylla	*Antennaria parviflora*
Astragalus adsurgens ssp. *robustior*	*Astragalus striatus*
Astragalus agrestis	*Astragalus dasyglottis*
Clematis occidentalis ssp. *grosseserrata*	*Clematis occidentalis* var. *grosseserrata*
Coeloglossum viride ssp. *bracteatum*	*Habenaria viridis* var. *bracteata*
Hackelia deflexa ssp. *americana*	*Hackelia americana*
Hackelia micrantha	*Hackelia jessicae*
Helianthus rigidus var. *subrhomboideus*	*Helianthus subrhomboideus*
Hieracium scouleri var. *griseum*	*Hieracium cynoglossoides*
Hypopitys monotropa	*Monotropa hypopitys*
Lactuca tatarica ssp. *pulchella*	*Lactuca pulchella*
Leucanthemum vulgare	*Chrysanthemum leucanthemum*
Linaria genistifolia ssp. *dalmatica*	*Linaria dalmatica*
Linum perenne ssp. *lewisii*	*Linum lewisii*
Matricaria discoidea	*Matricaria matricarioides*
Papaver radicatum ssp. *kluanensis*	*Papaver freedmanianum*
Papaver radicatum ssp. *kluanensis*	*Papaver kluanensis*
Petasites frigidus var. *palmatus*	*Petasites palmatus*
Petasites frigidus var. *frigidus*	*Petasites nivalis*
Petasites frigidus var. *x vitifolius*	*Petasites vitifolius*
Petasites frigidus var. *sagittatus*	*Petasites sagittatus*
Piperia unalascensis	*Habenaria unalascensis*
Platanthera dilatata	*Habenaria dilatata*
Platanthera hyperborea	*Habenaria hyperborea*
Platanthera obtusata	*Habenaria obtusata*
Platanthera orbiculata	*Habenaria orbiculata*
Platanthera stricta	*Habenaria saccata*
Polemonium caeruleum	*Polemonium acutiflorum*
Rumex salicifolius	*Rumex triangulivalvis*
Saussurea nuda ssp. *densa*	*Saussurea nuda* var. *densa*
Scirpus maritimus var. *paludosus*	*Scirpus paludosus*
Sedum integrifolium	*Tolmachevia integrifolia*
Solidago gigantea ssp. *serotina*	*Solidago gigantea* var. *serotina*
Tanacetum bipinnatum ssp. *huronense*	*Tanacetum huronense*
Trollius laxus	*Trollius albiflorus*
Vaccinium oxycoccos	*Oxycoccus microcarpus*
Veratrum viride ssp. *eschscholtzii*	*Veratrum eschscholtzii*
Veronica wormskjoldii	*Veronica alpina*

ACHENE ↝ A dry, single-seeded fruit that remains closed at maturity.

ALKALINE ↝ Refers to a soil with a pH higher than 7.0 and/or high sodium salt content.

ALKALOID ↝ A group of complex nitrogen-based chemicals that are thought to protect plants against insect predation. Some well-known examples of alkaloids derived from plants include cocaine, morphine and strychnine.

ALTERNATE ↝ Refers to a type of leaf arrangement, where leaves are borne singly, staggered along the stem.

ANGIOSPERM ↝ The most highly evolved flowering plants, in which the seeds are fully encased by fruits.

ANNUAL ↝ A plant that completes its life cycle (germination to seed production and death) in a single growing season.

ANTHER ↝ The part of a stamen that bears the pollen, usually consisting of one or two pollen sacs and a connecting layer between them. See flower parts illustration, page 332.

APPRESSED ↝ Pressed flat or lying close against a surface, leaves of western and white mountain-heather, for example (see illustration on page 165).

AXIL ↝ The angle formed where a leaf or branch is attached to the stem. See leaf parts illustration, below.

AXILLARY ↝ Growing out of the *axil*, referring to clusters of leaves or flowers.

BEAK ↝ A prolonged, usually slender projection on a bigger structure such as a fruit or *seed*. See illustration of beak on keel of locoweed flower, page 110.

BERRY ↝ A fleshy, many-seeded fruit.

BIENNIAL ↝ A plant that takes two growing seasons to complete its life cycle (germination to seed production and death).

LEAF PARTS

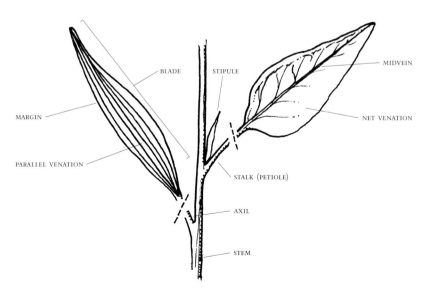

MARGIN

PARALLEL VENATION

BLADE

STIPULE

MIDVEIN

NET VENATION

STALK (PETIOLE)

AXIL

STEM

BIPINNATE ✺ Twice pinnate. See leaf arrangement illustration, page 336.

BLADE ✺ The body of the leaf, excluding the leaf stalk. See leaf parts illustration, page 331.

BOG ✺ Acidic wetland area, also called peatland, with a high water table; often low in oxygen and nutrients. Alberta bogs are often populated by *Sphagnum* mosses, sedges and black spruce.

BRACT ✺ A specialized (often reduced) leaf, associated with (but not part of) the flower or inflorescence.

BULB ✺ An underground shoot with modified leaves or thickened leaf bases that acts as a food-storage organ and may allow for vegetative reproduction or survival of the plant from one season to the next. Several members of the lily family have bulbs.

BULBIL ✺ Here, a bulb-like structure functioning in vegetative reproduction, produced by some plants instead of, or in addition to, flowers, for example, Geyer's onion.

CALCAREOUS ✺ Soils high in calcium carbonate.

CALYX (PL. CALYCES) ✺ Part of the flower surrounding the *corolla*, composed of *sepals*. See flower parts illustration, below.

CAPSULE ✺ A type of fruit with more than one compartment, that splits open to release the seeds.

CILIATE ✺ With a fringe of hairs on the margins (often referring to leaves). See leaf margins illustration, page 334.

CIRCUMBOREAL ✺ Occupying boreal regions around the world.

CONIFEROUS ✺ Conifers (coniferous trees and shrubs) bear their reproductive structures in cones. The seeds are usually loosely attached to the cone scales, rather than being enclosed by the *ovary*.

CONTIGUOUS ✺ Adjacent, close; refers here to dense forest growth as opposed to scattered clumps of trees above treeline.

CORM ✺ A short, thickened, underground stem that functions as a food-storage organ, in western spring beauty, for example. It lacks the modified leaves or leaf bases associated with bulbs. Corms may sometimes be used in propagating new plants.

FLOWER PARTS

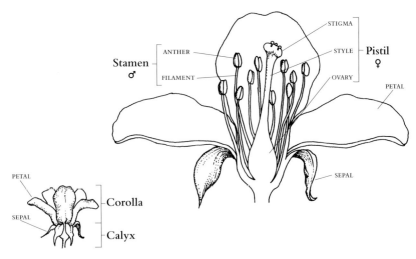

COROLLA ❧ The collective term for the petals of a flower. See flower parts illustration, page 332.

DECIDUOUS ❧ Falling off at the end of the growing season. In Alberta, deciduous species lose their leaves prior to winter.

DEHISCENT ❧ Bursting or splitting open at maturity, for example, the fruit of caragana.

DIGITATE ❧ Like fingers (digits) on a hand. Another term for *palmate*.

DISK FLORETS ❧ The tubular florets (lacking petals) found in some members of the composite family. See illustration on page 236.

DRUPE ❧ Fleshy *fruit* with a stony inner seed-covering, for example, a plum.

ESSENTIAL OILS ❧ Volatile oils are odorous substances containing complex combinations of terpenes, alcohols, phenols, aldehydes, ketones, oxides and other chemicals. They are found in various plant parts, including flowers, leaves, seeds, bark and roots. When separated by distillation and combined with oils, these chemicals are referred to as essential oils and may be used by aromatherapists to treat various ailments.

FEN ❧ Wetland area fed by streams and groundwater; less acidic and usually higher in nutrients than bogs. Often populated with sedges, grasses, willows and tamarack.

FILAMENT ❧ The stalk supporting the *anther* in a *stamen*. See flower parts illustration, page 332.

FLOODPLAIN ❧ A flat plain adjacent to a river, composed of sediments deposited during floods.

FLORET ❧ One of the individual small flowers of a clustered *inflorescence*, for example, in the composite family.

FLOWER ❧ In *angiosperms*, the structure involved in sexual reproduction: *stamen*, *pistil* and the surrounding *corolla* and *calyx*. For flower parts, see illustration on page 332 and individual part definitions.

FOLLICLE ❧ A dry *fruit* composed of a single compartment that splits open along one side to release the seeds, blue columbine, for example.

FROND ❧ The leaf of a fern, including *stipe* and *blade*. See illustration on page 5.

FRUIT ❧ The ripe *ovary* with the enclosed seeds.

GALEA ❧ The concave or helmet-shaped upper lip of some two-lipped *corollas*, for example, Indian paintbrush.

GAMETE ❧ A mature reproductive cell capable of uniting with another to form a fertilized cell that can develop into a new plant or animal. Each gamete has only half the number of chromosomes of other body cells.

GAMETOPHYTE ❧ The gamete-producing form or generation of a plant that reproduces by alternation of generations. In lower plants, the gametophyte is the dominant form.

GENUS (PL. GENERA) ❧ A taxonomic group between family and *species*; includes one or more species with certain characteristics in common.

GLAUCOUS ❧ With a fine, waxy (usually white) coating that may be rubbed off; often characteristic of berries, leaves or twigs.

GLUCOSIDES ❧ A *glycoside* formed from glucose.

GLYCOSIDES ❧ The product obtained when a sugar reacts with an alcohol or phenol.

HALLUCINOGEN ❧ Chemicals that produce changes in perception, thought and mood.

HERBACEOUS ❧ Non-woody plants whose stems die back to the ground at the end of the growing season.

HUMUS ↝ More or less stable decomposed organic matter.

HYPANTHIUM ↝ A cup-like, saucer-shaped or tube-like enlargement, often surrounding or enclosing the *ovaries* and bearing the *sepals*, *petals* and even the *stamens* on its margin.

INDUSIUM ↝ The membraneous covering over the cluster of spore sacs (*sori*) in some species of ferns. See illustration on page 5.

INFLORESCENCE ↝ Arrangement of flowers on a stem. See illustration on page 338.

INTERNODE ↝ Between nodes. Nodes are points of leaf or branch attachment.

INVOLUCRE ↝ Refers collectively to the bracts below the *inflorescence*. See illustration on page 236.

KEEL ↝ May refer to the V-shape of a leaf, or to two partly united specialized petals in the pea family. The latter is illustrated on page 108.

KRÜPPELHOLZ ↝ Scattered clumps of stunted, bushy trees and shrubs near treeline in upper subalpine and alpine zones.

LATEX ↝ Liquid produced in specialized tissues by some plants, for example, goat's-beard. It contains *terpenes* dispersed in water and may be colourless, white, red or yellow.

LEAF ↝ A thin, usually green, expanded organ, typically attached to the stem of a plant and comprised of a *blade* and *stalk*. Leaves are the main site of photosynthesis. For leaf parts, see illustration below and individual part definitions.

LEAFLET ↝ A unit of a compound leaf. See illustration on page 336.

LEAF MARGINS

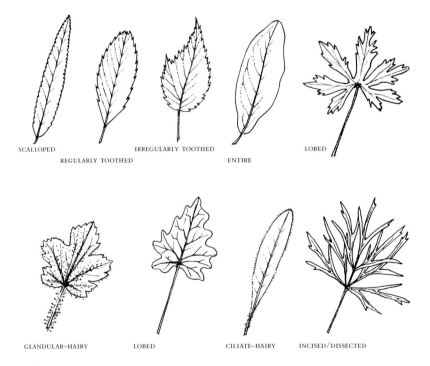

SCALLOPED

REGULARLY TOOTHED

IRREGULARLY TOOTHED

ENTIRE

LOBED

GLANDULAR-HAIRY

LOBED

CILIATE-HAIRY

INCISED/DISSECTED

LINEAR ☙ Like a line. Long, narrow and parallel-sided. Usually refers to leaf (occasionally petal) shape; see leaf shapes, page 337.

LIP ☙ The divisions of a two-lipped *corolla* or *calyx*; or may refer to the characteristic upper petal (appearing lower) of many members of the orchid family (see illustration on page 35).

LOMENT ☙ A type of *fruit* seen in the pea family (for example in sweet-vetch), usually characterized by constrictions between the seeds. See illustration on page 115.

MARGIN ☙ The edge of a leaf or petal. See leaf margin illustrations, pp 331 and 334.

MARSH ☙ A basically treeless area of grasses, sedges, reeds and low shrubs, either permanently or periodically inundated by standing or slow-moving water and typically divided into pools and channels by vegetation.

MEGASPORE ☙ Spore that gives rise to a female *gametophyte* (usually larger than a *microspore*).

MESIC ☙ Moist, but about halfway between very moist and very dry.

MICROSPORE ☙ Spore that gives rise to a male *gametophyte* (usually smaller than a *megaspore*).

MIDVEIN ☙ The middle vein of a leaf. See leaf parts illustration, page 331.

MIXEDWOOD ☙ Forest composed of both broad-leaved *deciduous* and *coniferous* trees.

MUSKEG ☙ Poorly drained, wooded peatland characterized by black spruce and *Spaghnum* moss.

NATURALIZED ☙ Not native to an area but capable of growing and reproducing there without human help.

NECTARY ☙ A structure that secretes nectar, usually attached to a flower, for example in blue columbine.

NITRATES, NITRITES ☙ As material decomposes in the soil, ammonia may be oxidized to form nitrites (NO_2) and subsequently nitrates (NO_3). These processes release energy that is used to reduce carbon dioxide to carbohydrate.

NODE ☙ A joint on a stem, usually where a leaf or branch arises.

NOXIOUS WEED ☙ A plant that is detrimental to agriculture.

NUT ☙ A hard, dry, single-seeded *fruit* that does not split open at maturity. Larger and with a firmer wall than an *achene*.

NUTLET ☙ A small nut.

OCREA (PL. OCREAE; ALSO OCHREA, OCHREAE) ☙ A sheath around the stem above the base of the leaf; as found in the buckwheat family. See illustration on page 49.

OPPOSITE ☙ Refers to a type of leaf arrangement where leaves are attached to the stem in pairs at each node. See leaf arrangement illustration, page 336.

OVARY ☙ The enlarged basal portion of the female reproductive organs; the ovary becomes the *fruit*. See flower parts illustration, page 332.

OVATE ☙ Egg-shaped.

OXALIC ACIDS ☙ A poisonous organic acid occurring in various plants, for example, mountain sorrel.

PALMATE ☙ Lobed or divided, with three or more lobes, nerves, leaflets or branches arising from a common point. Palmately compound leaves are illustrated on page 336.

PANICLE ☙ A type of branched inflorescence. See illustration on page 338.

PAPILLA (PL. PAPILLAE) ↬ Short, rounded, blunt projections, for example, on the fruit of rough-fruited fairybells.

PAPPUS ↬ The modified *calyx* at the top of the *achene* in the composite family. The pappus may be composed of scales, hairs or bristles and is sometimes lacking (see illustration on page 236).

PARASITIC ↬ A plant that derives its food or water mainly through attachment to a host plant, for example, clustered broom-rape.

PERENNIAL ↬ A plant that lives for more than two years.

PERIANTH ↬ All of the *sepals* and *petals* of a plant, collectively. This term is frequently used when referring to plants where the sepals and petals are alike in appearance, western wood lily, for example.

PETAL ↬ Part of the *corolla*, often brightly coloured. See flower parts illustration, page 332.

PINNA (PL. PINNAE) ↬ The primary division of a fern leaf. See illustration on page 5.

PINNATE ↬ Leaflets arranged on both sides of a central stalk in a compound leaf. See leaf arrangement illustration, below.

PISTIL ↬ The female reproductive organ of a flower; usually composed of *stigma*, *style* and *ovary*. See flower parts illustration, page 332.

PISTILLATE ↬ A flower with female reproductive parts (*pistil*) but not male (*stamens*) is said to be pistillate. Pearly everlasting is an example of a plant with either pistillate or staminate flowers. In some cases, both pistillate and staminate flowers occur on the same plant, as in common cattail.

LEAF ARRANGEMENT

Simple Leaves

ALTERNATE   OPPOSITE   WHORLED   ROSETTE (BASAL)

Compound Leaves

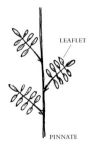

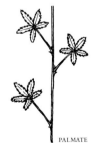

LEAFLET

PINNATE   BIPINNATE   TRIPINNATE   PALMATE

Pɪᴛʜ ᪥ Spongy tissue occupying the central part of the stem of certain plants, red elderberry or common annual sunflower, for example.

Pᴏᴅ ᪥ Any kind of dry, dehiscent *fruit*.

Rᴀᴄᴇᴍᴇ ᪥ A type of *inflorescence* with an elongated flower cluster with flowers attached to a central main stalk by shorter stalks nearly equal in length. See illustration, page 338. Pine-drops is an example of a plant with a raceme type of inflorescence.

Rᴀʏ (ᴏꜰ ᴜᴍʙᴇʟs) ᪥ One of the branches of an *umbel* (see illustration on page 338).

Rᴀʏ ꜰʟᴏʀᴇᴛ ᪥ The outer florets with strap-shaped petals seen in many members of the composite family. See illustration on page 236.

Rᴇᴄᴇᴘᴛᴀᴄʟᴇ ᪥ The part of the flower-stalk on which the flowers are borne in composites.

Rᴇꜰʟᴇxᴇᴅ ᪥ Bent backward. Refers to sepals, bracts, petals or the stalks on which flowers or fruits are borne.

Rᴇsɪɴ ᪥ A substance consisting of *terpenes* and other similar compounds exuded by some plants, for example, dogbanes. Resins are initially liquid but become solid after prolonged exposure to air.

Rʜɪᴢᴏᴍᴀᴛᴏᴜs ᪥ Plants with creeping underground stems (*rhizomes*) that can develop roots and send up new shoots. Examples include quackgrass and Canada thistle.

Rʜɪᴢᴏᴍᴇ ᪥ Creeping underground stem that can develop roots and send up new shoots.

Rɪᴠᴇʀɪɴᴇ ᪥ Moist habitats along river banks.

Rᴏᴏᴛsᴛᴏᴄᴋ ᪥ *Rhizome*; creeping underground stem.

Rᴏsᴇᴛᴛᴇ ᪥ A cluster of leaves or other structures arranged in a circle, often at the base of a plant. See leaf arrangement illustration on page 336.

Sᴀʟɪɴᴇ ᪥ Soils with a high soluble salt content (usually calcium or magnesium, but not sodium—soils with a high sodium salt content are usually referred to as *alkaline*).

Sᴀᴘᴏɴɪɴ ᪥ A type of *glycoside* that can form a foamy solution in water. Plants containing saponins are sometimes used to make simple soaps, for example, yucca.

Sᴀᴘʀᴏᴘʜʏᴛɪᴄ ᪥ A plant that lives on dead organic matter, for example, coral-roots.

Sᴄᴀᴘᴇ ᪥ A leafless flower stalk arising from ground level. Early yellow locoweed is an example of a plant with a scape.

Sᴄʀᴇᴇ ᪥ Loose, fragmented rock rubble often seen below a rock wall. Used interchangeably with *talus*.

LEAF SHAPES

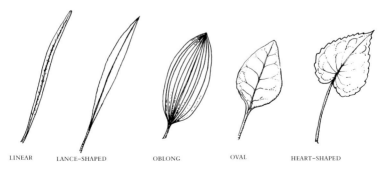

LINEAR   LANCE–SHAPED   OBLONG   OVAL   HEART–SHAPED

SELENIUM ∽ A chemical element essential for animal health and muscle development in small amounts but toxic in large doses. Some plants, particularly certain milk-vetches, can concentrate selenium and therefore pose a problem for grazing animals.

SEPAL ∽ Leaf-like, usually green appendages that surround the petals. Collectively, the sepals make up the *calyx*. When petals are missing, the sepals are sometimes coloured like *petals*, for example, cut-leaved anemone. See flower parts illustration, page 332.

SILICLE ∽ A pod-like *fruit* characteristic of the mustard family. It differs from a *silique* in being about as long as wide.

SILIQUE ∽ A pod-like *fruit* characteristic of the mustard family. It differs from a *silicle* in being much longer than wide.

SPADIX ∽ A spike of small, crowded flowers on a thickened, fleshy stalk. Water arum is an example of a plant with a spadix.

SPATHE ∽ A large, usually solitary bract surrounding the *spadix* or other *inflorescence* type in certain plant *genera*. Water arum is an example of a plant with a spathe.

SPECIES ∽ A kind of organism; subdivision of a *genus*.

SPHAGNUM ∽ A genus of mosses characteristic of wet, boggy, acidic habitats. Peat moss is usually composed of *Sphagnum*.

SPIKE ∽ A more or less elongate inflorescence type, with flowers attached directly to the central stalk, for example, dotted blazingstar. See illustration below.

SPORANGIUM (PL. SPORANGIA) ∽ A case that contains reproductive bodies called *spores*.

SPORE ∽ A one to many-celled reproductive structure capable of giving rise to a new plant.

SPOROPHYLL ∽ A modified leaf that bears or surrounds one or more *sporangia*. See illustration on page 1.

SPUR ∽ A hollow extension of the *corolla* or *calyx*; often acts as a *nectary*.

STALK ∽ Any slender, supporting or connecting part of a plant. A flower or leaf blade may have a stalk.

STAMEN ∽ The male reproductive structure of a flower that produces the pollen; composed of *anther* and *filament*. See flower parts illustration, page 332.

INFLORESCENCE TYPES *(only those types referred to in text are shown)*

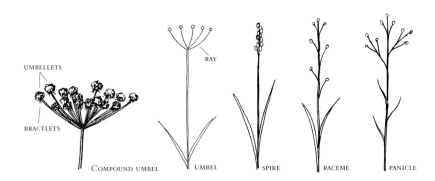

UMBELLETS

RAY

BRACTLETS

COMPOUND UMBEL UMBEL SPIKE RACEME PANICLE

STAMINATE ❧ A flower with one or more *stamens* but no *pistil*. Pearly everlasting is an example of a flower with either staminate or *pistillate* flowers, but not both. In some cases, both staminate and pistillate flowers may be borne separately on the same plant, as in common cattail.

STAMINODE (PL. STAMINODIA) ❧ A sterile *stamen*, as seen in lady's-slippers, for example (see illustration on page 35).

STANDARD ❧ The uppermost petal of a pea family flower. See illustration on page 108.

STEM ❧ The main axis of a plant, that bears buds, leaves and flowers.

STIGMA ❧ The part of the female reproductive organ that receives the pollen. See flower parts illustration, page 332.

STIPE ❧ The leaf stalk of a fern. See illustration on page 5.

STIPULE ❧ Paired leaf-like appendages found at the bases of the leaves in some plants. See leaf parts illustration, page 331.

STOLON ❧ Creeping above-ground stems, capable of sending up new plants. Strawberry plants have conspicuous stolons.

STOLONIFEROUS ❧ A plant with *stolons* is said to be stoloniferous.

STROBILUS (PL. STROBILII) ❧ The cluster of *sporophylls* on an axis. Seen in common horsetail.

STYLE ❧ The slender stalk connecting the *stigma* to the *ovary* in the female reproductive organ of a flower. See flower parts illustration, page 332.

SUCCULENT ❧ Fleshy or juicy. Often applied to a plant that can accumulate reserves of water in the leaves or stems, stonecrop, for example.

SWAMP ❧ Wetland where the water is either standing or flowing gently through pools and channels. Trees and tall shrubs are typically present, and the ground is usually covered with herbs and mosses.

TALUS ❧ See *scree*.

TANNINS ❧ Complex acidic compounds in plants that function to make them unpalatable to grazing animals. Tannins can be used in tanning and dyeing.

TAP ROOT ❧ A primary descending root, for example in carrots.

FLOWER ARRANGEMENT

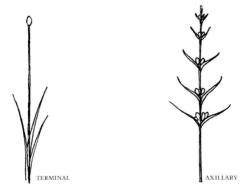

TERMINAL   AXILLARY

TENDRIL ✂ A slender, twining appendage found in some plants that allows them to attach to other objects or plants for support, for example cream-coloured vetchling (see illustration on page 116).

TERMINAL ✂ At the end. A flower cluster is said to be terminal if it occurs at the top of the plant, as opposed to in the leaf axils. See flower arrangement illustration on page 339.

TERPENES ✂ Certain carbon-containing compounds found in plants.

TERRACE ✂ A relatively level surface cut into the face of a steep, natural slope along the side of a valley.

TRANSLUCENT ✂ The property of letting light through without being transparent.

TREELINE ✂ The limit of continuous tree cover in the mountains. Above treeline, trees may occur in occasional, scattered small clumps.

TRIPINNATE ✂ Three times pinnate, in reference to compound leaf arrangement. See leaf arrangement illustration, page 336.

TRUNCATE ✂ With the tip or base appearing as if cut straight off, often in reference to leaves.

TUBER ✂ A swollen stem or root that functions as an underground food-storage organ. Yampa is an example of a plant with edible tubers.

TUBERCLES ✂ Small swellings or projections, usually distinct in colour and texture from the part of the plant on which they are growing, for example seen on the fruits of some dock and stickseed species.

UMBEL ✂ A type of *inflorescence* with several flower stalks arising from a single point; may be compound. See illustration on page 338.

UMBELLET ✂ One of the ultimate clusters of a compound umbel. See illustration on page 338.

UNISEXUAL ✂ Some flowers are unisexual, having either male parts or female parts but not both. Some plants are also unisexual, having either male flowers or female flowers, but not both.

VALVE ✂ One of the portions of the *ovary* wall into which a capsule separates at maturity; or, in some *stamens*, the portion of the *anther* wall covering the pore. In the genus *Rumex*, the inner *sepals* may be enlarged and noticeably veiny in fruit and are referred to as valves.

VENATION ✂ The pattern of veins in a leaf, net-veined or parallel-veined, for example. See leaf parts illustration, page 331.

VOLATILE OILS ✂ Plant oils capable of evaporating to a gas; often used in making herbal preparations.

WHORL ✂ A ring of three or more similar structures radiating out from a common point, often referring to leaf arrangement.

WINGS ✂ Refers either to the two lateral petals on a pea family flower (see illustration on page 108) or to the thin, flattened projections on the sides of some stems, leaf stalks or fruits.

Selected References

Note: ★ denotes references most suitable for those with some botanical training.

Alberta Agriculture and Alberta Environmental Protection. 1988. *Weeds of the Prairies*. Edmonton, Alberta.

Alberta Environmental Protection. 1993. Alberta plants and fungi—Master species list and species group checklists. Edmonton, Alberta.

★Alberta Natural Heritage Information Centre. November 1996 edition. Plant Species of Special Concern.

Alberta Native Plant Council. 1996. Native plant source list & collection and use guidelines. Alberta Native Plant Council, Edmonton, Alberta.

Angier, Bradford. 1974. *Field guide to edible wild plants*. Stackpole Books, Harrisburg, Pennsylvania.

Bailey, L.H. 1963. *How plants get their names*. Dover Publications Inc., New York, N.Y.

★Cherniawsky, Donna M. 1994. Systematics of North American *Petasites* (Asteraceae: Senecioneae). M.Sc. thesis, Department of Biological Sciences, University of Alberta, Edmonton, Alberta.

★Cherniawsky, Donna M. 1998. Systematics of North American *Petasites* (Asteraceae: Senecioneae). I. Morphometric Analyses. *Canadian Journal of Botany*. 76 (1998): 23–26.

Clark, Lewis J. 1976. *Wild flowers of the Pacific Northwest*. Gray's Publishing Ltd, Sidney, British Columbia.

Coffey, Timothy. 1993. *The History and Folklore of North American Wildflowers*. Houghton Mifflin Company, New York, N.Y.

★Douglas, G.W., G.B. Straley, D. Meidinger. 1989-1994. *The vascular plants of British Columbia*. Research Branch, B.C. Ministry of Forests, Victoria, British Columbia.

Durant, M.B. 1976. *Who named the daisy? Who named the rose? A roving dictionary of North American wildflowers*. Dodd, Mead & Co., New York, N.Y.

★Flora of North America Editorial Committee. 1993-1997. *Flora of North America north of Mexico*. Vols 1-3. Oxford University Press.

Ford, Gillian. 1984. *Plant names explained*. Publication No. 16. Friends of the Devonian Botanic Garden, University of Alberta, Edmonton, Alberta.

Gibbons, E. & G. Tucker. 1979. *Euell Gibbon's handbook of edible wild plants*. Donning Co., Publishers, Virginia Beach, Virginia.

Harrington, H.D. 1967. *Edible native plants of the Rocky Mountains*. University of New Mexico Press, Albuquerque, New Mexico.

Hart, Jeff. 1976. *Montana - native plants and early peoples*. Montana Historical Society and Montana Bicentennial Administration, Helena, Montana.

Hellson, J.C. & M. Gadd. 1974. *Ethnobotany of the Blackfoot Indians*. Canadian Ethnology Service Paper No. 19. National Museum of Man, Ottawa, Ontario.

★Hitchcock, C.C., A. Cronquist, M. Ownbey & J.W. Thompson. 1977. *Vascular plants of the Pacific Northwest*. Parts 1-5. University of Washington Press, Seattle, Washington.

Johnson, D., L. Kershaw, A. Mackinnon, and J. Pojar. 1995. *Plants of the Western Boreal Forest and Aspen Parkland*. Lone Pine Publishing and Canadian Forest Service, Edmonton, Alberta.

Johnston, A. 1982. *Plants and the Blackfoot*. Occasional Paper No. 15. Lethbridge Historical Society, Lethbridge, Alberta.

★Kartesz, J.T. 2nd ed. 1994. *A synonymized checklist of the vascular flora of the United States, Canada and Greenland*. Vols 1-2. Timber Press, Portland, Oregon.

Kerik, Joan. 1985. *Living with the land: use of plants by the native people of Alberta*. Provincial Museum of Alberta Travelling Exhibits Program. Alberta Culture, Edmonton, Alberta.

Kingsbury, J.M. 1964. *Poisonous plants of the United States and Canada*. Prentice-Hall Inc., Englewood Cliffs, New Jersey.

Kuijt, Job. 1972. *Common coulee plants of southern Alberta*. University of Lethbridge, Lethbridge, Alberta.

*Kuijt, Job. 1982. *A Flora of Waterton Lakes National Park*. The University of Alberta Press, Edmonton, Alberta.

Lampe, Kenneth E. 1985. *American Medical Association Handbook of poisonous and injurious plants*. American Medical Association, Chicago, Illinois.

*Moss, E.H. 1983. *Flora of Alberta*. 2nd edition, revised by J.G. Packer. University of Toronto Press, Toronto, Ontario.

*Packer, J.G. & C.E. Bradley. 1984. *A checklist of the rare vascular plants in Alberta*. Provincial Museum of Alberta Natural History Occasional Paper No. 5. Edmonton, Alberta.

Parkinson, John. 1629. *A garden of pleasant flowers*. As quoted in Coffey, T. 1993. *The history and folklore of North American wildflowers*. Houghton Mifflin Company, New York, N.Y.

Porsild, A.E. 1974. *Rocky Mountain Wildflowers*. National Museum of Natural Sciences, National Museums of Canada; and Parks Canada, Department of Indian and Northern Affairs, Ottawa, Ontario.

Scotter, G. & H. Flygare. 1986. *Wildflowers of the Canadian Rockies*. Hurtig Publishers, Edmonton, Alberta.

Shaw, R.J. & D. On. 1979. *Plants of Waterton-Glacier National Parks and the Canadian Rockies*. Summerthought Ltd., Banff, Alberta.

*Stearns, W.T. 1966. *Botanical Latin*. Thomas Nelson and Sons (Canada) Ltd, London, England.

Szczawinski, A.F. & N.J. Turner. 1978. *Edible garden weeds of Canada*. National Museum of Natural Sciences, Ottawa, Ontario.

Szczawinski, A.F. & N.J. Turner. 1980. *Wild green vegetables of Canada*. National Museum of Natural Sciences, Ottawa, Ontario.

Turner, N.J. 1978. *Food plants of British Columbia Indians. Part 2/Interior Peoples*. British Columbia Provincial Museum Handbook No. 36. Victoria, British Columbia.

Turner, N.J. 1979. *Plants in British Columbia Indian technology*. British Columbia Provincial Museum Handbook No. 38. Victoria, British Columbia.

Turner, N.J. 1982. *Food plants of British Columbia Indians. Part 1/Coastal Peoples*. British Columbia Provincial Museum Handbook No. 34. Victoria, British Columbia.

Turner, N.J. & A.F. Szczawinski. 1978. *Wild coffee and tea substitutes of Canada*. National Museum of Natural Sciences, Ottawa, Ontario.

Turner, N.J. & A.F. Szczawinski. 1979. *Edible wild fruits and nuts of Canada*. National Museum of Natural Sciences, Ottawa, Ontario.

*Vitt, D.H., J.E. Marsh & R.B. Bovey. 1988. *Mosses, lichens and ferns of Northwest North America*. Lone Pine Publishing, Edmonton, Alberta.

Weiner, M.A. 1990. *Earth medicine-earth food*. Fawcett Book Group, Division of Ballantine Books, New York, N.Y.

Wilkinson, Kathleen. 1990. *A habitat field guide to trees and shrubs of Alberta*. Lone Pine Publishing, Edmonton, Alberta.

Willard, Terry. 1992. *Edible and medicinal plants of the Rocky Mountains and neighbouring territories*. Wild Rose College of Natural Healing Ltd, Calgary, Alberta.

The 1990 United States Pharmacopeia and the National Formulary. 1995. Pharmacopeial Convention Incorporated, Rockville, Maryland.

* Some plants are found under more than one heading.

Greenish or Inconspicuous Flowers

Blue or
Purple Flowers

Yellow Flowers

Species Index

Photography credits

Lorna Allen (LA)

Blaine Andrusek (BA)

Cheryl Bradley (CB)

Terry Clayton (TC)

Olga Droppo (OD)

Lorne Fitch (LF)

Robert Frisch (RF)

Robert Gregg (RG)

Hole's Greenhouses & Gardens (HO)

Julie Hrapko (JH)

Derek Johnson (DJ)

Edgar Jones (EJ)

Linda Kershaw (LK)

Ian Macdonald (IM)

Orval Pall (OP)

Jim Pojar (JP)

Stanley Rach (SR)

Cliff Wallis (CWA)

Cleve Wershler (CWE)

Kathleen Wilkinson (KW)

KATHLEEN WILKINSON was born in Winnipeg and received her Bachelor of Agriculture degee in plant science from the University of Manitoba, followed shortly after by a Master of Science degree in plant ecology from the University of Calgary. For the past twenty-five years, she has lived in Calgary with her husband and son and has worked primarily as an environmental consultant, studying vegetation from Manitoba to British Columbia. Kathleen's previous book, *Habitat Field Guide to Trees and Shrubs of Alberta*, was published in 1990 by Lone Pine Publishing. Her interests include natural history, gardening, reading and travel.